Advanced Information and Knowledge Processing

Also in this series

Manuel Graña, Richard Duro, Alicia d'Anjou
and Paul P. Wang (Eds)

Information Processing with Evolutionary Algorithms

From Industrial Applications to Academic Speculations

With 137 Figures

 Springer

Manuel Graña, BSc, MSc, PhD
Universidad del Pais Vasco, San Sebastian, Spain
Richard J. Duro, BSc, MSc, PhD
Universidad da Coruña, La Coruña, Spain
Alicia d'Anjou, BSc, MSc, PhD
Universidad del Pais Vasco, San Sebastian, Spain
Paul P. Wang, PhD
Duke University, Durham, North Carolina, USA

Series Editors
Xindong Wu
Lakhmi Jain

British Library Cataloguing in Publication Data
Information processing with evolutionary algorithms : from
   industrial applications to academic speculations. —
   (Advanced information and knowledge processing)
   1. Evolutionary computation   2. Computer algorithms
   I. Graña, Manuel
   005.1

Library of Congress Cataloging-in-Publication Data
Information processing with evolutionary algorithms : from industrial applications to
   academic speculations / Manuel Graña ... [et al.].
      p. cm. — (Advanced information and knowledge processing)
      1. Evolutionary programming (Computer science)   2. Genetic algorithms.   3. Electronic
   data processing.   I. Graña, Manuel, 1958–   II. Series.
   QA76.618.I56   2004
   006.3'36—dc22   2004059333

AI&KP ISSN 1610-3947

ISBN 978-1-84996-937-6   e-ISBN 978-1-84628-117-4
Springer Science+Business Media
springeronline.com

© Springer-Verlag London Limited 2010

34/3830-543210   Printed on acid-free paper

Preface

The last decade of the 20th century has witnessed a surge of interest in numerical, computation-intensive approaches to information processing. The lines that draw the boundaries among statistics, optimization, artificial intelligence and information processing are disappearing, and it is not uncommon to find well-founded and sophisticated mathematical approaches in application domains traditionally associated with ad-hoc programming. Heuristics has become a branch of optimization and statistics. Clustering is applied to analyze soft data and to provide fast indexing in the World Wide Web. Non-trivial matrix algebra is at the heart of the last advances in computer vision.

The breakthrough impulse was, apparently, due to the rise of the interest in artificial neural networks, after its rediscovery in the late 1980s. Disguised as ANN, numerical and statistical methods made an appearance in the information processing scene, and others followed. A key component in many intelligent computational processing is the search for an optimal value of some function. Sometimes, this function is not evident and it must be made explicit in order to formulate the problem as an optimization problem. The search often takes place in high-dimensional spaces that can be either discrete, or continuous or mixed. The shape of the high-dimensional surface that corresponds to the optimized function is usually very complex. Evolutionary algorithms are increasingly being applied to information processing applications that require any kind of optimization. They provide a systematic and intuitive framework to state the optimization problems, and an already well-established body of theory that endorses their good mathematical properties. Evolutionary algorithms have reached the status of problem-solving tools in the backpack of the engineer. However, there are still exciting new developments taking place in the academic community. The driving idea in the organization of this compilation is the emphasis in the contrast between already accepted engineering practice and ongoing explorations in the academic community.

After the seminal works of Holland, Goldberg and Schwefel, the field of evolutionary algorithms has experienced an explosion of both researchers and publications in both the application-oriented and the fundamental issues. It is obviously difficult to present in a single book a complete and detailed picture of the field. Therefore, the point of view of this compilation is more modest. Its aim has been to provide a glimpse of the large variety of problems tackled with evolutionary approximations and of the diversity of evolutionary algorithms themselves based on some of the papers presented at the Frontiers on Evolutionary Algorithms Conference within JCIS 2002 and complemented with some papers by well-known authors in the field on topics that were not fully covered in the sessions. Following the general trend in the field, most of the papers are application-oriented. However, we have made an effort to include some that refer to fundamental issues as well as some that provide a review of the state of the art in some subfield.

As the subtitle "From industrial applications to academic speculations" suggests, the organization of the compilation follows an axis of nearness to practical applications. We travel from industrial day-to-day problems and practice to the more speculative works. The starting collection of papers is devoted to immediate applications of clear economical value at present.

- The chapter by T. Bäck is an example of successful consulting with a toolbox of computational methods that include evolutionary algorithms addressing nontrivial industrial problems. Although the emphasis of the chapter is on Evolutionary Strategies, Bäck's work is a bright example of a host of evolutionary solutions to everyday problems being developed at both universities and the industry RD labs.
- The general approach of Deschaine and Francone is to reverse engineer a system with Linear Genetic Programming at the machine code level. This approach provides very fast and accurate models of the process that will be subject to optimization. The optimization process itself is performed using an Evolutionary Strategy with completely deterministic parameter self-adaptation. The authors have tested this approach in a variety of academic problems. They target industrial problems, characterized by low formalization and high complexity. As a final illustration they deal with the design of an incinerator and the problem of subsurface unexploded ordnance detection.
- Nowadays there is a big industry of 3D computer modeling based on several 3D scanning methods. The rendering of these 3D structures from a cloud of scanned points requires a triangulation defined on them which may be very costly, depending on the number of scanned points, and subject to noise. Smooth and efficient approximations are therefore desired. In the chapter by Weinert et al. we find the application of Evolution Strategies to the problem of finding optimal triangulation coverings of a 3D object described by a cloud of points. The authors introduce a special encoding of the triangulation on a real-valued vector, a prerequisite for the application of Evolution Strategies. This encoding consists of the modeling of the triangulation as grid of springs and masses of varying coefficients. These coefficients and the Z coordinate of the mass points result in a problem

encoding that is closed under conventional Evolution Strategy genetic operators.

- Another practical application domain of current interest is the exploitation of hyperspectral images, especially those that arise in remote sensing. The recent advances in hyperspectral sensors and the space programs that include them in modern and future satellites imply that a large amount of data will be available in the near future. Fast, unsupervised analysis methods will be needed to provide adequate preprocessing of these data. Graña, Hernandez and d'Anjou propose an evolutionary algorithm to obtain an optimal unsupervised analysis of hyperspectral images given by a set of endmembers identified in the image. The identification is based on the notion of morphological independence, and Morphological Associative Memories serve as detectors of this condition.

- The processing of digital images is already an exploding application domain of computational methods. One of the issues of current interest, especially in the medical image domain and Magnetic Resonance Imaging (MRI), is the correction of illumination inhomogeneity (bias). Algorithms for illumination correction may be parametric or nonparametric. The latter are more computationally demanding. The formers require an appropriate modeling framework. Fernandez et al. present a gradient-driven evolution strategy for the estimation of the parameters of an illumination model given by a linear combination of Legendre polynomials. The gradient information is used in the mutation operator and seems to improve the convergence of the search, when compared with similar approaches.

- Job shop scheduling is a classical operations research problem and a recurrent problem in many industrial settings, ranging from the planning of a small workshop to the allocation of computing resources. Varela et al. propose an encoding that allows the modular decomposition of the problem. This modular decomposition is of use for the definition of new genetic operators that always produce feasible solutions. In addition, the new genetic operators benefit from the local/global structural tradeoffs of the problem, producing an implicit search of local solutions, akin to the local search in memetic approaches, but carried out in a parallel fashion.

The next batch of chapters includes works that present interesting and innovative applications of evolutionary approaches. The emphasis is on the departure of the application from the conventional optimization problems. Topics range from archeology to mobile robotics control design.

- The starting work is a fascinating application of evolution to the creation of a computational model that explains the emergence of an archaic state, the Zapotec state. The model is composed of the ontogenies evolved by specific agents dealing with the data about the sites in the Oaxaca valley, embodied in a GIS developed in the project. One of the basic results is the search for sites that may have been subject to warfare. A GA-driven

Rough Set data mining procedure was realized and its results compared with a decision tree approach.

- Phylogenetic is the search of evolutionary pathways between species based on biological data. The phylogenic relations take the form of trees. Species are characterized by several attributes, and the construction of phyloge-netic trees is somehow reminiscent of decision tree construction. Attributes usually consist of phenotypic data, although recent approaches also use ge-netic data. Measures of the quality of phylogenetic trees are based on the parsimony evolutive relation representation. These parsimonious objective functions have been used to guide heuristic search algorithms applied to phylogenetic tree construction. C.B. Congdon proposes an evolutionary approach to their construction. A GA is applied because only binary val-ued attributes are considered. A canonical tree is introduced to compare phylogenies, and the genetic mutation and crossover operators are defined accordingly. Besides the comparison of the evolutionary approach with standard algorithms, the effect of the genetic operators is studied.

- An active area in evolutionary robotics is the field of evolutionary devel-opment of robotic controllers. The need to test these controllers on the real robot to evaluate the fitness function imposes stringent constraints on the number of fitness evaluations allowable. Therefore, the convergence problems of conventional evolutionary approaches are worsened because of the poor sampling of the fitness landscape. Becerra et al. introduce Macroevolutionary Algorithms for the design of robot controllers in the domain of mobile robotics. Robot controllers take the form of artificial neural networks and the intended task is robust wall following in food or poison rewarding environment. The Macroevolutionary Algorithms parti-tion the population into races that may evolve independently and, some-times, become extinct. The chapter studies the setting of the colonization parameters that produce different exploitation/exploration balances.

- Parsing based on grammars is a common tool for natural language under-standing. The case of sublanguages associated with a specific activity, like patent claiming, is that many features of the general language do not ap-pear, so that simplified grammars could be designed for them. Learning of grammars from a corpus of the sublanguage is possible. Statistical learning techniques tend to produce rather complex grammars. Cyre applies evolu-tion algorithms to the task of finding optimal natural language context-free statistical grammars. Because of the obvious difficulties in coding entire grammars as individuals, Cyre's approach is a GA whose individuals are grammar rules, endowed with bucket-brigade rewarding mechanisms as in the classical Holland classifier systems. The evolutionary algorithm uses only mutation in the form of random insertion of wildcards in selected rules. The discovery of new rules is performed by instantiating the wild-card and evaluating the resulting rules. The fitness of a rule is the number of parsed sentences it has contributed to parse. Rules with small fitness are deleted in a culling step. Positive results are reported in this chapter with some large corpora.

- Discovering the spatial structure of proteins from their spectral images is a result that may be influential to pharmacological and biological studies. Gamalielsson and Olsson present the evaluation of protein structure models with off-lattice evolutionary algorithms. The type of evolutionary algorithms applied are evolution strategies with and without fitness sharing for premature convergence avoidance. The encoding of the protein structure is carried out by means of the angles between the residues. The main experimental argument of the paper is to study the effect of the fitness function definition. The best results are obtained with a fitness function that assumes knowledge of the actual spatial structure. This is equivalent to a supervised training problem. Unsupervised structure discovery is realized by fitness functions defined on characteristics of the composing amino acids.

- Classification is the most basic intelligent process. Among the diversity of approaches, the decision trees and related rule-based systems have enjoyed a great deal of attention, with some big success. Riquelme presents the generation of hierarchical decision rules by evolutionary approaches, comparing it to classical C4.5 decision trees over a well-known benchmark collection of problems. The hierarchical decision rules possess some nice intrinsic features, such as the parsimonious number of tests performed to classify a data pattern. They are in fact a decision list, which is constructed incrementally with the evolutionary algorithm serving as the rule selector for each addition to the list. Individuals correspond to candidate rules. Continuous-valued attributes are dealt with by the definition of intervals that quantize the attribute value range. Crossover and mutation are accordingly defined to deal with interval specifications. The fitness function computation involves the correctly classified examples, the erroneously classified examples and the coverage of the problem space by the rule.

- Evolvable hardware is an active field of research that aims at the unsupervised generation of hardware fulfilling some specifications. A fruitful area in this field is that of evolving designs of gate circuits implementing Boolean functions specified by truth tables, with great potential for application to circuit design. Hernandez Aguirre reviews the evolutionary approaches developed to handle this problem, which include classical binary GA and modifications, Ant Colony Systems and variations of the GP. Future lines of research include the design of appropriate platforms, because most present work is performed in an extrinsic mode, while the desired goal would be to perform the evolutionary search embedded in the hardware being optimized, that is, in an intrinsic way.

- System identification is the estimation of the parameters and structure of a system processing an input signal, on the basis of the observed input/output pairs. It is used in the context of designing control for processes whose models are unknown or highly uncertain. Montiel et al. present an approach to system identification using breeder genetic algorithms, an evolutionary algorithm with features of Genetic Algorithms and Evolutionary Strategies. They present a learning strategy and experimental results on the identification of an IIR filter as the unknown system that show great promise.

We have clustered under the label of Issues in Evolution Algorithm Foundations a collection of papers that deal with some fundamental aspects of evolutionary algorithms. Fundamental properties are usually related with convergence properties and domain of application.

- The starting work is the state of the art review on multiobjective optimization by C.A. Coello et al. This tutorial paper provides a comprehensive introduction to the history and present state of the field, giving a clear picture of the avenues for future research. A special emphasis is made on the approaches followed in the literature to introduce elitism in multiobjective evolutionary algorithms (MOEA). Elitism poses specific problems in MOEA, because of the need to preserve nondominated solutions, and the subtleties that appear when trying to combine them with the new generations of solutions. In addition, a case is made for the use of constrained single objective optimization problems as benchmarks for MOEAs, and, conversely, of the power of MOEAs as constraint satisfaction optimization algorithms.
- Premature convergence is one of the key problems in GAs, trapping them in local optima. Kubalik et al. lead us through a good review of approaches to avoid premature convergence. They propose and test a GA with Limited Convergence (GALCO) to solve this convergence problem. The GALCO imposes a restriction of the difference between the frequencies of ones and zeros of each gene across the population. The replacement strategy is designed so as to ensure the preservation of the convergence restriction. No mutation is performed. Only one crossover operator is applied to each generation. Empirical evaluations over deceptive functions are provided.
- When dealing with dynamic environments, the fitness function driving the evolutionary algorithm involves probing this environment, a process that may not result in a steady response. A time-varying fitness function appears in control-related applications, namely in mobile robotics. Two questions arise: (1) how much information do we need about the time evolution of the fitness response to ensure appropriate knowledge of it to drive the evolutionary algorithm? and (2) how to synchronize the evolutionary algorithm and the environment? That is, how frequent must the sampling of the environment be to ensure its tracking by the evolutionary algorithm. Bellas et al. deal with these questions in the setting of evolution based learning of time-dependent functions by artificial neural networks. Their results provide insights to more complex and realistic situations.

The closing collection of chapters includes the more speculative approaches that induce glimpses of the open roads for future developments. Some of the approaches are loosely related to evolutionary algorithms except for the fact that they are population-based random global optimization algorithms.

- Molecular Computing deals with the realization through molecular interaction of complex computational processes. The work of Liu and Shimohara presents a molecular computing method based on the Rho family of GTPases, that can be realized in situ (on living cells). They apply it at the simulation level to a 3SAT problem, obtaining linear dependencies of the execution time and space requirements on the number of clauses and propositions. The justification lies in the fact that the computational units are the molecular pathways that grow exponentially with the number of molecules.
- Evolutionary games play a central role in the Artificial Life paradigm. Cases and Anchorena present several developments of the theory of evolutionary games that that try to bridge the conceptual chasm between Dynamical Systems and Artificial Life, two rich research areas that involve divergent modeling of dynamical systems. Among the propositions in the paper is the formalization as a grammatical model of two-person evolutionary games.
- Al-kazemi and Mohan present a discrete version of the Particle Swarm Optimization (PSO) that involves the partition of the population of particles into coherent subpopulations, the definition of repulsive and attractive phases and a greedy local search. PSO is a random, population-based search algorithm, where particle motion can be assimilated to mutations in evolutionary algorithms. The results to benchmarck difficult discrete and continuous functions improve over other enhancements of PSO and GA.

As indicated above, the present compilation started with the FEA'2002 workshop, embedded in the JCIS'2002 celebrated in Research Triangle Park, NC. Most of the chapters correspond to extended versions of selected papers presented at the workshop. Some chapters have been requested of the authors with the aim of obtaining a view of some specific issue not present at the workshop. We want to express our gratitude to the members of the scientific committee that volunteered their time and insights to evaluate the papers submitted to the workshop:

Jarmo Alander, Enrique Alba, Thomas Bäck, Helio J.C. Barbosa, Hilan Bensusan, Peter Bentley, Maumita Bhattacharya, Stefano Cagnoni, Erick Cantu-Paz, Yuehui Chen, Carlos A. Coello Coello, Marie Cottrell, Kelly Crawford, Alicia d'Anjou, Dipankar Dasgupta, Kalyanmoy Deb, Marco Dorigo, Gerry V. Dozier, Richard Duro, Candida Ferreira, Alex Freitas, Max Garzon, Andreas Geyer-Schulz, Christophe Giraud-Carrier, Robert Ghanea-Hercock, David Goldberg, Manuel Graña, Darko Grundler, Francisco Herrera, Vasant Honavar, Frank Hoffmann, Spyros A. Kazarlis, Tatiana Kalganova, Sami Khuri, Hod Lipson, Evelyne Lutton, John A.W. McCall, J.J. Merelo, Jae

C. Oh, Bjorn Olsson, Ian C. Parmee, Frank Paseman, Andres Perez-Uribe, Jennifer L. Pittman, Alberto Prieto, Robert G. Reynolds, Leon Rothkrantz, Marco Ruso, Francisco Sandoval, Jose Santos, Marc Schoenauer, Shigeyoshi Tsutsui, J. Luis Verdegay, Thomas Villmann, Klaus Weinert, Man Leung Wong, Xin Yao, and Yun Seog Yeun.

Finally, we acknowledge the financial support of the Ministerio de Ciencia y Tecnología of Spain through grants TIC2000-0739-C04-02, TIC2000-0376-P4-04, MAT1999-1049-C03-03, DPI2003-06972 and VEMS2003-2088-c04. The Universidad del Pais Vasco has supported us through grant UPV/EHU 00140.226-TA-6872/1999. Manuel is grateful to Caravan, Juan Perro, Amaral, Terry Pratcher and Stanislaw Lem for adding spice to our lives.

San Sebastian, Spain   *Manuel Graña*
January 2004   *Richard Duro*
                                              Alicia d'Anjou
                                              Paul P. Wang

Contents

List of Contributors

J. Aguilar-Ruiz
Dept. of Computer Science
University of Sevilla
Avda. Reina Mercedes Mercedes
41012 Sevilla, Spain

B. Al-kazemi
Dept. of EECS
Syracuse University
Syracuse, NY 13244-4100, USA

S.O. Anchorena
Dept. of LSI
Universidad Pais Vasco
Apdo. 649, 20080,
San Sebastián, Spain

T. Bäck
NuTech Solutions
Martin-Schmeisser-Weg 15 8401
D-44227 Dortmund, Germany

J.A. Becerra
Grupo de Sistemas Autónomos
Universidade da Coruña
Spain

F. Bellas
Grupo de Sistemas Autónomos
Universidade da Coruña
Spain

B. Cases
Dept. of LSI
Universidad Pais Vasco
Apdo. 649, 20080,
San Sebastián, Spain

O. Castillo
Dept. of Computer Science
Tijuana Institute of Technology
Tijuana, Mexico

C.A. Coello Coello
CINVESTAV-IPN
Av. Instituto Politécnico
Nacional No. 2508
México, D.F. 07300, Mexico

C.B. Congdon
Dept. of Computer Science
Colby College
5846 Mayflower Hill Drive
Waterville, ME 04901, USA

W. Cyre
Department of Electrical and
Computer Engineering
Virginia Tech
Blacksburg, VA 24061, USA

A. d'Anjou
Dept. CCIA
Universidad Pais Vasco
Spain

L.M. Deschaine
Science Applications Int. Co.
360 Bay Street, Suite 200
Augusta, GA 30901, USA

R.J. Duro
Grupo de Sistemas Autónomos
Universidade da Coruña
Spain

E. Fernandez
Dept. CCIA
Universidad Pais Vasco
Spain

F.D. Francone
RML Technologies, Inc.
11757 Ken Caryl Ave., F-512
Littleton, CO 80127, USA

J. Gamalielsson
Department Comp. Science
University of Skövde
Box 408
541 28 Skövde, Sweden

M. Graña
Dept. CCIA
Universidad Pais Vasco
Spain

A. Hernández-Aguirre
Center Math. Research
Computer Science Section
Callejón Jalisco S/N,
Guanajuato, Gto. 36240 México

C. Hernandez
Dept. CCIA
Universidad Pais Vasco
Spain

J. Kubalík
Department of Cybernetics
CTU Prague
Technicka 2, 166 27 Prague 6
Czech Republic

J. Lažanský
Department of Cybernetics
CTU Prague
Technicka 2, 166 27 Prague 6
Czech Republic

A. Lazar
Artificial Intelligence Laboratory
Wayne State University
Detroit, MI 48202, USA

J.-Q. Liu
ATR Human Information
Science Laboratories
Hikaridai, Seika-cho, Soraku-gun
Kyoto, 619-0288, Japan

J. Mehnen
Inst. Machining Technology
University of Dortmund
Baroper Str. 301
D-44227 Dortmund, Germany

P. Melin
Dept. of Computer Science
Tijuana Institute of Technology
Tijuana, Mexico

E. Mezura Montes
CINVESTAV-IPN
Av. Instituto Politécnico
Nacional No. 2508
México, D.F. 07300, Mexico

C.K. Mohan
Dept. of EECS
Syracuse University
Syracuse, NY 13244-4100, USA

O. Montiel
CITEDI
National Polytechnic Institute
Tijuana, Mexico

B. Olsson
Dept. Computer Science
University of Skövde
Box 408
541 28 Skövde, Sweden

J. Puente
Centro de Inteligencia Artificial
Universidad de Oviedo
Campus de Viesques
E-33271 Gijon, Spain

R.G. Reynolds
Artificial Intelligence Laboratory
Wayne State University
Detroit, MI 48202, USA

J. Riquelme
Dept. of Computer Science
University of Sevilla
Avda. Reina Mercedes Mercedes
41012 Sevilla, Spain

L. Rothkrantz
Knowledge Based Systems G.
Dept. Mediamatics, TU Delft
P.O. Box 356, 2600 AJ Delft
The Netherlands

J. Ruiz-Cabello
U. Resonancia Magnetica
Universidad Complutense
Paseo Juan XXIII, 1, Madrid
Spain

J. Santos
Grupo de Sistemas Autónomos
Universidade da Coruña
Spain

M. Schneider
Inst. of Machining Technology
University of Dortmund
Baroper Str. 301
D-44227 Dortmund, Germany

R. Sepulveda
CITEDI
National Polytechnic Institute
Tijuana, Mexico

D. Serrano
Centro de Inteligencia Artificial
Universidad de Oviedo
Campus de Viesques
E-33271 Gijon, Spain

K. Shimohara
ATR Human Information
Science Laboratories
Hikaridai, Seika-cho, Soraku-gun
Kyoto, 619-0288, Japan

A. Suarez
Centro de Inteligencia Artificial
Universidad de Oviedo
Campus de Viesques
E-33271 Gijon, Spain

G. Toscano Pulido
CINVESTAV-IPN
Av. Instituto Politécnico
Nacional No. 2508
México, D.F. 07300, Mexico

R. Varela
Centro de Inteligencia Artificial
Universidad de Oviedo
Campus de Viesques
E-33271 Gijon, Spain

C.R. Vela
Centro de Inteligencia Artificial
Universidad de Oviedo
Campus de Viesques
E-33271 Gijon, Spain

K. Weinert
Inst. of Machining Technology
University of Dortmund
Baroper Str. 301
D-44227 Dortmund, Germany

1

Adaptive Business Intelligence Based on Evolution Strategies: Some Application Examples of Self-Adaptive Software

T. Bäck

Summary. Self-adaptive software is one of the key discoveries in the field of evolutionary computation, originally invented in the framework of so-called Evolution Strategies in Germany. Self-adaptability enables the algorithm to dynamically adapt to the problem characteristics and even to cope with changing environmental conditions as they occur in unforeseeable ways in many real-world business applications. In evolution strategies, self-adaptability is generated by means of an evolutionary search process that operates on the solutions generated by the method as well as on the evolution strategy's parameters, i.e., the algorithm itself. By focusing on a basic algorithmic variant of evolution strategies, the fundamental idea of self-adaptation is outlined in this paper. Applications of evolution strategies for NuTech's clients include the whole range of business tasks, including R & D, technical design, control, production, quality control, logistics, and management decision support. While such examples can, of course, not be disclosed, we illustrate the capabilities of evolution strategies by giving some simpler application examples to problems occurring in traffic control and engineering.

1.1 Introduction

Over the past 50 years, computer science has seen quite a number of fundamental inventions and, coming along with them, revolutions concerning the way how software systems are able to deal with data. Although the special focus is debatable, we claim that some of the major revolutions, roughly associated with decades of the past century, can be summarized as follows:

- **1950s:** Von Neumann architecture, simple operating systems, most basic programming languages.
- **1960s:** Improved operating systems (especially UNIX), structured programming, object-oriented programming, functional and logic programming.
- **1970s:** Relational model of Codd, relational database management systems (RDBMS).
- **1980s:** Enterprise resource planning (ERP) systems, production planning (PPS) systems, reflecting an integrated toolbox on top of the RDBMS-level.

- **1990s:** World Wide Web and Internet programming, facilitating a world-wide integrating access to ERP- and PPS-systems.
- **Now:** Semantic exploitation of data by means of **computational intelligence technologies**, facilitating **adaptive business intelligence** applications.

The hierarchy outlined above is meant to be data-oriented, as data are usually the driving force in business applications. Growing with the pure amount of data, the universal accessibility of data over the Internet, and the interconnetion of heterogenous databases, a pressing need emerged to deal with data not only in a syntactic way, but also to treat it semantically by new technologies, i.e., to deal with incomplete, imprecise, redundant, dynamic, and erroneous data. To mention just a few examples, consider the problem of identifying relevant information in the set of results returned by an Internet search engine (INFERNOsearch, developed by NuTech Solutions, Inc., solves this problem in a fundamentally new way by applying, among others, rough set technologies), or the problem of eliminating duplicates from enterprise databases, i.e., identifying semantically identical but syntactically different entries.

Assigning meaning to data, deriving knowledge from data, building the appropriate models from and about the data, and deriving optimal management decision support are the key activitities to support companies in business processes from all fields of the process chain, including R & D, technical design, control, production, quality control, logistics, and strategic management. This set of key activities is summarized under the term **adaptive business intelligence** and implemented by means of technologies summarized under the term **computational intelligence**. **Evolutionary algorithms** and, in particular, **evolution strategies** are one of the key technologies in the field of computational intelligence. In Section 1.2, we will explain the concept of adaptive business intelligence. In Section 1.3, we concentrate on evolution strategies and explain the basic idea of self-adaptive software. Section 1.4 then presents some application examples of the concept of adaptive business intelligence and evolution strategies in particular, and a brief outlook is given in Section 1.5.

1.2. Adaptive Business Intelligence

The general concept of the adaptive business intelligence approach is outlined in Figure 1.1. The methodology focuses completely on the business relevant aspects, i.e., on the business input and the business output. Business input means the problem to be treated and solved, together with the corresponding data, while business output is the problem knowledge or problem solution generated by the approach, which can be turned into business operations to improve desired aspects of the business.

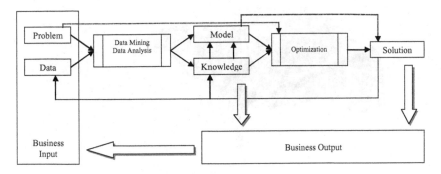

Figure 1.1 Adaptive Business Intelligence.

The critical tasks on the way from problem and data to an optimal business solution are the **data mining/data analysis** and **optimization** tasks. For these tasks, computational intelligence today offers technologies that allow us to treat problems of a complexity that could not be treated before, to derive knowledge in a way that was not accessible before, and to find optimized solutions of much better quality than before.

In data analysis and **data mining** [1], the task is to discover hidden knowledge from large amounts of data (e.g., in financial applications, chemical processes, marketing data, and many other fields). The term "knowledge" implies that the output should be compact, readable (i.e., presented in a symbolic way), interpretable, and highly relevant to the data, reflecting the fact that one is often more interested in understandable knowledge (so-called explicative models in terms of systems analysis) than in mathematical models (so-called descriptive models) but of course the latter kind of models, mostly derived by statistical methods, also play an important role. Derived knowledge and mathematical models are also often used together in a way such that knowledge is incorporated into the model. Technologies from computational intelligence that support various aspects of the data mining process include especially classifier systems, genetic programming, fuzzy logic, and rough sets.

Sometimes, knowledge or models derived from data can be used to generate business output directly by human interpretation in the light of the business processes of a company, but often an even more intensive exploitation of the knowledge / model combination is possible by adding an additional optimization step.

In the **optimization** step [7], an objective function $Y = f(y_1,...,y_m)$ is used, where $y_1,...,y_m = M(x_1,...,x_n)$ denote the model output when the model M is given the input $x_1,...,x_n$. Here, $x_1,...,x_n$ are the influencing factors, i.e., the process variables that can be controlled by management within a certain process window. The objective function f typically aggregates the model output $y_1,...,y_m$ into a criterion such as product quality, production costs, profit per production unit, etc., or a combination of them. The goal of the optimization step then is to find a set of values $x^*_1,...,x^*_n$ of the influencing factors, which minimizes or maximizes (mathematically, both

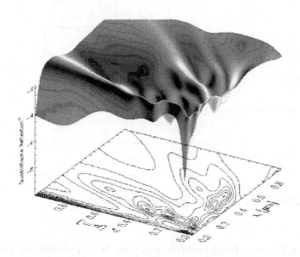

Figure 1.2 A nonlinear objective function

problems are equivalent) the objective function value; written usually as $Y \to \min(\max)$.

The need for accurate models that reflect all relevant aspects of reality implies that the optimization task becomes extremely complex, characterized by high-dimensional, nonlinear dependencies between process variables $x_1,...,x_n$ and objective function values $Y = f(M(x_1,...,x_n))$. Moreover, the functional dependency is often discontinuous, noisy, or even time-dependent in case of dynamical optimization problems, and it might be very time-consuming to evaluate Y for one set of values $x_1,...,x_n$, such that only a small number of pairs $((x_{1i},...,x_{ni}),\ Y_i)$ can be generated. Figure 1.2 illustrates a very simplified 2-dimensional cut from a real-world minimization problem, where the objective function value Y is plotted as a function of two real-valued process variables only. As one can see directly, a greedy minimization procedure might easily "get stuck" in a suboptimal "hole" without finding the sharp peak if the method is not allowed to accept temporarily a worsening of Y at the benefit of overcoming such a locally optimal hole.

While a large number of special-purpose optimization methods is available for simplified subclasses of the optimization problem, empirical research of the past decade has demonstrated that technologies from the field of computational intelligence, so-called evolutionary algorithms, are especially powerful for solving real-world problems characterized by this one or even by more of the above-mentioned features. In particular, this includes evolution strategies and genetic algorithms (see e.g., [3, 2, 7]).

In many business applications, dynamics of the real-world business processes is of paramount importance as it requires timely adaptation of the process to changing conditions (consider, e.g., plane and crew scheduling problems of big airlines, which require adaptations of the schedule on daily, weekly, monthly, quarterly, etc. time frames). Self-adaptability of software as implemented, e.g., in evolution strategies, one of the key computational intelligence technologies, is a key technology to guarantee adaptation even under fast-changing environmental conditions [6].

1.3 Self-Adaptive Software: Evolution Strategies

One of the key features of evolution strategies is that they adapt themselves to the characteristics of the optimization problem to be solved, i.e., they use a feature called self-adaptation to achieve a new level of flexibility. Self-adaptation allows a software to adapt itself to any problem from a general class of problems, to reconfigure itself accordingly, and to do this without any user interaction. The concept was originally invented in the context of evolution strategies (see, e.g., [6]), but can of course be applied on a more general level [5]. Looking at this from the optimization point of view, most optimization methods can be summarized by the following iterative procedure, which shows how to generate the next vector $(x_{1(t+1)},...,x_{n(t+1)})$ from the current one:

$$(x_{1(t+1)},...,x_{n(t+1)}) = (x_{1(t)},...,x_{n(t)}) + s_t \cdot (v_{1(t)},...,v_{n(t)}).$$

Here, $(v_{1(t)},...,v_{n(t)})$ denotes the direction of the next search step at iteration $t+1$, and s_t denotes the step size (a scalar value) for the search step length along this direction. Of course, the key to the success of an optimization method consists of finding effective ways to determine, at each time step t, an appropriate direction and step size (and there are hundreds of proposals how to do this). An evolution strategy does this in a self-adaptive way.

The basic idea of an evolution strategy, like other evolutionary algorithms as well, consists of using the model of organic evolution as a process for adaptation and optimization. Consequently, the algorithms use a "population of individuals" representing candidate solutions to the optimization problem, and evolutionary operators such as variation (e.g., recombination and mutation) and selection in an iterative way such as it is outlined in Figure 1.3. In evolution strategies, populations can be rather small, like, e.g., in the example of a *(1,10)*-strategy. The notation indicates that 10 offspring solutions are generated by means of mutation from one parent solution, and the best (according to the objective function value) of the offspring individuals is chosen as the parent for the next iteration. It should be noted that discarding the parent is done intentionally, because it allows the algorithm to accept temporary worsenings in quality to overcome locally optimal solutions (cf. Figure 1.2). For the mutation operator, the basic variants of evolution strategies use normally distributed variations $z_i \approx N_i(0,\sigma)$ where $N_i(0,\sigma)$ denotes a normally distributed random sample with expectation zero and standard deviation σ, i.e., the mutation operator modifies a solution candidate $(x_{1(t)},...,x_{n(t)})$ by setting $x_{i(t+1)} = x_{i(t)} + z_i$, where $i = \{1,...,n\}$. The mutation is normally distributed with expected value zero and variance σ^2, i.e., step size and direction are implicitly defined by means of the normal distribution (here, the direction is random while the step size is approximately $\sigma(n)^{1/2}$). The fundamental approach for self-adaptation is to adapt σ itself online while optimizing by extending the representation of solutions by the step size σ, i.e., $((x_{1(t)},...,x_{n(t)}), \sigma)$, where σ now is a component of the in-

6   Thomas Bäck

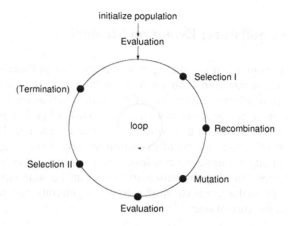

Figure 1.3. The evolutionary loop.

dividual (and different for each individual of a population), and the mutation operator proceeds according to the rule

$$\sigma' = \sigma \cdot \exp(\tau \cdot N(0,1)),$$

$$x_{i(t+1)} = x_{i(t)} + N_i(0,\sigma')$$

forming the new individual $((x_{1(t)},...,x_{n(t)}),\ \sigma')$. In other words, σ is mutated first, and the mutated step size is then used to generate the offspring. There is no external control of step sizes at all. Instead, they are completely controlled by the algorithm itself, based on an autonomous adaptation process using the implicit feedback of the quality criterion. A theoretical analysis for an analyzable objective function has proven that, for this special case, self-adaptation generates an optimal σ at any stage of the search process (see, e.g., [4] for a complete introduction to evolution strategy theory). In the above formulation, the special parameter τ denotes a "learning rate", which defines the speed of adaptation on the level of standard deviations σ. According to the theoretical knowledge about the process, a value of $\tau = 1/(2n)^{1/2}$ is a robust and generally useful setting.

The method outlined above is only the most basic version of self-adaptation. Much more elaborate variants are in use, which allow for the self-adaptation of general, n-dimensional normal distributions, including correlations between the variables, and also self-adaptive population sizes are currently under investigation. The resulting algorithms have no external parameters that need to be tuned for a particular application.

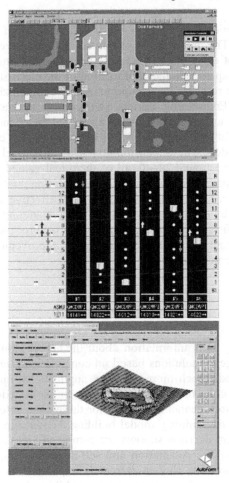

Figure 1.4. Examples of applications of evolution strategies: traffic light control (top), elevator control optimization (middle), metal stamping process optimization in automobile industry (bottom).

1.4 Examples

All adaptive business intelligence solutions provided by NuTech Solutions for its clients are characterized by applying the most suitable combination of traditional and computational intelligence technologies to achieve the best possible improvement of business processes. In all cases, the technical aspects of the implementation and client's problem are subject to nondisclosure agreements. Concerning the applications of self-adaptive evolution strategies, the following three examples (see Figure 1.3) illustrate the capabilities of these algorithms: the optimization of traffic light schedules at street intersections to dynamically adapt the traffic light control to the actual traffic situation (executed for the Dutch Ministry of Traffic, Rotterdam, The Netherlands). The optimization of control policies for elevator controllers to dynamically adapt elevator control to the actual traffic situation (executed for Fujitec Ltd., Osaka, Japan), and the optimization of the metal stamping process to improve quality of the resulting car components while minimizing metal losses (executed for AutoForm Engineering, Zürich, Switzerland). In these examples, the model is implemented by a simulation software already at the client's disposal, i.e., the optimization part (right part) of Figure 1.1 is executed by NuTech Solutions on the basis of existing models. The dimensionality n of the model input is in the small to middle range, i.e., around 20–40, all of them real-valued. The two traffic control problems are dynamic and noisy, and the evolution strategy locates and continuously maintains very high-quality solutions in an effective and flexible way that cannot be achieved by other methods. In the metal stamping simulation, the evolution strategy is the first algorithm at all that makes the process manageable by means of optimization, and the method yields strong improvements when compared to hand-optimized processes.

1.5 Outlook

In this chapter, only very little information about the actual industrial impact of adaptive business intelligence solutions based on computational intelligence technologies can be disclosed. Much more complex applications, implementing the whole scenario outlined in Figure 1.1, are presently in use by clients of NuTech Solutions, with an enormous economic benefit for these companies. In particular, those applications where data mining, model building, knowledge discovery, optimization, and management decision support are combined yield a new quality in business process optimization. Adaptation and self-adaptation capabilities of the corresponding software products play an extremely important role in this context, as many applications require a dynamic response capability of the applicable solution software. The modern business environment clearly demonstrates the growing need for adaptive business intelligence solutions, and computational intelligence has proven to be the ideal technology to fulfill the needs of companies in the new century. Adaptive business intelligence is the realization of structured management technologies (e.g., 6 Sigma, TQM) using technologies of the 21st century.

References

1. Adriaans P., D. Zantinge, Data Mining, Addison-Wesley, 1996.
2. Bäck T., D.B. Fogel, Z. Michaewicz, Handbook of Evolutionary Computation, Institute of Physics, Bristol, UK, 2000.
3. Bäck T., Evolutionary Algorithms in Theory and Practice, Oxford University Press, New York, 1996.

4. Beyer H.-G., The Theory of Evolution Strategies, Series on Natural Computation, Springer, Berlin, 2001.
5. Robertson P., H. Shrobe, R. Laddaga (eds.), Self-Adaptive Software. Lecture Notes in Computer Science, Vol. 1936, Springer, Berlin, 2000.
6. Schwefel H.-P., Collective Phenomena in Evolutionary Systems. In Preprints of the 31st Annual Meeting of the International Society for General System Research, Budapest, Vol. 2, 1025-1033.
7. Schwefel H.-P., Evolution and Optimum Seeking, Wiley, New York, 1995.

2

Extending the Boundaries of Design Optimization by Integrating Fast Optimization Techniques with Machine Code Based, Linear Genetic Programming

L. M. Deschaine, F.D. Francone

2.1 Introduction

Engineers frequently encounter problems that require them to estimate control or response settings for industrial or business processes that optimize one or more goals. Most optimization problems include two distinct parts: (1) a model of the process to be optimized; and (2) an optimizer that varies the control parameters of the model to derive optimal settings for those parameters.

For example, one of the research and development (R&D) case studies included here involves the control of an incinerator plant to achieve a high probability of environmental compliance and minimal cost. This required predictive models of the incinerator process, environmental regulations, and operating costs. It also required an optimizer that could combine the underlying models to calculate a real-time optimal response that satisfied the underlying constraints. Figure 2.1 shows the relationship of the optimizer and the underlying models for this problem.

The incinerator example discussed above and the other case studies below did not yield to a simple constrained optimization approach or a well-designed neural network approach. The underlying physics of the problem were not well understood; so this problem was best solved by decomposing it into its constituent parts—the three underlying models (Figure 2.1) and the optimizer.

This work is, therefore, concerned with complex optimization problems characterized by either of the following situations.

First: Engineers often understand the underlying processes quite well, but the software simulator they create for the process is slow. Deriving optimal settings for a slow simulator requires many calls to the simulator. This makes optimization inconvenient or completely impractical. Our solution in this situation was to reverse engineer the existing software simulator using Linear Genetic Programming (LGP)—in effect, we simulated the simulator. Such "second-order" LGP simulations are frequently very accurate and almost always orders of magnitude faster than the hand-coded simulator. For example, for the Kodak Simulator, described below, LGP reverse engineered that simulator, reducing the time per simulation from hours to less than a second. As a result, an optimizer may be applied to the LGP-derived simulation quickly and conveniently.

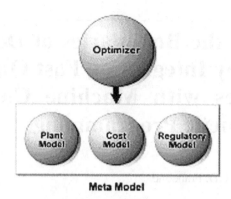

Figure 2.1 How the optimizer and the various models operate together for the incinerator solution.

Second: In the incinerator example given above, the cost and regulatory models were well understood, but the physics of the incinerator plant were not. However, good-quality plant operating data existed. This example highlights the second situation in which our approach consistently yields excellent results. LGP built a model of plant operation directly from the plant operation data. Combined with the cost and regulatory models to form a meta-model, the LGP model permits real-time optimization to achieve regulatory and cost goals.

For both of the above types of problems, the optimization and modeling tools should possess certain clearly definable characteristics:

- The optimizer should make as few calls to the process model as possible, consistent with producing high-quality solutions,
- The modeling tool should consistently produce high-precision models that execute quickly when called by the optimizer,
- Both the modeling and optimizing tools should be general-purpose tools. That is, they should be applicable to most problem domains with minimal customization and capable of producing good to excellent results across the whole range of problems that might be encountered; and
- By integrating tools with the above characteristics, we have been able to improve problem-solving capabilities very significantly for both problem types above.

This work is organized as follows. We begin by introducing the Evolution Strategies with Completely Derandomized Self-Adaptation (ES-CDSA) algorithm as our optimization algorithm of choice. Next, we describe machine-code-based, LGP in detail and describe a three-year study from which we have concluded that machine-code-based, LGP is our modeling tool of choice for these types of applications. Finally, we suggest ways in which the integrated optimization and modeling strategy may be applied to design optimization problems.

2.2 Evolution Strategies Optimization

ES was first developed in Germany in the 1960s. It is a very powerful, general-purpose, parameter optimization technique [25,26,27]. Although we refer in this work to ES, it is closely related to Fogel's Evolutionary Programming (EP) [7, 1]. Our discussion here applies equally to ES and EP. For ease of reference, we will use the term "ES" to refer to both approaches.

ES uses a population-based learning algorithm. Each generation of possible solutions is formed by mutating and recombining the best members of the previous generation. ES pioneered the use of evolvable "strategy parameters." Strategy parameters control the learning process. Thus, ES evolves both the parameters to be optimized and the parameters that control the optimization [2].

ES has the following desirable characteristics for the uses in our methodology:

- ES can optimize the parameters of arbitrary functions. It does not need to be able to calculate derivatives of the function to be optimized, nor does the researcher need to assume differentiability and numerical accuracy. Instead, ES gathers gradient information about the function by sampling. [12]
- Substantial literature over many years demonstrates that ES can solve a very wide range of optimization problems with minimal customization. [25, 26, 27, 12]

Although very powerful and not prone to getting stuck in local optima, typical ES systems can be very time-consuming for significant optimization problems. Thus, canonical ES often fails the requirement of efficient optimization.

But in the past five years, ES has been extended using the ES-CDSA technique [12]. ES-CDSA allows a much more efficient evolution of the strategy parameters and cumulates gradient information over many generations, rather than single generation as used in traditional ES.

As a rule of thumb, where n is the number of parameters to be optimized, users should allow between 100 and $200(n+3)2$ function evaluations to get optimal use from this algorithm [12]. While this is a large improvement over previous ES approaches, it can still require many calls by the optimizer to the model to be optimized to produce results. As a result, it is still very important to couple ES-CDSA with fast-executing models. And that is where LGP becomes important.

2.3 Linear Genetic Programming

Genetic Programming (GP) is the automatic creation of computer programs to perform a selected task using Darwinian natural selection. GP developers give their computers examples of how they want the computer to perform a task. GP software then writes a computer program that performs the task described by the examples. GP is a robust, dynamic, and quickly growing discipline. It has been applied to diverse problems with great success—equaling or exceeding the best human-created solutions to many difficult problems [14, 3, 4, 2].

This chapter presents three years of analysis of machine-code-based, LGP. To perform the analyses, we used Versions 1 through 3 of an off-the-shelf commercial software package called Discipulus™ [22]. Discipulus is an LGP system that operates directly on machine code.

2.3.1 The Genetic Programming Algorithm

Good, detailed treatments of GP may be found in [2, 14]. In brief summary, the LGP algorithm in Discipulus is surprisingly simple. It starts with a population of randomly generated computer programs. These programs are the "primordial soup" on which computerized evolution operates. Then, GP conducts a "tournament" by selecting four programs from the population—also at random—and measures how well each of the four programs performs the task designated by the GP developer. The two programs that perform the task best "win" the tournament.

The GP algorithm then copies the two winner programs and transforms these copies into two new programs via crossover and mutation transformation operators—in short, the winners have "children." These two new child programs are then inserted into the population of programs, replacing the two loser programs from the tournament. GP repeats these simple steps over and over until it has written a program that performs the selected task.

GP creates its "child" programs by transforming the tournament winning programs. The transformations used are inspired by biology. For example, the GP mutation operator transforms a tournament winner by changing it randomly—the mutation operator might change an addition instruction in a tournament winner to a multiplication instruction. Likewise, the GP crossover operator causes instructions from the two tournament winning programs to be swapped—in essence, an exchange of genetic material between the winners. GP crossover is inspired by the exchange of genetic material that occurs in sexual reproduction in biology.

2.3.2 Linear Genetic Programming Using Direct Manipulation of Binary Machine Code

Machine-code-based, LGP is the direct evolution of binary machine code through GP techniques [15, 16, 17, 18, 20]. Thus, an evolved LGP program is a sequence of binary machine instructions. For example, an evolved LGP program might be comprised of a sequence of four, 32-bit machine instructions. When executed, those four instructions would cause the central processing unit (CPU) to perform operations on the CPU's hardware registers. Here is an example of a simple, four-instruction LGP program that uses three hardware registers:

```
register 2 = register 1 + register 2
register 3 = register 1 - 64
register 3 = register 2 * register 3
register 3 = register 2 / register 3
```

While LGP programs are apparently very simple, it is actually possible to evolve functions of great complexity using only simple arithmetic functions on a register machine [18, 20].

After completing a machine-code LGP project, the LGP software decompiles the best evolved models from machine code into Java, ANSI C, or Intel Assembler programs [22]. The resulting decompiled code may be linked to the optimizer and compiled or it may be compiled into a DLL or COM object and called from the optimization routines.

The linear machine code approach to GP has been documented to be between 60 to 200 times faster than comparable interpreting systems [10, 15, 20]. As will be developed in more detail in the next section, this enhanced speed may be used to conduct a more intensive search of the solution space by performing more and longer runs.

2.4 Why Machine-Code-based, Linear Genetic Programming?

At first glance, it is not at all obvious that machine-code, LGP is a strong candidate for the modeling algorithm of choice for the types of complex, high-dimensional problems at issue here. But over the past three years, a series of tests was performed on both synthetic and industrial data sets—many of them data sets on which other modeling tools had failed. The purpose of these tests was to assess machine-code, LGP's performance as a general-purpose modeling tool.

In brief summary, the machine-code-based LGP software [22] has become our modeling tool of choice for complex problems like the ones described in this work for several reasons:

- Its speed permits the engineer to conduct many runs in realistic timeframes on a desktop computer. This results in consistent, high-precision models with little customization;
- It is well-designed to prevent overfitting and to produce robust solutions; and
- The models produced by the LGP software execute very quickly when called by an optimizer.

We will first discuss the use of multiple LGP runs as a key ingredient of this technique. Then we will discuss our investigation of machine-code, LGP over the past three years.

2.5 Multiple Linear Genetic Programming Runs

GP is a stochastic algorithm. Accordingly, running it over and over with the same inputs usually produces a wide range of results, ranging from very bad to very good. For example, Figure 2.2 shows the distribution of the results from 30 runs of LGP on the incinerator plant modeling problem mentioned in the introduction—the R^2 value is used to measure the quality of the solution. The solutions ranged from a very poor R^2 of 0.05 to an excellent R^2 of 0.95. Our investigation to date strongly suggests the typical LGP distribution of results from multiple LGP runs includes a distributional tail of excellent solutions that is not always duplicated by other learning algorithms.

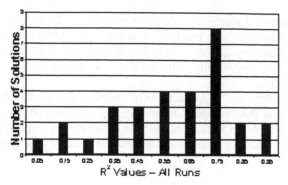

Figure 2.2 . Incinerator control data. Histogram of results for 30 LGP runs.

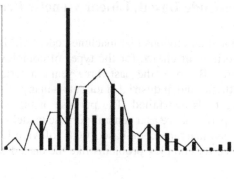

Better Solutions ➤

Figure 2.3 Typical comparative histograms of the quality of solutions produced by LGP runs (bars) and Neural Network runs (lines). Discussed in detail in [8].

For example, for three separate problem domains, an LGP system produced a long tail of outstanding solutions, even though the average LGP solution was not necessarily very good. By way of contrast, and in that same study, the distribution of many neural networks runs on the same problems often produced a good average solution, but did not produce a tail of outstanding solutions like LGP [4,8].

Figure 2.3 shows a comparative histogram of LGP results versus neural network results derived from 720 runs of each algorithm on the same problem. Better solutions appear to the right of the chart. Note the tail of good LGP solutions (the bars) that is not duplicated by a comparable tail of good neural network solutions. This same pattern may be found in other problem domains [4,8].

To locate the tail of best solutions on the right of Figure 2.3, it is *essential* to perform many runs, regardless whether the researcher is using neural networks or LGP. This is one of the most important reasons why a machine-code approach to GP is preferable to other approaches. It is so much faster than other approaches, that it is possible to complete many runs in realistic timeframes on a desktop computer. That makes it more capable of finding the programs in the good tail of the distribution.

2.6 Configuration Issues in Performing Multiple LGP Runs

Our investigation into exploiting the multiple run capability of machine-code-based LGP had two phases—largely defined by software versioning. Early versions of the Discipulus LGP software permitted multiple runs, but only with user-predefined parameter settings.

As a result, our early multiple run efforts (described below as our Phase I investigation) just chose a range of reasonable values for key parameters, estimated an appropriate termination criterion for the runs, and conducted a series of runs at those selected parameter settings. For example, the chart of the LGP results on the incinerator CO2 data sets (Figure. 2.2) was the result of doing 30 runs using different settings for the mutation parameter.

By way of contrast, the second phase of our investigation was enabled by four key new capabilities introduced into later versions of the LGP software. Those capabilities were

- The ability to perform multiple runs with randomized parameter settings from run to run;
- The ability to conduct hillclimbing through LGP parameter space based on the results of previous runs;
- The ability to automatically assemble teams of models during a project that, in general, perform better than individual models; and
- The ability to determine an appropriate termination criterion for runs, for a particular problem domain, by starting a project with short runs and automatically increasing the length of the runs until longer runs stop yielding better results.

Accordingly, the results reported below as part of our Phase II investigation are based on utilizing these additional four capabilities.

2.7 Investigation of Machine-Code-Based, Linear Genetic Programming—Phase I

We tested Versions 1.0 and 2.0 of the Discipulus LGP software on a number of problem domains during this first phase of our investigation. This Phase I investigation covered about two years and is reported in the next three sections.

2.7.1 Deriving Physical Laws

Science Applications International Corporation's (SAIC's) interest in LGP was initially based on its potential ability to model physical relationships. So the first test for LGP to see if it could model the well-known (to environmental engineers, at least) Darcy's law. Darcy's law describes the flow of water through porous media. The equation is

$$Q=K*I*A, \tag{2.1}$$

where $Q = flow\ [L3/T]$, $K = hydraulic\ conductivity\ [L/T]$, $I = gradient\ [L/L]$, and $A = area\ [L2]$.

To test LGP, we generated a realistic input set and then used Darcy's law to produce outputs. We then added 10% random variation to the inputs and outputs and ran the LGP software on these data. After completing our runs, we examined the best program it produced.

The best solution derived by the LGP software from these data was a four-instruction program that is precisely Darcy's law, represented in ANSI C as

```
Q = 0.0
Q += I
Q *= K
Q *= A
```

In this LGP evolved program, Q is an accumulator variable that is also the final output of the evolved program.

This program model of Darcy's law was derived as follows. First, it was evolved by LGP. The "raw" LGP solution was accurate though somewhat unintelligible. By using intron removal [19] with heuristics and evolutionary strategies the specific form of Darcy's law was evolved. This process is coded in the LGP software; we used the "Interactive Evaluator" module, which links to the "Intron Removal" and automatic "Simplification" and "Optimization" functions. These functions combine heuristics and ES optimization to derive simpler versions of the programs that LGP evolves [22].

2.7.2 Incinerator Process Simulation

The second LGP test SAIC performed was the prediction of CO_2 concentrations in the secondary combustion chamber of an incinerator plant from process measurements from plant operation. The inputs were various process parameters (e.g., fuel oil flow, liquid waste flow, etc.) and the plant control settings. The ability to make this prediction is important because the CO_2 concentration strongly affects regulatory compliance.

This problem was chosen because it had been investigated using neural networks. Great difficulty was encountered in deriving any useful neural network models for this problem during a well-conducted study [5].

The incinerator to be modeled processed a variety of solid and aqueous waste, using a combination of a rotary kiln, a secondary combustion chamber, and an off-gas scrubber. The process is complex and consists of variable fuel and waste inputs, high temperatures of combustion, and high-velocity off-gas emissions.

To set up the data, a zero- and one-hour offset for the data was used to construct the training and validation instance sets. This resulted in a total of 44 input variables. We conducted 30 LGP runs for a period of 20 hours each, using 10 different random seeds for each of three mutation rates (0.10, 0.50, 0.95) [3]. The stopping criterion for all simulations was 20 hours. All 30 runs together took 600 hours to run.

Two of the LGP runs produced excellent results. The best run showed a validation data set R2 fitness of 0.961 and an R2 fitness of 0.979 across the entire data set.

The two important results here were (1) LGP produced a solution that could not be obtained using neural networks; and (2) only two of the 30 runs produced good solutions (see Figure 2.2), so we would expect to have to conduct all 30 runs to solve the problem again.

2.7.3 Data Memorization Test

The third test SAIC performed was to see whether the LGP algorithm was memorizing data, or actually learning relationships.

SAIC constructed a known, chaotic time series based on the combination of drops of colored water making their way through a cylinder of mineral oil. The time series used was constructed via a physical process experimental technique discussed in [24].

The point of constructing these data was an attempt to deceive the LGP software into predicting an unpredictable relationship, that is, the information content of the preceding values from the drop experiment is not sufficient to predict the next value. Accordingly, if the LGP technique found a relationship on this chaotic series, it would have found a false relationship and its ability to generalize relationships from data would be suspect.

The LGP was configured to train on a data set as follows:

• The inputs were comprised of eight consecutive values from the drop data; and
• The target output was the next-in-sequence value of the drop data.

Various attempts were tried to trick the LGP technique, including varying parameters such as the instructions that were available for evolving the solution.

The results of this memorization test are shown on Figure 2.4. The "step" function shown in Figure 2.4 represents the measured drop data, sorted by value. The noisy data series is the output of the best LGP model of the drop data. It is clear that the LGP algorithm was not fooled by this data set. It evolved a program that was approximately a linear representation of the average value of the data set. But it did not memorize or fit the noise.

2.8 Investigation of Machine-Code-based, Linear Genetic Programming—Phase II

Phase II of our investigation started when we began using Version 3.0 of the LGP software [22]. As noted above, this new version automated many aspects of conducting multiple runs, including automatically randomizing run parameters, hill-climbing to optimize run parameters, automatic determination of the appropriate termination criterion for LGP for a particular problem domain, and automatic creation of team solutions.

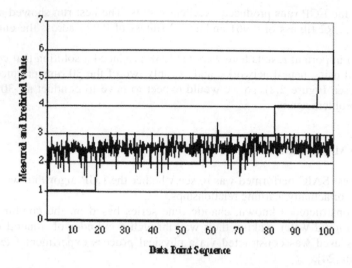

Figure 2.4 Attempt to model a chaotic time series with LGP.

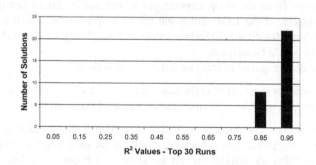

Figure 2.5 Distribution of 30 best LGP runs using randomized run parameters for 300 runs on incinerator problem

2.8.1 Incinerator Problem, Phase II

SAIC used the new software version and reran the R&D problem involving CO2 level prediction for the incinerator plant problem (described above). A total of 901,983,797 programs was evaluated to produce the distribution of the best 30 program results shown in Figure 2.5.

The enhanced LGP algorithm modeled the incinerator plant CO_2 levels with better accuracy and much more rapidly than earlier versions. The validation-data-set, seven-team, R^2 fitness was 0.985 as opposed to 0.961 previously achieved by multiple single runs. The CPU time for the new algorithm was 67 hours (using a PIII-800 MHz/100 MHz FSB machine), as opposed to 600 hours (using a PIII 533 MHz /133 FSB machine) that was needed in Phase I. It is important to note that the team solution approach was important in developing a better solution in less time.

2.8.2 UXO Discrimination

The preceding examples are regression problems. The enhanced LGP algorithm was also tested during Phase II on a difficult classification challenge the determination of the presence of subsurface unexploded ordnance (UXO).

The Department of Defense has been responsible for conducting UXO investigations at many locations around the world. These investigations have resulted in the collection of extraordinary amounts of geophysical data with the goal of identifying buried UXO.

Evaluation of UXO/non-UXO data is time-consuming and costly. The standard outcome of these types of evaluations is maps showing the location of geophysical anomalies. In general, what these anomalies may be (i.e., UXO, non-UXO, boulders, etc.) cannot be determined without excavation at the location of the anomaly.

Figure 2.6 shows the performance of 10 published industrial-strength, discrimination algorithms on the Jefferson Proving Grounds UXO data—which consisted of 160 targets [13]. The horizontal axis shows the performance of each algorithm in correctly identifying points that *did not* contain buried UXO. The vertical axis shows the performance of each algorithm in correctly identifying points that *did* contain buried UXO. The angled line in Figure 2.6 represents what would be expected from random guessing.

Figure 2.6 points out the difficulty of modeling these data. Most algorithms did little better than random guessing; however, the LGP algorithm derived a best-known model for correctly identifying UXO's and for correctly rejecting non-UXO's using various data set configurations [5, 13]. The triangle in the upper right-hand corner of Figure 2.6 shows the range of LGP solutions in these different configurations.

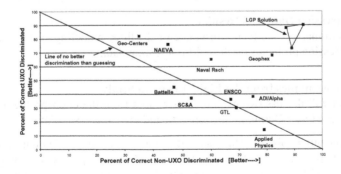

Figure 2.6 LGP and 10 other algorithms applied to the UXO discrimination data [13].

2.8.3 Eight-Problem Comparative Study

In 2001, we concluded Phase II of our LGP study with a comparative study using machine-code-based, LGP, back-propagation neural networks, Vapnick Statistical Regression (VSR) [28], and C5.0 [21] on a suite of real-world modeling problems.

The test suite included six regression problems and two classification problems. LGP and VSR were used on all problems. In addition, on regression problems, neural networks were used and on classification problems, C5.0 was used.

Space constraints prevent us from detailing the experimental protocol in detail. That detail may be obtained in [9]. In summary, each algorithm was trained on the same data as the others and was also tested on the same held-out data as the others. The figures reported below are the performance on the *held-out, testing data*. Each algorithm was run so as to maximize its performance, except that the LGP system was run at its default parameters in each case.

2.8.3.1 Classification Data Sets Results
Table 2.1 reports the comparative classification error rates of the best LGP, VSR, and C5.0 results on the classification suite of problems on the held-out, testing data.

Table 2.1 Comparison of Error Rates of Best LGP, C5.0, and Vapnick Regression Results on Two Industrial Classification Data Sets. Reported Results Are on Unseen Data. Lower is Better.

Problem	Linear Genetic Programming	C5.0 Decision Tree	Vapnick Regression
Company H spam filter	3.2%	8.5%	9.1%
Predict income from census data	14%	14.5%	15.4%

2.8.3.2 Regression Data Sets Results
Table 2.2 summarizes the R^2 performance of the three modeling systems across the suite of regression problems on the held-out testing data.

2.8.3.3 Two Examples from the Eight-Problem Study
This section will discuss two examples of results from the eight-problem comparison study—the Laser Output prediction data and the Kodak Simulator data.

Laser Output Problem. This data set comprises about 19,000 data points with 25 inputs. This is sequential data so the last 2,500 data points were held out for testing. The problem is to predict the output level of a ruby laser, using only previously measured outputs.

Table 2.2 Comparison of LGP, Neural Networks, and Vapnick Regression on Six Industrial Regression Problems. Value Shown is the R^2 Value on Unseen Data Showing Correlation between the Target Function and the Model's Predictions. Higher Values Are Better.

Problem	Linear Genetic Programming	Neural Network	Vapnick Regression
Dept. of Energy, cone penetremeter,	0.72	0.618	0.68
Kodak, software simulator	0.99	0.9509	0.80
Company D, chemical batch process control	0.72	0.63	0.72
Laser output prediction	0.99	0.96	0.41
Tokamak 1	0.99	0.55	N/A
Tokamak 2	0.44	.00	.12

This is an easy data set to do well upon; but it is very difficult to model the phase with precision. Most modeling tools pick up the strong periodic element but have a difficult time matching the phase and/or frequency components—they generate their solutions by lagging the actual output by several cycles. Figures 2.7 and 2.8 show the output of VSR and LGP, respectively, plotted against a portion of the unseen laser testing data.

Figure 2.7 is the result from the Vapnick tool. It picks up the strong periodic element but, critically, the predicted output lags behind the actual output by a few cycles. By way of contrast, Figure 2.8 shows the results from LGP modeling. Note the almost perfect phase coherence of the LGP solution and the actual output of the laser both before and after the phase change. The phase accuracy of the LGP models is what resulted in such a high R^2 for the LGP models, compared to the others.

Simulating a Simulator. In the Kodak simulator problem, the task was to use LGP to simulate an existing software simulator. Past runs of the existing simulator provided many matched pairs of inputs (five production-related variables) and the output from [23]. The data set consisted of 7,547 simulations of the output of a chemical batch process, given the five input variables common to making production decisions. Of these data points, 2,521 were held out of training for testing the model.

The results on the testing or held-out data for LGP, VSR, and neural networks are reported in Table 2.2. Figures 2.9 and 2.10 graph the LGP and Vapnick models against the target data.

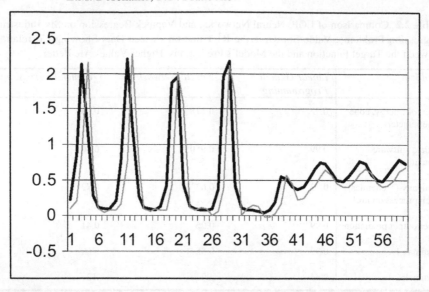

Figure 2.7 Best VSR model on laser problem (light gray line) compared to target output (heavy line) on held-out data.

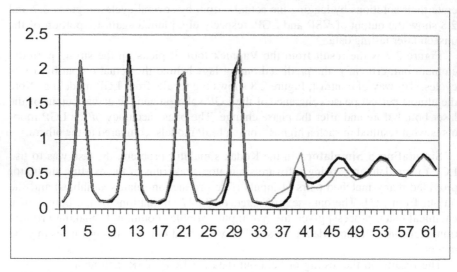

Figure 2.8 Best LGP model (light gray line) on laser problem compared to target output (dark line) on held-out testing data.

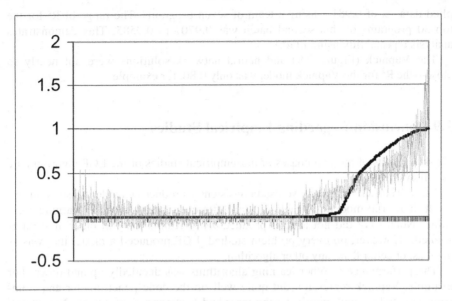

Figure 2.9 Best Vapnick predictions of Kodak simulator data (light-gray series) vs. the target data (dark line) on held-out data.

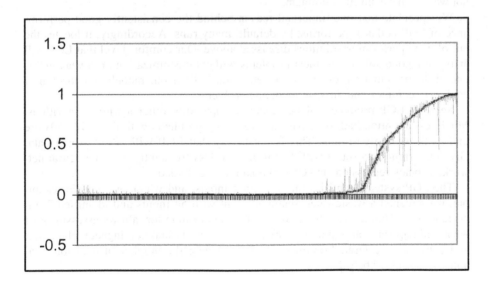

Figure 2.10 Best LGP model of company K simulator problem (light gray series) vs. target data (dark series) on the held-out data.

The LGP solution (Figure 2.10) so closely models the target output that the predictions completely obscure the target output line. In fact, for all but six of the 2,521 data points, the agreement between the LGP prediction and the actual value is very good. The R^2 fitness on the applied data set for the best team solution was 0.9889. (A second batch of 232 LGP runs achieved a similar R^2 fitness on the applied data set of 0.9814, using a team of seven programs. The range of R^2 for the top 30 programs of this second batch was 0.9707 to 0.9585. This demonstrates analysis repeatability using LGP.)

The Vapnick (Figure 2.9) and neural network solutions were not nearly so close—the R^2 for the Vapnick model was only 0.80, for example.

2.9 Conclusion Regarding Empirical Studies

The key results of the two phases of our empirical studies of the LGP algorithm are as follows.

First: The LGP software we used consistently produces excellent results on difficult, industrial modeling problems with little customization of the learning algorithm. Note: LGP did not always produce *better* results than all other algorithms studied. However, on every problem studied, LGP produced a model that was as good as, or better than, any other algorithm.

The performance of other learning algorithms was decidedly up-and-down. For example, Vapnick regression did quite well on the cone penetrometer and Company D data but quite poorly on the laser and Company K problems. Neural networks did quite well on the laser and Company K problems but not so well on the Tokamak and incinerator CO_2 data sets. C5.0 did well on the census problem but not well on the spam filter problem.

We speculate that one important reason behind the consistently good performance of LGP is that it performs, by default, many runs. Accordingly, it locates the tail of good performing solutions discussed above. Our comfort level that LGP will arrive at a good solution to most problems without customization or "tweaking" is one of the principal reasons we have settled on LGP as our modeling algorithm of choice for complex and difficult modeling problems.

Second: LGP produces robust models compared to other learning algorithms. Much less attention had to be paid to overfitting problems with the LGP software than with other algorithms. This is not to say that LGP will never overfit data. Given the right data set, it will. But it does so less frequently than the neural network, Vapnick regression, and C5.0 alternatives we studied

The LGP system identifies the important inputs, and which are not. For example, we screened a wastewater treatment plant with 54 inputs and identified 7 important ones. This reduces the number of inputs to monitor, allows assessment of what will happen if an input goes off-line (for security and contingency planning), and enhances accelerated optimization by reducing the number of decision variables, as discussed below.

2.10 Integrated System Analysis

This work is concerned with the building of a system comprised of integrated modeling and optimization tools. The integrated tool suite, comprised of (1) machine-code-based LGP for creating predictive models, and (2) ES-CDSA, is expected to ably handle a wide range of the complex problems with which we are concerned.

The remainder of this paper is devoted to discussing two application areas for the integration of these tools using two of the problems mentioned above—the incinerator R&D problem and the UXO discrimination problem.

2.10.1 Optimizing the Incinerator Model

The incinerator project was conceived from the beginning as a real-time control project. The models built with LGP predicted CO_2 levels in the secondary combustion chamber as a function of (1) The measured state of the plant at several previous time iterations; and (2) the plant control settings at previous time iterations.

Because plant control settings are part of the evolved LGP models, they may be optimized in response to each new state of the plant. That optimization may optimize for lowest cost operation, operation with a high probability of regulatory compliance, or both. Space limitations prevent a detailed description of the optimizer operation. However, details, including screenshots of the optimizer application, may be found in [4].

In terms of speed, optimization of these fast LGP models is practical and useful. The control programs evolved by LGP contain no more than 200 instructions, so they will execute on a modern Pentium computer in far less than a millisecond. So, during optimization, each call to the optimizer occupies less than a millisecond. According to the formula given above for ES-CDSA optimization, $200*(n+3)^2$ should suffice to derive an optimal setting for a new plant state. So, to optimize five parameters would take no more than 1.3 seconds—easily enough time to determine a new group of five control settings for the plant (the LGP model predicts an hour in advance).

2.10.2 Optimizing the LGP-derived UXO Models

The problem of UXO or land mines affects millions of acres worldwide and includes both training areas and former battlefields. The estimated cost for remediating the U.S. training ranges alone is at least $14 billion, and this number is likely understated [11]. The very real cost of clean-up (or nonclean-up) is the injury or death to people.

Currently, too large a portion of the resources available for responding to UXO challenges is expended by digging up sites where UXOs are predicted, but which turn out to be false alarms—that is, false positives. This, in turn, limits funding available for remediating genuine UXOs.

Machine-code-based, LGP has derived the most accurate UXO discriminator among published results to date [Jefferson Proving Grounds 1999] by a wide margin. This LGP UXO/non-UXO identification success opens up the assessment and optimization of response to the UXO issue on both the program and the project levels:

- The presence or absence of UXO can be assessed using remote, non-destructive technology such as land- or air-based sensors, including geophysics and various wave length sensors. Developed to a high degree of accuracy, wide areas can be screened and analyzed to reduce the footprint of areas needing further investigation. This will help manage the sheer size of this challenge.

- Areas of interest identified as requiring further investigation can be prioritized and ranked using good information on the probability or absence of UXO. This ranking would integrate the LGP UXO solution with multi-criteria/multi-objective decision support models; and
- Site-specific remedial action plans, known as "dig sheets," can be optimally designed to focus efforts on high probability, UXO-containing areas. When the decreased predicted likelihood of UXO presence and the field verified absence of UXO are demonstrated, a stopping point for remedial activities, based on scientific principals and field validation, is provided.

2.11 Summary and Conclusions

We are in the early stages of building a comprehensive, integrated optimization and modeling system to handle complex industrial problems. We believe a combination of machine-code-based, LGP (for modeling) and ES CDSA (for optimization) together provides the best combination of available tools and algorithms for this task.

By conceiving of design optimization projects as integrated modeling and optimization problems from the outset, we anticipate that engineers and researchers will be able to extend the range of problems that are solvable, given today's technology.

Acknowledgments

The results presented in this work are part of a three-plus-year collaborative effort between SAIC and Register Machine Learning Technologies to advance the state of the art of evolutionary computation as applied to complex systems. Specifically thanked for funding and latitude from SAIC are Joseph W. Craver, John Aucella, and Janardan J. Patel. Dr. Gregory Flach, Dr. Frank Syms, and Robert Walton are gratefully acknowledged for providing the input data sets used in some of the work – as are the researchers who need to keep their identity confidential for business reasons. Christopher R. Wellington, Ad Fontes Academy, Centreville, Virginia, conducted the chaotic drop experiment. All computations were performed by, and responsibility for their accuracy lies with, the authors.

References

1.   Bäck, T., Schwefel, H.P. (1993) An Overview of Evolutionary Algorithms for Parameter Optimization, Evolutionary Computation, 1(1):1-23.

2. Banzhaf, W., Nordin, P., Keller, R., Francone, F. (1998) Genetic Programming, An Introduction, Morgan Kauffman Publishers, Inc., San Francisco, CA.

3. Deschaine, L.M. (2000) Tackling real-world environmental challenges with linear genetic programming. PCAI Magazine,15(5):35-37.

4. Deschaine, L.M., Patel, J.J., Guthrie, R.G., Grumski, J.T., Ades, M.J. (2001) "Using Linear Genetic Programming to Develop a C/C++ Simulation Model of a Waste Incinerator," The Society for Modeling and Simulation International: Advanced Simulation Technology Conference, Seattle, WA, USA, ISBN: 1-56555-238-5, pp. 41-48.

5. Deschaine, L.M., Hoover, R.A. Skibinski, J. (2002) Using Machine Learning to Complement and Extend the Accuracy of UXO Discrimination Beyond the Best Reported Results at the Jefferson Proving Grounds, (in press), Proceedings of Society for Modeling and Simulation International.

6. Fausett, L.V. (2000). A Neural Network Approach to Modeling a Waste Incinerator Facility, Society for Computer Simulation's Advanced Simulation Technology Conference, Washington, DC, USA.

7. Fogel, D.B. (1992) Evolving Artificial Intelligence. Ph.D. thesis, University of California, San Diego, CA.

8. Francone, F., Nordin, P., and Banzhaf. W. (1996) Benchmarking the Generalization Capabilities of a Compiling Genetic Programming System Using Sparse Data Sets. In Koza et al. Proceedings of the First Annual Conference on Genetic Programming, Stanford, CA.

9. Francone F. (2002) Comparison of Discipulus™ Genetic Programming Software with Alternative Modeling Tools. Available at www.aimlearning.com.

10. Fukunaga, A., Stechert, A., Mutz, D. (1998) A Genome Compiler for High Performance Genetic Programming. In Proceedings of the Third Annual Genetic Programming Conference, pp. 86-94, Morgan Kaufman Publishers, Jet Propulsion Laboratories, California Institute of Technology, Pasadena, CA.

11. Government Accounting Office (2001) DOD Training Range Clean-up Cost Estimates are Likely Understated, Report to House of Representatives on Environmental Liabilities, USA General Accounting Office, April, Report no. GAO 01 479.

12. Hansen, N., Ostermeier, A. (2001) Completely derandomized self-adaptation in evolution strategies. Evolutionary Computation 9(2):159-195.

13. Jefferson Proving Grounds (1999) Jefferson Proving Grounds Phase IV Report: Graph ES-1, May, Report No: SFIM-AEC-ET-CR-99051.

14. Koza, J., Bennet, F., Andre, D., and Keane, M. (1999) Genetic Programming III. Morgan Kaufman, San Francisco, CA.

15. Nordin, J.P. (1994) A Compiling Genetic Programming System that Directly Manipulates the Machine Code. In Advances in Genetic Programming, K. Kinnear, Jr. (ed.), MIT Press: Cambridge MA.

16. Nordin, J.P. (1999). Evolutionary Program Induction of Binary Machine Code and its Applications, Krehl Verlag.

17. Nordin, J.P., Banzhaf , W. (1995). Complexity Compression and Evolution. In Proceedings of Sixth International Conference of Genetic Algorithms, Morgan Kaufmann Publishers, Inc.

18. Nordin, J.P., Banzhaf, W. (1995). Evolving Turing Complete Programs for a Register Machine with Self Modifying Code. In Proceedings of Sixth International Conference of Genetic Algorithms, Morgan Kaufmann Publishers, Inc.

19. Nordin, J.P., Francone, F., and Banzhaf, W. (1996) Explicitly Defined Introns and Destructive Crossover in Genetic Programming. Advances in Genetic Programming 2, K. Kinnear, Jr. (ed.), MIT Press: Cambridge, MA.

20. Nordin, J.P., Francone, F., and Banzhaf, W. (1998) Efficient Evolution of Machine Code for CISC Architectures Using Blocks and Homologous Crossover. In Advances in Genetic Programming 3, MIT Press, Cambridge, MA.
21. Quinlan, R. (1998) Data Mining Tools See5 and C5.0. Technical report, RuleQuest Research.
22. Register Machine Learning Technologies, Inc. (2002) Discipulus Users Manual, Version 3.0. Available at www.aimlearning.com.
23. Brian S. Rice and Robert L. Walton of Eastman Kodak. Company, Industrial Production Data Set.
24. Scientific American (Nov. 1999). Drop Experiment to Demonstrate a Chaotic Time Series.
25. Rechenberg, I. (1994). Evolutionsstrategie '93, Fromann Verlag, Stuttgart, Germany.
26. Schwefel, H.P. (1995). Evolution and Optimum Seeking. Sixth-Generation Computer Technology Series, John Wiley & Sons, New York.
27. Schwefel, H.P. and Rudolph, G. (1995). Contemporary Evolution Strategies. In Advances in Artificial Life, pp. 893-907, Springer-Verlag, Berlin.
28. Vapnick V. (1998) The Nature of Statistical Learning Theory, Wiley-Interscience Publishing.

Evolutionary Optimization of Approximating Triangulations for Surface Reconstruction from Unstructured 3D Data

K. Weinert, J. Mehnen, and M. Schneider

Summary. The aim of surface reconstruction is to transfer the shape of physical objects, which have been sampled by tactile or optical scanning techniques, into computer-processable descriptions. Triangulation is the most common surface model used in CAD/CAM systems. The processing time of a triangulation is decisively influenced by the number of sampling points. Hence, either the sampling points have to be reduced or efficient triangulations have to be found. Due to the fact that for interpolating triangulations the optimal distribution of the sampling points is generally difficult to find, here, self-organizing dynamic meshes are applied. The complex problem to find the best discrete approximation of a surface using a dynamic triangulation and a simple distance measure is solved by an evolution strategy. A special node-spring description always encodes valid triangulations.

3.1 Introduction

The problem of triangulation can be classified into two possible categories. The first class – and the most commonly known – is piecewise linear interpolation. This class of triangulations interpolates a set of unstructured points P in $\mathbb{R}^3$ with a surface consisting of triangular facets. The number of possible valid triangulations increases drastically with the number of points in P. The task of optimal triangulation is to find a representation that renders the true surface structure as realistic as possible. This problem is algorithmically very complex [5, 8]. In practical surface reconstruction the number of digitizing points can reach several million samples. In CAD/CAM systems the respective triangulations become very large and difficult to handle. In fact, a lot of digitizing points are redundant (e.g., plane areas) and can be eliminated from the original point set. In practical applications, 75% to 90% of the original points can be eliminated while high-tolerance demands are still met. The problem of automatic point reduction is to find filtering criteria that efficiently select relevant sampling points [10].

The second triangulation class, called *Approximating Triangulation (AT)* (also known under the term "mesh optimization" [4]), will be the subject matter of this article. AT avoids the need to preselect sampling points. In fact, the more sampling points are used for AT, the better. In contrast to interpolating triangulations, the 3D surface of an approximating triangulation fits a "flexible" triangular surface into a set of sampling points as close as possible. The number of vertices of the AT is fixed and usually a lot smaller than the number of sampling points of P. In contrast to interpolating triangulations, where only the graph structure of the edges is changed via edge flipping, in the case of AT the positions of the vertices are varied in 3D space while the connections in the graph structure remain unchanged. Here, the approximation problem is solved by an evolutionary optimization algorithm. This class of probabilistic algorithms is known to be robust and able to find good solutions also in cases where deterministic strategies fail. A special encoding will be introduced which allows us to interpret a triangulation as a vector of real values. The EA in combination with a simple distance function is able to find triangulations that are automatically adapted to the shape of a surface. This evolutionary approach reduces the influence of perhaps misleading human assumptions about the search problem structure to a minimum and, hence, allows us to find "unbiased" solutions.

3.2 Problem Definition

Typically, tactile as well as optical digitizing systems generate discrete point sets that do not have undercuts. Due to technical reasons, in die and mold making undercuts are not allowed. This restriction is often used in surface reconstruction and also applied in the following applications.

Let P be a set of discrete unstructured points in $\mathbb{R}^3$ that describe a functional surface. The number of points in P is n. Let S be a set of points in $\mathbb{R}^3$ with $r := |S|$ elements ($|S|$ is arbitrary but fixed and usually a lot smaller than n). No two points in S have the same z value.

A triangulation T of a set of $r \in \mathbb{N}$ vertices $S = \{s_i = (x_i, y_i, z_i) \in \mathbb{R}^3 | 1 \leq i \leq r\}$ in the 3D space is a set $T = \{T_j = (s_\alpha, s_\beta, s_\gamma)_j | \alpha, \beta, \gamma \in \{1, \ldots, r\}, 1 \leq j \leq m\}$ of m triangles, where

1. $(s_\alpha, s_\beta, s_\gamma)_j$, $1 \leq j \leq m$, are the vertices of a not degenerated (e.g., the points are not collinear) triangle T_j.
2. Each triangle is defined by exactly three vertices of S.
3. Each two triangles T_j and T_k of T, $j \neq k$, do not intersect.
4. The union of all triangles forms the convex hull of S.

The problem of AT is to find a triangulation T_S that approximates P best. The vertices of T_S (i.e., the points of S) can be changed arbitrarily in 3D space with the only restriction that T_S has to be a valid triangulation without undercuts.

Generally, the definition of an adequate quality criterion for triangulations that yields the best, i.e., highly realistic and efficient, descriptions of the original shape, is not easy to find [9, 5]. Smoothness criteria like the total absolute curvature [11] have been optimal for interpolating triangulations. For AT the simple sum of squared errors (SSE) was successful and yielded structurally similar results. Of course, only in special cases an AT represents a surface as exact as an interpolating triangulation. The idea to use an AT is that it gives hints about selection criteria where to select points for interpolating triangulations rather than to represent a surface with an AT directly. The SSE is defined by the sum of each distance d_i (measured in parallel to the z-axis) of a point $P_i \in P$ to a triangle $T_i = (s_1, s_2, s_3)_i$ of T_S:

$$SSE(P, T_S) = \sum_{i=1}^{|P|} d_i^2. \tag{3.1}$$

The SSE is calculated point by point. Because the triangulation T_S always covers the complete point set P, it is always possible to find a triangle that lies above or below a specific point. Due to the dynamic structure of the triangulation T_S, the reverse case must not be true. These triangles with no corresponding point will not influence the SSE. In practice, this case does not appear very often but can cause problems. These triangles may arrange freely in the 3D space, because their position does not undergo the selection process. Due to the fact that the triangles are always interconnected with each other, the total structure of the AT is only affected locally.

3.3 Encoding the AT

Approximating a triangulation T_S into a point set P is an optimization problem of the type

$$SSE(P, T_S) \longrightarrow \min_{S \in D_{T_S}} \tag{3.2}$$

D_{T_S} denotes the space of possible (restricted) positions of the vertices of S of the triangulation T_S. The positions of the vertices S of T_S have to be chosen in a way that the SSE-distance of T_S and P is minimized.

In order to map D_{T_S} into an *unrestricted* real valued space, the triangulation T_S is interpreted as a net of masses and springs (see Figure 3.1). In order to avoid solving time-consuming dynamic differential equations, the static equilibrium case is considered. The masses in the system are all zero.

The positions of the inner points (here, A, B, C) depend uniquely on the position of the supports (here, $s_1, \ldots, s_5$) and the spring coefficients (here, $c_1, \ldots, c_8$). A change in one of the spring coefficients implies a change in the position of all other mass points. Thus, a variation of one of the coefficient has always a global effect, although the influence weakens linearly with the distance.

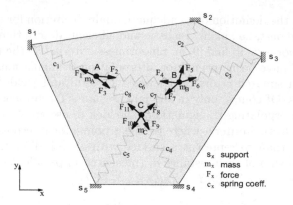

Figure 3.1. Planar node-spring system (masses all equal zero).

The basic structure of T_S for the optimization process is arbitrary. Here, the initial triangulation has been calculated by Delaunay's algorithm [3]. The structure of T_S mapped into the xy-plane is uniquely defined by the position of the convex hull of the border vertices and the set of spring coefficients $C = \{c_k \in \mathbb{R} | \ k = 1, \ldots, |E|\}$. Here $|E|$ denotes the number of inner edges of the triangulation T_S. Due to the fact that undercuts are not allowed, the z-components z_i of the vertices $s_i \in S$, $i = 1, \ldots, r$, of the triangulation T_S can be chosen arbitrarily in $\mathbb{R}$. Thus, T_S can be encoded as follows:

$$T_S = \{c_1, \ldots, c_{|E|}, z_1, \ldots, z_{|S|}\}. \tag{3.3}$$

All coefficients can vary arbitrarily in $\mathbb{R}$ while they always encode valid triangulations. This special mapping from $D_{T_S} \rightarrow \mathbb{R}^{|E|+|S|}$ allows us to use real valued vectors. This is a precondition for the application of an evolution strategy without explicit restrictions. Restrictions in the fitness function are usually time-consuming and increase the complexity of the optimization problem. The mapping $D_{T_S} \rightarrow \mathbb{R}^{|E|+|S|}$ can also be interpreted as a genotype-phenotype mapping. The *genotype* encoding describes all possible triangulations in a *vector*. The vector is manipulated by evolutionary operators. The mapping transforms the vector into the respective *3D triangulation*. This *phenotype* can be evaluated by the fitness function (e.g., the SSE).

3.4 Deterministic AT Optimization

Terzpoulos and Vasilescu [8] use dynamic graphs for triangulations. The authors use a mass-spring system with spring coefficients that are adjusted according to the estimated curvature of the point set to be approximated. The equilibrium state is calculated by solving a differential equation system. In their experiments a point set P of 128×128 sampling points is approximated by a triangulation with $|S| = 30 \times 30$. Typical for this approach is that it uses (manmade) assumptions about the correlation between the optimal position of the vertices and the curvature estimated from the point cloud.

Hoppe [4] uses a deterministic approximation scheme that utilizes least-square distances as well as varying numbers of edges for a dynamic mass-spring-based triangulation model. An additional regularization term in the fitness function generates regular distribution of the vertices. This additional term supports the search for the minimum of an energy function. The strength of the spring coefficients is decreased continuously in order to allow triangles with tapered-off edges. The approach of Hoppe does not make explicit use of a priori assumptions about curvature properties, etc. It just needs the evaluation of an unbiased distance function.

Algorri and Schmitt [1] introduce a different mass-spring model. The relation between the vertices and the sampling points is realized by a connection between the vertex and its next-nearest sampling point. A nonlinear equation system models a dynamically oscillating net structure. The spring values of the system are calculated deterministically after each oscillation step. The definition of the damping factor is not easy to adjust because on the one hand the system should remain long enough in oscillation to find a good global solution and on the other hand it should "anneal" fast enough to find a good solution.

3.5 Evolutionary AT Optimization

All algorithms described in the last paragraph follow deterministic schemes. These approaches assume that the implemented algorithmic solution leads directly and without any deterioration to the optimum solution. This implies that the general criteria to find a solution are already known and can be implemented algorithmically. An evolutionary algorithm does not make any assumptions about the path to the solution and, thus, is able to find the desired optimum with only very little a priori knowledge.

The evolution strategy (ES) is a special form of the superset called evolutionary algorithms (EA). EA also comprise methods like genetic algorithms (GA), evolutionary programming (EP), and genetic programming (GP). EA, fuzzy logic, and neural networks belong to the general set called CI (computational intelligence) techniques [12]. Evolutionary algorithms are probabilistic optimization strategies that adopt the paradigms of evolution as introduced by Darwin. The surprisingly robust and beautiful solutions of nature are the motivation to use this sophisticated approach.

The evolution strategy is described in its basic form by the nomenclature $(\mu/\rho \overset{+}{,} \lambda)$-ES [2]. Here, $\mu \in \mathbb{N}_+$ denotes the number of parents, $\lambda \in \mathbb{N}_+$ the number of offspring, and $\rho \in \mathbb{N}_+$ a coefficient that defines the number of parents involved in recombination. In the special case where two parents mate to form an offspring, the two commonly known short forms $(\mu + \lambda)$-ES and (μ, λ)-ES are used. The "+" sign denotes that offspring as well as parents are used by selection. The sign "," denotes that only the offspring will be used to form the next parent population. In the case of a (μ, λ)-selection the relation $1 \leq \mu < \lambda$ is necessary. An individual I consists of a set of n real-valued parameters (so called objective variables), which can be evaluated by an n-dimensional fitness function (generally, $f : \mathbb{R}^n \to \mathbb{R}$), and 1 to n strategy parameters $\sigma_i, i = 1, \ldots, n_\sigma, n_\sigma \in \{1, \ldots, n\}$ of the ES. Two additional global parameters τ' and τ characterize the strength of the normal distributed random mutation, which is applied to the objective variables of each individual. If only one step size σ is used, τ' equals zero. A rotation matrix of correlation coefficients as elements of the strategic parameters is introduced by Schwefel [11] but is not used in this context. Each complete individual consisting of both parameter sets is adapted by the evolutionary process. Hence, an external deterministic adaptation of the step sizes is not necessary, because the strategy parameters also undergo the selection process. Recombination interchanges the genetic data of two or more parent individuals by intermediate or discrete exchange schemes.

An *Evolutionary Algorithm*

$$EA = (I, \Phi, \Omega, \Psi, s, \iota, \mu, \lambda) \tag{3.4}$$

is called an $(\mu \overset{+}{,} \lambda)$-*ES*: $\Leftrightarrow$

(1) individual: $I = \mathbb{R}^n \times \mathbb{R}_+^{n_\sigma}, n_\sigma \in \{1, \ldots, n\}$
(2) fitness function: $\Phi = f, \Phi : I \to \mathbb{R}$
(3) probabilistic genetic operators:
$\Omega = \{r_{r_x r_\sigma} : I^\mu \to I^\lambda\} \cup \{m_{\{\tau, \tau'\}} : I^\lambda \to I^\lambda\}$
(4) selection: $\Psi(P) = s(Q \cup m_{\{\tau, \tau'\}}(r_{r_x r_\sigma}(P)))$,
where $Q = \emptyset$ in case of (μ, λ) selection and
$Q = P$ in case of $(\mu + \lambda)$ selection.
(5) truncation selection: $s \in \{s_{(\mu+\lambda)}, s_{(\mu,\lambda)}\}$
The individuals are ordered by their fitness evaluated by Φ.
The μ best $P \cup Q$ survive.
(6) termination criterion: ι (e.g., a maximum number of generations)

The algorithm iterates the following steps:
(A) initialization: $P = I^\mu$
(B) recombination: $P' = r_{r_x r_\sigma}(P)$
(C) mutation: $P'' = m_{\{\tau, \tau'\}}(P')$
(D) evaluation: $\Phi : P'' \rightarrow \mathbb{R}^\lambda$
      $\Phi : P \rightarrow \mathbb{R}^\mu$
(E) $(\mu \dagger \lambda)$ selection: $s(Q, P) \rightarrow P$
(F) test termination criterion: either $\rightarrow$ (B) or end.

Mutation is realized by first varying the n step size parameters:

$$\sigma'_i = \sigma_i \cdot exp(\tau' \cdot N(0, 1) + \tau \cdot N_i(0, 1)). \tag{3.5}$$

In a second step the objective variables are changed:

$$x_i = x_i + \sigma'_i \cdot N_i(0, 1). \tag{3.6}$$

The vector σ can be initialized arbitrarily in $\mathbb{R}^n$ (e.g., $\sigma_i = 1.0$). The factors τ and τ_i depend on the dimension of the problem. A classic choice is $\tau \propto \left(\sqrt{2\sqrt{(n)}}\right)^{-1}$ and $\tau' \propto (\sqrt{2n})^{-1}$, respectively [13]. $N(0, 1)$ denotes the normal distribution with expectation 0 and variance 1.

Typically, either discrete or intermediate recombination is used. This operator is applied separately to the objective and the strategic parameters. Bisexual discrete recombination generates one new offspring individual I_O by mating two randomly selected parent individuals I_{P_1} and I_{P_2}. The components $I_{P_{1i}}$ or $I_{P_{2i}}$ of the parents are chosen by chance. Bisexual intermediate recombination generates a new offspring individual by application of the formula: $I_{O_i} = I_{P_{1i}} + (I_{P_{2i}} - I_{P_{1i}})/2$. From empirical results it is known that intermediate recombination of the objective parameters and discrete recombination of the step sizes are a good choice.

The ES for optimizing an AT was implemented as follows:

- The initial population I^μ is formed by μ triangulations (e.g., by Delaunay triangulation [3]) of the point set S. The individuals I are encoded according to the description of T_s (see paragraph *Encoding the AT*). In the beginning, an equidistant point set in the plane is used to build S.
- A set of sampling points P of artificially designed objects is used.
- The fitness function $f = SSE(P, T_S)$ (see paragraph *Problem Definition*) is applied.
- The termination criterion ι holds if a limiting maximum number of generations is exceeded.
- $\mu = 30$ and $\lambda = 100$. The complete set of step sizes is used, i.e., $n_\sigma = n$. Intermediate recombination of the objective parameters and discrete recombination of the step sizes was the best choice during initial experiments

and, thus, this setting is kept for all experiments. τ and τ_i have been set according to the dimensions (e.g., $\tau = 0.01$, $\tau_i = 0.04$ for $n = 8 \times 8$).

3.6 Results

The experiments have been designed to illustrate the behavior of the algorithm regarding the influence of the structure and density of the sampling points, the exactness of the reconstruction, and time and space complexity of the algorithm.

Hemisphere A hemisphere was sampled with $|P| = 50 \times 50$ points. Figure 3.2 shows the reconstruction of the artificial object using a set S of 8×8 vertices.

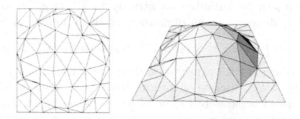

Figure 3.2. Reconstruction of a hemisphere.

The initial triangulation started with an equidistant point set. The optimized triangulation shows triangles with nearly equal edge lengths (left-hand side of Figure 3.2). This result is typical for surfaces with homogenous curvature. The algorithm distributes the vertices equally over the surface. The border edge between the sphere and the plane is interpolated by a regular linear polygon. The best fitness measured for 5 runs was $SSE_{min} = 9.18 \cdot 10^{-3}$, the minimum punctiform distance was $9.27 \cdot 10^{-7}$, and the maximum punctiform distance was $9.4 \cdot 10^{-3}$.

Half-Cylinder A cylinder lying in the plane has a lateral area with one constant zero and one constant nonzero curvature. The front and rear faces stand vertically on the plane and form two sharp circular edges with the lateral area of the cylinder. Again a set P of 50×50 equally spaced sampling points has been used to describe the object surface. A subset $S \subset P$ of 8×8 vertices was used for the triangulation.

On the right-hand side of Figure 3.3 the insufficient approximation of the front face as well as the cut curve of the cylinder and the plane are obvious.

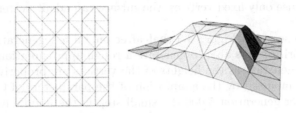

Figure 3.3. Delaunay triangulation of a half-cylinder using the initial regular grid.

The triangulation algorithm of Delaunay used for the initial individual tries to generate triangles with equal edge lengths. On a regular point grid this yields the typical structures that can be seen in the left-hand side of Figure 3.3.

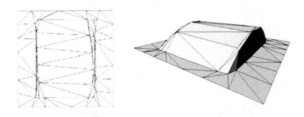

Figure 3.4. Optimized reconstruction of a half cylinder.

The optimized approximating triangulation is shown in Figure 3.4. The vertices are distributed in a more efficient way than during the initialization. Long triangles are generated automatically only by application of the simple SSE fitness function. This is especially noteworthy, because interpolating triangulations often generate small triangles. Even optimized interpolating triangulations need special fitness functions to be able to evolve long triangles [9]. The ability of the algorithm to generate nearly vertical triangles should also be noticed.

The special property of the EA is that it forms optimal structures just by evaluating the fitness function and selecting the best solutions. It does not follow fixed deterministic rules.

Skew Steps Sharp edges that do not exactly follow the orientation of the scanning lines may become problematic for 3D interpolating triangulations. Due to aliasing effects and the fixed vertex structure, these algorithms sometimes tend to generate harmonica-shaped vertical structures. Leaving the restriction to use only fixed vertices, the surface can adapt better to the surface structure.

One can see from Figure 3.5 that after only a few generations the evolutionary algorithm was able to generate a rough approximation of the object. After 5.000 generations the heights of the vertices are properly set. Then the structure is modeled by the adaptation of the parameters of the mass-spring system. After generation 5.000 the small step in the middle has evolved. After 30.000 generations a maximum distance of $1.2046 \cdot 10^{-2}$ and a fitness of $5.397 \cdot 10^{-2}$ are reached.

Figure 3.6 shows exemplarily the convergence behavior of the optimization algorithm. The fitness values and the step sizes are displayed. The trend of the curves is representative for the reconstruction of surfaces with a complex topology. The best case, linearly (in a logarithmic scale) decreasing fitness values, can only be achieved for simple structured surfaces. The result of the automatic adaptation process of the step sizes can be seen in the lower part of Figure 3.6.

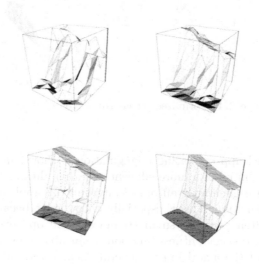

Figure 3.5. Evolution of a step structure. Generations 100 (upper left), 1.000 (upper right), 5.000 (lower left) and 30.000 (lower right).

Influence of the Sample Point Density. The density of the digitized points has a direct influence on the calculation time because the next-nearest triangle to a given point has to be identified. This problem can be solved efficiently by the method of Preparata [6], which has $O(n_P \log n_i) + O(m \log m)$ time and

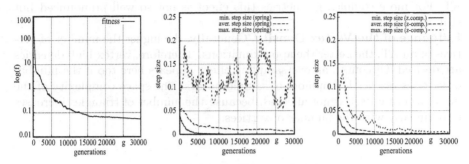

Figure 3.6. Fitness function and step sizes.

$O(n)$ space complexity (n_i number inner edges, m number of triangles, n_P number of sampling points).

In the experiments the sample points of the half-cylinder have been used. The number of the equidistant points is varied from 10×10 to 90×90. The initial triangulation of the AT has 8×8 vertices. In order to allow a comparison of the triangulations, the distance of the resulting surfaces to a 100×100 sample point set was calculated. All runs stopped after 30.000 generations.

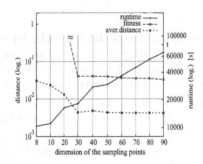

Figure 3.7. Influence of the number of sampling points on the fitness and the run time.

Figure 3.7 shows the average distances of 5 runs and the amount of time (logarithmic scaling). The figure supports the experience that a non-linear relation between the amount of time and the number of points exists. It should be noted that an increasing number of points does not have a relevant influence on the fitness, if the proportion of the number of triangles to the number of sampling points exceeds a certain limit (here about $1/14$). This oversampling phenomenon is also typical for reconstructions with Non-Uniform Rational B-Splines (NURBS) [10] and gives a hint about the necessary resolution of an

AT. For more complex geometries this effect is not so well pronounced but still exists.

Influence of the Vertex Density. Generally, the higher the number of vertices of an AT, the better the approximations. Therefore, vertex high densities are desired. Of course, an oversampling effect appears here too if the number of vertices reaches the number of sample points. The space complexity of the data structure itself is not affected, because the number of triangles increases only linearly with the number of vertices.

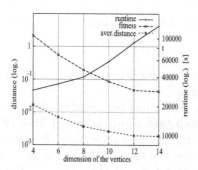

Figure 3.8. Influence of the vertex density on the fitness and the run time.

In the experiment the geometry of the half-cylinder with 50×50 sampling points has been used. The number of vertices has been increased from 4 to 14. Figure 3.8 shows the fitness and the run time in relation to the number of vertices. The experiments show that the number of vertices has a cubic influence on the run time. Therefore, the parameter settings for the AT should be adequately chosen in order to find a compromise between run time and surface quality. Vertex numbers over 30×30 lead to unreasonable run times. Furthermore, instability problems may appear. Small vertical triangles evolve that fit between the scan lines. These triangles do not contribute directly to the fitness and therefore cannot be adapted. A different encoding of the z-parameters of an individual may help to handle this problem.

Experiments with large objects show that, due to the fact that long triangles should be evolvable, generally it is not possible to split the surface into smaller patches without losses in the reconstruction quality.

3.7 Conclusions and Outlook

The technique of approximating triangulations is an important tool to find the optimal distribution and density of sampling points. This data can be estimated by the positions of the vertices organized by an evolutionary algorithm.

A special genotype-phenotpye mapping for triangulations using a node-spring system has been introduced. This encoding was necessary for the application of the evolution strategy. The experiments give evidence that a simple distance criterion is sufficient to find good approximating triangulations. In order to find optimal structures, it is necessary to allow the algorithm to evolve long triangles. Due to fact that high-dimensional and complex problems generally take long run times, the reconstruction of complex freeform surfaces using AT is not appropriate. However, the application of an EA is necessary because deterministic optimization algorithms, e.g., the SIMPLEX algorithm (in [11]), generally yielded insufficient surface qualities. Depending on the shape of the surface and the initial triangulation, the EA had a much higher convergence probability than the comparatively fast SIMPLEX algorithm. This evolutionary approach may also help to create new ideas for efficient point selection schemes.

Acknowledgments

This research was supported by the Deutsche Forschungsgemeinschaft as part of the Collaborative Research Center "Computational Intelligence" (SFB 531). Many thanks for the contributions of Markus Heller. His work was essential for this article. Also many thanks to W. Banzhaf and M. Brameier, who have been very important for this work.

References

1. M.-E. Algorri, F. Schmitt (1993) Surface reconstruction from unstructured 3D data, Computer Graphics Forum, 15(1):47-60.
2. H.-G. Beyer (2001) The Theory of Evolution Strategies. Springer, Heidelberg.
3. M. de Berg, M. van Kreveld, M. Overmars, O. Schwarzkopf (1998) Computational Geometry: Algorithms and Applications, Springer, Berlin.
4. H. Hoppe, T. DeRose, T. Duchamp (1993) Mesh optimization. Proc. Computer Graphics SIGGRAPH '93, pp. 21-26.
5. J. Mehnen (2000) Evolutionäre Flächenrekonstruktion, Ph.D. Thesis, University of Dortmund, Germany, K. Weinert (ed.), Vulkan Verlag, Essen.
6. F. Preparata, I. Shamos (1985) Computational Geometry: An Introduction, Springer, New York.
7. H.-P Schwefel (1995) Evolution and Optimum Seeking, Wiley Interscience, New York.
8. D. Terzopoulos, M. Vasilescu (1991) Sampling and Reconstruction with Adaptive Meshes. In Proc. IEEE Comp. Soc. Conf. Computer Vision and Pattern Recognition, pp. 70-75.
9. K. Weinert, J. Mehnen, P. Drerup (1998) New Solutions for Surface Reconstructions from Discrete Point Data by Means of Computational Intelligence. In CIRP, ICME'98, Capri, Italy, 1.7-3.7.1998, S.431-438.

10. K. Weinert, J. Mehnen (2000) Comparison of Selection Schemes for Discrete Point Data for Evolutionary Optimized Triangulations and NURBS Surface Reconstructions, ISA 2000, Wollongong, Australia, F. Nagdy and F. Kurfess (eds.), pp. 104-110, Dec. 11-15.
11. R. van Damme and L. Alboul (1994) Polyhedral metrics in surface reconstruction. Tight Triangulations, Technical report. University of Twente, Dep. of Applied Mathematics, Twente, The Netherlands.
12. J. C. Bezdek (1994) Computational Intelligence: Imitating Life. Chapter: What is Computational Intelligence. pp. 1-12, IEEE Press, New York.
13. T. Bäck (1996) Evolutionary Algorithms in Theory and Practice, Oxford University Press, New York.

An Evolutionary Algorithm Based on Morphological Associative Memories for Endmember Selection in Hyperspectral Images

M. Graña, C. Hernandez, A. d'Anjou

Summary. In previous works we have introduced Morphological Autoassociative Memories (MAM) as detectors of morphologically independent patterns and their application to the task of endmember determination in hyperspectral images. After shifting the hyperspectral image data to the mean and taking the signs of the resulting hyperspectral patterns, we obtain a binary representation of the image pixels. Morphologically independent binary patterns can be seen as representations of the vertices of a convex region that covers most of the data. The MAMs are used as detectors of morphologically independent binary patterns and the selected binary patterns are taken as the guides for the selection of endmembers for spectral unmixing between the image pixels. This process was defined in a greedy suboptimal fashion, whose results depend largely on the initial conditions. We define an Evolutionary Algorithm for the search of the set of endmembers based on the morphological independence condition and we compare it with a conventional Evolutionary Strategy tailored to the endmember detection task over a multispectral image.

4.1 Introduction

In this chapter we are concerned with the definition of spectral endmembers for spectral unmixing of hyperspectral images. We study the application of evolutionary algorithms combined with a morphological approach that uses Morphological Associative Memories (MAMs) to detect the endmember spectra in the image.

Passive remote sensing evolution has produced measurement instruments with ever-growing spectral breadth and resolution. Multispectral sensing allows the classification of pixels. However, the recognition that pixels of interest are frequently a combination of materials has introduced the need to quantitatively decompose the pixel spectrum into their constituent material spectra. Hyperspectral sensor measurements in hundreds of spectral bands allow us to perform such "spectral unmixing" [13]. The reasons for the mixture of several spectra in a single pixel are (1) the spatial resolution of the sensor implies that different land covers are included in the area whose radiance measurement results in an image pixel, and (2) distinct materials are intimately mixed (e.g., a beach). The second situation is independent of the sensor spatial resolution and produces nonlinear mixtures, which are difficult to analyze. The first situation produces mixtures that, often can be adequately modeled by a linear mixing model. In a previous chapter [10] we assume that the linear model is correct, and we present an approach to the detection of endmembers for spectral unmixing in hyperspectral image processing through the application of MAMs.

Briefly introduced, Morphological Neural Networks are those that involve somehow the maximum and/or minimum operators. Some fuzzy approaches are included in this definition. The kind of Morphological Neural Networks range from pattern classifiers [5], [15], [23], [28], target detection [7], [9], [17], [27], to associative memories for image restoration [19], [20], [21]. The MAMs [19], [20], [21] are the morphological counterpart of the Linear Associative Memories (LAM) [14] and the well known Hopfield Autoassociative Memories [11]. Like the LAMs, MAMs are constructed as correlation matrices but with the substitution of the conventional matrix product by a min or max matrix product from Image Algebra [22]. Dual constructions can be made using the dual min and max operators. In [10] we propose the MAMs as detectors of morphological independent binary patterns and, therefore, as the endmember selection tool. The described algorithm is a local search process, highly sensitive to the initial conditions of the process. In this chapter we explore the definition of an Evolutionary Algorithm devoted to the task of endmember selection from a given image that uses the MAMs as detectors of morphological independences. This new algorithm is a Genetic Algorithm [8] that searches the space of binary patterns that correspond to representations of the endmembers looked for, which must be sets of morphologically independent patterns. Through the chapter we call this algorithm GA with Morphological Independence restriction (GA-MI). Mutation is the genetic operator used. We use the MAM to test the morphological independence of the children. Because mutation does not preserve the morphological independence and there is not any established procedure for its correction, the children that do not conform to the morphological independence requisite are discarded. For comparison we propose an Evolution Strategy [2], [3], [4] for the same task of endmember design. In both evolutionary approaches, the objective function to be minimized is the combination of the reconstruction error of the image pixels and the satisfaction of the properties of a true abundance image: the full additivity and nonnegativity of all the abundance image pixels.

The structure of the chapter is as follows: In Section 4.2 we review the definition of the linear mixing model. Section 4.3 provides a review of basic results of MAMs. Section 4.4 describes our evolutionary algorithm of endmember selection for remote sensing hyperspectral images, and a competing conventional evolution strategy approach. Section 4.5 presents some experimental results of the proposed algorithm and the competing evolution strategy. Section 4.6 gives our conclusions and directions of future work.

4.2 The Linear Mixing Model

The linear mixing model can be expressed as follows:

$$\mathbf{x} = \sum_{i=1}^{M} a_i \mathbf{s}_i + \mathbf{w} = \mathbf{S}\mathbf{a} + \mathbf{w}, \tag{4.1}$$

where $\mathbf{x}$ is the d-dimensional received pixel spectrum vector, $\mathbf{S}$ is the $d \times M$ matrix whose columns are the d-dimensional endmembers $\mathbf{s}_i, i = 1, .., M$, $\mathbf{a}$ is the M-dimensional fractional abundance vector, and $\mathbf{w}$ is the d-dimensional additive observation noise vector. The linear mixing model is subjected to two constraints on the abundances. First, to be physically meaningful, all abundances must be nonnegative $a_i \geq 0, i = 1, ..., M$. Second, to account for the entire composition the abundances must be fully additive $\sum_{i=1}^{M} a_i = 1$.

Often the process of spectral unmixing is performed on transformations of the data intended to reduce the computational burden [13] or to enhance some properties of the data [12]. We do not apply any dimension reduction transformation here. The task of endmember determination is the focus of this chapter. In an already classical chapter [6], Craig starts with the observation that the scatter plots of remotely sensed data are tear-shaped or pyramidal if two or three spectral bands are considered. The apex lies in the so-called dark point. The endmember detection becomes the search for nonorthogonal planes that enclose the data, forming a minimum volume simplex, hence the name of the method. Besides its computational cost the method requires the prespecification of the number of endmenbers. Another step to the automatic endmember detection is the Conical Analysis method proposed in [12] and applied to target detection. The extreme points in the data after a principal component transformation are the searched for endmember spectra. The method is geometrically similar to Craig´s one but does not require costly linear programming. It also requires the prespecification of the desired number of endmembers. Another approach is the modeling by Markov Random Fields and the detection of spatially consistent regions whose spectra will be assumed as endmembers [18]. A quite standard approach to endmember determination is the use of standard libraries of spectra [13]. This approach requires great expertise and a prori knowledge of the data. Finally, there are interactive exploration algorithms that are supported by specific software packages.

Once the endmembers have been determined, the last task is the computation of the inversion that gives the fractional abundance and, therefore, the spectral unmixing. The simplest approach is the unconstrained least-squared error estimation given by

$$\widehat{\mathbf{a}} = \left(\mathbf{S}^T \mathbf{S}\right)^{-1} \mathbf{S}^T \mathbf{x}. \tag{4.2}$$

The abundances that result from this computation do not fulfill the non-negative and full additivity conditions. It is possible to enforce each condition separately, but rather difficult to enforce both simultaneously [13]. As our aim is to test an endmember determination procedure, therfore we will use unconstrained estimation (4.2) to compute the abundance images. We will show intensity scaled and shifted images of the abundances to evaluate our results. As a measure of the quality of the decomposition obtained it is useful to introduce the reconstruction error:

$$\varepsilon^2 = \|\mathbf{x} - \mathbf{S}\widehat{\mathbf{a}}\|^2. \tag{4.3}$$

4.3 Morphological Associative Memories

The work on MAMs stems from the consideration of an algebraic lattice structure $(\mathbb{R}, \vee, \wedge, +)$ as the alternative to the algebraic $(\mathbb{R}, +, \cdot)$ framework for the definition of Neural Networks computation [19] [20]. The operators $\vee$ and $\wedge$ denote, respectively, the discrete max and min operators (resp., sup and inf in a continuous setting). The approach is termed morphological neural networks because $\vee$ and $\wedge$ correspond to the morphological dilation and erosion operators, respectively. Given a set of input/output pairs of pattern $(X, Y) = \{(\mathbf{x}^\xi, \mathbf{y}^\xi) ; \xi = 1, ..., k\}$, a heteroassociative neural network based on the pattern's cross correlation [14], [11] is built up as $W = \sum_\xi \mathbf{y}^\xi \cdot (\mathbf{x}^\xi)'$. Mimicking this construction procedure the works in [19], [20] propose the following constructions of heteroassociative morphological memories

$$W_{XY} = \bigwedge_{\xi=1}^{k} \left[\mathbf{y}^\xi \times \left(-\mathbf{x}^\xi \right)' \right], \qquad M_{XY} = \bigvee_{\xi=1}^{k} \left[\mathbf{y}^\xi \times \left(-\mathbf{x}^\xi \right)' \right], \tag{4.4}$$

where $\times$ is any of the $\veebar$ or $\barwedge$ operators. Here $\veebar$ and $\barwedge$ denote the max and min matrix product, respectively, defined as follows:

$$C = A \veebar B = [c_{ij}] \Leftrightarrow c_{ij} = \bigvee_{k=1..n} \{a_{ik} + b_{kj}\}, \tag{4.5}$$

$$C = A \barwedge B = [c_{ij}] \Leftrightarrow c_{ij} = \bigwedge_{k=1..n} \{a_{ik} + b_{kj}\}. \tag{4.6}$$

It follows that the weight matrices W_{XY} and M_{XY} are lower and upper bounds of the max and min matrix products $\forall \xi; W_{XY} \leq \mathbf{y}^\xi \times (-\mathbf{x}^\xi)' \leq M_{XY}$ and therefore the following bounds on the output patterns hold: $\forall \xi; W_{XY} \veebar \mathbf{x}^\xi \leq \mathbf{y}^\xi \leq M_{XY} \barwedge \mathbf{x}^\xi$, that can be rewritten as $W_{XY} \veebar X \leq Y \leq M_{XY} \barwedge X$. A matrix A is a $\veebar$-perfect ($\barwedge$-perfect) memory for (X, Y) if $A \veebar X = Y$ ($A \barwedge X = Y$). It can be proven that if A and B are $\veebar$-perfect and $\barwedge$-perfect memories, resp., for (X, Y), then W_{XY} and M_{XY} are also $\veebar$-perfect and $\barwedge$-perfect, resp.: $A \leq W_{XY} \leq M_{XY} \leq B$. Therefore, $W_{XY} \veebar X = Y = M_{XY} \barwedge X$. Conditions of perfect recall of the stored patterns are given by the following theorem [19],[20]:

Theorem 1. *Perfect recall of HMM. The matrix W_{XY} is $\veebar$-perfect if and only if $\forall\xi$ the matrix $\left[\mathbf{y}^\xi \times (-\mathbf{x}^\xi)'\right] - W_{XY}$ contains a zero at each row. Similarly, the matrix M_{XY} is $\barwedge$ -perfect if and only if $\forall\xi$ the matrix $\left[\mathbf{y}^\xi \times (-\mathbf{x}^\xi)'\right] - M_{XY}$ contains a zero at each row. These conditions are formulated for W_{XY} as $\forall\gamma\forall i\exists j; x_j^\gamma = \bigvee_{\xi=1}^{k}\left(x_j^\xi - y_i^\xi\right) + y_i^\gamma$, and for M_{XY} as $\forall\gamma\forall i\exists j; x_j^\gamma = \bigwedge_{\xi=1}^{k}\left(x_j^\xi - y_i^\xi\right) + y_i^\gamma$.*

Theorem 2. *Perfect recall of AMM. Both erosive and dilative AMMs have the perfect recall property: $W_{XX} \veebar X = X = M_{XX} \barwedge X$, for any X.*

These results hold when we try to recover the output patterns from the noise free input pattern. To take into account the noise, a special definition of the kinds of noise affecting the input patterns is needed. Let $\widetilde{\mathbf{x}}^\gamma$ be a noisy version of $\mathbf{x}^\gamma$. If $\widetilde{\mathbf{x}}^\gamma \le \mathbf{x}^\gamma$, then $\widetilde{\mathbf{x}}^\gamma$ is an eroded version of $\mathbf{x}^\gamma$. Alternatively, we say that $\widetilde{\mathbf{x}}^\gamma$ is subjected to erosive noise. If $\widetilde{\mathbf{x}}^\gamma \ge \mathbf{x}^\gamma$, then $\widetilde{\mathbf{x}}^\gamma$ is a dilated version of $\mathbf{x}^\gamma$. Alternatively, we say that $\widetilde{\mathbf{x}}^\gamma$ is subjected to dilative noise. Morphological memories are very sensitive to these kinds of noise. The conditions of *robust* perfect recall for W_{XY}, i.e., the retrieval of $\mathbf{y}^\gamma$ given a noisy copy $\widetilde{\mathbf{x}}^\gamma$, are given by the following theorem [19], [20].

Theorem 3. *Robust perfect recall of HMM. Given input/output pairs (X, Y), the equality $W_{XY} \veebar \widetilde{\mathbf{x}}^\gamma = \mathbf{y}^\gamma$ holds when the following relation holds:*

$$\begin{aligned}
\forall j; \widetilde{x}_j^\gamma \le x_j^\gamma \vee \bigwedge_i \left(\bigvee_{\xi\neq\gamma}\left(y_i^\gamma - y_i^\xi + x_j^\xi\right)\right), \\
\forall i\exists j_i; \widetilde{x}_{j_i}^\gamma = x_{j_i}^\gamma \vee \left(\bigvee_{\xi\neq\gamma}\left(y_i^\gamma - y_i^\xi + x_{j_i}^\xi\right)\right).
\end{aligned} \tag{4.7}$$

Similarly for the conditions of robust perfect recall for M_{XY} given a noisy copy $\widetilde{\mathbf{x}}^\gamma$ of $\mathbf{x}^\gamma$, that is, the equality $M_{XY} \barwedge \widetilde{\mathbf{x}}^\gamma = \mathbf{y}^\gamma$ holds when

$$\begin{aligned}
\forall j; \widetilde{x}_j^\gamma \ge x_j^\gamma \wedge \bigvee_i \left(\bigwedge_{\xi\neq\gamma}\left(y_i^\gamma - y_i^\xi + x_j^\xi\right)\right), \\
\forall i\exists j_i; \widetilde{x}_{j_i}^\gamma = x_{j_i}^\gamma \wedge \left(\bigwedge_{\xi\neq\gamma}\left(y_i^\gamma - y_i^\xi + x_{j_i}^\xi\right)\right).
\end{aligned} \tag{4.8}$$

The associative memory matrix W_{XY} is robust against controlled erosions of the input patterns while the associative memory matrix M_{XY} is robust against controlled dilations of the input patterns. In the case of autoassociative memories the conditions for perfect recall of noisy patterns are a corollary for Theorem 3:

Corollary 1. *Given patterns X, the equality $W_{XX} \veebar \widetilde{\mathbf{x}}^\gamma = \mathbf{x}^\gamma$ holds when the noise affecting the pattern is erosive $\widetilde{\mathbf{x}}^\gamma \le \mathbf{x}^\gamma$ and the following relation holds*

$\forall i \exists j_i; \widetilde{x}_{j_i}^\gamma = x_{j_i}^\gamma \vee \left(\bigvee_{\xi \neq \gamma} \left(x_i^\gamma - x_i^\xi + x_{j_i}^\xi \right) \right)$. *Similarly, the equality* $M_{XY} \overline{\wedge} \widetilde{\mathbf{x}}^\gamma = \mathbf{x}^\gamma$ *holds when the noise affecting the pattern is dilative* $\widetilde{\mathbf{x}}^\gamma \geq \mathbf{x}^\gamma$ *and the following relation holds:* $\forall i \exists j_i; \widetilde{x}_{j_i}^\gamma = x_{j_i}^\gamma \wedge \left(\bigwedge_{\xi \neq \gamma} \left(x_i^\gamma - x_i^\xi + x_{j_i}^\xi \right) \right)$.

The AMM will fail in the case of noise being a mixture of erosive and dilative noise. To obtain general robustness, the kernel method has been proposed [19], [21], [25]. A kernel for (X, Y) is defined as a set of patterns Z that satisfy the following conditions: (1) $Z \neq X$, (2) $M_{ZZ} \overline{\wedge} X = Z$, and (3) $W_{ZY} \underline{\vee} Z = Y$. Kernels are, therefore, selective erosions of the input patterns designed to ensure that the robustness against dilation of the M memories will allow the recovering of Z patterns from either eroded and dilated versions of the input patterns, and the W memory will produce the desired output response. That is, for corrupted inputs $\widetilde{\mathbf{x}}^\gamma \geq \mathbf{z}^\gamma$ we are guaranteed that $W_{ZY} \underline{\vee} (M_{ZZ} \overline{\wedge} \widetilde{\mathbf{x}}^\gamma) = \mathbf{y}^\gamma$. Note that $\widetilde{\mathbf{x}}^\gamma > \mathbf{z}^\gamma$ does not guarantee correct recall.

In order to characterize kernels and to obtain a constructive definition, the notion of morphological independence and strong morphological independence is introduced in [21]. Here we distinguish erosive and dilative versions of this definition:

Definition 1. *Morphological independence. Given a set of pattern vectors* $X = (\mathbf{x}^1, ..., \mathbf{x}^k)$, *a pattern vector* $\mathbf{y}$ *is said to be morphologically independent of* X *in the erosive sense if* $\mathbf{y} \not\leq \mathbf{x}^\gamma; \gamma = \{1, ..., k\}$, *and morphologically independent of* X *in the dilative sense if* $\mathbf{y} \not\geq \mathbf{x}^\gamma; \gamma = \{1, ..., k\}$. *The set of pattern vectors* X *is said to be morphologically independent in either sense when all the patterns are morphologically independent of the remaining patterns in the set.*

The strong morphological independence is introduced in [21] to give a construction for minimal kernels with maximal noise robustness. For binary-valued vectors, morphological independence and strong morphological independence are equivalent. For the current application we want to use AMMs as detectors of the set extreme points, to obtain a rough approximation of the minimal simplex that covers the data points. We need to establish first a simple fact in the following remark:

Remark 1. Given a set of pattern vectors $X = (\mathbf{x}^1, ..., \mathbf{x}^k)$ and the erosive W_{XX} and dilative M_{XX} memories constructed from it. Given a test pattern $\mathbf{y} \notin X$, if $\mathbf{y}$ is morphologically independent of X in the erosive sense, then $W_{XX} \underline{\vee} \mathbf{y} \notin X$. Also, if $\mathbf{y}$ is morphologically independent of X in the dilative sense, then $M_{XX} \overline{\wedge} \mathbf{y} \notin X$.

The endmembers that we are searching for are the corners of a high-dimensional box centered at the origin of the space. They are morphologically independent vectors both in the erosive and dilative senses, and they enclose the remaining vectors. The endmember detection process would apply the erosive and dilative AMMs constructed from the already detected endmembers to detect the new ones as suggested by the previous remark. Working with integer-valued vectors, a desirable property is that vectors already inside the box defined by the endmembers would be detected as such. However, given a set of pattern vectors $X = \left(\mathbf{x}^1, ..., \mathbf{x}^k \right)$ and the erosive W_{XX} and dilative M_{XX} memories constructed from it. A test pattern $\mathbf{y} < \mathbf{x}^\gamma$ for some $\gamma \in \{1, .., k\}$ would give $W_{XX} \underline{\vee} \mathbf{y} \notin X$. Also, if the test pattern $\mathbf{y} > \mathbf{x}^\gamma$ for some $\gamma \in \{1, .., k\}$, then $M_{XX} \overline{\wedge} \mathbf{y} \geq \notin X$. Therefore, working with integer-valued patterns the detection of the morphologically independent patterns would be impossible. However, if we consider the binary vectors obtained as the sign of the vector components, then morphological independence would be detected as suggested by the above remark. Let us denote by the expression $\mathbf{x} > \mathbf{0}$ the construction of the binary vector $(\{b_i = 1 \text{ if } x_i > 0; b_i = 0 \text{ if } x_i \leq 0\}; i = 1, .., n)$.

4.4 The Detection of Spectral Endmembers

In this section we describe both the approach based on the GA with morphological independence restriction (GA-MI) and the standard Evolution Strategy defined for the problem at hand. The endmembers of a given hyperspectral image under the linear mixture assumption correspond to the vertices of the minimal simplex that encloses the data points [6]. The region of the space enclosed by a set of vectors, simultaneously morphologically independent in both erosive and dilative senses resulting from the GA-MI, is a high-dimensional linear convex region (i.e., bounded by hyperplanes). The result of the Evolution Strategy is also a set of vertices that may define a convex region. It is difficult to give a quantitative measure of the goodness of a given set of endmembers, which is needed for the definition of evolutionary approaches. The positive and full addition properties are the basic restriction to fulfill, so that they are the basis for the definition of the fitness function. We have chosen the reconstruction error in (4.3) as the regularization term. Let us formalize first the fitness function.

Let us denote $\left\{ \mathbf{f}\left(i, j\right) \in \mathbb{R}^d; \ i = 1, .., n; j = 1, .., m \right\}$ the hyperspectral image, $\boldsymbol{\mu}$ and $\boldsymbol{\sigma}$ the vectors of the mean and standard deviations of each band computed over the image, α the noise correction factor, and E the set of M endmembers whose fitness is to be quantified. Let $\left\{ \widehat{\mathbf{a}}\left(i, j\right) \in \mathbb{R}^M; \ i = 1, .., n; j = 1, .., m \right\}$ and $\left\{ \varepsilon^2\left(i, j\right) \in \mathbb{R}^M; \ i = 1, .., n; j = 1, .., m \right\}$ be the abundance estimations and reconstrucion error computed applying (4.2) and (4.3) at each pixel with E as the endmember collection. The fitness function to be minimized is defined as follows:

$$F\left(\mathbf{f}, E\right) = \sum_{i=1}^{n} \sum_{j=1}^{m} \varepsilon^2\left(i, j\right) + \sum_{i=1}^{n} \sum_{j=1}^{m} \left(1 - \|\widehat{\mathbf{a}}\left(i, j\right)\|\right)^2 \qquad (4.9)$$

$$+ \sum_{i=1}^{n} \sum_{j=1}^{m} \sum_{\mathbf{k}} abs\left(\widehat{a}_k\left(i, j\right)\right).$$

In this equation $\mathbf{k} = \{k \,|\, \hat{a}_k\,(i,j) < 0\}$. Both evolutionary approaches have a population P of N individuals, each consisting of a set of endmembers of size K. In the GA-MI we have a population of binary individuals

$$P_t = \{\mathbf{B}_i; i = 1, ..., N\}.$$

Each one of the individuals $\mathbf{B}_i = \{\mathbf{b}_{ij}; j = 1, ..., M\}$ corresponds to a set of endmembers, where each $\mathbf{b}_{ij} \in \{0,1\}^d$ encodes the directions of the convex region vertices. Each collection $\mathbf{B}_i$ is morphologically independent in both erosive and dilative senses. The GA-MI evolves the population using a conventional mutation operator and a roulette wheel selection. However, each time a new individual is generated, it is tested for morphological independence, and if it fails to pass the test it is rejected and a new individual is generated. The test for morphological independence proceeds as follows:

1. Consider initially $X = \{\mathbf{x}_1\} = \{\mathbf{b}_{i,1}\}$.
2. Construct the AMMs based on the morphologically independent binary signatures: M_{XX} and W_{XX}. Define orthogonal binary codes Y for the endmembers and construct the identification HMM[1]: M_{XY}.
3. Consider the next endmember code: $\mathbf{b}_{i,k}$
   a) Compute the vector of the signs of the Gaussian noise corrections $\mathbf{f}^+(i,j) = (\mathbf{f}^c(i,j) + \alpha\boldsymbol{\sigma} > 0)$ and $\mathbf{f}^-(i,j) = (\mathbf{f}^c(i,j) - \alpha\boldsymbol{\sigma} > 0)$.
   b) Compute $y^+ = M_{XY} \,\overline{\wedge}\, (M_{XX} \,\overline{\wedge}\, \mathbf{b}_{i,k})$.
   c) Compute $y^- = M_{XY} \,\overline{\wedge}\, (W_{XX} \,\overline{\wedge}\, \mathbf{b}_{i,k})$.
   d) If $y^+ \notin Y$ and $y^- \notin Y$, then $\mathbf{b}_{i,k}$ is morphologically independent in both senses. Go to step 2 adding $\mathbf{b}_{i,k}$ to X and resume the test, increasing k. If not, the test fails and the individual is rejected.

To compute the set of endmembers E_i corresponding to each $\mathbf{B}_i$ we need first to consider the zero mean image

$$\{\mathbf{f}^c(i,j) = \mathbf{f}(i,j) - \boldsymbol{\mu}; i = 1, ..., n; j = 1, ..., m\}. \qquad (4.10)$$

Then the endmember pixels are determined as the extreme points in the directions specified by the $\mathbf{B}_i$. The final set of endmembers is the set of original spectral signatures $\mathbf{f}(i,j)$ of the pixels selected as members of E_i.

The Evolution Strategy follows the conventional definition and dynamics [4]. Population individuals are given by a set of endmember hypothesis and their mutation variances $P_t = \{(E_i, \sigma_i); i = 1, ..., N\}$. Initial endmembers are generated by a random perturbation about the mean spectrum of the image, and the following generations are produced by the conventional schema of perturbation and self-adaptation of the mutation variances. A $(\mu + \lambda)$ strategy is used for selection, where the next generation is obtained as the best ones from the joint set of parents and children.

---

[1] Although we have no formal proof of the perfect recall of the HMM when the input patterns are morphologically independent, it is very likely and fits nicely to use the HMM as the endmember identifier. In practice, we search the set X directly.

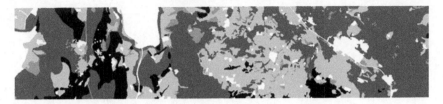

Figure 4.1. Ground truth of the experimental image.

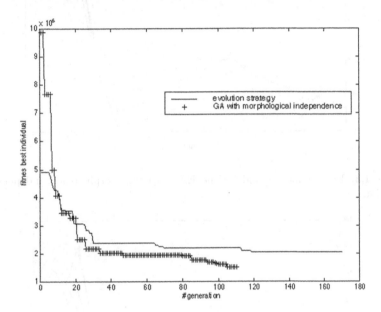

Figure 4.2. Evolution of the fitness function of the best individual of the GA with morphological independence restriction and the evolution strategy.

4.5 Experimental results

The data used for the experimental work correspond to a multispectral image of size of 710×4558 pixels which covers a large area including vegetation, cultivated land areas, and urban areas. This image has been acquired through a CASI (Compact Airborne Spectrographic Imager) sensor using a general configuration of 14 bands, that is, each pixel is represented by a vector of 14 8-bpp gray scale values. From all the 14 bands of the original image, a smaller region of 448×2048 pixels has been selected (cropped). For the operation of both the Evolutionary Algorithm and the Evolution Strategy a 8:1 subsampled version of this region has been used to compute the fitness function value. However, final abundance results were computed over the 448×2048 pixels region.

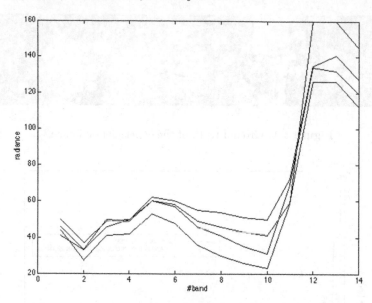

Figure 4.3. Endmembers found by the EA with the morphological independence restriction.

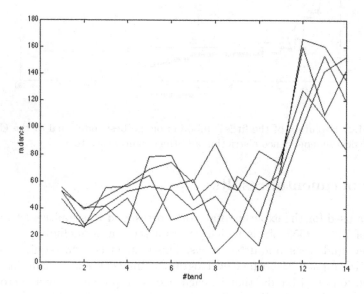

Figure 4.4. Endmembers found by the Evolution Strategy tailored to the endmember determination task.

Figure 4.5. Abundance images corresponding to the endmembers discovered by the GA with the morphological independence restriction: GA-MI.

The ground truth of the image is composed of the following categories of land cover: **A** evergreen trees, **B** deciduous trees, **C** brushwoods, **D** meadows and crops, **E** urban areas. The ground truth is visualized in Figure 4.1 assigning an increasing intensity to the land cover categories: black corresponds to evergreen trees and white to urban areas. Figure 4.2 shows the plot of an evolution of the fitness value of the best individual for the GA-MI and the Evolution Strategy. In both algorithms the population size was 10, the number of endmembers per individual was 5, and the number of mutations allowed was 30. It can be appreciated that the GA-MI finally obtains better quantitative results than the ES approach. However, the qualitative assessment of the results must be done on the abundance images computed from the obtained endmember spectra.

The monitoring of the evolution of GA-MI shows that, although all the individuals are collections of morphologically independent binary vectors, the codifications seldom have a corresponding extreme point in the image. Therefore, GA-MI initially has collections of only one or two endmembers. The

Figure 4.6. Abundance images corresponding to the endmembers discovered by the Evolutionary Strategy.

evolution adds new meaningful endmembers to the best individuals. In the final best individual we have found 4 endmembers, whose spectra are plotted in Figure 4.3. The Evolution Strategy performs better most of the time according to Figure 4.2. However, it stagnates at the end. It gives 5 endmembers plotted in Figure 4.4. The endmember spectra found are like noisy versions of the ones found in the image. It is worth noting that the GA-MI is performing spontaneously a process of selection of the appropriate number of endmembers, always below the upper bound fixed in the simulation. The number of endmembers was fixed at $M = 5$, like the population size $N = 10$ and the number of children generated $\lambda = 10$.

The qualitative results are given by the abundance images computed using the endmember spectra found by both approaches. The abundance images obtained from the spectral unmixing with the GA-MI endmembers are shown in Figure 4.5. Figure 4.6 presents the abundance images obtained from the ES endmembers. We find that the results are quite parallel: the abundance image of endmember #1 found by the GA-MI is similar to the one of endmember #2 found by the Evolutionary Strategy, and the corresponding endmembers seem to be good detectors of vegetal cover including crops. Abundance image #2 of GA-MI is similar to the abundance image #5 of the Evolution Strategy. However, these images seem of little value. There are no interesting spatial structures discovered in these images. It seems that the corresponding endmember spectra are noise detectors. The abundance images #3 and #4 of the GA-MI correspond to the abundance images #3 and #4 of the Evolutionary Strategy, respectively. The endmembers seem to correspond to detectors of artificial constructs like buildings and roads.

An interesting result is that the GA-MI has obtained the same qualitative results with fewer endmembers than the ES. From a dimensionality reduction viewpoint, the GA-MI has been able to obtain a transformation of the image data from the original 14-dimensional space into a 4-dimensional space, preserving much of the qualitative information of the image and obtaining an optimized reconstruction of the original image. We assert that the qualitative information has been preserved because the main spatial features of the imaged scene are detectable in the transformed images, and correspond to cover classes defined in the ground truth. We may say that GA-MI outperforms the ES in the sense of obtaining a more parsimonious representation of the image data.

4.6 Conclusions and Further Work

We have proposed an Evolutionary Algorithm that uses the notion of morphological independence and the Morphological Autoassociative Memory for testing it, for the task of hyperspectral image linear unmixing. Linear unmixing is both a detection process and a dimension reduction process. It is very efficient for the detection of small features, which can be blurred by other methods, like clustering-based unsupervised analysis of the images. The Evolutionary Algorithm ensures some degree of optimality of the endmembers extracted from the image, in the sense of minimum unmixing (and reconstruction) error. We have found that our algorithm improves over an Evolutionary Strategy tailored to the problem, in the sense of the minimization of the proposed fitness function. We have also found that the GA-MI algorithm spontaneously performs a selection of the appropriate number of endmembers. An added appeal of the approach proposed is that it uses the spectra found in the image. Using the actually measured spectra may reduce the interpretation problems when trying to decide the actual physical materials present in the scene.

Further work must be addressed to the experimentation with other hyperspectral images, and the extensive testing of the parameter sensitivities of the approach, keeping in mind that hyperspectral images are very large and need speedy analysis methods.

Acknowledgments

The authors received partial support from projects of the Ministerio de Ciencia y Tecnologia MAT1999-1049-C03-03, TIC2000-0739-C04-02, and TIC2000-0376-P4-04, and UPV/EHU 00140.226-TA-6872/1999 of the University of The Basque Country (UPV/EHU). The Center for Ecological Research and Forestry Applications (CREAF) of the UAB kindly provided the experimental multispectral image and corresponding ground truth.

References

1. Asano A., K. Matsumura, K. Itoh, Y. Ichioka, S. Yokozeki (1995) Optimization of morphological filters by learning, Optics Comm. 112 : 265-270
2. Bäck T., H.P. Schwefel (1993) An overview of Evolution Algorithms for parameter optimization. Evolutionary Computation, 1:1-24.
3. Bäck T., H.P. Schwefel (1996) Evolutionary computation: An overview. IEEE ICEC'96, pp.20-29.
4. Th. Bäck (1996) Evolutionary Algorithms in Theory and Practice, Oxford University Press, New York.
5. Carpenter G.A., S. Grossberg, D.B. Rosen (1991) Fuzzy ART: Fast stable learning of analog patterns by an adaptive resonance system, Neural Networks, 4:759-771,
6. Craig M., Minimum volume transformations for remotely sensed data, IEEE Trans. Geos. Rem. Sensing, 32(3):542-552.
7. Gader P.D., M.A. Khabou, A. Kodobobsky (2000) Morphological regularization neural networks, Pattern Recognition, 33:935-944.
8. Goldberg D.F. (1989) Genetic Algorithms in Search, Optimization & Machine Learning, Addison-Wesley, Reading, MA.
9. Graña M., B. Raducanu (2001) On the application of morphological heteroassociative neural networks. Proc. Intl. Conf. on Image Processing (ICIP), I. Pitas (ed.), pp. 501-504, Thessaloniki, Greece, October, IEEE Press.
10. Graña M., B. Raducanu, P. Sussner, G. Ritter (2002) On endmember detection in hyperspectral images with Morphological Associative Memories, Iberamia 2002, LNCS Springer-Verlag, in press.
11. Hopfield J.J. (1982) Neural networks and physical systems with emergent collective computational abilities, Proc. Nat. Acad. Sciences, 79:2554-2558,
12. Ifarraguerri A., C.-I Chang (1999) Multispectral and hyperspectral image analysis with convex cones, IEEE Trans. Geos. Rem. Sensing, 37(2):756-770.
13. Keshava N., J.F. Mustard (2002) Spectral unimixing, IEEE Signal Proc. Mag. 19(1):44-57
14. Kohonen T., (1972) Correlation Matrix Memory, IEEE Trans. Computers, 21:353-359.

15. Pessoa L.F.C , P. Maragos, (1998) MRL-filters: a general class of nonlinear systems and their optimal design for image processing, IEEE Trans. on Image Processing, 7(7):966 -978,

16. Pessoa L.F.C , P. Maragos (2000) Neural networks with hybrid morphological/rank/linear nodes: A unifying framework with applications to handwritten character recognition, Patt. Rec. 33:945-960

17. Raducanu B., M. Graña, P. Sussner (2001) Morphological neural networks for vision based self-localization. Proc. of ICRA2001, Intl. Conf. on Robotics and Automation, pp. 2059-2064, Seoul, Korea, May, IEEE Press.

18. Rand R.S., D.M. Keenan (2001) A Spectral Mixture Process conditioned by Gibbs-based partitioning, IEEE Trans. Geos. Rem. Sensing, 39(7):1421-1434.

19. Ritter G.X., J.L. Diaz-de-Leon, P. Sussner. (1999) Morphological bidirectional associative memories. Neural Networks, 12:851-867.

20. Ritter G.X., P. Sussner, J.L. Diaz-de-Leon. (1998) Morphological associative memories. IEEE Trans. on Neural Networks, 9(2):281-292.

21. Ritter G.X., G. Urcid, L. Iancu (2002) Reconstruction of patterns from noisy inputs using morphological associative memories, J. Math. Imag. Vision, submitted.

22. Ritter G.X., J.N. Wilson, Handbook of Computer Vision Algorithms in Image Algebra, CRC Press:Boca Raton, Fla.

23. Rizzi A.,M. ,F.M. Frattale Mascioli (2002) Adaptive resolution Min-Max classifiers, IEEE Trans. Neural Networks 13(2):402-414.

24. Salembier P. (1992) Structuring element adaptation for morphological filters, J. Visual Comm. Image Repres., 3:115-136.

25. Sussner P. (2001) Observations on Morphological Associative Memories and the Kernel Method, Proc. IJCNN'2001, Washington, DC, July

26. Sussner P. (2002) , Generalizing operations of binary autoassociative morphological memories using fuzzy set theory, J. Math. Imag. Vision, submitted.

27. Won Y., P.D. Gader, P.C. Coffield (1997) Morphological shared-weight neural network with applications to automatic target detection, IEEE Trans. Neural Networks, 8(5):1195-1203.

28. Yang P.F., P. Maragos, (1995) Min-max classifiers: Learnability, design and application, Patt. Rec., 28(6):879-899.

29. Zhang X.; C. Hang; S. Tan; PZ. Wang (1996) The min-max function differentiation and training of fuzzy neural networks, IEEE tTrans. Neural Networks 7(5):1139 -1150.

5

On a Gradient-based Evolution Strategy for Parametric Illumination Correction

Elsa Fernández, Manuel Graña, Jesús Ruiz-Cabello

Abstract. This chapter deals with the issue of illumination inhomogeneity correction in images. The approach followed is that of estimating the illumination bias as a parametric model. The model is a linear combination of Legendre polynomials in the 2D or 3D space. The estimated bias is, therefore, a smooth function characterized by a small set of parameters that define a search space of lower dimension than the images. Our work is an enhancement of the PABIC algorithm, using gradient information in the mutation operator hence we name it GradPABIC. We apply our algorithm, the PABIC, and a conventional Evolution Strategy (ES) over a set of synthetic images to evaluate them, through the comparison of the correlation between the recovered images and the original one. The PABIC and the EE are allowed the same number of fitness computations, while the Grad PABIC number of fitness evaluations is two orders of magnitude lower, because of the gradient computation added complexity. Finally, we present some results on slices of a synthetic MRI volume.

5.1 Introduction

Illumination bias correction is a key problem in several domains, above all in medical imaging and Magnetic Resonance Imaging (MRI). The bias correction is critical in some cases to obtain meaningful image segmentations, because these segmentations are usually done on the basis of a known catalog of MR responses of specific tissues. Pixels are classified according to their intensities and a set of known values. Besides the partial volume effect, the intensity inhomogeneities are the main difficulty to obtain precise automatic segmentations. The contribution of the illumination to the image formation is multiplicative; therefore, its effect cannot be removed easily through traditional linear filtering algorithms. In this chapter we will not consider other noise contributions [6]. The classic approach to solve this problem is the homomorphic filtering [3] that filters out the low-frequency components of the logarithm image Fourier transform. Illumination gradients are usually smooth functions. Therefore, it is expected that the lowest components of the logarithm image will correspond to the illumination bias. Working over the logarithm image trying to isolate the illumination components of the image is common to many other illumination correction algorithms. Few algorithms perform the correction, computing the division of the corrupted image by the estimated bias. Among them, the straightforward approaches consist of taking an image of the background and dividing the new images by it.

There has been broad interest in this problem, which has produced a number of algorithms. A coarse taxonomy distinguishes between parametric and nonparametric methods. On the nonparametric class of algorithms, a well-founded approach is the one applying Bayesian image modeling to the image logarithm and using some minimization method to estimate the most likely bias field logarithm. The estimation task [10] applies an EM algorithm, while [4] applies a minimization of an entropy criterion. These works try to isolate the bias field. On the other hand, [1] introduces the effect of the bias field inside the classification adding a bias term into the fuzzy c-means that they apply to the image pixels classification in order to obtain image segmentations. On the whole, nonparametric methods are computer-intensive and require huge amounts of memory in some cases. An approach that gives good results based on the iterative deconvolution with Gaussian kernels is described in [8].

Parametric methods assume some mathematical model of the illumination bias, whose estimation becomes fitting the model surface to the image intensity function. The model surfaces are always very smooth and the fitness criterion involves the approximation error. In [5] the bias model consists of multiplicative and additive components that are modeled by a combination of smoothly varying basis functions. The parameters of this model are optimized such that the information of the corrected image is minimized while the global intensity statistics are preserved. In [9] the illumination bias is modeled by a linear combination of 2D or 3D Legendre polynomials. The coefficients of this combination are estimated by a random search, called PABIC, that looks like an oversimplified Evolution Strategy (ES) [2]. The ES are, as all the evolutionary algorithms, rather sensitive to the population size and the number of mutations. Small populations lead to premature convergence, and the PABIC is an extreme case. Therefore, premature convergence may be an issue for PABIC. In fact, this phenomenon shows itself in the computational experiments by the high variance of the results of replicating the PABIC search. The application of an ES of equivalent computational complexity (allowing the same overall number of fitness evaluations) leads to some improvement and a lower variance of the results. However, the "single solution per population" approach of PABIC remains appealing for its simplicity. We have devised a modification of the PABIC that uses the gradient information in the mutation operator, directing the algorithm to the search in the directions of greater promise of improvement. We call this approach GradPABIC. It is a kind of instantaneous memetic algorithm [11]. The computational experiments show the improvements of GradPABIC both in the mean accuracy of the recovered image and in the reduction of the result's variance.

The chapter structure is as follows: Section 5.2 recalls the formal statement of the illumination correction problem, and the basic homomorphic algorithm. Section 5.3 presents ES, and the PABIC as a specific instance, as well as the GradPABIC. Section 5.4 presents experimental results that confirm our discussion. Finally, Section 5.5 presents some conclusions and lines of further work.

5.2 Homomorphic Filtering

A classical image model is given by the equation:

$$f(x,y) = i(x,y) \cdot r(x,y) + n(x,y). \tag{5.1}$$

The observed (sensed) image $f(x,y)$ is the product of the "real" image $r(x,y)$ and the illumination field $i(x,y)$. Besides it is perturbed by a random additive noise $n(x,y)$, which is assumed usually as having zero-mean Gaussian distribution. This model implies that the effects of the illumination in the frequency space are spread over all the range of frequencies, because of the duality of product and convolution on the Fourier transform. Linear filtering is able to remove sections of the frequency space but not to deconvolve the illumination effect. Early approaches tried to convert the nonlinear problem into a linear one working on the logarithm of the image. This is the homomorphic filtering approach [3].

If we discard the Gaussian additive noise, Eq. (5.1) becomes: $f(x,y) = i(x,y) \cdot r(x,y)$. The logarithm of the image is computed to obtain a linear expression: $g(x,y) = \ln i(x,y) + \ln r(x,y)$. The Fourier transform of this expression is $G(u,v) = I(u,v) + R(u,v)$. The linear filtering of the image with a filter $H(u,v)$ is given by

$$S(u,v) = H(u,v) \cdot G(u,v) = H(u,v) \cdot I(u,v) + H(u,v) \cdot R(u,v). \tag{5.2}$$

From this expression it becomes clear that we can remove the illumination component by linear filtering of the logarithm image, assuming that the illumination logarithm is band-limited. A high-pass filter would allow to recover the real image after exponentiation of the filtered image in Eq. (5.2). If the filter applied is a low-pass filter, we would obtain the estimation of the illumination field. A weakness of the method is the assumption that low-frequency components are only due to illumination effects. This is especially bad in MRI images where the tissues are assumed to correspond to constant-intensity regions.

5.3 Evolution Strategies and the Illumination Correction Problem

The initial discussion for any application of evolutionary algorithms is the function to be minimized. In the case of parametric approaches to illumination inhomogeneity correction, the objective function will be related to the approximation error. In [9] the model of the illumination bias is a linear combination of Legendre polynomials, denoted $P_i(.)$, where i is the order of the polynomial. The reason for this choice is that they are orthogonal, thus they constitute a basis of smooth functions, ideal to model the smooth variations of the illumination gradient. The 2D bias field is modeled as follows:

$$\hat{b}(\underline{x}, \underline{p}) = \sum_{i=0}^{m-1} p_i f_i(\underline{x}) = \sum_{i=0}^{l} \sum_{j=0}^{l-i} p_{ij} P_i(x) P_j(y).$$ (5.3)

Therefore, the 2D fields $P_i(x)P_j(y)$ remain smooth and it can be proved that they are orthogonal. In the case of the 3D volumes, needed for medical imaging, the generalization is straightforward. The true illumination bias is unknown, so it is impossible to define the error of approximation related to it. The approach is then to assume (1) that we know the classes of objects present in the image, (2) that each region in the image corresponding to an object has the same and constant intensity, and (3) that we know this intensity value. This is generally true for medical images where the tissues have a known response to a given imaging method. A noise term could be needed for model completeness but it is of no use in the following, so it is neglected. The error is then defined as the approximation to an image whose pixels have exactly the class-defined intensities.

$$e = \sum_{x,y} \prod_k valley(\hat{r}(x,y) - \mu_k),$$ (5.4)

where $valley()$ is an smooth convex function and $\hat{r}(x,y)$ is the estimated reflectance obtained after correction. Many of the expressions in the original paper [9] refer to the modeling of the illumination as an additive term, which can be explained in the framework of the homomorphic filtering. In this case the algorithm would be estimating the filter to be applied to the logarithm image. We have preferred to assume that the Legendre polynomials are multiplicative modulations of the image. Therefore, they must be normalized in the [0,1] range. The image correction is performed by dividing the observed image by the estimated bias: $\hat{r}(x,y) = f(x,y)/\hat{b}(x,y)$. It must be noted that the corrected image will have a greater signal-to-noise-ratio (SNR) in the regions of low estimated bias. The global minima of Eq. (5.4) will be configurations of pixel intensities such that each one belongs to one of the predefined intensity classes μ_k. The expression of the error that we use in the derivation of the gradient is a special case of Eq. (5.4), when $valley$ is a quadratic function:

$$e = \sum_{x,y} \prod_k (\hat{r}(x,y) - \mu_k)^2 = \sum_{x,y} \prod_k \left(\frac{f(x,y)}{\hat{b}(x,y)} - \mu_k \right)^2.$$ (5.5)

It is easy to deduce an expression of the gradient of the error relative to each parameter of the linear combination of Legendre polynomials.

$$\frac{\partial e}{\partial p_{ij}} = \sum_{x,y} \left[\left[\prod_k \left(\frac{f(x,y)}{\hat{b}(x,y)} - \mu_k \right) \right] \frac{-f(x,y)P_i(x)P_j(y)}{\hat{b}(x,y)^2} \right]$$

(5.6)

This expression is the basis for the GradPABIC proposed below. Once the error function has beenidentified, the formulation of an ES needs the definition of the individuals and the search space. In the present case, the search space is that of the linear combination parameters of Legendre polynomials, and each individual will consist of a set of such parameters. We assume that the typical ES [2] is well known by the reader. We will use a $(\mu + \lambda)$ strategy that consists of the selection of the new population over the set of parents and offsprings. This strategy is elitist and its convergence is guaranteed. The sensitive parameters of these algorithms are the number of mutations and the population size. We will not use recombination. Observe that the number of fitness computations is $O(\mu + \lambda G)$, with G the number of generations. That is, the population size is not very influential on the computation time (unless it grows exponentially). The PABIC proposed by [9] is basically an ES with a population of an individual, and a restricted version of the self-adaptive mutation variance: a (1+1) ES. We reproduce below the expressions that define the algorithm:

$$\underline{r}_t \approx N(\underline{0}, I),$$

$$\underline{x}_{t+1} = \underline{x}_t + A_t \cdot \underline{r}_t,$$

$$A_{t+1} = \begin{cases} A_t (I + (c_g - 1)\frac{r_t r_t'}{r_t' r_t})) & \text{if } f(\underline{x}_{t+1}) < f(\underline{x}_{opt}), \\ A_t (I + (c_s - 1)\frac{r_t r_t'}{r_t' r_t})) & \text{otherwise,} \end{cases}$$

$$\underline{x}_{opt} = \begin{cases} \underline{x}_{t+1} & \text{if } f(\underline{x}_{t+1}) < f(\underline{x}_{opt}), \\ \underline{x}_{opt} & \text{otherwise,} \end{cases}$$

where $\underline{x}_t$ is the population of the algorithm, given by the set of linear combination parameters of the Legendre polynomial, $\underline{r}_t$ is a random vector whose components follow independent normal $N(0,1)$ distributions. The A_t is the mutation covariance matrix, which is self-adapted along the evolution. The magnitude of the matrix is increased or decreased depending on the finding of new optimal solutions. We have applied the algorithm with the parameters recommended in the paper. The GradPABIC algorithm has the same outline as the PABIC, but the mutation operator is given by a random sampling along the gradient of the error function on the search parameters:

$$\underline{r}_t \approx N(\underline{0}, I),$$

$$\underline{x}_{t+1} = \underline{x}_t + \left[\frac{\partial f(x_t)}{\partial x_i} \right] \cdot \underline{r}_t,$$

$$\underline{x}_{opt} = \begin{cases} \underline{x}_{t+1} & \text{if } f(\underline{x}_{t+1}) < f(\underline{x}_{opt}), \\ \underline{x}_{opt} & \text{otherwise.} \end{cases}$$

5.4 Experimental Results

To test the algorithms we have generated several instances of corrupted images from a chessboard image. We know the original uncorrupted image and the illumination bias field, and therefore we can compute the correlation between them and the estimated ones. The goal of the algorithms is to estimate the bias fields and to recover a clean chessboard image. PABIC parameters were set according to the nominal values recommended in [9]: c_{grow} in the interval $[1.01, 1.1]$ and $c_{shrink} = c_{grow}^{-1/4}$. The number of PABIC iterations is 9000. The maximum order of the Legendre polynomials was 3. The ES was tested with $\mu = 100, \lambda = 300$ and the number of generations is 30, which gives the same number of fitness evaluations of PABIC. The GradPABIC was allowed only 300 fitness evaluations because of the cost of computing the gradient. We computed 30 replications of the algorithm on each image. We computed the correlation between the recovered chessboard images and the original ones, as well as the correlation between the original illumination bias and the ones estimated by the correction algorithms. The results are summarized in Figures 5.1, 5.2, 5.3, and 5.4. Figure 5.1 plots the average correlation between the original image and the recovered one for each image and algorithm. The results of GradPABIC are better than the PABIC and ES in all cases. Figure 5.2 plots the standard deviation of the correlation between the recovered image and the ground truth for each image and algorithm. High standard deviation implies low confidence in the algorithm results.

Again GradPABIC provides the best results in the sense of lower variance of the results for each image, but for some images where the ES improves it. The worst results in terms of variance are the ones provided by the PABIC. The ES is less variable than PABIC, which is natural because of the improved convergence properties implied by the larger population. The PABIC, being a single individual or single-solution algorithm, has a poorer ability to escape bad local optima than ES. The good results of GradPABIC are more surprising, because it is also a single-solution algorithm. It seems that the gradient information improves the convergence of the algorithm.

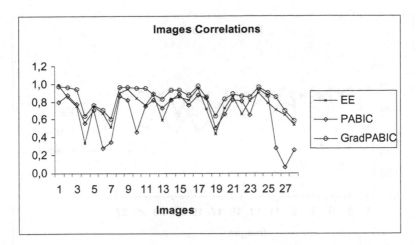

Figure 5.1. The correlations between the ground truth chessboard image and the ones recovered after correction with the different methods from the synthetically corrupted image. The results are the averages over the 30 replications of the algorithms.

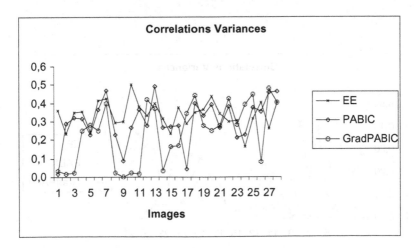

Figure 5.2. The variances of the correlations between the corrected images and the original ones, computed over the 30 replications of the algorithm on each image.

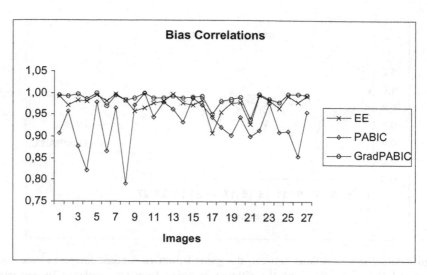

Figure 5.3. The correlations between the ground truth illumination bias images and the ones estimated by the correction methods. The results are the averages over the 30 replications of the algorithm.

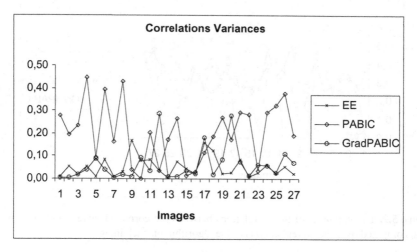

Figure 5.4. The standard deviations of the different correlations between the obtained bias images and the original ones over the 30 replications of the algorithms.

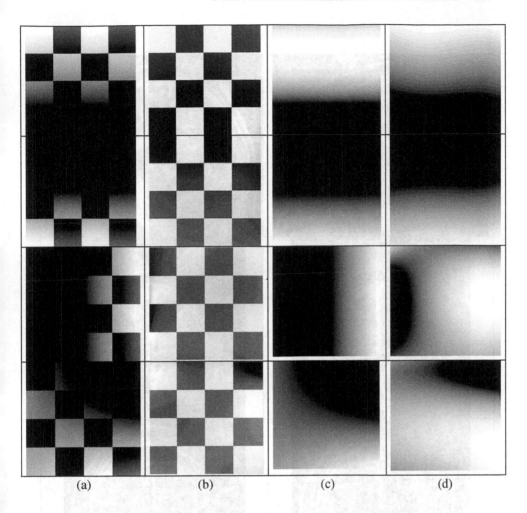

| (a) | (b) | (c) | (d) |

Figure 5.5. Several instances of the chessboard image experiments. (a) Corrupted image, and (b) recovered images by GradPABIC. (c) Original synthetic illumination bias used to produce the images in (a) and (d) the illumination bias estimated by GradPABIC.

Figure 5.3 plots the correlation between the ground truth illumination bias and the estimated ones. The ES and the GradPABIC are competing for the best results, while the PABIC is clearly worse in almost all the images. The cause of the little differences between the results is that the illumination biases are very smooth functions. Figure 5.4 shows the standard deviations of the correlations between the estimated bias and the ground truth. Again, the PABIC is worse than the ES and the GradPABIC. There is no significant difference between the ES and the GradPABIC, which is a good result for a single-solution algorithm. To give a qualitative appraisal of the algorithm proposed, Figure 5.5 shows several instances of the corrupted image (Fig. 5.5a) and the recovered clean images that result from the GradPABIC (Fig. 5.5b). It also shows the original bias field (Fig. 5.5c) and the ones estimated by the GradPABIC (Fig. 5.5d).

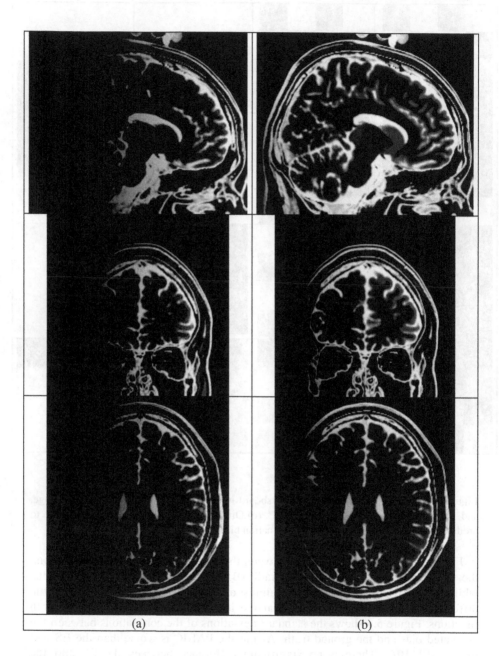

(a)   (b)

Figure 5.6. (a) Slices from a corrupted MRI voume, (b) corresponding slices of the corrected volume given by the GradPABIC algorithm.

Figure 5.6 shows the results of the GradPABIC on an MRI synthetic volume of the brain corrupted with a known illumination bias. The slices correspond to selected axial, sagital, and coronal cuts of the corrupted and the restored volumes.

5.5 Conclusions

The PABIC algorithm for parametric illumination inhomogeneity correction in images is a special case of ES. We have proposed GradPABIC as an improvement that consists in using the gradient information of the error in the mutation operator. This is similar to an instantaneous memetic algorithm. GradPABIC gives better results and a smaller variance on a collection of synthetic images tested. Besides the improvement in accuracy of the image restoration, the reduction in variance of the results of the algorithm is very significant. As GradPABIC is a single-solution evolutionary strategy, equivalent to reducing the population to a single individual, big variances are to expected. The reduction in variance points to GradPABIC as an especially good combination of the local search power of the gradient-based algorithms and the random search of evolutive algorithms.

Acknowledgments

We would like to acknowledge the Ministerio de Ciencia y Tecnología of Spain through grants TIC2000-0739-C04-02 and TIC2000-0376-P4-04. The Universidad del Pais Vasco has supported us through a special grant as a consolidated research group in the years 2004 to 2006.

References

1. Ahmed M.N., S.N. Yamany, N. Mohamed, A.A. Farag, T. Moriarty, (2002) A modified fuzzy C-means algorithm for bias field estimation and segmentation of MRI data, IEEE Trans. Med. Imag. 21(3): 193-199.

2. Back T., H.-P. Schwefel, (1993) An overview of evolutionary algorithms for parameter optimization, Evolutionary Computation, 1(1):1-23.

3. Gonzalez R.C., R.E Woods, (1990) Digital Image Processing, Academic Press, New York.

4.. Guillemaud, R.; Brady, M. (1997) Estimating the bias field of MR images, IEEE Trans. Med. Imag., 16(3); 238-251.

5. Likar B., M.A. Viergever, F. Pernus, (2001) Retrospective correction of MR intensity inhomogeneity by information minimization. IEEE Trans Med. Imag., 20(12):1398-1410.

6. Macovski A., (1996) Noise in MRI, Magn.Reson.Med. 36,(3):494-497.

7. Sled J.G., G.B. Pike, (1998) Standing-wave and RF penetration artifacts caused by elliptic geometry: An electrodynamic analysis of MRI, IEEE Trans Med Imag, 17(4):653-662.

8. Sled J.G., A.P. Zijdenbos, A.C. Evans, (1998) A nonparametric method for automatic correction of intensity nonuniformity in MRI data, IEEE Trans Med Imag, 17(1):87-97.

9. Styner M., G. Gerig, C. Brechbühler, G. Szekely, (2000) Parametric estimate of intensity inhomogeneities applied to MRI. IEEE Trans. Med. Imag. 19(3):153-165.

10. Wells, W.M., III; Grimson, W.E.L.; Kikinis, R.; Jolesz, F.A. (1996) Adaptive segmentation of MRI data, IEEE Trans. Med. Imag., 15(4): 429-442.

11. http://www.densis.fee.unicamp.br/~moscato/memetic_home.html.

6

A New Chromosome Codification for Scheduling Problems

Ramiro Varela, Camino R. Vela, Jorge Puente, David Serrano, Ana Suárez

Summary. In this chapter we confront the Job Shop Scheduling problem by means of Genetic Algorithms. Our aim is twofold: first to envisage a codification schema that makes it clear what we consider the basic building blocks of a chromosome, that is the partial schedules of the set of tasks requiring the same resource; and then to design a scheduling policy that maintains as long as possible these partial schedules. The expected utility of this new codification is that it allows us to design knowledge-based operators and initialization strategies. We report results from an experimental study on a small set of selected problems showing that our proposed codification and scheduling algorithm layouts produce similar results to other conventional schemas. And at the same time this codification facilitates the design of genetic operators focused to produce promising building blocks.

6.1 Introduction

The application of GAs to scheduling problems has interested many researchers [1-4, 8, 11, 13] due to the fact that they seem to offer the ability to cope with the huge search spaces involved in optimization of constraint satisfaction problems [6]. Because conventional GAs provide rather poor results for medium- and large-size problems, a number of enhancements like elitism, local search, and structured population techniques have been proposed that improve their performance.

In this work we propose a new codification schema and a scheduling strategy for solving Job Shop Scheduling (JSS) problems. The intuition behind this codification is that partial schedules, i.e., schedules of the set of tasks requiring the same machine, are the basic building blocks that contribute to a problem solution. Therefore, we first codify a chromosome as a set of partial schedules from which a problem solution is built by the scheduling strategy. Whenever two or more partial schedules are not compatible, a number of them should be modified in order to restore compatibility. To do that we enhance the codification by means of a resource ordering vector that expresses a priority among resources, so that partial schedules of low-priority resources are broken first.

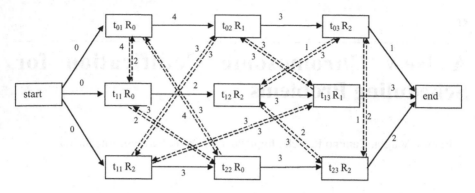

Figure 6.1. A directed graph representation of a *JSS* problem instance with three jobs. The resource requirement of every task is indicated within the boxes. Arcs are weighted with the processing time of the task at the outcoming node.

We report experimental results from two implementations of conventional or genuine GAs to compare our proposed codification against a well-known and widely used schema: the permutations with repetition proposed by C. Bierwirth in [1]. What we expect of this new codification schema is that it will allow us to introduce new genetic operators that better cope with issues as epistasis and that facilitate the exploitation of heuristic knowledge from the problem domain.

The remainder of this chapter is organised as follows: in Section 6.2 we introduce the JSS problem. Section 6.3 summarizes a conventional approach to JSS problems based on the permutation with repetition schema proposed in [1]. In Section 6.4 we describe our proposed codification schema: the Task and Resource Ordering (TRO), and the scheduling algorithm. Section 6.5 reports the results from an experimental study on a set of well-known problems. Finally, in Section 6.6 we summarize the main conclusions and propose some ideas for further work.

6.2 The JSS Problem

The JSS requires scheduling a set of jobs $\{J_0, ..., J_{n-1}\}$ on a set of physical resources

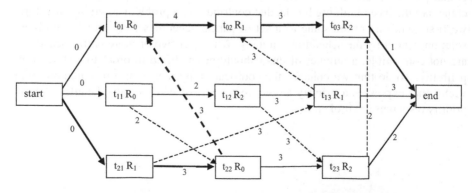

Figure 6.2. A solution to the problem of Figure 6.1. The makespan is 14

or machines $\{R_0,...,R_{m-1}\}$. Each job Ji consists of a set of tasks $\{t_{i0},...,t_{i(m-1)}\}$ or operations to be sequentially scheduled. Each task has a fixed duration or processing time du_{il} and requires the exclusive use of a single resource. The objective is to come up with a feasible schedule such that the completion time of the whole set of tasks, i.e., the makespan, is minimized. Figure 6.1 shows a problem instance in a usual graphic representation. From this representation a solution to the problem is an acyclic subgraph that includes every node as well as every arc from sequential constraints, but only a Hamiltonian selection from each resource, that is a subgraph that expresses a linear ordering among the set of tasks requiring the resource. The cost of the solution is the cost of the longest path from the start node to the end node in the solution graph. Figure 6.2 shows a solution subgraph to the problem of Figure 6.1.

This representation of the JSS problem suggests that partial schedules of the subset of tasks requiring the same resource are the actual basic building blocks. Hence we have tried to envisage a codification schema that allows us to design genetic operators to explicitly manipulate partial schedules. The long-term objective is that these operators can exploit knowledge from the problem domain.

6.3 Conventional Codification Schemas and Scheduling Algorithms

Here we consider the codification schema proposed by C. Bierwirth [1]: the permutation with repetition schema. According to this representation, a chromosome is codified by a permutation of the whole set of tasks of the problem at hand. Consider, for example, the problem depicted in Figure 6.1 and the permutation of its tasks $(t_{31}\ t_{11}\ t_{12}\ t_{32}\ t_{01}\ t_{33}\ t_{13}\ t_{02}\ t_{03})$. From this permutation an individual is obtained by replacing every task identifier by the corresponding job number; therefore we obtain (3 1 1 3 0 3 1 0 0). Consequently, this codification should be understood to mean the following: the first 2 represents the first task of the second job, the first 3 is the first task of the third job, the second 2 is the second task of the second job, and so on. One of the main reasons to introduce this codification is that the genetic operators always produce feasible chromosomes, as we will see in the following paragraphs. The mutation operator we use in this work is the *order-based mutation (OX)* proposed by Syswerda [8]: two tasks are selected at random and their positions are interchanged. At the same time, we use the *generalized position crossover (GPX)* proposed by Bierwirth [1]. In order to clarify how GPX works, consider the following two parents:

Parent1   (3 1 <u>1 3 0 3</u> 1 0 <u>0</u>)   Parent2   (<u>0</u> 3 <u>3</u> 0 1 <u>1</u> 0 1 <u>3</u>).

A substring is selected at random from parent1, for example the underlined substring that includes the second 1, the second and third 3, and the first 0. The offspring is constructed by inserting that substring at the position it has in parent1 and filling the remaining positions with the remaining tasks, in this case maintaining the ordering they have in parent2. Hence, in this case we obtain the offspring

(3 0 <u>1 3 0 3</u> 1 0 1).

76   Ramiro Varela et al.

The intuition behind the GPX operator is that the offspring inherits characteristics from both of the two parents by maintaining the relative ordering and position of a number of tasks from parent1, and only the relative order of the remaining ones from parent2. However, the meaning of an allele might change during crossover; for example, the 0 of the former substring selected from parent1 represents the task t_{01}, while after being inserted into the offspring it represents t_{02}. This effect is known as implicit mutation of the crossover operator and in practice makes it difficult to characterize the effect of the genetic operators on the basic building blocks that in this codification are considered as the partial ordering of subsequences.

In order to evaluate chromosomes a scheduling strategy must be defined that translates the chromosome codification into a schedule. The fitness value is, in principle, the inverse of the makespan of this schedule given that we have a minimization problem. In this work we used the following scheduling algorithm.

```
for each task in the chromosome from left to right do
    set its start time to lowest value compatible with
    the assignments made to the previous tasks in the
    chromosome;
```

This algorithm has a complexity that in the worst case is $O(N^2)$, N being the total number of the problem tasks. The start time of a task is calculated as the maximum value of the completion time of the previous task in the job and the completion times of the scheduled tasks requiring the same resource. Figure 6.3 shows the Gantt chart of the schedule produced for this algorithm when it is applied to the chromosome (3 1 1 3 0 3 1 0 0).

The above fitness function can be adjusted in order to better discriminate between good and bad chromosomes. Here we consider the *scaling*. This is a common technique, as pointed out in [9]. The objective is either to accentuate or to soften the difference between good and bad chromosomes in order to obtain a more accurate discrimination. The underlying idea is that small relative differences among the fitness of good and bad chromosomes do not facilitate the selection of the best chromosomes and the elimination of the worse ones, whereas large relative differences

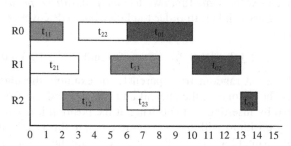

Figure 6.3. Solution produced to the problem of Figure. 6.1 by the former scheduling algorithm from the chromosome (3 1 1 3 0 3 1 0 0). The makespan is 14. It is the same solution represented in the graph of Figure 6.2

might produce the dominance of semi-optima chromosomes and hence the premature convergence of the GA. Here, we consider a linear scaling that consists of replacing the original fitness f by

$$f' = f + b, \tag{6.1}$$

b being a parameter that may be provided by the user or automatically determined from the problem. Here we use the following strategy to compute the value of the parameter b. The objective is to establish a constant relation C among the *best* and *mean* fitness values at each generation. Hence we calculate the parameter b for a given generation so that

$$C = (mean + b)/(best + b). \tag{6.2}$$

Consequently, for each generation we will have

$$b = (mean - best * C)/(C - 1). \tag{6.3}$$

C is the *scaling parameter*: its value must be greater than 1 and, in principle, is given by the user as the reminder parameters of the GA.

6.4 The TRO Codification Schema

In principle, a chromosome is represented by a *Resource Matrix (RM)*. This is an $m \times n$ matrix where the jth row represents a partial schedule for the tasks requiring the resource R_j. From a RM a schedule can be built by merging all of the partial schedules so that every precedence constraint is also satisfied. Unfortunately, sometimes this is not possible because of the lack of compatibility among partial schedules and hence a number of them should be modified. In order to do that, we take up a priority schema for resources so that partial schedules of low-priority resources are modified first. To represent priorities we include into the chromosome representation a *Resource Priority* vector *(RP)* that codifies a resource ordering, from high to low rescheduling priority. Figure 6.4a shows an RM representing partial schedules for the problem of Figure 6.1, and Figure 6.4 b shows an RP of priorities among resources.

The genetic operators we have used in this work are a natural extension of the former GPX and OX. Given two chromosomes we first apply the GPX operator to the pair composed by the i*th* row of each RM component, and then to the pair of RP components. At the same time, the OX operator is applied to the RP component and to every row of the RM component of the offspring. Nevertheless, the design of genetic operators allows other possibilities, for example we could exploit any heuristic information about either promising partial schedules or criticality measures of the resources as an alternative choice of making random crossovers and mutations.

$$\begin{pmatrix} t_{11} & t_{22} & t_{01} \\ t_{21} & t_{13} & t_{02} \\ t_{12} & t_{13} & t_{03} \end{pmatrix} \qquad\qquad \begin{pmatrix} R_0 & R_1 & R_2 \end{pmatrix}$$

a. The Resource Matrix (RM) component   **b.** The vector of Resource Priorities (RP) component

Figure 6.4. A TRO codification chromosome for the problem of Figure 6.1.

To evaluate chromosomes we have envisaged a scheduling algorithm that is a variant of the well-known G&T algorithm proposed in [5] and used, for example, in [8]. The G&T algorithm selects nondeterministically the next task to be scheduled. We solve this nondeterminism by taking into account partial schedules of resources, as expressed in the *MR* component and the priorities among resources expressed in the *RP*. The algorithm tries to preserve the partial orderings of resources with highest priority at the cost of breaking the partial schedules of lower-priority ones. The rationale behind this strategy is that the priority of a resource is a measure of the reliance on its partial schedule.

Figure 6.5 shows the scheduling algorithm. This algorithm is a variant of the well-known G&T algorithm proposed by Giffler and Thomson in [5]. The main difference is the way of selecting the task $t\theta'$ at the beginning. In the G&T algorithm this task is selected as the one with the lowest completion time possible in case it was scheduled next. By working in this way, the G&T algorithm constrains the search to the subset of active schedules, i.e. no matter how the task $\theta*$ is finally selected from the set B, the resulting schedule is active. A schedule is active if it is not possible to change the starting of a task toward a lower time, without delaying another one, requiring in consequence swapping the relative ordering of at least two tasks. Constraining the search to the set of active schedules is, in principle, a good idea because it is proved that there is at least an optimal solution belonging to this set. Even though our proposed algorithm does not constrain the search to the set of active schedules, we have obtained experimental results a little bit better than the results obtained with the genuine G&T algorithm.

The algorithm that selects the task $\theta*$ from the set B to be scheduled next needs some more explanations. This algorithm tries to maintain the partial schedules as expressed in the rows of the matrix RM. Therefore, if the set B contains a number of tasks whose ancestors in the partial schedule have been already selected $(B \cap TR \neq \varnothing)$, one of these task is scheduled next. Moreover, ties are broken in favor of the most critical resources in order to give a higher chance of maintaining their partial schedules on further selections. On the other hand, when the set B does not contain any task whose precedents in the row of matrix RM were already selected $(B \cap TR = \varnothing)$ at least a partial schedule must be broken. In this situation, the algorithm tries to select the task in B belonging to the same job as the task in the set

Scheduling algorithm

$A = \{t_{01},...,t_{0(m-1)}\}$; /* first task of each of the jobs, at each step A is the set of
                       unscheduled tasks whose precedents in the job are scheduled*/

while $A \neq \varnothing$ **do** {

Determine $\theta' \in A$ such that $t\theta' \leq t\theta, \forall \theta \in A$, where $t\theta$ is the lowest start time if task θ was scheduled next;

Let M' be the machine required by θ', and B the subset of tasks in A requiring M';

Delete from B those tasks that cannot start at a time lower than $t\theta' + du\theta'$;

Select $\theta *$ **from** B to be scheduled next;

Delete $\theta *$ from A and insert the next task of the same job as $\theta *$ if $\theta *$ is not the last one of its job;

}

end.

Algorithm to **Select** $\theta *$ **from B**

TR = set of unscheduled tasks such that all their precedents in the corresponding row of RM are already scheduled;

if $\left(B \cap TR \neq \varnothing \right)$

then $\theta * =$ task of $B \cap TR$ requiring the most critical resource, i.e, the one with highest priority in RP;

else JB = set of jobs to which the tasks of B belongs;

TRB = subset of tasks of TR belonging to a job of JB;

if $\left(TRB \neq \varnothing \right)$

then R* = set of resources required by the tasks of TRB;

$\theta =$ task of TRB requiring to the most critical resource of R* (see RP);

J* = job containing the task θ;

$\theta * =$ task of B belonging to J*;

else $\theta * =$ task of B requiring the least critical resource (see RP);

end.

Figure 6.5. Scheduling algorithm. $t\theta$ refers to the start time of task θ and $du\theta$ to its processing time.

TB that requires the most critical resource, hence giving a chance to maintain the partial schedule of this resource. Finally if there is not any task in the set $B \cap TB$ with the same resource requirement, the task of *B* requiring the lowest-priority resource is selected, therefore breaking its partial schedule.

Table 6.1 Results of an experimental study on 11 selected problems from the OR-library comparing the permutations with repetition against the TRO codification. Every experiment was repeated 40 times and shows the best solution found, the mean solution, and the standard deviation in percent. The size of the problem refers to the number of jobs (N) and the number of machines (M).

Problem instance	Problem size		Best solution known	Permutations with repetition codification			TRO codification		
	N	M		Best found	Mean	sd%	Best found	Mean	sd%
FT10	10	10	930	953	1023	3.1	936	977	1.8
FT20	20	5	1165	1244	1309	2.8	1175	1203	1.4
abz7	20	15	665	728	759	1.7	699	731	1.6
abz8	20	15	670	760	780	1.8	721	747	1.1
abz9	20	15	686	780	802	2.1	745	764	1.0
la21	15	10	1046	1115	1172	2.1	1070	1118	1.9
la24	15	10	935	1002	1047	2.1	970	1004	1.5
la25	15	10	977	1024	1078	2.2	1012	1042	1.3
la27	20	10	1235	1305	1390	2.1	1291	1337	2.3
la29	20	10	1153	1275	1326	2.1	1236	1282	2.6
la38	15	15	1196	1344	1398	2.0	1257	1292	1.8

6.5 Experimental Study

In this section we report results from an experimental study on a subset of selected problems from the OR-library comparing our proposed codification and scheduling algorithm against the permutation with repetition codification and the scheduling algorithm proposed in Section 6.3. In both cases we implement a genuine GA, that is, a GA that does not exploit any knowledge from the problem domain and that is not enhanced with common techniques that contributes to improve the performance, such as elitism, local search or structured populations. Table 6.1 summarizes the results of this study. In any case, we run the GA so that a number of about 10,000 chromosomes are evaluated and repeat each experiment 40 times. As we can observe, our proposed codification presents a little bit better results, but on the other hand the run time required is higher. For example, solving the FT10 problem requires about of 1.5 sec when using permutations with repetition codification, whereas it requires about 6 sec when using TRO, on a Pentium III at 750 Mhz.

6.6 Final Remarks

In this chapter we proposed both a new chromosome codification and a scheduling algorithm for JSS problems: the TRO schema, and a variant of the G&T algorithm. From the experimental results we can assume that the performance of this schema is similar to the codification of permutations with repetition in conjunction with the conventional scheduling algorithm proposed in Section 6.2, when both of them are used with a genuine GA. Even though the reported experimental results are a little bit better when using our proposed approach, this improvement might be a consequence of the scheduling algorithm. Of course, this algorithm could be used in conjunction with the permutation schema. On the other hand, the TRO codification makes the partial schedules of the resources clear and therefore it is expected that it will allow us to envisage genetic operators and initialization strategies focused to obtain promising partial schedules. In order to do that we plan to exploit the heuristic proposed in [10] that we have already used to design the initialization strategy proposed in [12]. Therefore, we expect that the proposed TRO schema and the scheduling algorithm provide a useful way to hybridize a genetic algorithm by means of knowledge from any heuristic strategy.

References

1.   Bierwirth, C... (1995) A generalized perutation approach to job shop scheduling with genetic algorithms. OR Spektrum, 17:87-92.
2.   Bierwirth, C., D. C. Mattfeld (1999) Production scheduling and rescheduling with Genetic algoritms, Evolutionary Computation, 7(1):1-17.
3.   Dorndorf, U., E. Pesch, (1995) Evolution based learning in a job shop scheduling environment, Computers & Operations Research, 22:25-40.
4.   Fang, H.L., P. Ross, D. Corne, (1993) A promising genetic algorithm approach to job-shop scheduling, rescheduling, and open-shop scheduling problems, Proc. Fifth Intel. Conf. Genetic Algorithms, 375-382.
5.   Giffler, B., G.L Thomson,. (1960) Algorithms for solving production scheduling problems, Operations Reseach, 8:487-503.
6.   Goldberg, D. (1985) Genetic Algorithms in Search, Optimization & Machine Learning, Addison-Wesley, Reading, MA.
7.   Grefenstette, J. J. (1987) Incorporating problem specific knowledge in genetic algorithms, in: Genetic Algorithms and Simulated Annealing, Morgan Kaufmann, pp. 42-60.
8.   Matfeld, D. C. (1995) Evolutionary search and the job shop. Investigations on Genetic Algorithms for Production Scheduling. Springer-Verlag.
9.   Michalewicz, Z. (1994) Genetic Algorithms + Data Structures = Evolution Program. Second, Extended Edition, Springer-Verlag.
10. Sadeh, N., M.S. Fox, (1996) Variable and value ordering heuristics for the Job Shop Scheduling Constraint Satisfaction Problem, Artificial Intelligence, 86:1-41.
11. Syswerda, G. (1991) Schedule Optimization Using Genetic Algorithms, in Handbook of Genetic Algorithms, (ed.) L. Davis, Van Nostrand Reinhold, New York, pp.1332-13490.

12.   Varela, R., C. R. Vela, J. Puente, A. Gómez (2003) A Knowledge-Based Evolutionary Strategy for Scheduling Problems with Bottlenecks. European Journal of Operational Research. 145(1): 57-71.

13.   Yamada, T. and Nakano, R. (1996) Scheduling by Genetic Local Search with multistep crossover. In: Fourth Int. Conf. On Parallel Problem Solving from Nature (PPSN IV), Berlin, Germany, pp. 960-969.

7

Evolution-based Learning of Ontological Knowledge for a Large-scale Multi-agent Simulation

A. Lazar, R.G. Reynolds

7.1 Introduction

The results of the data mining [1] process can be used in many different ways. Therefore, the form of the knowledge collected will have a major impact on the efficiency and effectiveness of its use in a given application. In this paper we examine the problem of extracting knowledge for use by agents in a large-scale multi-agent system [2]. Here, the knowledge is ontological knowledge that represents constraints that the physical and social environments placed upon the agents and their interactions. The ontological knowledge represents the semantic building blocks around which the world models are formed. For an agent in a particular model, only the things in his ontology can exist and it cannot perceive things that are not represented in the ontology. An *ontology* [3] is a basic level of knowledge representation scheme, a formal definition of entities and their properties, interactions, behaviors, and constraints. Each agent's decisions need to be checked against these constraints prior to their execution. In a complex multi-agent system, hundreds of thousands of agents may need to check these constraints regularly, which means that a successful data mining activity will need to produce a relatively small set of syntactically simple rules for the process to be efficient. Fox et al. [3] have used data mining techniques to produce corporate ontogenies.

Several factors can influence the nature of the ontological constraints that are produced: first, the nature of the data collection and measurement process and the uncertainty induced into the data set by the presence of noise, second, the nature of the representation used to express the extracted patterns; e.g.,. whether it allows for uncertainty or not, third, the data mining technique employed and the assumptions that it makes about the collected data, fourth, how these constraints will be stored, accessed, and used by the agents involved.

For a given data set one can compare the different data mining techniques in terms of the syntactic and semantics of the induced constraints. In this application we are interested in simulating the emergence of the archaic state in the Valley of Oaxaca, Mexico. A state is among the most sophisticated and powerful structures that has emerged from the social evolution process. In the modern world these are termed "nation states" with a government composed of a hierarchical decision-making structure where the decision-makers are either elected or appointed. States are supported by various economies and are able to interact with each other via warfare, trade, etc. Most states in the ancient world-often called archaic states-were ruled by hereditary royal families. These archaic states exhibited much internal diversity with populations numbering from tens of thousands to millions. They had a bureaucracy, organized religion, a military presence, large urban centers, public buildings, public works, and services provided by various professional specialists. The state itself could enter into warfare and trade-based relationships with other states and less complex neighbors.

The process by which complex social entities such as the state emerged from lower level structures and other supporting economies has long been of prime interest to anthropologists and other disciplines as well. This is because the emergence of such a social structure can have a profound impact on the society's physical and social environment. However, the task of developing realistic computational models that aid in the understanding and explanation of state emergence has been a difficult one. This is the result of two basic factors:

1. The process of state formation inherently takes place on a variety of temporal and spatial scales. The emergence of hierarchical decision-making [4, 5] can be viewed as an adaptation that allows decision-makers to specialize their decisions to particular spatial and temporal scales.
2. The formation of the state is a complex process that is fundamentally directed by the social variables but requiring dynamic interaction between the emergent system and its environment. Identifying the nature of these interactions is one of the reasons why the process of state formation is of such interest.

The goal of this project is to produce a large-scale knowledge-based computational model of the origins of the Zapotec State [6], centered at Monte Alban, in the Valley of Oaxaca, Mexico. State formation took place between 1400 B.C. and 300 B.C. While archaic states have emerged in various parts of the world, the relative isolation of the valley allowed the processes of social evolution to be more visible there. Extensive surveys [7, 8, 9] of the 2,100-square-kilometer valley were undertaken by the Oaxaca Settlement Pattern Project in the 1970s and 1980s. The location and features of over 2,700 sites dating from the archaic period (8000 B.C.) to Late Monte Alban V (just prior to the arrival of the Spaniards) were documented. Several hundred variables were recorded for each site. In addition, they surveyed the 6.5-square-kilometer urban center of Monte Alban, a site that contained over 2,000 residential terraces. This site was the focus for early state formation in the valley.

Both surveys provided the knowledge needed to create our multi-agent simulation model. We then produced a spatial temporal database that contained the results of both surveys and used data mining techniques from Artificial Intelligence [2] to produce knowledge about site location, warfare, trade, and economic decisions to be used for the construction of the multi-agent model. However, in order to do this we needed to add more data about the spatial and temporal context to both the regional and urban center surveys. Specifically, we had to add variables that allowed us to locate each site spatially and temporally to a level of precision consistent with the scale of our simulation. For example, temporal periods are characterized by the presence of pottery of different styles. That data was available only in text form.

All of this pottery data, over 130 variables for each residential terrace, was scanned into the computer, corrected for errors, and added to the Monte Alban data set. This data allowed us to identify the periods that each terrace was occupied. Pottery data was also integrated into the regional data set.

In addition, the survey had produced hundreds of pages of hand-drawn maps for both the Monte Alban and regional surveys that contained the spatial context for the location of each site. Since our goal was to ask specific questions about the spatial and temporal context, we needed to tie each site into its mapped location. We then proceeded to digitize each of the maps and to associate each site object with its corresponding data record. This allowed us to produce a geographical information system (GIS) that serves as our "virtual valley of Oaxaca". This acts as a vehicle for our data mining activities and as a knowledge base for the multi-agent simulation and allows the results of the simulation to be displayed and compared with the actual data in a spatial context. It is envisioned that the resultant GIS system will be a useful tool for researchers and students from various fields to study the emergence of complexity in the future.

In order to perform the data mining activities, we extended traditional data mining techniques and developed new ones in order to deal with the complexities inherent in the Oaxaca database. At the regional level we used Utgoff's incremental decision tree algorithm (IDTI) [10] to generate the decision trees for each region and phase of the valley. The approach was used to generate decision trees that discriminated between sites that were targets for warfare and those that were not for a given period [11, 12].

However, given the many disparate steps under which the data was collected and organized, it was felt that perhaps some improvements might be made by using a technique that took into account the presence of uncertainty in the data, especially in regions and periods when the social and settlement patterns were complex and prone to data collection error. To test this hypothesis we selected a period of time just before the emergence of the state, Rosario, where there was evidence of increased social strife brought about in part by increased population growth. The part of the valley that exhibited the greatest population at the time, Etla, was also selected. Since the majority of the data was discrete rather than continuous in nature, we selected rough sets as a vehicle for representing uncertainty here.

We employed an evolutionary technique, Genetic Algorithms [13, 14], to control the search in this case because Genetic Algorithms had been successfully used with Rough Sets previously. The decision systems or rule sets produced by both approaches were then compared in terms of their ability to decide about the location of sites that are targets for warfare in this period. We then compared the two approaches over all relevant phases of social evolution in the valley.

In Section 7.2 we begin with an overview of decision trees and their generation. Next Section 7.3 discusses the ways in which noise was introduced into the data here. In Section 7.4 a general framework for the generation and description of decision systems is briefly presented. In Section 7.5 rough sets are introduced and embedded within an evolutionary search engine based upon Genetic Algorithms. Section 7.6 provides a comparison of a specific decision system for the Etla region in the Rosario phase as produced by decision trees and rough sets, respectively.

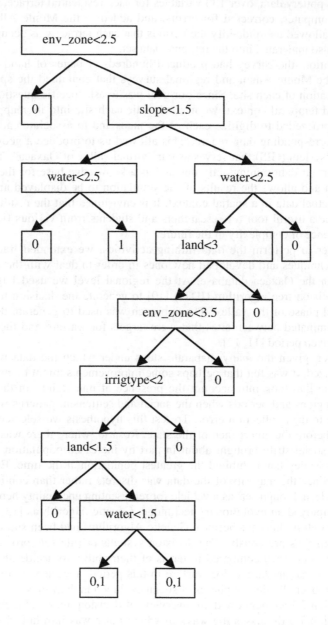

Figure 7.1 The decision tree for the locations of sites with evidence of raiding in Rosario phase in the Etla region of the valley.

Section 7.7 compares the two approaches together over all phases in the Etla region. The rough set approach appears most useful in those phases with the most evidence for change in social complexity. Section 7.8 gives our conclusions.

7.2 Decision Tree

Decision tree induction is a very good method for high-dimensional applications. It is a fast, nonlinear prediction method and employs dynamic feature selection. The solution complexity is expressed in terms of the number of terminal nodes. The most complex tree covers all cases in the training data. Pruning the tree and measuring the errors in progressively smaller trees find less complex solutions.

Any decision tree can be rewritten in a form of decision rule set. An implied decision rule in a tree is a complete path to a terminal node. Because these rules are not mutually exclusive, the size of the decision rule set can be much larger than the logic needed for overlapping rules. One rule can combine a large number of terms or true-false conditions, which takes a lot of time for evaluation, when the rule set is used in an agent-based simulation.

One of the advantages of logic-based solutions as decision trees and corresponding decision rules is their powerful explanatory capabilities. Table 7.1 gives all of the relevant periods of social evolution in the valley. Tierras Largas marks the beginning of early village settlement there. The state emerged at Monte Alban in period Monte Alban Ia. The valley came under control of the state by Monte Alban II, and Monte Alban IIIa signaled the decline of the state and its succession by a collection of city-states localized in different parts of the valley.

Table 7.1 Number of Terminal Nodes for Each Phase

Period	Approximate date
Tierras Largas	1400 - 1150 BC
San Jose	1150 - 850 BC
Guadalupe	850 - 700 BC
Rosario	700 - 500 BC
Monte Alban Ia	500 - 300 BC
Monte Alban Ic	300 - 150/100 BC
Monte Alban II	150/100 BC - AD 200
Monte Alban IIIa	AD 200 - 500
Monte Alban IIIb	AD 500 - 700/750
Monte Alban IV	AD 700/750
Monte Alban V	AD 1000 - 1521

For some periods there were several hundred rules produced just for the warfare constraint alone. Adding in the other constraints would produce a knowledge base of several thousand rules at a minimum. However, since the data were collected over a ten-year period over varying landscapes using different surveyors and recording equipment, it was felt that a significant amount of noise might be present in the data. The original technique did not account explicitly for uncertainty in the measurement data. Thus, it was possible that certain rules or rule conditions were present only to deal with the specific noise introduced into the process by the survey methods and data transformation activities.

Table 7.2 Decision Rule Set Induced from the Decision Tree

	Rules
1	env_zone<2.5 => decision(0)
2	env_zone>=2.5 and slope<1.5 and water<2.5 => decision(0)
3	env_zone>=2.5 and slope<1.5 and water>=2.5 => decision(1)
4	env_zone>=2.5 and slope>=1.5 and water<2.5 and land<3 and env_zone<3.5 and irrigtype<2 and land<1.5 => decision(0)
5	env_zone>=2.5 and slope>=1.5 and water<2.5 and land<3 and env_zone<3.5 and irrigtype<2 and land>=1.5 and water<1.5 => decision(0) or decision(1)
6	env_zone>=2.5 and slope>=1.5 and water<2.5 and land<3 and env_zone<3.5 and irrigtype<2 and land>=1.5 and water>=1.5 => decision(0) or decision(1)
7	env_zone>=2.5 and slope>=1.5 and water<2.5 and land<3 and env_zone<3.5 and irrigtype>=2 => decision(0)
8	env_zone>=2.5 and slope>=1.5 and water<2.5 and land<3 and env_zone>=3.5 => decision(0)
9	env_zone>=2.5 and slope>=1.5 and water<2.5 and land>3 => decision(0)
10	env_zone>=2.5 and slope>=1.5 and water>=2.5 => decision(0)

If this was the case, then by using a representation and associated learning technique that dealt explicitly with uncertainty it might be that fewer rules would be needed in periods where the noise is most pronounced.

7.3 Uncertainty in Data

Uncertainty in a data set, which can occur during data collection or data entry, is referred to as noise in the data. One type of noise is the presence of missing attribute values. In this case, the objects containing missing attributes values can be discarded or the missing values can be replaced with the most common values. Another type of noise occurs because the available knowledge in many situations is incomplete and imprecise. This means that sometimes the attribute values for a set of objects are not sufficient and precise enough to differentiate between the desired classes of objects. In the Oaxaca data set, this may have occurred for many reasons. The ancient sites may be damaged because of plowing, erosion, pot hunting, and grazing. Also, human perception is subjective, and many people worked on the collection of the data. Some errors are also possible due to the scanning process since much of the data was available only from printed text and hand-drawn maps as described earlier.

Many different ways of representing and reasoning about uncertainty have been developed in Artificial Intelligence. These theories include belief networks, non-monotonic logic, fuzzy sets along with fuzzy logic and rough sets. One approach based on the rough set theory [15] provides a lower and upper approximation in terms of a set describing a target concept depending on how the relationship between two partitions of a finite universe is defined.

Given the discrete nature of the data set we selected the rough sets method for representing uncertainty here. Since the rough set algorithm is inherently intractable for large data sets like ours, an evolutionary based approach, here Genetic Algorithms, was employed to guide the search for the appropriate rough set rules.

7.4 Building Decision Systems

A *decision rule* is an assertion, of the form "if p then s", denoted by p=>s, where p and s are logical formulas in the first-order logic. For each object, certain values of the condition attributes determine the value of the decision attribute. We define a *decision system* as a finite collection or set of decision rules. In order to obtain a decision system with a minimum number of rules, superfluous decision rules associated with the same decision class can be eliminated without disturbing the decision-making process.

The problem of decision system construction is to induce a set of rule descriptors for decision classes from the input set of objects in a decision table. These sets of descriptors, named decision systems, consist of a set of decision rules. We can classify the decision system as follows:

1. Decision systems with a minimum set of rules. They are focused on describing input objects using a minimum number of necessary rules.
2. Decision systems with an exhaustive set of rules. These decision systems contain all possible decision rules.
3. Decision systems with a satisfactory set of rules. This category represents sets of decision rules, which satisfy given a priori user's requirement for an acceptable decision system.

One strategy to find a simple decision system with good classificatory capabilities is to first induce an exhaustive set of rules, and then to prune away those rules that do not lower the decision system's performance significantly. An exhaustive decision system can be generated from the reducts [16, 17].

Pruning can be done by identifying and removing components of the decision system that only explain small parts of the data, thereby preserving general trends in the underlying data material. In order to find a minimal decision system we can use a simple greedy heuristic algorithm as described by Lazar and Sethi [18]. This algorithm computes only one decision system. If more than one decision system is required, we can use a Genetic Algorithm, which solves the minimal cover set problem. Agotnes [19] proposed two algorithms for generating satisfactory decision systems, a quality-based rule filtering algorithm and a genetic rule-filtering algorithm. Rule filtering operates on an existing exhaustive decision system, pruning it while retaining a high performance. Both of the above solutions make no assumptions about the minimal set cover condition. As a result, the decision system may not be minimal.

7.5 Rough Set Theory

Pawlak [15] introduced rough set theory in the early 1980s as a tool for representing imprecise or uncertain information, and for reasoning about it. Based on the notion of indiscernability, rough set theory deals with the approximation of sets, using equivalence relations. These approximations can form model hypotheses. The basic concept of rough set theory is called a *reduct* [15]. A reduct is a minimal sufficient subset of features such that it will produce the same categorization of objects as the set of all features. By definition a *reduct* represents an alternative and simplified way of representing a set of objects. Following the rough set meth-

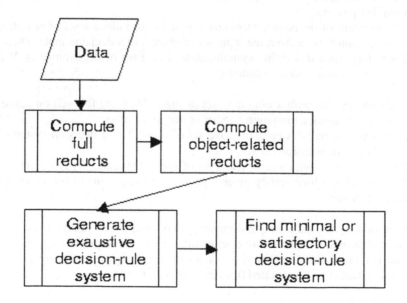

Figure 7.2 Model Construction
Phases

odology, the full set of reducts is computed, a minimal reduct is chosen, and the data table is vertically pruned. Then the object-related reducts are computed and the exhaustive decision rule system is generated.

At the end, a pruning method for the decision rule set is applied in order to obtain a performant decision system that possesses a good balance between the number of rules and the accuracy of the classifications. The process is shown in Figure 7.2.

7.5.1 Genetic Algorithm for the Reduct Problem

Multisets are unordered collections of elements where an element can occur as a member more than once. A *hitting set* [20, 21] for a given multiset, MS, of elements from $P(C)$ is a set B, $B \subset C B \subset C$, such that the intersection between B and every set in MS is nonempty.

$$HS(MS) = \left\{ B \subseteq C \mid B \cap MS_i \neq \varnothing \text{ for all } MS_i \in MS \right\}. \qquad (7.1)$$

The set $B \in HS(MS)$ is a minimal hitting set of MS, iff B is no longer a hitting set whenever any of its elements are removed. The set of minimal hitting sets is denoted by minHS(MS).

For the reduct problem using a minimal hitting set, the population for the Genetic Algorithm is a set P of N individuals, each from the space P(C), where C is the condition attributes set. Each individual is encoded as a binary vector, where each bit indicates the presence of an attribute in the set.

For this population, the fitness function rewards individuals hitting more sets in the collection of sets corresponding to the discernibility function.

A possible fitness function proposed by Vinterbo [21] is the following:

$$f(B) = \frac{|C| - |B|}{|C|} + \frac{\left| \left\{ MS_i \in MS \mid MS_i \cap B \neq \phi \right\} \right|}{|MS|}. \qquad (7.2)$$

The first term rewards smaller-sized individuals, and the second is used to ensure that we reward sets that are hitting sets.

The fitness function is a discrete, multimodal function. The algorithm used by Vinterbo and Ohrn [20] is the traditional Genetic Algorithm implementation. The genetic operators crossover, mutation, and inversion are used and selection is done by the "roulette wheel" process. The same selection of individuals is used in order to replace the individuals in the fixed-size population in the recombination step. Elitism and Boltzaman scaling are included. Initialization of the population is done randomly, and the process stops when no more improvement in the average fitness of the population is produced over a predefined number of generations.

7.6 Decision Trees and Rough Set Rules

Previously [12] computed decision trees from Tierras Largas phase through Monte Alban IIIa for all regions in the valley using Utgoff's decision tree algorithm. The goal was to diferentiate between the sites that are targets for attack and the those that are not. Three variables were used in order to compute the decision: the presence of burnt daubt at the site, other evidence of burning, and the presence of defensive walls. The variables used to predict these decisions from positive and negative examples in the training set were: Environmental zone, Slope, Hiltop or Ridge top, Soil Character, On the boundary between the loam and the swampy reagion, Water source, Depth of Water Table, Type of irrigation, and Land use type among others.

In section 7.2 we presented a decision tree (Figure 7.1) and a corresponding decision system (Table 7.2) for the Rosario phase (700-500 B.C.) generated by the decision tree approach. It is the fourth phase of occupation in the study, and at that time population size and warfare increased substantially [6]. For example, it was observed that chunks of burnt daub appear on the surface of the villages seven times more frequently than in the previous phases. There are 36 sites in the Rosario phase. The archaic state emerged in the period following this phase of increased warfare.

First, we performed a feature selection using the rough set guided by Genetic Algorithm with the variables above. The rough set approach extracted the same five variables as did the decision tree approach. They are: Environmental Zone, Slope, Hiltop or Ridge Top, Water Source, Type of Irrigation, and Land Use. We then computed the reducts, and the corresponding decision system is given in Table 7.3. This table represents the exhaustive set of rules produced. While it is clear that several of the rules are so simple that they can be easily combined to produce a smaller set of rules overall, it is sufficient for comparative purposes here.

Our focus here is on the impact of the use of a technique, such as rough sets, that explicitly is able to deal with uncertainty in the recognition decision. From this standpoint there are two basic points of comparison. First, how many of the rules identify a site for attack unambiguously and, what percentage of the rules that select sites for attack do they comprise? Second, in those cases in which the rule produces a split decision we will need to resolve the tie using other means. The question is, how much effort do we need to spend in order to find out that we must contact another source to resolve the question?

In answer to the first question, explicitly dealing with uncertainty using the rough set representation produced four rules that identify sites for attack as opposed to just three rules in the decision tree approach. Of these four rules, two of the four (11 and 16) result in unambiguous decisions. That is, 50% of the rules that can conclude that a site can be attacked are unambiguous whereas the other two need further clarification. The decision trees approach produces 3 rules that can conclude that a site can be attacked, with only one of them (rule 3) being conclusive. Thus, only 33% of the rules that identify a site for attack are conclusive as opposed to 50% for the rough set approach. By taking data uncertainty into account, the rough set approach not only produced more rules for the identification of the target concept, but also a higher percentage of unambiguous ones.

Table 7.3 Exaustive Decision System for the Rosario Phase in Etla Region

	Rules
1	env_zone(2) => decision(0)
2	water(1) AND land(2) => decision(0) OR decision(1)
3	env_zone(3) AND slope(2) AND water(2) AND irrig_type(0) AND land(2) => decision(0) OR decision(1)
4	slope(1) and water(2) => decision(0)
5	water(4) => decision(0)
6	land(1) => decision(0)
7	land(4) => decision(0)
8	env_zone(4) => decision(0)
9	irrig_type(3) => decision(0)
10	irrig_type(4) => decision(0)
11	slope(1) and water(3) => decision(1)
12	slope(2) and water(3) => decision(0)
13	water(0) => decision(0)
14	irrig_type(2) => decision(0)
15	irrig_type(1) => decision(0)
16	water(3) and irrig_type(0) => decision(1)

The other question concerns the relative amount of effort expended to produce an uncertain conclusion. In the decision system produced using Rough Sets, the inconclusive rules have fewer conditions to be checked than for those from the decision trees approach. Specifically, the inclusive rough set rules have 2 and 5 conditions respectively for a total of 7 conditions, one of which is shared between them (land type =2). In the decision tree system 8 conditions must be checked in the 2 inconclusive rules for a total of 16. However, each shares the same 8 so that the total number of unique conditions to be tested is 8 as opposed to 6 for the Rough Set approach. More effort must then be expended in order to check the inconclusive rules in the decision tree approach as opposed to that for Rough Sets.

Since both approaches extracted the same set of condition variables, the differences are likely to reflect the impact that noise in the data had on the relative performance of the approaches. By allowing for the presence of noise in the system the number and percentage of conclusive rules have been increased and the amount of effort spent on evaluating inconclusive rules decreased. This region and phase combination reflects an increased complexity in the warfare patterning when compared to previous periods. While the complexity isn't nearly as great in the subsequent periods when the state emerges, even in this case specific efficiencies accrue to the use of approaches that take uncertainty explicitly into account. In the next section we will investigate this hypothesis by comparing the performance of the two approaches over all periods of interest in the valley.

7.7 Results

The two representational approaches were compared over the seven periods that chronicle the emergence of social complexity in the valley. The decision trees results are based on the average of the best solution for each of 20 runs with Utgoff's Decision Tree algorithm. The Rough Set approach describes the best solution produced by the Genetic Algorithm-guided Rough Set algorithm using the performance function described earlier.

DT-#c and RS-#c refer to the number of conditions in an average rule for the best decision trees and rough sets rule set, respectively. For each of the 7 periods, the number of conditions in the rough set approach is never greater than that for decision tree approach. In fact, aside from period II the number of terms in the rough set representation is less than that for decision trees. Rosario through Monte Alban Ic correspond to periods of escalating warfare associated with the emergence of a state centered at the site of Monte Alban in the valley. Period II corresponds to a period in which the entire valley is under control of the state and the focus of warfare moves outside of the valley as the Oaxacan state attempted to subdue neighboring areas. Thus, the amount of warfare present in the valley at that time is markedly reduced, and the simplicity of its patterns is equally characterized by both approaches.

During the periods in which warfare patterns were the most complex (Rosario, Monte Alban Ia, Monte Alban Ic), the rough set representation produced rules with a total of 143 conditions as opposed to a total of 223 conditions for decision trees, a significant reduction in complexity. In terms of the simulation, if these rules need to be checked every time step for each of several thousand sites and several thousand agents per site, the computational time saved can be significant.

DT-depth and RS-depth correspond to the maximum number of conditions in a rule in the best rule set. In this case the rough set representation always has fewer conditions on average than the decision tree representation. The increased number of conditions in the decision tree representation corresponds to that fact that explicit sources of noise are included as terms in the rules as opposed to being removed in the rough set representation. Variation can be produced by different surveyors and different landscapes and if their charcaterization is not part of our goal, an approach such as Rough Sets that works to exclude these terms will be more successful.

Dt-#var and RS-#var correspond to the number of unique variables used as terms found in the best rule set of each. What is interesting here is that although the rough set approach produces a rule set with fewer rules and fewer conditions per rule, the number of variables never differs by more than one between the two approaches. They are both using the same information to a different effect in each. This is, in fact, what we observed in the previous section where both approaches used the same subset of variables for their rule conditions. But, we observed that the actual behavior of the rules that were produced was different in terms of identifying the target concept.

Table 7.4 A comparison of the rules produced by using strict (DT) and rough set (RS) constraint representations. # is the average number of conditions in each rule of a rule set. Depth is the maximum length of the rules in the rule set. #var corresponds to the number of different variables used in each of the rules in the rule set.

Phase	DT - #c	RS - #c	DT - #r	RS - #r	DT - Depth	RS - Depth	DT - #var	RS - #var
Tierras Largas	8	6	4	5	3	2	2	2
San Jose	20	11	6	8	5	4	3	4
Rosario	48	25	10	16	8	5	4	5
Monte Alban Ia	80	64	13	34	9	6	6	6
Monte Alban Ic	95	54	16	35	11	6	7	7
Monte Alban II	23	24	7	16	5	4	5	5
Monte Alban IIIa	13	9	5	8	4	2	3	2

7.8 Conclusions

In this chapter, the goal was to employ evolution-based techniques to mine a large-scale spatial data set describing the interactions of agents over several occupational periods in the ancient valley of Oaxaca, Mexico. Specifically, we want to extract from the data set spatial constraints on the interaction of agents in each temporal period. These constraints will be used to mediate the interactions of agents in a large-scale social simulation for each period and will need to be checked many times during the course of the simulation.

One of the major questions was how to represent the constraint knowledge. Popular data mining methods such as decision trees work well with data collected in a quantitative manner. However, the conditions under which the surface survey data was collected here introduced some uncertainty into the data. Would a representation that explicitly incorporated uncertainty into its structure produce a more efficient representation of the constraints here that one than did not? This is important since the complexity of the constraint set will impact the complexity of the simulation that uses those rules.

Here, we use Genetic Algorithms to guide the search for a collection of rough set rules to describe constraints on the location of particular types of warfare in the valley. Since warfare was a major factor in the social evolution in the valley, the constraints reflecting its spatial and temporal patterning are important ingredients in the model. The rules generated are compared sy with those produced by a Utgoff's Decision Tree algorithm. In each of the phases examined, the best rule set that used the rough set representation always had fewer conditions in it, and the average rule length was less than that for the decision tree approach in every case but one. In that case they were equal. The differences were most marked in those periods where the warfare patterns were most complex. It was suggested that the differences reflect the inclusion of noise factors as explicit terms in the decision tree representation and their exclusion in the rough set approach.

A comparison of two decision systems from the first period where the two approaches begin to show larger differences in rule and condition number, Rosario, demonstrates that the rough set approach has a fewer percentage of inconclusive rules and a larger percentage of conclusive ones than for the decision tree approach. In addtion, the rough set approach needs to evaluate fewer conditions relative to the inconclusive ones than the decision tree approach. These differences, it is argued, result from the explicit consideration of uncertainty into a period that is more complex and more prone to the introduction of such uncertainty than previous periods.

The focus of the comparisons here was on the syntactic or structural differences in the decision systems produced. In future work a comparison of the semantic differences will be accomplished by using the approaches to produce alternative ontologies in the agent-based simulation and assess the differences that are produced. In other words, do the syntactic differences reflect semantic differences in simulation model performance? And, what impact does the use of uncertainty to represent ontological knowledge of the agents have on the basic simulation results?

References

1.   Weiss SM, Indurkhya N (1998). *Predictive Data Mining A Practical Guide*. Morgan Kaufmann Publishers, Inc., San Francisco, Ca.
2.   Russell SJ & Norvig P (1995). *Artificial Intelligence a Modern Approach*. Prentice Hall, Upper Saddle River, NJ.
3.   Fox M, Barbuceanu M, Gruninger M & Lin J (1998). An Organizational Ontology for Enterprise Modeling. *Simulation Organizations Computational – Models of Institutions and Groups*. Prietula, MJ, Carley KM, Grasser, L eds. AAAI Press/ MIT Press Menlo Park, Ca., Cambridge, Ma.
4.   Reynolds RG (1984). A computational model of hierarchical decision systems," *Journal of Anthropological Archaeology*, No. 3, pp. 159-189.
5.   Sandoe K (1998) Organizational Mnemonics Exploring the Role of Information Technology in Collective Remembering and Forgetting. *Simulation Organizations Computational – Models of Institutions and Groups*. Prietula, MJ, Carley KM, Grasser, L eds. AAAI Press/ MIT Press, Menlo Park, Ca, Cambridge, Ma.
6.   Marcus J, Flannery KV, (1996) *Zapotec Civilization – How Urban Societies Evolved in Mexico's Oaxaca Valley*, Thames and Hudson Ltd, London.
7.   Blanton RE (1989). *Monte Albán Settlement Patterns at the Ancient Zapotec Capital*. Academic Press.
8.   Blanton R.E, Kowalewski S, Feinman G, Appel J (1982) *Monte Albán's Hinterland, Part I, the Prehispanic Settlement Patterns of the Central and Southern Parts of the Valley of Oaxaca, Mexico*. The Regents of the Univerity of Michigan, The Museum of Anthropology.
9.   Kowalewski SA, Feinman, GM, Finsten L, Blanton RE & Nicholas LM (1989) *Monte Albán's Hinterland, Part II, Prehispanic Settlement Patterns in Tlacolula, Etla, and Ocotlan, the Valley of Oaxaca, Mexico*. Vol. 1. The Regents of the University of Michigan, The Museum of Anthropology.
10.   Utgoff P E. (1989) Incremental Induction of Decision Trees, in Machine Learning, P. Langley, (ed.) pp. 161-186 Boston Kluwer.

11. Reynolds RG, Al-Shehri H (1998) *Data Mining of Large-Scale Spatio-Temporal Databases Using Cultural Algorithms and Decision Trees*, in Proceedings of 1998 IEEE World Congress on Computational Intelligence, Anchorage, Ak.

12. Reynolds RG (1999). The Impact of Raiding on Settlement Patterns in the Northern Valley of Oaxaca: An Approach Using Decision Trees. In *Dynamics in Human and Primate Societies* (T. Kohler and G. Gumerman, (eds.), Oxford University Press.

13. Goldberg DE (1989). *Genetic Algorithms in Search, Optimization, and Machine Learning*. Addison-Wesley Publishing Company, Inc.

14. Holland JH (1975). *Adaptation in Natural and Artificial Systems*. University of Michigan Press. Ann Arbor, MI

15. Pawlak Z (1991). *Rough Sets - Theoretical Aspects of Reasoning about Data*. Kluwer Academinc Publishers.

16. Øhrn A, Komorowski, J., Skowron, A., Synak, P. (1998). The Design and Implementation of a Knowledge Discovery Toolkit Based on Rough Sets: The Rosetta System. *Rough Sets in Knowledge Discovery* L. Polkovski & A. Skowron, (eds.), Physica Verlag, Heidelberg, Germany:.

17. Øhrn A (2000). Rosetta Technical Reference Manual. Tech. Rep., Department of Computer and Information Science, Norwegian University of Science and Technology (NTNU), Trondheim, Norway.

18. Lazar A, Sethi IK (1999). Decision Rule Extraction from Trained Neural Networks Using Rough Sets. *Intelligent Engineering Systems Through Artificial Neural Networks* CH Dagli, AL Buczak, & J Ghosh, (eds.), Vol. 9 pp. 493-498, ASME Press, New York, NY.

19. Ågotnes T (1999, February). Filtering Large Propositional Rule Sets While Retaining Classifier Performance, Master's thesis, Norwegian University of Science and Technology.

20. Vinterbo S & Øhrn A (1999). Approximate Minimal Hitting Sets and Rule Templates.

21. Vinterbo S (1999, December). *Predictive Models in Medicine: Some Methods for Construction and Adaptation*. Ph.D. Thesis, Norwegian University of Science and Technology, Department of Computer and Information Science.

22. Øhrn A & Komorowski J (1997, March). Rosetta - a Rough Set Toolkit for Analysis of Data. *Proceedings of Third International Joint Conference on Information Sciences, Durham, NC*, Vol. 3, pp. 403-407.

23. Komorowski J & Øhrn A (1999) Modelling prognostic power of cardiac tests using Rough Sets. *Artificial Intelligence in Medicine*, Vol. 15, No. 2, pp. 167-191.

24. Fogel DB (1995). *Evolutionary Computation - Toward a New Philosophy of Machine Learning*. IEEE Press.

25. Ågotnes T, Komorowski J and Øhrn A (1999). Finding High Performance Subsets of Induced Rule Sets: Extended Summary. *Proceedings Seventh European Congress on Inteligent Techniques and Soft Computing (EUFIT'99), Aachen, Germany* H. J. Zimmermann and K. Lieven, (eds.).

26. Crowston K (1994) Evolving Novel Organizational Forms. *Computational Organization Theory*. Carley KM, Prietula MJ, eds. Lawrence Erlbaum Associates Publisher, Hillsdale, NJ.

8

An Evolutionary Algorithms Approach to Phylogenetic Tree Construction

C. B. Congdon

Summary. Phylogenetics is an approach used by biologists to investigate the evolutionary relationships among organisms. Typical software packages use heuristic search methods to navigate through the space of possible hypotheses (phylogenies) in an attempt to find one or more "best" hypotheses, as exhaustive search is not practical in this domain. We have developed a system called Gaphyl, which uses an evolutionary algorithms approach to search for phylogenies, and an evaluation metric from a common phylogenetics software package (Phylip). The evolutionary algorithms approach to search yields improvements over Phylip on the tasks investigated here.

8.1 Introduction

The human genome project and similar projects in biology have led to a wealth of data and the rapid growth of the emerging field of bioinformatics, a hybrid discipline between biology and computer science that uses the tools and techniques of computer science to help manage, visualize, and find patterns in this wealth of data. The work reported here is an application to evolutionary biology, and indicates gains from using evolutionary algorithms (EAs) as the search mechanism for the task.

Phylogenetics [7] is a method widely used by biologists to investigate hypothesized evolutionary pathways followed by organisms currently or previously inhabiting the Earth. Given a data set that contains a number of different species, each with a number of attribute values, phylogenetics software constructs phylogenies, which are representations of the possible evolutionary relationships between the given species. A typical phylogeny is a tree structure: the root of a tree can be viewed as the common ancestor, the leaves are the species, and subtrees are subsets of species that share a common ancestor. Each branching of a parent node into offspring represents a divergence in one or more attribute values of the species within the two subtrees. In an alternate approach, sometimes called "unrooted trees" or "networks", the root of the tree is not assumed to be an ancestral state, although these hypotheses are often drawn as trees as a convenience. In this case, the tree represents a hypothesis about the relationships between the species and does not attempt to model ancestral relationships.

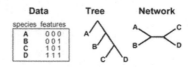

Figure 8.1. A toy example data set, sample phylogeny, and sample network. In this example, there are four species and three features. The tree formed shows the hypothesis that species B is related to species A, gaining the third feature. Similarly, C and D are more closely related to B than to A, also acquiring new features.

An example phylogeny for a toy data set is shown in Figure 8.1. In this example, species A is the common ancestor in the tree, and B is the common ancestor of the subtree below A (assuming the tree is rooted). The relationships between species is also shown in the network representation, to better understand the "unrooted tree".

Phylogenies are evaluated using metrics such as parsimony: a tree with fewer evolutionary steps is considered better than one with more evolutionary steps. The work reported here uses Wagner parsimony. Wagner parsimony is straightforward to compute (requiring only a single pass through the tree) and incorporates few constraints on the evolutionary changes that will be considered. (For example, some parsimony approaches require the assumption that species will only grow more complex via evolution — that features will be gained, but not lost in the process.) Although originally used with phenotype data (physical attributes of the species), it is increasingly common to do genetic studies of related species and construct phylogenies with the genetic data.

The typical phylogenetics approach uses a deterministic hill climbing methodology to find a phylogeny for a given data set, saving one or more "most parsimonious" trees as the result of the process. (The most parsimonious trees are the ones with a minimum number of evolutionary changes connecting the species in the tree. Multiple "bests" correspond to equally plausible evolutionary hypotheses, and finding more of these competing hypotheses is an important part of the task.) The tree-building approach adds each species into the tree in sequence, searching for the best place to add the new species. The search process is deterministic, but different trees may be found by running the algorithm with different random "jumbles" of the order of the species in the data set.

The evolutionary algorithms (EA) approach to problem solving has shown improvements to hill climbing approaches on a wide variety of problems [25] [4] [12]. In this approach, a population of possible solutions to the problem "breed", producing new solutions; over a number of "generations", the population tends to include better solutions to the problem. The process uses random numbers in several different places, as will be discussed later.

This research is an investigation into the utility of using evolutionary algorithms as on the problem of finding parsimonious phylogenies.

8.2 Design Decisions

To hasten the development of our system, we used parts of two existing software packages. Phylip [6] is a phylogenetics system widely used by biologists. In particular, this system contains code for evaluating the parsimony of the phylogenies (as well as some helpful utilities for working with the trees). Using the Phylip source code rather than writing our own tree-evaluation modules also helps to ensure that our trees are properly comparable to the Phylip trees. Genesis [9] is a genetic algorithms (GA) package intended to aid the development and experimentation with variations on the GA. In particular, the basic mechanisms for managing populations of solutions and the modular design of the code facilitate implementing a GA for a specific problem. We named our new system Gaphyl, a reflection of the combination of GA and Phylip source code.

The research described here was conducted using published data sets available over the Internet [5] and was done primarily with the families of the superorder of Lamiiflorae data set [1], consisting of 23 species and 29 attributes. This data set was chosen as being large enough to be interesting, but small enough to be manageable. A second data set, the major clades of the angiosperms [3], consisting of 49 species and 61 attributes, was used for further experimentation.

These data sets were selected because the attributes are binary, which simplified the tree-building process. As a preliminary step in evaluating the GA as a search mechanism for phylogenetics, "unknown" values for the attributes were replaced with 1's to make the data fully binary. This minor alteration to the data does impact the meaningfulness of the resulting phylogenies as evolutionary hypotheses, but does not affect the comparison of Gaphyl and Phylip as search mechanisms.

8.3 The Genetic Algorithm Approach

There are many variations on the GA approach[1], but a standard methodology proceeds as follows:

1. Generate a population of random solutions to the problem. (These are not assumed to be particularly good solutions to the problem, but serve as a starting point.)
2. The GA proceeds through a number of "generations". In each generation:
   a) Assign a "fitness" to each solution, so that we know which solutions are better than others.
   b) Select a "parent" population through a biased random (with replacement) process, so that higher fitness solutions are more likely to be parents.
   c) Use operators such as crossover, which combines parts of two parent solutions to form new solutions, and mutation, which randomly changes part of a solution, to create a new population of solutions.

The algorithm terminates after a predetermined number of generations or when the solutions in the population have converged within a preset criterion (that is, until they are so similar that little is gained from combining parents to form new solutions).

Several factors should be evaluated when considering the utility of GAs for a particular problem:

1. Is there a more straightforward means of finding a "best" solution to the problem? (If so, there is no point in using the GA approach.)
2. Can potential solutions to the problem be represented using simple data structures such as bit strings or trees? (If not, it may be difficult to work with the mechanics of the GA.)
3. Can a meaningful evaluation metric be identified that will enable one to rate the quality of each potential solution to your problem? (Without such a measure, the GA is unable to determine which solutions are more promising to work with.)
4. Can operators be devised to combine parts of two "parent" solutions and produce (viable) offspring solutions? (If the offspring do not potentially retain some of what made the parents "good", the GA will not be markedly better than random trial and error.)

In the phylogenetics task, there is a standard approach to forming the phylogenies, but that process also has a stochastic element, so the standard approach is not guaranteed to find "the best" phylogenies for a given data set. In the phylogenetics task, solutions to the problem are naturally represented as trees. In addition, a standard metric for evaluating a given tree is provided

---

[1] As is the custom in the evolutionary computation community, the author distinguishes different forms of evolutionary computation and is working specifically within the "genetic algorithms" framework.

with the task (parsimony). However, there is a challenge for implementing the phylogenetics task using the GA approach: devising operators that produce offspring from two parent solutions while retaining meaningful information from the parents.

8.4 The GA for Phylogenetics

The typical GA approach to doing "crossover" with two parent solutions with a tree representation is to pick a subtree (an interior or root node) in both parents at random and then swap the subtrees to form the offspring solution. The typical mutation operator would select a point in the tree and mutate it to any one of the possible legal values (here, any one of the species). However, these approaches do not work with the phylogenies because each species must be represented in the tree exactly once.

Operators designed specifically for this task are described in the following sections and in more detail in [2].

8.4.1 Crossover Operator

The needs for our crossover operator bear some similarity to traveling sales-person problems (TSPs), where each city is to be visited exactly once on a tour. There are several approaches in the literature for working on this type of problem with a GA. However, the TSP naturally calls for a string represen-tation, not a tree. In designing our own operator, we studied TSP approaches for inspiration, but ultimately devised our own. We wanted our operator to attempt to preserve some of the species relationships from the parents. In other words, a given tree contains species in a particular relationship to each other, and we would like to retain a large degree of this structure via the crossover process.

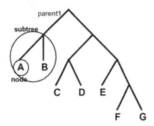

Figure 8.2. An example parent tree for a phylogeny problem with seven species. A subtree for crossover has been identified.

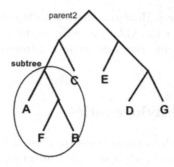

Figure 8.3. A second example parent tree for a phylogeny problem with seven species. A subtree for crossover has been identified.

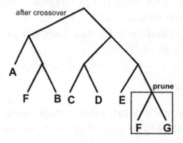

Figure 8.4. The offspring initially formed by replacing the subtree from parent1 with the subtree from parent2.

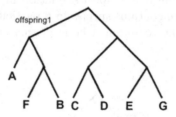

Figure 8.5. The offspring tree has been pruned to remove the duplicate species F.

Our crossover operator proceeds as follows:

1. Choose a species at random from one of the parent trees. Select a subtree at random that includes this node, excluding the subtree that is only the leaf node and the subtree that is the entire tree. (The exclusions prevent meaningless crossovers, where no information is gained from the operation.)
2. In the second parent tree, find the smallest subtree containing all the species from the first parent's subtree.
3. To form an offspring tree, replace the subtree from the first parent with the subtree from the second parent. The offspring must then be pruned (from the "older" branches) to remove any duplicate species.
4. Repeat the process using the other parent as the starting point, so that this process results in two offspring trees from two parent trees.

This process results in offspring trees that retain some of the species relationships from the two parents, and combine them in new ways.

An example crossover is illustrated in Figures 8.2 through 8.5. The parents are shown in Figures 8.2 and 8.3; Figure 8.4 shows the offspring formed via the crossover operation and identifies the subtree that must now be pruned, and Figure 8.5 shows the resulting offspring (after pruning species F). (Note that in the phylogenies, swapping the left and right children does not affect the meaning of the phylogeny.)

8.4.2 Canonical Form

The Wagner parsimony metric uses "unrooted" trees, leading to many different possible representations of "the same" phylogeny that are anchored at different points. Furthermore, flipping a tree (or subtree) left to right (switching the left and right subtrees) does not alter the parsimony of a phylogeny (nor represent an alternative evolutionary hypothesis). Therefore, it soon became clear that Gaphyl would benefit from a canonical form that could be applied to trees to ascertain whether trees in the population represented the same or distinct phylogenies.

The canonical form we instituted picks the first species in the data set to be an offspring of the root and "rotates" the tree (and flips, if necessary) to keep the species relationships intact, but to reroot the tree at a given species. (To simplify comparisons, we followed the default Phylip assumption of making the first species in the data set the direct offspring of the root of the tree.) Secondly, the subtrees are (recursively) rearranged so that left subtrees are smaller (fewer nodes) than right subtrees and that when left and right subtrees have the same number of nodes, a preorder traversal of the left subtree is alphabetically before a preorder traversal of the right subtree. This process is carried out when saving the "best" trees found in each generation, to ensure that no equivalent trees are saved among the best ones. Canonical form is illustrated in Figure 8.6.

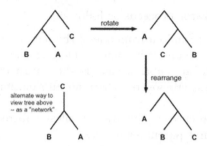

Figure 8.6. An illustration of putting a tree into canonical form. The tree starts as in the top left; an alternate representation of the tree as a "network" is shown at the bottom left. First, the tree is rotated, so that the first species is an offspring of the root. Second, subtrees are rearranged so that smaller trees are on the left and alphabetically lower species are on the left.

Trees are put into a canonical form when saving the best trees found in each generation, to ensure that no equivalent trees are saved among the best ones.

8.4.3 Mutation Operators

The typical GA "mutation" operator takes a location in the solution at random and mutates it to some other value. Again, the standard operator was not suited to our representation, where each species must appear exactly once in the tree. Instead, for our mutation operator, we selected two leaf nodes (species) at random, and swapped their positions in the tree.

A second mutation operator picks a random subtree and a random species within the subtree. The subtree is rotated to have the species as the left child of the root and reconnected to the parent. This second operator is based on the mechanisms of the canonical form and was found empirically to help the search process.

8.4.4 Immigration

Early runs with Gaphyl on the larger data set yielded trees with a parsimony of 280, but not 279 (lower parsimony is better). Reflection on the process and inspection of the population determined that the process seemed to be converging too rapidly — losing the diversity across individuals that enables the crossover operator to find stronger solutions. "Premature convergence" is a known problem in the GA community, and there are a number of good approaches for combating it. In Gaphyl, we opted to implement parallel populations with immigration. Adding immigration to the system allowed Gaphyl to find the trees of fitness 279.

The immigration approach implemented here is fairly standard. The population is subdivided into a specified number of subpopulations, which, in most generations, are distinct from each other (crossovers happen only within a given subpopulation). After a number of generations have passed, each population migrates a number of its individuals into other populations; each emigrant determines at random which population it will move to and which tree within that population it will uproot. The uprooted tree replaces the emigrant in the emigrant's original population. The number of populations, the number of generations to pass between migrations, and the number of individuals from each population to migrate at each migration event are determined by parameters to the system.

8.5 Experimental Results

Recall that both Gaphyl and Phylip have a stochastic component, which means that evaluating each system requires doing a number of runs. In Phylip, each distinct run first "jumbles" the species list into a different random order. In Gaphyl, there are many different effects of random number generation: the construction of the initial population, parent selection, and the selection of crossover and mutation points. For both systems, a number of different runs must be done to evaluate the approach.

8.5.1 Comparison of Gaphyl and Phylip

1. With the Lamiiflorae data set, the performance of Gaphyl and Phylip is comparable. Phylip is more expedient in finding a single tree with the best parsimony (72), but both Gaphyl and Phylip find 45 most parsimonious phylogenies in about 20 minutes of run time.
2. With the angiosperm data set, a similar pattern emerges: Phylip is able to find one tree with the best fitness (279) quite quickly, while Gaphyl needs more run time to first discover a tree of fitness 279. However, in a comparable amount of run time, Gaphyl is able to find 250 different most parsimonious trees of length 279 (approximately 24 hours of run time). Phylip runs for comparable periods of time have not found more than 75 distinct trees with a parsimony of 279. Furthermore, the trees found by Phylip are a proper subset of the trees found by Gaphyl.

In other words, Gaphyl is more successful than Phylip in finding more trees (more equally plausible evolutionary hypotheses) in the same time period.

The first task is considerably easier to solve, and Gaphyl does not require immigration to do so. Example parameter settings are a population size of 500, 500 generations, 50% elitism (the 250 best trees are preserved into the next generation), 100% crossover, 10% first mutation, and 100% second mutation.

Empirically, it appears that 72 is the best possible parsimony for this data set, and that there are not more than 45 different trees of length 72.

The second task, as stated above, seems to benefit from immigration in order for Gaphyl to find the best-known trees (fitness 279). Successful parameter settings are 5 populations, population size of 500 (in each subpopulation), 2000 generations, immigration of 5% (25 trees) after every 500 generations, 50% elitism (the 250 best trees are preserved into the next generation), 100% crossover, 10% first mutation, and 100% second mutation. (Immigration does not happen following the final generation.) We have not yet done enough runs with either Phylip or Gaphyl to estimate the maximum number of trees at this fitness, nor a more concise estimate of how long Phylip would have to run to find 250 distinct trees, nor whether 279 is even the best possible parsimony for this data set. In two days of run time, Phylip runs have not found more that 100 distinct trees of fitness 279.

The pattern that emerges is that as the problems get more complex, Gaphyl is able to find a more complete set of trees with less work than what Phylip is able to find. The work done to date illustrates that Gaphyl is a promising approach for phylogenetics work, as Gaphyl finds a wider variety of trees on this problem than Phylip does. This further suggests that Gaphyl may be able to find solutions better than those Phylip is able to find on data sets with a larger number of species and attributes, because it appears to be searching more successful regions of the search space.

8.5.2 Contribution of Operators

To evaluate the contributions of the GA operators to the search, additional runs were done with the first data set (and no immigration). Empirically, crossover and the second mutation operator had been found to be the largest contributors to successful search, so attention was focused on the contributions of these operators.

In the first set of experiments, the first mutation rate was set to be 0%. First, the crossover rate was varied from 0% to 100% at increments of 10% while the second mutation rate was held constant at 100%. Second, the second mutation rate was varied from 0% to 100% at increments of 10% while the crossover rate was held constant at 100%. at each parameter setting 20 experiments were run; each experiment of 500 generations.

Figure 8.7 illustrates the effects of varying the crossover rate (solid line) and second mutation rate (dashed line) on the average number of generations taken to find at least one tree of the known best fitness (72). Experiments that did not discover a tree of fitness 72 are averaged in as taking 500 generations. For example, 0% crossover was unable to find any trees of the best fitness in all 20 experiments, and so its average is 500 generations.

This first experiment illustrates that, in general, higher crossover rates are better. There is not a clear preference, however, for high rates of the second form of mutation. To look at this operator more closely, the final populations

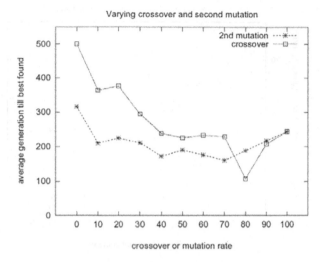

Figure 8.7. The effect of varying crossover rate while holding second mutation constant and of varying the second mutation rate while holding the crossover rate constant. The average generation at which the best fitness (72) was found is illustrated.

of the 20 experiments were looked at to determine how many of the best trees were found in each run.

Figure 8.8 illustrates the effects of varying the crossover rate (solid line) and second mutation rate (dashed line) on the average number of best trees found. Experiments that did not discover a tree of fitness 72 are averaged in as finding 0 trees. For example, 0% crossover was unable to find any trees of the best fitness in all 20 experiments, and so its average is 0 of the best trees.

As Figure 8.9 illustrates, runs with a higher second mutation rate tend to find more of the best trees than runs with a lower second mutation rate.

The impact of the first mutation operator had seemed to be low based on empirical evidence. So another set of experiments was done to assess the contribution of this operator. In both, the crossover rate was set at 100%; in one, the second mutation rate was set at 0% and in the other, the second mutation rate was set at 100%.

The results of this experiment clearly indicate that higher rates of this form of mutation are not beneficial. Furthermore, this operator is not clearly contributing to the search.

In the final set of experiments, the first experiments of varying crossover rate while holding second mutation rate constant and vice versa were repeated, but this time with a first mutation rate of 10%. The results are illustrated in Figure 8.10.

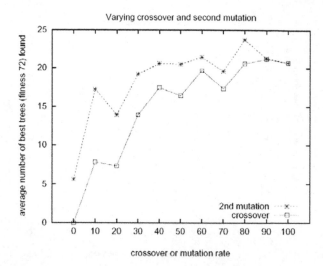

Figure 8.8. The effects of varying crossover rate while holding second mutation constant and of varying the second mutation rate while holding the crossover rate constant. The average number of best trees (45 max) found by each parameter setting is illustrated.

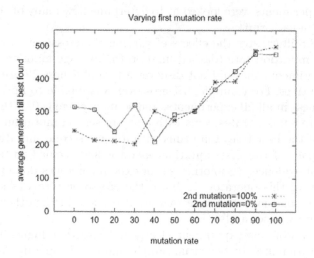

Figure 8.9. The effect of varying the first mutation rate while holding crossover and second mutation constant. The crossover rate is 100% for both graphs; second mutation rates of 100% and 0% are shown. The average generation at which the best fitness (72) was found is illustrated.

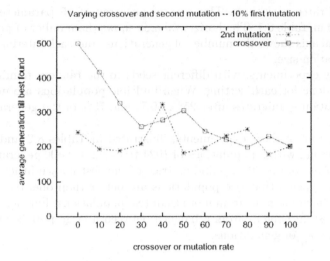

Figure 8.10. The effect of varying crossover rate while holding second mutation constant and of varying the second mutation rate while holding the crossover rate constant, this time with a first mutation rate of 10%. The average generation at which the best fitness (72) was found is illustrated.

8.5.3 Contribution of Other Parameters

An additional set of experiments were designed to assess tradeoffs in terms of putting a fixed number of trees in one population or distributing them across a number of populations and tradeoffs between having larger population sizes or doing more generations, for a fixed number of evaluations in all cases. These experiments were done using the angiosperms data set.

Table 8.1. The population size for each experiment described in Section 8.5.3. When there are multiple populations, the number shown refers to the number of trees in each distinct population.

Gens	Number of populations				
	1	2	4	8	16
1600	1024	512	256	128	64
800	2048	1024	512	256	128
400	4096	2048	1024	512	256

The base case may be thought of as 1 population of 1024 individuals, and 1600 generations. Then, along one dimension, the population is divided across 2, 4, 8, and 16 populations, a total of five variations. Along the other dimension the number of generations is halved as the population size is doubled, for a total of three variations. This creates an array of 15 parameter settings, illustrated in Table 8.1. The horizontal axis shows the number of populations, the vertical axis shows the number of generations, and each interior cell shows the population size.

Twenty experiments, with different seeds to the random number generator, were done for each setting. When multiple populations are used, 5% of the population immigrates after 25%, 50%, and 75% of the generations have completed.

The results of these experiments, illustrated in Tables 8.2 and 8.3, show the best results with 2 populations of 1024 trees run for 800 generations, with a total of 7 out of the 20 runs finding trees of the best-known fitness of 279. In general, it appears that two populations are better than one, but that there might not be great gains from more than two populations. Further, it appears that the system benefits from a balance between a large population size and a large number of generations.

Table 8.2. The number of runs that found the best solution found across 20 runs, varying the number of populations and number of generations, with a constant 1024 trees (split across the specified number of populations).

Gens	Number of populations					sum
	1	2	4	8	16	
1600	1	2	1	2	1	7
800	5	7	2	5	2	21
400	3	3	4	0	0	10
sum	9	12	7	7	3	

Table 8.3. Average fitness of final populations found across 20 runs, varying the number of populations and number of generations, with a constant 1024 trees (split across the specified number of populations).

Gens	Number of populations				
	1	2	4	8	16
1600	281.70	281.55	281.10	280.85	280.95
800	280.60	279.95	280.25	279.95	280.15
400	280.45	280.15	280.45	281.15	281.95

8.5.4 Exploration of Hybrid Possibilities

We have noted that Phylip is relatively quick to find at least one of the best solutions, but that over a span of time it does not find as many of the bests as Gaphyl does. Therefore, it seems that investigating the possibility of a hybrid system would be beneficial. The hybrid variation explored here is to use Phylip runs to seed the initial population of the GA run.

In these experiments, the point of comparison is the starting point for the system. Four variations were explored, using the angiosperms data set:

1. Starting with an entirely random initial population.
2. Starting with an initial population comprised of a random selection of trees found by running one Phylip jumble.
3. Starting with an initial population comprised of half Phylip trees from one jumble and half random trees.
4. Starting with an initial population comprised of 20 Phylip trees, one of the best from each of 20 different jumbles, and the remainder random trees.

We ran 25 experiments for each variation. One population was used, so as not to confound the effects of multiple populations. The population size was 2000 trees, run for 1000 generations. Other parameters are as reported previously.

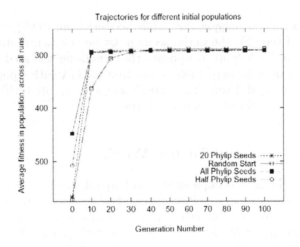

Figure 8.11. Trajectories for the four experiments with seeding the initial population.

Of these runs, the 4th variation fared the best, finding at least one tree with the 279 fitness in 14 of the 25 runs. Secondly, the first variation found at least one tree with 279 fitness in 5 of the 25 runs. The second and third variations did not find any trees of 279 fitness in the 25 runs. Trajectories of average fitnesses across all runs are shown in Figure 8.11. The results in the saturation region are more closely presented in Figure 8.12.

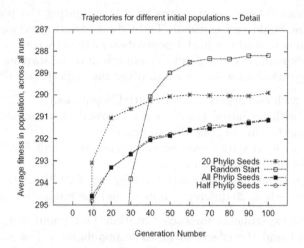

Figure 8.12. More detail on the trajectories for the four experiments with seeding the initial population.

These experiments suggest that while seeding from Phylip runs may help the progress of the GA, the initial seeds must be sufficiently diverse for this "jump start" to be helpful. It appears that choosing the seed trees from a single Phylip jumble is comparable to starting the GA with a population that has already converged. (Note: This experiment was repeated with five distinct Phylip jumbles, always with similar results.)

8.6 Conclusions and Future Work

The GA search process as implemented in Gaphyl represents an improvement over Phylip's search process in its ability to find more trees than Phylip in the same run time. One possible facet of this success is that the Gaphyl search process is independent of the number of attributes (and attribute values); the complexity of the search varies with the number of species (which determines the number of leaf nodes in the tree). Phylip uses attribute information in its search process.

The first mutation operator is perhaps the "obvious" form of mutation to implement for this problem, and yet its use (at high levels) appears to detract from the success of the search. This points to the importance of evaluating the contributions of operators to the search process.

There is obviously a wealth of possible extensions to the work reported here. First, more extensive evaluations of the capabilities of the two systems must be done on the angiosperms data set, including an estimate of the maximum number of trees of fitness 279 (and, indeed, whether 279 is the most parsimonious tree possible). This would entail more extensive runs with both approaches. Furthermore, as evidenced by the unexpected result with the mutation operator, the effect of the immigration operator in Gaphyl must be explored further.

Second, more work must be done with a wider range of data sets to evaluate whether Gaphyl is consistently able to find a broader variety of trees than Phylip, and perhaps able to find trees better than Phylip is able to find.

Third, Gaphyl should be extended to work with nonbinary attributes. This is particularly important in that phylogenetic trees are increasingly used by biologists primarily with the A, C, G, T markers of genetic data.

Finally, we need to compare the work reported here to other projects that use GA approaches with different forms of phylogenetics, including [10] and [11]. Both of these projects use maximum likelihood for constructing and evaluating the phylogenies. The maximum likelihood approach (which is known as a "distance-based method") is not directly comparable to the Wagner parsimony approach (which is known as a "maximum parsimony" approach).

Acknowledgments

I would like to thank Emily F. Greenfest, who worked with me in the initial design and implementation of this project. Thanks also to Judy L. Stone and Randall Downer for sharing their knowledge of phylogenetic theory and software. Thanks to Randolph M. Jones, Joshua R. Ladieu, and the anonymous reviewers for comments on previous versions of this paper.

References

1. L. An-Ming. (1990) A preliminary cladistic study of the families of the superorder lamiiflorae. *Biol. J. Linn. Soc.*, 103:39–57 .
2. C. B. Congdon. (2001) Gaphyl: A genetic algorithms approach to cladistics. In L. De. Raedt and A. Siebes, editors, *Principles of Data Mining and Knowledge Dicovery (PKDD 2001)*, Lecture notes in artificial intelligence 2168, pages 67–78, New York. Springer.
3. R. Dahlgren and K. Bremer (1985) Major clades of the angiosperms. *Cladistics*, 1:349–368.
4. L. Davis (1991) *Handbook of Genetic Algorithms*. Van Nostrand Reinhold, New York, NY.
5. M. J. Donaghue (2000) Treebase: A database of phylogenetic knowledge. web-based data repository. Available at http://phylogeny.harvard.edu/treebase.
6. J. Felsenstein. (1995) Phylip source code and documentation. Available via the web at http://evolution.genetics.washington.edu/phylip.html.
7. P. L. Forey, C. J. Humphries, I. L. Kitching, R. W. Scotland, D. J. Siebert, and D. M. Williams (1993) *Cladistics: A Practical Course in Systematics*. Number 10 in The Systematics Association. Clarendon Press, Oxford.

8. D. E. Goldberg (1989) *Genetic Algorithms in Search, Optimization and Machine Learning.* Addison-Wesley, Reading, MA.
9. J. J. Grefenstette (1987)   A user's guide to GENESIS.   Technical report, Navy Center for Applied Research in AI, Washington, DC.   Source code updated 1990; available at `http://www.cs.cmu.edu/afs/cs/project/ai-repository/ai/areas/genetic/ga/systems/genesis/`.
10. P. O. Lewis (1998) A genetic algorithm for maximum-likelihood phylogeny inference using nucleotide sequence data. *Mol. Biol. Evol.*, 15(3):277–283.
11. H. Matsuda (1996) Protein phylogenetic inference using maximum likelihood with a genetic algorithm. In L. Hunter and T. E. Klein, editors, *Pacific Symposium on Biocomputing '96*, pages 512–523. World Scientific, London.
12. M. Mitchell (1996) *An Introduction to Genetic Algorithms.* MIT Press, Cambridge, MA.

9

Robot Controller Evolution with Macroevolutionary Algorithms

J. A. Becerra, J. Santos, R.J. Duro

Summary There are certain problems that require using small populations to explore fitness landscapes that are mostly flat, thus offering very little information, where the solutions appear as sparsely distributed narrow peaks. This is the case of the evolution of controllers for many problems in evolutionary robotics. Consequently, for these types of problems it should be useful to consider the use of evolutionary algorithms that cluster the few individuals in the surroundings of the local good solutions permitting an adequate trade-off between exploration and exploitation. Macroevolutionary algorithms cover this need, and through the appropriate selection of the values for its parameters they perform in general better than genetic algorithms for the case of very low population values. In this work we study the influence of the two main parameters governing the search performed by macroevolutionary algorithms as well as the influence of dividing populations into races.

9.1 Introduction

Due to the large computational requirements for calculating the fitness of each solution (possible robot controller), and in order to make computing times bearable, most processes in evolutionary robotics imply very small populations. This is because every individual must live its life out in a real or simulated environment and this life implies complex interactions incurring large computational costs per individual. It becomes especially critical when the evolution is carried out in the real robot.

In traditional methods of simulated evolution such as GAs, selective pressure determines how fast the population converges to a solution. The more pressure, the faster the convergence, at the cost of increasing the probability of the solution found being suboptimal. Consequently, in this type of methodologies an exploration/exploitation dilemma is present whereby a designer can choose to consider the evaluation of a large number of candidates throughout the search space or concentrate the search in the direction of a good, possibly suboptimal, solution. The choice of a good equilibrium between exploration and exploitation is even more important when the computational requirements of the evaluation of the individuals are very high as in the case of evolutionary robotics. Obviously, if an evolutionary roboticist requires reasonable solutions in bearable amounts of time, populations with a restricted number of individuals must be considered. As a consequence of the small size of the populations, the evolutionary dynamics for these systems stray from those established for so-called *infinite population* evolutionary systems, and the convergence properties become more brittle. This problem becomes even more noticeable when the fitness functions lead to landscapes that are mostly flat except for a very sparse distribution of peaks where fit individuals are located. Much research is needed on the interplay of the different parameters that control the evolutionary process and on the best possible solutions for this extreme low population, low information fitness function case. What we will need is to use evolutionary algorithms that cluster the few individuals in the surroundings of the local good solutions and allow a control of an adequate trade-off between exploration and exploitation.

One promising avenue out of the exploration/exploitation dilemma is an intermediate alternative in which the search is concentrated on or covers an adequate number of candidate solutions, not only one. A first possible approximation to this objective is the use of parallel evolutionary algorithms, imposing geographic constraints on the evolutionary search of different subpopulations. Although it is not the same as concentrating on several candidate solutions, it can be an approximation, especially if the subpopulations cover different areas of the search space, at least at the beginning of the evolution process, as studied in [6]. Obviously, after a few generations, some subpopulations may contain individuals outside their assigned space due to mutations or migrations of best individuals from other subpopulations, but, in general, the procedure implies a more exhaustive search of the solution space and, thus, there is a tendency to prevent the premature convergence problem.

Another possibility to avoid the problem of ill-convergence is to obtain selection procedures that produce the desired clustering or concentration of the search efforts on the different candidate solutions of the fitness landscape. This is called "niching" in biology. In this biological sense, Goldberg [2] defines a niche as an organism's job or role in an environment, and a species as a type of organisms with similar characteristics. At the computational level it means that these groups can be formed around each of the local fitness peaks of the solution space. In most evolutionary methods this effect does not appear due to the way in which evolutionary pressure is applied in traditional selection schemes such as the roulette wheel or tournament selection. The most classical solution in this line is to consider the use of the so-called *crowding* operator 1: when a new individual is generated, it replaces the most similar individual of the population, which prevents the possibility of having many similar individuals ("crowds") at the same time in the population. Thus, the key point in this approach seems to take into account some measure of similarity among the individuals. For example, Menczer et al. [5] use a local selection scheme for evolving neural networks in problems that require multicriteria fitness functions. For each individual in the population the authors consider a solution similar to itself. This individual is evaluated in an environment with shared resources that are consumed and replenished in time. If the energy of the new agent, considering the cost of creating it, is higher than a threshold, the new individual remains in the population with half the energy. In any other case, the parent and the new individual die. The population is kept constant on average thanks to an adequate conservation of the total energy in the environment.

Another more formal solution in the same line, which is the one we have followed in this work, is the one proposed by Marín and Solé [4]. The authors consider a new temporal scale, the "macroevolutionary" scale, in which the extinctions and diversification of species are modeled. The population is interpreted as a set of species that model an ecological system with connections between them, instead of a number of independent entities as in classical GAs. The species can become extinct if their survival ratio with respect to the others is not higher than a *survival coefficient*. This ratio measures the fitness of a species with respect to the fitness of the other species. When species become extinct, a diversification operator colonizes the holes with species derived from those that survived or with completely new ones.

This paper deals with the study of several parameters and techniques that are of interest in order to make the evolutionary processes used to obtain robot controllers more efficient. This problem must be handled using small populations, and its fitness landscapes present huge areas with very low values and sparse hyper-dimensional peaks. This involves delimiting when a Macroevolutionary Algorithm (MA) performs better on average than a Genetic Algorithm. That is, defining the best parameters in MAs so as to adequately balance exploration and exploitation, and how a population should be divided into races in order to optimize the search for an optimal solution.

9.2 Description of Macroevolutionary Algorithms

Here, we summarize the model proposed by Marín and Solé [4], which explains the dynamics of an ecosystem based only on the relation between species. Thus, the individuals in the population are referred to as species. They can survive or become extinct in each generation of the evolutionary process. The number of species is a constant. The relation between them is established by a matrix in which the term $W_{i,j}(t)$ represents the influence of species j on species i at time t, which is a continuous value in a given range. This influence is a measure of the difference of the relative fitness of the two species, considering the distance between both in genotypic space:

$$W_{i,j} = \frac{f(p_i) - f(p_j)}{|p_i - p_j|},$$ (9.1)

where $p_i=(p_i^1,...,p_i^d)$ is the genotype of species i, with its parameters in a d-dimensional space. f represents the fitness of each species. Thus, the influence is the difference in fitness with a normalization factor that weighs the distance between the two.

Two operators are applied to each generation:

1. **Selection operator**: defines which species survive and which species become extinct. To determine this, the "state" of each individual is calculated as

$$S_i(t+1) = \begin{cases} 1 & \text{if } \sum_{j=1}^{p} W_{i,j}(t) \geq 0, \\ 0 & \text{otherwise,} \end{cases} \qquad (9.2)$$

that is, if the sum of the influences of a species relative to all the other species in the population is positive, the species survives. Otherwise, it becomes extinct.

2. Colonization operator: it defines how the extinct species are replaced. The authors define a probability Γ to determine if a new solution p_n is generated. Otherwise exploitation of surviving solutions takes place through *colonization*. One of the surviving solutions, p_b, is chosen as a base to replace the extinct solution p_i, and the new species that replaces the extinct one is attracted toward p_b, in the following manner:

$$p_i(t+1) = \begin{cases} p_b(t) + \rho\lambda\big(p_b(t) - p_i(t)\big) & \text{if } \xi > \Gamma \\ p_n & \text{if } \xi \leq \Gamma \end{cases} \qquad (9.3)$$

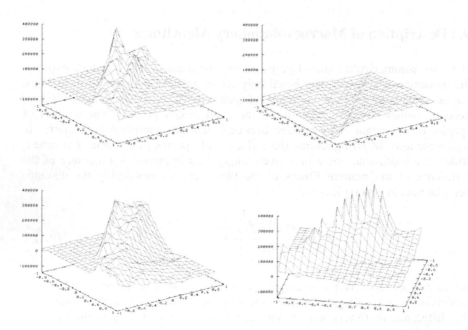

Figure 9.1 Different views of the fitness landscape with the variation of four genes (connection weights in the neural controller) while the others are fixed. Top-Left: different peaks in a well-defined area. Top right: flat landscape with a small change in the surface level. Bottom left: another similar area of concentrated peaks. Bottom right: Another area, viewed from a different reference point, that denotes a periodic distribution of peaks in a small area.

where ξ is a random number in [0,1], λ a random number in [-1,1], both with uniform distribution, ρ describes a maximum radius around the surviving solution and Γ controls the percentage of random individuals. This parameter may act as a temperature, because it can decrease in evolutionary time so as to perform a type of simulated annealing process. That is, when the temperature is low, the randomness is low, and, consequently, there is a tendency toward increased exploitation around the surviving individuals and reduced exploration of new species. Thus, when using a macroevolutionary algorithm one can tweak with basically two parameters. On one hand, Γ determines what proportion of the species are randomly generated, that is, how much exploitation or exploration we perform in a given generation. On the other, one can modify ρ and thus juggle with the size of the attractor basin around p_b, that is, it permits deciding how the exploitation is carried out.

9.3 Experimental Setup for Testing the MA-based Evolution

As commented before, the comparison between GAs and MAs will be carried out in a problem where robot controllers, made up of artificial neural networks, are the end product. This is a very typical problem that implies a sparse fitness function and a large amount of processing per individual. In particular, all the examples presented here correspond to the evolution of a wall following controller for a Pioneer II robot. The fitness is defined with hints in the environment that represent food or poison. This procedure allows more freedom than many handcrafted fitness functions for the robot controller evolution to discover good behaviors, at the cost of a more difficult fitness landscape. The controller is a neural network with a 6-node hidden layer, 8 inputs, and 2 outputs, which implies a total of 76 genes representing the connection weights, slope of the sigmoid functions and bias in the different nodes. Figure 9.1 displays partial views of the fitness landscape where 4 out of the 76 genes that make up the chromosome are modified while the rest are maintained constant at values corresponding to the best solution obtained. The chosen genes are two connection weights between the inputs and a node in the hidden layer, and the two weights between this hidden node and the two output nodes. It is well known that with genetic encodings of the parameters of distributed structures such as neural networks, there can be a lot of different parameter sets that obtain similar input-output mappings. As a consequence, several fitness peaks can appear in the search space. This is what is shown in Figure 9.1, where the fitness was obtained testing each individual in 20 different life situations. The axes x and y correspond to the variation of two of the genes, while the four views correspond to four different selected combination values on the other two genes (weights connecting the hidden node with the output nodes), while the rest of the genes remain fixed. This analysis is similar to the one carried out by Janson and Frenzel [3], who show slices of the error surface in a neural network with the variation of only one gene, to demonstrate the difficulty for discovering the global optimum. Their neural network must predict the optimal transistor width for a CMOS switch. What the figure demonstrates is that the search space has a lot of different peaks in a lot of different areas, surrounded by flat surfaces with different levels.

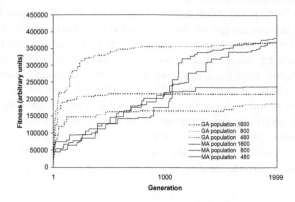

Figure 9.2. Evolution of the fittest for a GA and a
MA with different population sizes (8 races).

With that in mind in the experiments we describe evolution was carried out
using two types of algorithms. One of them was a pure genetic algorithm, with a
0.8 crossover probability and a 0.1 mutation probability. Crossover was a standard
one point crossover and mutation was random. The selection strategy employed
was tournament. The GA used a diagonal distribution for the initial population, as
it has been shown to provide the best usage of resources [6]. This algorithm was
taken as a standard in order to compare different aspects. The other one was a
macroevolutionary algorithm as commented before.

9.4 GA Versus MA

The first consideration one should make is how well GAs and MAs compare when
evolving solutions to a problem such as the one we are tackling, a problem that
must be solved using small populations. In Figure 9.2 we display the results
comparing the performance of a GA and a MA for different population sizes. Two
main characteristics stand out at first sight. On one hand, GAs display the classical
evolution curve for the best individual, that is, very fast fitness increase at the
beginning, when the GA is making use of the genetic material present in the initial
population and recombining it to obtain the best possible individuals from this
material, that is, very fast exploitation of the initial population, and a very slow,
almost flat second part, where evolution is driven by mutation, as new genetic
material is required in order to find new combinations that provide better fitness, in
a sense we have a second stage of exploration. This behavior, as pointed out in [6]
makes GAs very dependent on the distribution of the initial population. This would
not be a big problem when large populations are used, as an initial random
distribution would probably introduce enough genetic elements in the population to
allow the algorithm paths for reaching the optimum, or close to it. When using
small populations, the best possible distribution of the initial population would be a

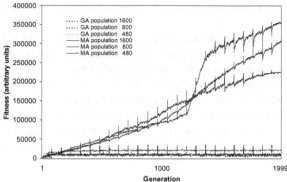

Figure 9.3. Evolution of the average fitness for a GA and an MA with different population sizes (8 races).

diagonal, as it maximizes the spread of the gene variety, but it still constrains evolution and makes it dependent on mutation (basically random search) after a short period.

In the case of MAs, as mentioned before, exploration takes place first, and exploitation comes into play slowly throughout the process (when annealing is used). In fact, due to the way in which exploitation is carried out in this type of algorithms, new genetic material arises throughout the exploitation phase. This leads to a slower evolution in the beginning, but it is much more constant as shown in the figure. In fact, it usually leads to better results than GAs, especially in the low population cases, such as those with 480 and 800 individuals.

In Figure 9.3 we see the very different behavior in terms of average fitness in both types of evolutionary algorithms. In the GA, average fitness is far below maximum fitness and it never converges to it. The search space in this problem could be described as a flat surface with sporadic high peaks. This particular search space leads to most of the individuals in the population, resulting from crossover or random mutation, being quite poor when performing the desired task. In the MA case, this is very different. Because of the way exploitation is carried out in this algorithm, individuals tend to concentrate in the high peaks as time progresses.

9.5 Effect of Distribution into Races

Distributing the individuals into subpopulations that evolve independently and only communicate through a periodic migration of best individuals between them can be shown to improve the evolution process. From the point of view of implementation it also permits distributing subpopulations among processors adding a concurrency level that leads to an acceleration of the process. We have tried this strategy both for GAs and MAs applied to the current problem. The case of GAs was presented in [6]. In both cases, the subdivision of the population into races led to improvements in the final fitness of the best individuals. The evolution of fitness for the best individuals and for the average of the whole population in MAs are shown in Figures 9.4 and 9.5 as we change the number of races for a given population size.

Obviously, as the number of races increases, the number of individuals in a race decreases. In fact, when too many races are considered, that is, when each race reaches a number of individuals below a critical point (related to the selective pressure in that population), evolution in the case of GAs has very little initial genetic variety and is mostly driven by mutation, that is, a random walk, and basically tends to get stuck in a suboptimal individual. In the case of MAs the behavior is quite similar: too few individuals cannot provide enough genetic variety for exploitation to work well, as shown in the 16 races case of the figure.

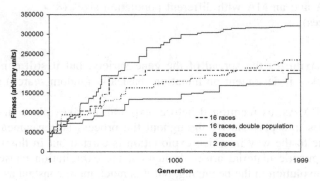

Figure 9.4. Evolution of the fittest in an MA with 800 individuals for different numbers of races.

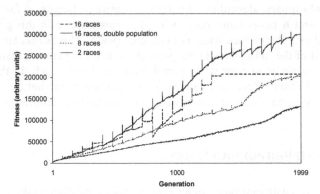

Figure 9.5. Evolution of the average fitness for an MA with 800 individuals distributed into different numbers of races.

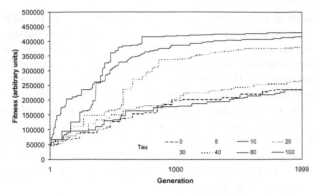

Figure 9.6. Evolution of fittest individuals for different values of NR.

Another important observation that may be extracted from this data is that in the beginning of MA evolution, every time there is a migration, as shown in the average fitness graphs of Figure 9.5, it provides new genetic material that helps to maintain a steady improvement in the fitness of the population. The slope of this improvement is related to the number of individuals that can combine their genetic material with the immigrant, i.e., the subpopulation size. After a migration, average fitness usually increases because the better individuals of other races replace the worst individuals of each race, but after that, average fitness may decrease. This is especially notable in MAs at the end of evolution if different races are exploiting different candidate solutions, because almost all the individuals are quite good and, when a foreign individual arrives, its descendants with other individuals from the original race will probably fall to the plain, outside the high peaks.

In general, MAs improve with races in the same way as GAs do, although evolution is more fluid and usually leads to better results for the same population sizes, as shown in the previous section.

9.6 Influence of parameters Γ and ρ on the MA

From the point of view of exploration vs. exploitation, as we have commented above, this dichotomy is regulated in MAs through parameter Γ. This parameter may take any value throughout the evolution process, but in order to study its effect on problems such as the ones stated above, we have decide to modify it linearly from all random to no random individuals in the population but keeping a number of generations with no random individuals at the end of evolution where, consequently, the MA is performing pure exploitation. This number of generations was controlled through a parameter we called NR (Non Randomness), that is, the percentage of generations with no random individuals.

Figure 9.6 shows the fitness results of running the MA with different values for NR. It can be clearly seen that it seems to be quite useful to let the MA perform pure exploitation before ending the evolutionary process. It usually leads to better results due to the landscape of the fitness function. This can be interpreted from the point of view of a cloud of samplings of the solution space for the MA. Initially, we want the algorithm to explore as much of the solution space as possible so that it does not miss any possible promising region. Once the main promising regions have been found, the directional properties of MAs, which lead them to cluster test points around better solutions, will end up leading to clusters that will tend to converge to a good solution. Thus, in this second part it is interesting to reduce randomness and perform more exploitation, that is, better coverage of promising regions. In particular, for very flat fitness landscapes the initial exploration for promising regions becomes more a problem of delimiting the important areas (which is much less costly than covering the whole region). Then, through the particular exploitation phase of the MA by creating offspring located in between the parents in the solution hyperspace, a fine-grained search is performed, leading to the individuals clustering around the peaks.

Finally, we have experimented with parameter ρ, which defines the neighborhood considered in the exploitation or colonization phase of the MA. The tests carried out for different values of this parameter do not display a clear tendency in the MA behavior, which agrees with the same results of Marín and Solé [4] for the search in two landscapes, one with some local maxima of close heights, and another one with infinite maxima around the global maximum. The authors conclude that "in most cases simulated annealing seems to be the best choice, being the specific ρ-value less important. Because of that, the authors choose in their comparison with GAs a value of 0.5 for the parameter, the same one we have used in the NR tests.

9.7 Conclusions

In this article we have provided some results on evolving complex controllers with small populations for fitness functions with flat landscapes where sparse narrow peaks are distributed. The basic idea is that macroevolutionary algorithms permit obtaining better results due to the way in which they handle the exploration/exploitation equilibrium, which, in effect, implies a lower selective pressure at the beginning than traditional GAs, preventing, in most cases, the premature convergence effects displayed by GAs. When these algorithms are combined with the use of races and their NR parameter adjusted to appropriate values, the results obtained are quite comparable to GAs with much larger populations. Thus, using macroevolutionary algorithms and a race scheme, evolutions of systems whose individual fitness is very costly to calculate can be achieved in reasonable computation times through the use of small populations and the inherent parallelization level provided by the race scheme.

Acknowledgments

This work was supported by the MCYT of Spain through project TIC2000-0739C0404 and Xunta de Galicia through project PGIDIT02PXIB10501PR.

References

1. De Jong, K.A. (1975) *An Analysis of the Behavior of a Class of a Genetic Adaptive Systems*, Ph. Thesis, University of Michigan, Ann Arbor.
2. Goldberg, D.E. (1989) *Genetic Algorithms in Search, Optimization and Machine Learning*, New York, Addison-Wesley.
3. Janson, D.J., Frenzel, J.F. (1993) Training product unit neural networks with genetic algorithms", *IEEE Expert* 26-32.
4. Marín, J., Solé, R.V. (1999) Macroevolutionary algorithms: A new optimization method on fitness landscapes, *IEEE Transactions on Evolutionary Computation* 3(4):272-286.
5. Menczer, F., Street, W.N., Degeratu, M. (2001) Evolving heterogeneous neural agents by local selection, *Advances in the Evolutionary Synthesis of Intelligent Agents*, M.J. Patel, V. Honavar and K. Balakrishnan (eds.), MIT Press, 337-365.
6. Santos, J., Duro, R.J., Becerra, J.A., Crespo, J.L., and Bellas F. (2001) Considerations in the application of evolution to the generation of robot controllers, *Information Sciences*, 133:127-148.

10

Evolving Natural Language Grammars

W. Cyre

10.1 Introduction

Most approaches to natural language understanding depend on a grammar to perform the syntactic analysis of sentences. Manually developing a consistent, context-free grammar that accurately parses a good portion of a natural language requires considerable expertise and diligence and is a tedious task. Presently, statistical and machine learning methods are popular. Statistical grammars may have over tens of thousands of rules, which results in a high computational cost for parsing.

The problem of developing a grammar is simplified somewhat when the natural language documents are limited to a particular domain. Examples of such restricted domains are medical records, weather reports, patents, and legal reports. A language used in a restricted domain is called a sublanguage and tends to have a limited vocabulary, syntax, and semantics. For example, the sublanguage of interest to the present author is that used in manufacturer's data sheets and U.S. patents that describe microprocessor system components. These documents have vocabularies limited to a narrow technical domain, and many sentence constructions of general English (such as questions and imperatives) do not occur. On the other hand, sentences tend to be quite complex. Four examples of sentences from patents that could not be parsed by an initial grammar, but that were parsed by an evolved grammar, are reproduced below.

"Once the subsystem controller has been set up, the central processing unit is then free to carry out other operations in the system while the subsystem device controller itself controls the transfers between memory and the peripheral device."   (1)

"Another object of the invention is to provide an improved data processing system as described above and further including a counter in the shared direct memory access controller; selection means responsive to the address recognition means and an output instruction from the microprocessor for loading a value on the common data bus into the counter; and, gating means connecting the counter to the common address bus so that the contents of the counter may directly address the memory."   (2)

"On the other hand, if the signal RADR-0 is at the low level, then a low level signal on lead 326 enables counters 322 and 323 so that they are loaded with data from the outputs of QUAD MUX's 302 and 303.   (3)

"The probe signal is applied to Figure 3A where it enables the decoder 318 controlling the loading of the address pointer counter, and further controls MUX's 302 and 303 so as to gate the data on the system data bus 200 through the MUX's to the address pointer counter."   (4)

The conventions of a sublanguage may also depart from standard English. For example, computer engineers generally nominalize verbs to the infinitive form ("a memory write", "generates an interrupt") rather than a gerund ("a writing to memory", "generates an interruption") as is done in general English. What is needed for automated analysis of a sublanguage is a context-free grammar tailored to the specific sublanguage. The problem of parsing the sublanguage may be exacerbated by the need for results that are amenable to later semantic analysis. The semantic analysis approach in the present example employs verb-centered templates called case frames [1]. A case frame for a particular verb, such as transfer, has slots for semantic roles such as the agent, operand, source, and destination. These slots are filled by noun phrases, which may include other frames that represent nominalizations of other verbs. Semantic analysis is performed by tracing a parse tree from top to bottom, instantiating a case frame whenever a verb structure is encountered, and filling the frame's slots with syntactically related noun phrases. Thus it is important in this application to develop a context-free, phrase-structured grammar that focuses on verb structures and noun phrases, as well as their syntactic connectives (subject/object position, prepositions, and subordinating conjunctions). Unfortunately, the manual development of sublanguage grammars is a difficult and expensive task. Statistical techniques are not attractive because large, manually parsed training sets in sublanguages are generally not available and are expensive to produce.

The approach investigated here is to evolve sublanguage grammars. The initial grammar has a small number of manually developed rules with the desired, context-free, phrase-structured style. But, this grammar parses only a small fraction of the sublanguage corpus. These initial rules represent the general rules of the sublanguage, and the genetic algorithm discovers the more specialized or exception rules. In experiments described later, the parsing ability of the evolved grammar was much greater than that of the initial grammar after a relatively short number of generations. In some cases, parsing capability grew from 17% to 90%, and yet, the number of rules remained relatively small. In addition, the evolution tends to preserve the style of the initial grammar.

10.2   Related Research

Recently, statistical methods and machine learning for generating grammars have become popular in natural language understanding [2]. Supervised learning methods require a large database of manually analyzed sentences (tree bank), from which the grammar is derived. A large general database is available from the Linguistic Data Consortium, and one grammar derived from the data is a 14,000-rule probabilistic grammar [3]. The style of the statistically derived grammars is constrained to the manual parsing style used when creating the training corpus, which in the above case has very shallow trees. Unsupervised methods [4] have also been used. In these cases, the set of all possible grammar rules is constructed (incrementally) and the training algorithm discovers the rule probabilities. The grammar growth is made incremental by ordering the training corpus on sentence length. Without additional constraints, these methods do not produce consistent results, even with quite small languages.

Earlier experiments in grammar evolution focused on very small context-free grammars. Wyard [5] evolved a population of context-free grammars for two-symbol palindromes, and another population for a language with even numbers of two symbols. Each grammar of the population was evaluated based on its ability to distinguish positive and negative strings. (Negative strings are examples that are not in the target language.) The initial grammars were generated randomly. Elitist selection from the most fit 10% of grammars was used. Grammar rules were subject to mutation with low probability, and the crossover point could occur anywhere in a grammar, except inside the list of constituents of a right-hand side of a rule. With populations of 1000 grammars and limited computational resources, the algorithm found the palindrome grammar 40% of the time but never discovered an acceptable grammar for the second language. Some early experiments by the present author on natural language sentences with a similar approach were not encouraging.

Lucas [6] followed a similar path, but developed a binary encoding of his normal-form grammars. He evolved grammars that proved 80% to 100% competent for two- and three-symbol palindromes. His population was much smaller (40 grammars), and fitness was also evaluated on positive and negative strings. His initial grammars were random.

Smith and Witten [7] used a binary and/or tree representation of the grammars. Their language consisted of several five-word English sentences on a vocabulary of about eight words. In their approach, the lexicon (parts of speech of the words) was evolved at the same time as the grammar rules. They also used bootstrapping (actually co-evolution of the evaluation test set) with a population of grammars but did not require a constant size population. Their hybrid algorithm used an initial population of 10 random grammars, each of which could parse one initial sentence. During each generation, another sentence was added to the test set. Selection for reproduction was based on grammar size, since each grammar could parse all current sentences. The selected grammars were either mutated or crossed over using standard tree operations of genetic programming, and the offspring were immediately added to the population. Reproduction proceeded until at least one grammar could parse all sentences, including the new one. Then all grammars that could not parse all sentences were culled from the population. For the next generation, a new sentence was added and the cycle repeated. This approach attempts to solve a very large problem in discovering the grammar and lexicon simultaneously. Each word in the grammar must be represented as a leaf in a tree chromosome for each of its parts of speech. In the automatic design problem, this means each tree would have over 300,000 nodes! The approach reported here uses a single grammar (the population consists of rules) and also performs part-of-speech tagging as well as syntactic analysis.

10.3 The Evolutionary Algorithm

This section describes a genetic algorithm developed for evolution of sublanguage grammars of English. The population to be evolved by the Genetic Algorithm (GA) consists of a set of grammar rules (productions) of a context-free, phrase-structured grammar. Each grammar rule is a chromosome, so the GA actually operates on the phenotypes. This GA has some of the features of a classifier system [8] in that the grammar rules are rewarded by a bucket-brigade, and the GA has separate rule discovery and grammar evaluation phases. First, it is helpful to define context-free grammars.

A Context-Free, Phrase Structured Grammar (CFPSG) consists of

- a finite set of **terminals**, T, also called the alphabet,
- a finite set of **nonterminals**, V,
- a special nonterminal, s, called the **start symbol**, and
- a finite set of **rules** or productions, P, of the form $R \rightarrow w$, where $R \in V$ and $w \in (V \cup T)^*$. [9]

For convenience, we will call the nonterminal, R, on the left-hand side of a rule the **result** of the rule, and each terminal and nonterminal, w_i, of the sequence, $w = (w_1, w_2, \ldots, w_n)$, on the right-hand side of the rule will be called a **constituent** of the rule. In this study, a CFPSG that will parse a sublanguage of English is being sought. The language for which a grammar is desired is defined by a corpus of sentences, and the percentage of sentences in the language that the grammar parses will be called the **competence** of the grammar. The corpus in this study was a collection of descriptive text from patents issued on direct memory access controllers for digital computers. It is well known that a deterministic grammar cannot be generated from only positive examples (sentences) of a language [10], but statistical grammars can be. The present approach evolves grammar rules and with a small extension can generate the probabilities.

During evolution, rule discovery and fitness evaluation employ a form of bottom-up, parallel chart parser that can find all parses of a sentence simultaneously. This parsing method also performs part-of-speech tagging, so the initial grammar formally includes a very large set of rules that map nonterminals onto English words, such as *processor* → *noun*. Parts of speech in this study include noun, verb, preposition, conjunction, determiner, adjectives, adverbs, and identifiers. These "rules" are in the form of a dictionary. In the domain of interest, an identifier is a proper name, an acronym, or any other unknown character string. To simplify the discussion here, however, we will consider the parts of speech to be terminals of the grammar to be evolved. Since English words often have more than one part of speech, the input to the parser is actually graph, called an (initial) chart, rather than a string. In an initial chart, each node corresponds to position between words, and the arcs are labeled by the parts of speech of the words. Since English is syntactically ambiguous, grammars to approximate English are also ambiguous and produce multiple parses for most sentences. Another goal of grammar evolution is to minimize the ambiguity of the grammar to the extent it is possible.

Genetic Algorithm for Grammar Evolution

0. Initialize population.

1. Repeat until stopping criterion.

a) *Add* **rule schemata.**

b) *Discover* **new rules.**

c) *Replace* **rule schemata by new rules.**

d) *Evaluate* **grammar.**

e) *Cull* **unfit rules.**

Figure 10.1. The algorithm.

Each rule of the grammar may be considered a variable-length chromosome consisting of the rule's result, followed by its list of constituents. However, the rules are not evaluated individually, but as a cooperating set, and the fitnesses of the rules are called their strengths, after the tradition of classifier systems. Evaluation is performed by parsing a collection of sentences (the corpus) using the grammar, and rewarding the rules based on how often they participate in successfully parsing sentences. The individual grammar rules are rewarded by tracing each parse tree from the top down for a successfully parsed sentence. The leaf nodes are parts of speech, and each nonleaf node of a parse tree represents a phrase constructed by a rule. The top node of the tree receives a fixed reward. Each rule that formed a successor node in the tree is awarded a fraction of that node's reward. If for example, if the rule *sentence → noun – phrase predicate* was used in a parse of a sentence, it is given a reward, r, inversely proportional to the number of parse trees that sentence has. (This is done to reduce the ambiguity of the grammar.) Next, the two rules that formed the noun-phase and the predicate constituents are then each rewarded by k*r, for some constant k. This constant was determined empirically.

The genetic algorithm is outlined in Figure 10.1. Each iteration of Step 1 is a generation of the algorithm. It differs from general GAs in the discovery and culling steps. The genetic operations are performed during the discovery step.

As mentioned earlier, the initial population is derived manually. In the present project, this grammar was derived from several hundred sentences describing microprocessor products [11]. To facilitate a later step of semantic analysis [12], a case grammar style was used, so that the major nonterminals included verb sequence, nominal (high-level noun phrases), and adverbial. Other nonterminals used during analysis include noun phrase, clause, predicate, and prepositional phrase, as well as the parts of speech. It is very desirable during evolution of the grammar to maintain this style of analysis, and therefore, no new nonterminals were added during evolution. The initial grammar used in the present experiment has 131 rules and is evaluated by the parallel chart parser to determine rule strengths for later selection of parents. This initial grammar parses only a small fraction of the corpus.

During a generation of the algorithm, a set of *n* rule schemata is added to the grammar. During the **Add** step, *n* "parent" rules are selected with replacement using a tournament based on rule strengths. A copy of a parent rule is mutated by inserting one wildcard nonterminal at a random position in the constituent list (right-hand side of the rule). A wildcard nonterminal will match any nonterminal or terminal of the grammar during parsing, so a rule with wildcards is indeed a schema for rules. The wildcard may be inserted at the beginning of the constituent list or any other position except the end. (This is a practical matter to speed up evaluation speed.) For example, the rule *np → determiner adjective noun* might be mutated to *np → determiner wildcard adjective noun*, which would allow two adjectives to modify the noun or an adverb to modify the adjective, as in the phrases "an edge-triggered synchronous counter" and "a virtually asynchronous counter." When the set of *n* schemata has been generated, they are temporarily added to the grammar. Crossover is not used in this algorithm. First, it would not be reasonable to crossover a rule for a noun phrase with a rule for a verb sequence. Thus, crossover points should only occur in the constituent lists of rules having the same result nonterminal type. Since English does have constraints on word order, crossover would have some of the same difficulties as found in ordering problems, such as the traveling salesman problem. It was felt that crossover would introduce less desirable rules than would the specialized mutation above. Other possible mutation techniques such as random nonterminal insertion, exchange, and inversion were not used either. Random nonterminal insertion would only be a slow version of wildcard insertion. Inversion and exchange, like crossover, are reordering operations, though it would be interesting to experiment with the latter.

Next, the **Discover** step is performed to generate new, permanent grammar rules by instantiating the wildcards of schemata. This is done by parsing the unparsed sentences of the corpus with a fast version of the chart parser. When a sentence is parsed for the first time, a wildcard that was used during that parse is instantiated to the nonterminal it matched, and a new rule is generated from the schema. This new rule is added to a temporary list of new rules. Note that a single schema may generate multiple new rules if it matches more than one nonterminal, even in a single sentence. The Discovery step does not reconsider previously parsed sentences, since it is not desirable to increase the ambiguity of the grammar by finding additional rules that parse sentences. For a given set of *n* schemata, the number of new rules that are generated can vary from zero to several times *n*. For this study, the number of new rules was artificially limited to *10*n* in order to limit the growth rate of the grammar.

Having discovered a set of new grammar rules, the schemata are then deleted from the grammar, and the new rules that do not duplicate existing grammar rules are added in the **Replace** step. The list of new rules is then cleared. Notice that unlike most GA applications, the population (of grammar rules) is allowed to grow. We start here with a very small grammar of 131 rules. Grammars that have been developed for general English may have tens of thousands of rules, particularly probabilistic grammars [10], but the grammars evolved here remain relatively small, as described later.

Next, the grammar is evaluated by the parallel parser to determine the strengths of the rules for selection in the next generation. As mentioned earlier, each sentence-level rule that participates in a successful parse is given a reward that is inversely proportionally to the ambiguity of the sentence (number of parse trees). In addition, a percentage of the reward is then added to each rule that formed a constituent necessary to satisfy the rule, in a chained bucket-brigade fashion. Hence when a sentence is parsed, every rule that participated in forming any parse tree for it is rewarded. There is an exception: if the number of parse trees exceeds a preset threshold, then none of the participating rules is rewarded for that sentence. This is done to minimize the growth of ambiguity in the grammar. Finally, any rules, except those in the initial grammar, that have very low strength are deleted from the grammar in the *Cull* step. This prevents the grammar from accumulating rules that are used very infrequently or that add significant ambiguity. It is assumed that discovered rules that are essential for parsing some sentence will be rediscovered in a more general or less ambiguous manner later.

10.4 Experiments

The experiments with a C++ implementation of the algorithm were run on text selected from U.S. patents on a type of digital device called a direct memory access controller. The text was selected from the summary and detailed description sections of the patents. This avoided many of the nonsentential structures in patents such as numbers, references, names, and legal claims. The corpora still contained a small amount of nonsentential structures from tables and headings. The dictionary used to tag tokens with parts of speech included about 5000 words and was developed manually. Not all words in the patents were in the dictionary. The unknown words plus acronyms and identifiers were classified as identifiers during preprocessing. A corpus may have several thousand instances of identifiers. Three sets of experiments were run, one on some large corpora of several thousand sentences, and two sets of experiments on a small corpus of about 400 sentences. In most cases, the experimenter limited the algorithm runs to a relatively small number of generations to focus on the more interesting period of most rapid growth. In a few cases the algorithm was run for many generations to demonstrate that a reasonably competent grammar could be evolved from a seriously inadequate grammar.

A limited number of experiments were run on three large corpora having 3557, 3745, and 6943 sentences, respectively. The initial manual grammar parsed only 6% to 9% of the sentences in these corpora, requiring 5 to 7 hours each on a 500MHz Pentium PC for 30 generations of the algorithm. In each generation, 5 schemata were generated, so that up to 50 new rules could be produced per generation.

The other sets of experiments were performed on a small corpus of 385 sentences selected from the larger corpus. This corpus was cleaner than the large ones and intentionally contained more sentences that could be parsed with the initial grammar, i.e., 17%, or 69 sentences. One set of experiments used a constant number of schemata per generation ($n = 5$) to determine how repeatably the algorithm performed. A different random number generator seed was used in each run to

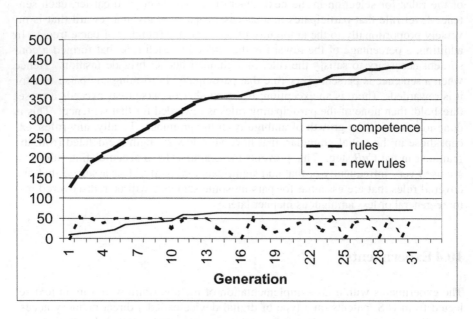

Figure 10.2 Grammar evolution.

provide a different set of schemata. Another set was run on with a varying number of schemata per generation to determine the effects of the number of schemata per generation on grammar growth. The results of the experiments are described in the next section.

10.5 Results

10.5.1 Large Corpora Experiments

The evolution of the grammar for one of the large corpora is shown in Figure 10.2. This corpus has 3745 sentences, of which the initial grammar parses 266, or 7%. Growth of the grammar and its competence in parsing the sentences is rapid at first and slows later, with the competence up to at 65% by the 20th generation and leveling to 71% by the 30th generation.

The size of the grammar grew to about 340% of its original size. Initially, more new rules were generated than the limit (50 for 5 schemata). As can be seen, the number of new rules produced in a generation is rather erratic. The algorithm performed similarly on one of the other large corpora, but did only half as well on the third corpus having 6943 sentences. In that run, the limit on the number of new rules was reached in nearly every generation.

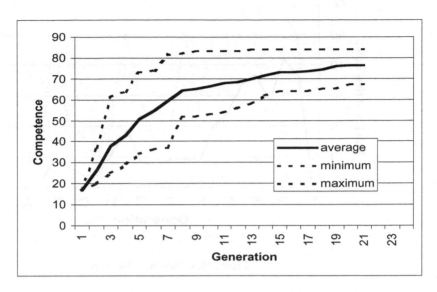

Figure 10.3 Growth of grammar competence.

10.5.2 Performance Variability

Seven experiments run with the same small corpus of 385 sentences and parameter values were performed to observe how consistently the algorithm performed.

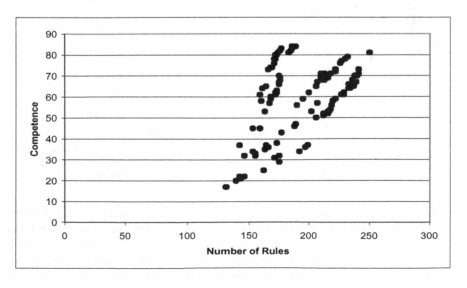

Figure 10.4. Competence versus number of rules.

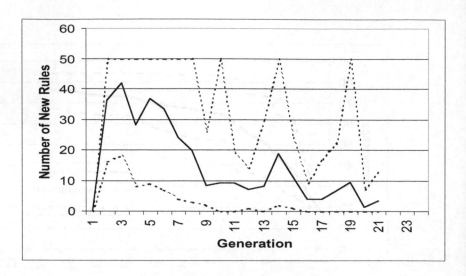

Figure 10.5. New rule discovery.

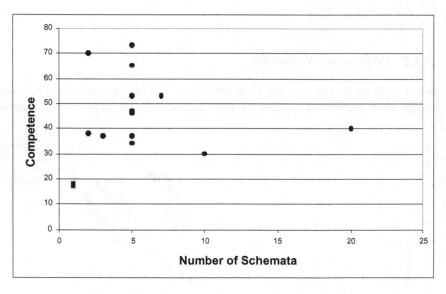

Figure 10.6. Competence versus number of schemata.

Figure 10.3 shows the average, maximum, and minimum percent competence versus generation of the algorithm. All the curves display the same growth trend, but as can be seen the growth rate of competence can vary considerably. The growth of the grammar itself is similar, and the sizes of the final grammars vary accordingly. The relationship between the number of rules in the grammar and the com-

petence of the grammar is shown in Figure 10.4 for the six runs with five schemata. The runs seem to have a nearly linear relationship between the number of
rules and competence, but with slightly different slopes. So, it appears that each
run should eventually reach a desired competence, regardless of the order in which
schemata are introduced, but the final grammars may be different sizes.

Figure 10.5 shows the rate at which new rules are discovered. Discovery is very
rapid at first and was even truncated to the *10n* limit. Discovery then tapers off. In
other runs, only an occasional new rule may be discovered in the later generations.
This may result from there being no mechanism for preventing the same schemata
from being introduced in generation after generation. The discovery peaks may be
due to the occasional introduction of a new and fruitful schema. The number of
new rules culled from the evolving grammars shows a similar pattern. While the
number of rules culled was not a fixed percentage of the number of new rules, it
was generally less than 25% but did reach 67% in one case.

10.5.3   Varying the Number of Schemata

The effects of varying the number of schemata was studied with the same corpus of
385 sentences by adding another 9 runs with the number of schemata varying between 1 and 20. In each case, the algorithm was run for 20 generations. The competence of the evolved grammars after twenty generations versus the number of
schemata per generation is shown in Figure 10.6. A plot of the number of grammar rules versus the number of schemata has a similar shape. From this sparse
data, it does not appear that the number of schemata per generation has much effect
on evolution. The runs in which only one schema was used, or where a large number of schema were used, did not do as well as the intermediate cases. In some
earlier experiments where only one schema could be introduced per generation, the
grammars generally leveled off at only twice their initial competence values.

10.5.4   Examples of Discovered Rules

A selection of the 568 new rules discovered by the genetic algorithm in the series
of seven runs with 5 schemata appears in Table 10.1. Rows 1 through 5 show a
single rule that was discovered in five of the seven runs. Note that the rule has different strengths in the runs. This useful rule allows an identifier to be appended to
the head of a noun phrase. This accepts constructions such as "Register X" and
"Pin AG4/2", which often occur in this domain. Rule 6 occurred in two runs and
allows a modal (can, may, should) to prefix an active verb. It is surprising that this
rule was not discovered in all runs. That may be due to other rules that prefixed
predicate structures with modals, such as Rule 7, which was discovered in two
runs. The discovered rule with greatest strength is shown in row 8 of the table.
This rule forms a sentence from a simple sentence followed by a nominal and a period. Its strength is twice the next-strongest rule and tenfold most other strong new
rules, and yet it was found in only one run. The rule in row 9 was found in two
runs and forms a predicate with an active verb structure and two nominals. This
accommodates sentences with both an indirect and direct object (a construct not

covered by the initial grammar). Note that Rule 8 serves a similar function provided the simple sentence contains no adverbials.

Rule 10 allows noun phrases to be strung together, which is useful in parsing long nominal compounds, such as "the computer multiplexer chip strobe pin of the processor." Rule 11 forms a coordinated noun phrase from three noun phrases and a coordinating conjunction, and allows for the grammatical error of omitting a comma. A similar rule was found in another run. Rule 13 constructs a nominal from an adjective preceding a noun phrase. This would appear to be a useful rule, but most word sequences accepted by this rule are also recognized by a combination of three rules in the initial grammar. So, while this rule may accommodate a few cases, it will also introduce additional ambiguity in the grammar by allowing multiple parses of some strings. Other rules that can introduce ambiguity were found among the discovered rules.

Table 10.1 Examples of Discovered Rules

#	Runs	Strength	Rule
1		0.9	head --> head id
2		20.3	head --> head id
3		1.8	head --> head id
4		0.5	head --> head id
5		8.8	head --> head id
6	2	-	avs --> mod verb
7	2	-	pred --> mod pvs d
8	1	220.1	s --> ss n .
9	2	-	pred --> avs n n
10	1	4.4	n --> np np of n
11	1	1.6	nc --> np np conj np
12	2	-	avs --> conj verb
13	4	-	n --> adjs np
14	4	-	np --> det det head
15	6	-	n --> prep np

The rules mentioned so far are consistent and desirable to the phrase-structured parsing goals. Not all discovered rules were desirable. Some rules introduce structures that are not attractive candidates for semantic analysis. For example rule 12 considers a conjunction followed by a verb to be an active verb structure. This rule was probably discovered to accommodate coordinated verbs, such as in "the device clears and loads the register", which were not accepted by the initial grammar. Since a wildcard matches only one symbol, there is no mechanism or introducing conjunctions in a single step. Mechanisms for accommodating conjunctions are being considered. The rule in row 14 was discovered in four runs and accepts a noun phrase with two determiners (a, an, the, this, that) and was probably generated by word sequences such as "that the register" or possibly by typographical errors. The last rule in Table 10.1 is particularly disturbing because it constructs a nominal from a preposition followed by a noun phrase. Such constructs are indeed phrases but should be classified as prepositional phrases (that modify nouns) or adverbials (phrases that directly modify verbs). Similar rules were discovered that form noun phrases from prepositions and nouns. This rule may have been discovered to work with higher-order rules such as Rule 8 above. Presently, a simple sentence may have only up to three nominals and adverbials after the verb. Rule 8 with Rule15 allows one additional adverbial.

Although the competence of the grammar evolves vigorously, and most new rules appear reasonable, some of the discovered rules do not appear desirable from the standpoint of conventional English grammar, or because they introduce ambiguity in the grammar. The "ungrammatical" or undesirable rules may be useful, however, in that they will enable semantic analysis of ungrammatical sentences. Ambiguity in the grammar is inconvenient because it increases the computation time for both grammatical and semantic analysis. Ambiguity is introduced in the grammar when the result nonterminal they construct can be synthesized by one or more existing rules. In any case, the manner in which these undesirable rules are introduced needs to be investigated so that they might be avoided.

10.6   Conclusions

A genetic algorithm has been presented for evolving context-free phrase-structured grammars from an initial, small, handcrafted grammar. The algorithm uses distinct discovery and evaluation steps, as well as a culling step to reduce the ambiguity of the grammar being evolved. The algorithm performs surprisingly well on developing grammars for very complex sentences in a restricted domain of English. The algorithm was generally run for a small number of generations to observe the initial growth of the grammar, but even then, it reached 90% competence in some cases.

Much remains to be investigated in this area. First, a method is needed to cull or avoid rules that form undesirable phrase structures from the semantic analysis perspective. This might be done by interaction with a user who affirms desirable parsings from time to time, as with the occasional environmental rewards in classifier systems. This interactive feedback could have the effects of negative training strings. Alternatively, a semantic analyzer can be run on some of the parse trees and have the rules that participated in parse supporting a successful semantic analysis rewarded enthusiastically. A mechanism needs to be added that will allow conjunction to be introduced in the form $X conj X$, rather than in two separate rules.

The competence of the evolving grammars seems to encounter ceilings below 100% competence. This barrier must be overcome. It would also be interesting to increase the number of schemata introduced in a generation as the grammar evolves. While this would tend to sustain rapid growth during the later generations, it would also increase the evaluation time substantially, since that time depends heavily on the size of the grammar.

142   W. Cyre

Acknowledgments

The research reported here was supported in part by the National Science Foundation, Grant MIP-9707317.

References

1.   W. A. Cook, (1989) Case Grammar Theory, Georgetown University Press, Washington, DC.
2.   C. Manning and H. Schütze, (1999) Foundations of Statistical Natural Language Processing, MIT Press, Cambridge, MA.
3.   E. Charniak, (1996) Tree-bank Grammars, Proceedings of the Thirteenth National Conference on Artificial Intelligence, AAAI Press/MIT Press, Menlo Park, pp.1031-1036.
4.   G. Carroll and E. Charniak, (1992) Two Experiments on Learning Probabilistic Dependency Grammars from Corpora, Workshop Notes, Statistically-Based NLP Techniques, 1-13, AAAI Press, Menlo Park, CA,.
5.   P. Wyard, (1991) Context free grammar induction using genetic algorithms, Proceedings of the 4th International Conference on Genetic Algorithms, 514–518.
6.   S. Lucas, (1994) Structuring Chromosomes for Context-Free Grammar Evolution, First IEEE Int'l Conf. on Evolutionary Computation, 130-135.
7.   T. Smith and I. Witten, (1995) A Genetic Algorithm for the Induction of Natural Language Grammars Proc. IJCAI-95 Workshop on New Approaches to Learning for Natural Language Processing,17-24, Montreal, Canada.
8.   L. Booker, D. Goldberg, J. Holland, (1989) Classifier Systems and Genetic Algorithms," Artificial Intelligence, 40, 235-282.
9.   K-S. Fu, T. Booth, (1986) Grammatical Inference: Introduction and Survey, IEEE Trans. Pattern Analysis and Machine Intelligence, 343-375, May
10.   M. Gold, (1967) Language Identification in the Limit, Information and Control, 10, 447-474.
11.   W. R. Cyre (1995) A Requirements Sublanguage for Automated Analysis, International Journal of Intelligent Systems, 10 (7), 665-689.
12.   W. R. Cyre, (1997) Capture, Integration, and Analysis of Digital System Requirements with Conceptual Graphs, IEEE Trans. Knowledge and Data Engineering, 9(1), 8-23.

11

Evaluating Protein Structure Prediction Models with Evolutionary Algorithms

J. Gamalielsson and B. Olsson

Summary. EAs are competent at solving complex, multimodal optimization problems in applications with large and badly understood search spaces. EAs are therefore among the most promising algorithms for solving the protein structure prediction problem. In this chapter, we use this insight to evaluate, and show the limitations of, simplified models for protein structure prediction. These simplified models, e.g., lattice-based models, have been proposed for their computational efficiency, and it has been proposed that simplified models will work if only a sufficiently competent optimization algorithm is developed. However, in this chapter we show that simplified models do not contain the biological information necessary to solve the protein structure prediction problem. This is demonstrated in two steps: first, we show that the EA finds the correct structure given a fitness function based on information of the known structure. This shows that the EA is sufficiently competent for accurate protein structure prediction. Second, we show that the same algorithm fails to find correct structures when any of the simplified models is used. Our main contribution is to have strengthened the hypothesis that solving the problem of protein structure prediction will require detailed models encoding information at the atomic level. We have also demonstrated that EAs indeed are promising algorithms for eventually solving the protein structure prediction problem.

11.1 Introduction

Protein structure prediction is the task of predicting the three-dimensional folded structure of a protein, given information only about its amino acid sequence. Computational methods for protein structure prediction have achieved limited success, due to the immense complexity of the task, and it is well-known that finding the lowest free-energy conformation of a protein is an NP-hard problem [14].

When designing a computational method for protein structure prediction, there are three main issues to address: *1)* how to represent candidate solutions, *2)* what algorithm to use, *3)* what evaluation function to use. Representation of candidate solutions includes issues such as what structure elements to model and whether to use a discrete or a continuous environment.

Solution representations that have been used for protein structure prediction can be classified into atomic level models (e.g. [11]) and amino acid level models (e.g. [13]). Atomic level models represent the individual atoms that make up each amino acid, while amino acid level models represent each amino acid as a single entity. An obvious advantage of atomic level models is the higher accuracy, which on the other hand results in increased computational complexity. Atomic level models are therefore intractable for large proteins, unless very efficient heuristics can be developed. It is therefore attractive to explore amino acid level models, to see if they are sufficiently detailed to at least allow approximate solutions, which are either useful directly or after further improvement by applying a more detailed model.

The structural elements that are modeled are spatially positioned in an environment. A distinction can be made between lattice and off-lattice environments. Lattice environments use a grid (Figure 11.1) where structural elements can be positioned only at intersections, whereas off-lattice environments position elements in a continuous space. There are different types of lattice environments in two- or three-dimensional space, which all limit the number of possible conformations of proteins. This reduces the computational complexity but limits the accuracy since the folding process of real proteins is not restricted to a gridlike environment. Continuous off-lattice environments offer a more realistic spatial representation, but give, on the other hand, a practically infinite number of possible conformations.

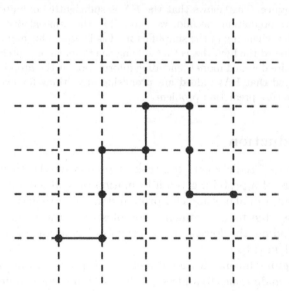

Figure 11.1. Lattice environment where structural elements can only be placed at intersections.

Algorithms that have been applied to protein structure prediction include several versions of EAs. In [12] and [13] a hybrid GA containing Monte Carlo components is compared with a pure Monte Carlo method on 2D and 3D HP models, where amino acids are classified as hydrophobic (H) or polar (P) [4]. On test sequences of 27 and 64 residues the hybrid GA was able to reach the global energy minimum in fewer time steps than the pure Monte Carlo method. A GA is used also in [8], which is based on [13] but avoid the use of nonstandard properties (which are used in [13]) and introduces an improved representation resulting in faster convergence.

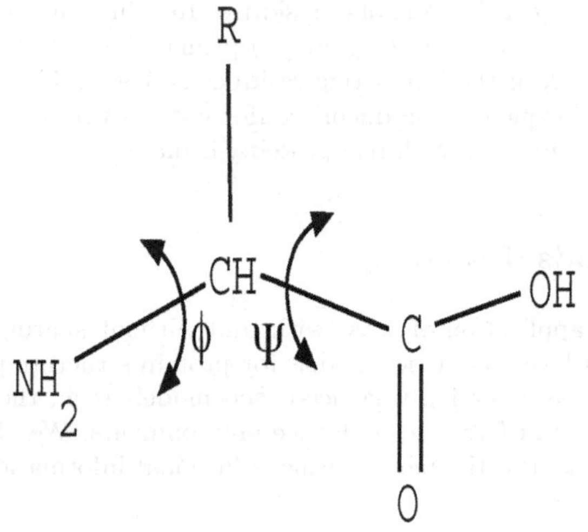

Figure 11.2. Generic amino acid structure with dihedral angles ϕ and ψ. The structure of the side chain R is unique for each of the 20 amino acids.

In [11] a GA is applied to protein structure prediction using a force field as fitness function and having structures being represented at the atomic level by dihedral angles (Figure 11.2). The angles ϕ and ψ are the main degrees of freedom when proteins fold, ϕ being located between the α-carbon atom and the NH group and ψ between the α-carbon and the CO group. In [11], total energy is calculated as $E = E_{tor} + E_{vdW} + E_{el} + E_{pe}$, where E_{tor} is torsion angle potential, E_{vdW} is van der Waals pair interactions, E_{el} is electrostatic potential, and E_{pe} is a pseudo-entropic term driving the protein to a globular state. Simulations using the 46-residue protein 1CRN gave structures with root mean square deviation RMSD $\simeq 9$Å from the native fold. Extensions to the approach reduced RMSD to 4.4Å.

In [2] an EA is applied in an off-lattice environment. Input to the algorithm are the residue sequence and the preferred secondary structural states for different residues. The backbone structure of the fittest solution in the last generation is compared with the native fold of the protein. Nineteen target proteins with fewer than 100 residues and mixed secondary structure compositions are used to test the prediction performance, giving average RMSD = 5.3Å.

An off-lattice environment and amino acid level model is used also in [9], which introduces a distance matrix representation of residue positions instead of the commonly used internal coordinate representation (dihedral angles). A distance matrix contains a distance for every residue pair. The fitness function has terms for punishment of residue clashes, for enforcement of correct distance between consecutive residues, and a term (E_{hyd}) rewarding closeness between hydrophobic residues. Residues are only classified as either hydrophobic or polar. E_{hyd} gives optimal interaction potential when the distance between the interacting residues is 3.80Å. The EA is tested on three 27-residue sequences, producing conformations with compact hydrophobic cores. No comparison with real proteins is made.

11.2 Methods Tested

We tested the application of EAs (with and without sharing) to simplified, i.e., amino acid level, off-lattice models for protein structure prediction, with the purpose of investigating if lattice-based models (e.g., the HP model [4]) can be usefully transferred to off-lattice environments. We also propose and test extensions to the HP model, using additional information about amino acid properties.

11.2.1 Solution Representation

The EA population P at iteration t contains N solutions $P(t) = \{s_1^t, \ldots, s_N^t\}$. A solution for a protein containing M residues is represented by an array of $M - 1$ angles $s_i^t = (\theta_1, \phi_1, \ldots, \theta_{M-1}, \phi_{M-1})$. To obtain the coordinates of the residues in 3D space, a transformation to rectangular coordinates is done using

$$x_i = x_{i-1} + R \cdot \sin \theta_i \cdot \cos \phi_i \quad (i = 2, \ldots, M), \tag{11.1}$$

$$y_i = y_{i-1} + R \cdot \sin \theta_i \cdot \sin \phi_i \quad (i = 2, \ldots, M), \tag{11.2}$$

$$z_i = z_{i-1} + R \cdot \cos \theta_i \quad (i = 2, \ldots, M), \tag{11.3}$$

where $x_1 = y_1 = z_1 = 0$. R is the distance between consecutive residues. Residue positions are approximated by their α-carbon atom positions, which are used to represent the shape of the backbone. This is a very simplified representation where the configurations of the sidechains are not taken into consideration.

We found empirically that the mean distance between consecutive α-carbon atoms for the proteins used in this work is 3.82Å with $\sigma = 0.04$Å. The distance between consecutive α-carbon atoms was therefore set to unit distance $R = 1$ in the algorithm, corresponding to an actual distance of 3.80Å. The distance of 3.80Å has also been used, e.g., by [2]. The angular representation is easy to implement and facilitates the application of genetic variation operators.

11.2.2 EA1. A Standard Evolutionary Algorithm

The EA uses a population $P(t)$ of 100 solutions, which are initialized as straight structures, with all angles set to 0 (cf. [13]). Fitness is assigned according to one of the evaluation functions in Section 11.2.4. We use standard tournament selection without replacement and tournament size $s = 10$. After selection, the new population $P(t)$ is divided into pairs of parent solutions, and standard single-point crossover is applied with $p_c = 0.7$. The crossover point may not split an angle pair (θ, ϕ) for a residue pair. Gaussian mutation is applied to all parameters (angles) of each individual with a probability $p_m = 4/n$, where n is the number of parameters. The mutation operator adds a random number r from a normal distribution ($\bar{r} = 0, \sigma^2 = 1$) to a parameter value.

Table 11.1. Parameter Values Used in the EA1 Experiments.

Protein	Residues	T	n	s	p_c	p_m	σ^2
1CRN	46	9000	100	10	0.7	0.0444	1
2ETI	28	5400	100	10	0.7	0.0741	1
1CTI	29	5600	100	10	0.7	0.0714	1
3ZNF	30	5800	100	10	0.7	0.0690	1
1PPT	36	7000	100	10	0.7	0.0571	1

After reproduction, all solutions s_i in $P(t)$ are evaluated and receive a fitness value $F(s_i)$, and elitism is applied by replacing the worst solution from time t with the best solution from time $t - 1$ if $F_{\max}(P(t)) < F_{\max}(P(t-1))$. The evolutionary cycle is repeated for $T = n \cdot 100$ iterations. The expressions for calculation of p_m and T were determined empirically. It is desirable to adjust p_m so that the same number of parameters are likely to be mutated irrespective of the number of parameters. T is proportional to n because a larger number of parameters usually gives a slower convergence rate. Table 11.1 shows the parameter settings used in simulations for the five different proteins studied.

11.2.3 EA2. An Evolutionary Algorithm with Sharing

The standard EA uses no method to ensure that solutions in a population are diverse, which may cause the algorithm to converge to a point where all solutions are very similar [6]. Hence, there is a risk for premature convergence and suboptimal solutions. EA2 is a modified version of EA1 that uses a fitness sharing strategy. Fitness sharing enforces diversity within a population by demanding that each solution share its fitness with other solutions that are within the same region of the search space. The principle of fitness sharing, as described in [6], is defined in Eqs. (11.4) and (11.5). The problem-specific distance measure used in this work is defined in equation 11.6.

$$F'(s_i) = \frac{F(s_i)}{\sum_{j=1}^{n} sh(d(s_i, s_j))} , \qquad (11.4)$$

$$sh(d) = \begin{cases} 1 - (\frac{d}{\sigma_{share}})^\alpha & \text{if } d < \sigma_{share} \\ 0 & \text{otherwise} , \end{cases} \qquad (11.5)$$

$$d(s_i, s_j) = \sqrt{\sum_{k=1}^{m} (rem(s_{i,k}, 360) - rem(s_{j,k}, 360))^2} . \qquad (11.6)$$

In Eq. (11.4), $F'(s_i)$ is the shared fitness for solution s_i, $F(s_i)$ is the raw fitness returned by the evaluation function for solution s_i, n is the population size ($n = 100$), $sh(d(s_i, s_j))$ is the sharing function value for the distance $d(s_i, s_j)$, which is the distance between solutions s_i and s_j. Hence, $F'(s_i)$ is used during the selection procedure instead of $F(s_i)$. In Eq. (11.5) σ_{share} defines the size of the neighborhood around solution s_i and α is a scaling parameter. In Eq. (11.6), $rem(s_{i,k}, 360)$ is the remainder after dividing parameter k of solution s_i with 360. Hence, Eq. (11.6) is a modified expression for Euclidean distance, taking into consideration that the remainder from a division $\frac{\psi}{360}$ encodes the same position as an angle ψ. The consequence of the sharing function in Eq. (11.5) is that the closer two solutions are to each other, the more each solution is penalized. Different parameter values for σ_{share} were tested during initial simulations and $\sigma_{share} = 16$ was found appropriate. The α parameter was set to 1.

EA2 was applied to all evaluation functions, but only one target protein (2ETI) was used. The number of iterations T was extended from 5400 to 9000, since the broader exploration done with a more diversified population may require more time until convergence. The other EA parameters were set to the same values as described in Table 11.1 for the EA1 algorithm: $n = 100$, $s = 10$, $p_c = 0.7$, $p_m = 0.0741$, and $\sigma^2 = 1$.

11.2.4 Evaluation Functions

This section describes the evaluation functions that we defined and tested.

Table 11.2. Amino Acid Properties

Amino acid	Hydrophobicity	Charge	Woese	Miller
Alanine	H	H	7.0	-0.20
Arginine	P	P	9.1	1.34
Asparagine	P	X	10.0	0.69
Aspartate	P	N	13.0	0.72
Cysteine	P	X	4.8	-0.67
Glutamine	P	X	8.6	0.74
Glutamate	P	N	12.5	1.09
Glycine	P	X	7.9	-0.06
Histidine	P	P	8.4	-0.04
Isoleucine	H	H	4.9	-0.74
Leucine	H	H	4.9	-0.75
Lysine	P	P	10.1	2.00
Methionine	H	H	5.3	-0.71
Phenylalanine	H	H	5.0	-0.67
Proline	H	H	6.6	-0.44
Serine	P	X	7.5	0.34
Threonine	P	X	6.6	0.26
Tryptophan	H	H	5.2	-0.45
Tyrosine	P	X	5.4	0.22
Valine	H	H	5.6	-0.61

HP is an adaptation of the lattice HP model [4] to off-lattice environments, using a similar approach as in [15] and [9]. We used the Rasmol (http://www.umass.edu/microbio/rasmol/) predefined sets "Hydrophobic" and "Polar"to classify amino acids, as shown in Table 11.2, in the column marked "Hydrophobicity". Table 11.3 shows the potential p_{ij} for the HP energy function for types of interactions between neighboring residues r_i and r_j in a lattice environment [10]. The off-lattice version uses a potential function taking the distance between interacting residues into account. An optimal interaction potential equivalent to the lattice interaction potential for neighboring hydrophobic residues occurs at unit distance (3.8Å). Smaller distances are penalized to enforce steric constraints, i.e., to avoid residue clashes. This approach has been used in both lattice [13] and off-lattice models [9, 15]. Total energy is calculated using

$$E = \sum_{i=1}^{M-2} \sum_{j=i+2}^{M} e_{ij} , \qquad (11.7)$$

$$e_{ij} = \begin{cases} \frac{1}{d_{ij}^\gamma} + p_{ij} - 1 & d_{ij} < 1 , \; p_{ij} \neq 0, \\ p_{ij} \cdot \exp(1 - d_{ij}^\epsilon) & d_{ij} \geq 1 , \; p_{ij} \neq 0, \\ \frac{1}{d_{ij}^\gamma} & p_{ij} = 0. \end{cases} \qquad (11.8)$$

where E is the total energy of a conformation, e_{ij} is energy potential between residues i and j, d_{ij} is the Euclidean distance between residues i and j, γ and ϵ are constants, and p_{ij} is the interaction potential according to Table 11.3.

Table 11.3. Interaction Potential p_{ij} for the HP Evaluation Function.

	r_i	
r_j	H	P
H	-1	0
P	0	0

Eq. (11.8) is visualised in Figure 11.3, plotting e_{ij} against d_{ij}. We tested different values for γ and ϵ before fixing them. Higher γ makes the penalty curve steeper. Mutation of a single angle may change e_{ij} dramatically around $d_{ij} = 1$ because of the steep penalty curve below this point. We found $\gamma = 6$ useful for achieving a high penalty effect to avoid residue clashes while also avoiding too high sensitivity to mutation. Higher ϵ yields a reward curve that approaches 0 quicker as a function of d_{ij}. We found that ϵ must not be too high ($\epsilon \geq 1$) as this results in weak guidance toward globular structures for long-distance interactions. $\epsilon = 0.5$ was found adequate.

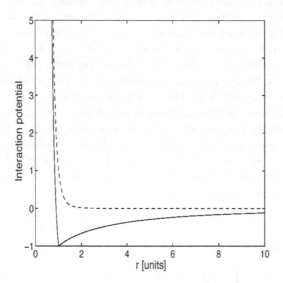

Figure 11.3. Off-lattice HP model interaction potential. *Solid line*: pairwise hydrophobic interactions (H-H). *Dashed*: all other types of interactions.

The fitness value returned by the evaluation function is negated total energy, since EAs strives to maximize fitness and the total free energy of the native fold is assumed to be at a minimum [1].

Table 11.4. Interaction Potential p_{ij} for the HPNX Evaluation Function.

			r_i	
r_j	H	P	N	X
H	-4	1	1	0
P	1	0	-1	0
N	1	-1	0	0
X	0	0	0	0

HPNX is an extension to HP to consider the charge of amino acids [10]. Amino acids are classified as hydrophobic (H), positively (P) or negatively (N) charged, or neutral (X), using the Rasmol predefined sets "Basic", "Acidic", and "Neutral" to subdivide the polar residues. The resulting classification is shown in the column marked "Charge" in Table 11.2. The interaction potentials in the HPNX function are illustrated in Table 11.4. The energy is otherwise calculated as in HP (see Eqs. (11.7) and (11.8)).

WOESE uses polar requirement values h^w, i.e., different degrees of polarity for different amino acids [16], which vary in the interval [4.8, 13.0]. A high h^w corresponds to a polar residue. The polar requirement values are shown in the column marked "Woese" in Table 11.2. As this evaluation function is more detailed than HP it should yield conformations structurally closer to target conformations. The energy calculation uses Eq. (11.7) and

$$
\mathbf{e_{ij}} = \begin{cases} \frac{1}{d_{ij}^{\gamma}} + c \cdot p_{ij} - 1 & \text{if } d_{ij} < 1, \\ c \cdot p_{ij} \cdot \exp(1 - d_{ij}^{\epsilon}) & \text{if } d_{ij} \geq 1, \end{cases} \tag{11.9}
$$

where $p_{ij} = 1/h_i^w + 1/h_j^w$ (so that hydrophobic interactions are rewarded), and $c = -1$.

MILLER uses degrees of hydrophobicity h^m, according to the empirical hydrophobicity scale of [5], where h^m varies in the range $[-0.74, 2.00]$ kcal/mol, and where negative values correspond to hydrophobicity. The h^m values are shown in the column marked "Miller" in Table 11.2. The energy calculation is defined by Eq. (11.9) with $c = 1$ and $p_{ij} = h_i^m + h_j^m$.

EMP uses empirically derived contact potentials for amino acid interactions. A contact potential describes the energy between two residues in proximity (typically, $d_{ij} \leq 6.5$ Å). In [7] a contact potential emp was determined for all pairs of amino acid types using 1168 known structures. The interaction between two Leucine residues gives the lowest emp of -7.37. Leucine is one of the most hydrophobic amino acids and this supports the assumption that hydrophobicity is the driving force in protein folding, largely determining the backbone structure of the protein [10]. Hence, EMP favors hydrophobic interactions like previous models. The energy calculations are the same as in Eq. (11.9), but with $c = 1$ and $p_{ij} = emp_{ij}$.

STRUCT uses structural information about the target protein, thus being a way to test if the EA is capable of producing folds structurally close to the native fold. Minimization of the Distance Matrix Error (DME) [3] between simulated and target structure, should result in a near-native fold. It is defined as

$$\mathbf{DME_{ab}} = \sqrt{\frac{2 \sum_{i=1}^{K-1} \sum_{j=i+1}^{K} |d_{ij}^a - d_{ij}^b|^2}{K(K-1)}}, \qquad (11.10)$$

where d_{ij}^a is Euclidean distance between atoms i and j in protein structure a, and K is the number of atoms used for the comparison. DME is the sum of all 2-combinations of interatomic distances between the structures. In the STRUCT evaluation function fitness it is defined as $F = 1/DME_{st}$, where s is the simulated structure and t is the target structure.

GLOB minimizes the greatest inter-residue distance, thus not having any biological plausibility. It was defined here to evaluate the biological relevance of the other functions. GLOB fitness is defined as

$$F = \frac{1}{d_{\max}} + E, \qquad (11.11)$$

$$e_{ij} = \begin{cases} 1 - \frac{1}{d_{ij}^7} & \text{if } d_{ij} < 1, \\ 0 & \text{otherwise,} \end{cases} \qquad (11.12)$$

where $d_{\max}$ is the maximum interresidue Euclidean distance for the simulated conformation and E is defined according to Eq. (11.7). e_{ij} is the penalty for the interaction between residues i and j. The penalty term is necessary in order to enforce steric constraints.

11.3 Results

Table 11.5 shows a summary of EA1 simulations using the five example proteins. Ten simulations were performed for each combination of evaluation function and protein (only five per protein for STRUCT). STRUCT gave near-native folds for all target proteins, which shows that the EA is competent and can produce native folds given a suitable evaluation function. This confirms our belief that EAs are promising algorithms for eventually solving the protein structure prediction problem.

The RAND function that is included in Table 11.5 creates randomized structures with residues being at least one unit distance apart. RAND gave higher average $\overline{DME}$ than all other functions except MILLER, which was an

Table 11.5. DME Results (in Ångstroms) for EA1.

	Protein	$\overline{DME}$	σ_{DME}	DME_{max}	DME_{min}
STRUCT	1CRN	< 0.05	< 0.05	< 0.05	< 0.05
STRUCT	2ETI	< 0.05	< 0.05	< 0.05	< 0.05
STRUCT	1CTI	< 0.05	< 0.05	< 0.05	< 0.05
STRUCT	3ZNF	0.3	0.2	0.4	< 0.05
STRUCT	1PPT	0.5	0.1	0.6	0.5
Avg.		< 0.19	< 0.09	< 0.23	< 0.14
RAND	1CRN	12.6	5.3	25.1	6.1
RAND	2ETI	9.0	2.2	12.9	6.6
RAND	1CTI	9.1	3.5	15.3	5.5
RAND	3ZNF	8.7	3.4	15.8	5.3
RAND	1PPT	9.4	3.0	14.2	4.9
Avg.		9.8	3.5	16.7	5.7
HP	1CRN	7.3	0.4	7.9	6.8
HP	2ETI	4.6	0.2	4.9	4.3
HP	1CTI	7.8	0.5	8.8	7.0
HP	3ZNF	5.0	0.2	5.2	4.6
HP	1PPT	7.2	0.3	7.7	6.9
Avg.		6.4	0.3	6.9	5.9
HPNX	1CRN	7.1	0.3	7.7	6.8
HPNX	2ETI	4.5	0.3	5.2	4.1
HPNX	1CTI	7.9	0.7	9.1	7.2
HPNX	3ZNF	4.8	0.3	5.3	4.4
HPNX	1PPT	7.4	0.1	7.6	7.3
Avg.		6.3	0.3	7.0	6.0
WOESE	1CRN	6.6	0.2	7.0	6.4
WOESE	2ETI	4.5	0.4	5.4	4.0
WOESE	1CTI	5.2	0.5	6.3	4.7
WOESE	3ZNF	4.6	0.2	5.0	4.3
WOESE	1PPT	7.5	0.4	8.1	6.9
Avg.		5.7	0.3	6.4	5.3
MILLER	1CRN	7.6	0.4	8.3	7.0
MILLER	2ETI	5.0	0.3	5.6	4.7
MILLER	1CTI	12.3	7.8	20.3	4.8
MILLER	3ZNF	36.8	0.0	36.8	36.8
MILLER	1PPT	41.3	0.0	41.3	41.3
Avg.		20.6	1.7	22.5	18.9
EMP	1CRN	7.4	0.1	7.6	7.3
EMP	2ETI	4.5	0.2	4.6	4.1
EMP	1CTI	5.1	0.1	5.2	4.9
EMP	3ZNF	5.6	0.2	5.9	5.2
EMP	1PPT	9.1	0.1	9.3	8.9
Avg.		6.3	0.1	6.5	6.1
GLOB	1CRN	6.1	0.3	6.6	5.5
GLOB	2ETI	4.0	0.3	4.5	3.5
GLOB	1CTI	4.4	0.3	4.8	3.7
GLOB	3ZNF	5.2	0.3	5.4	4.4
GLOB	1PPT	8.2	0.2	8.5	7.9
Avg.		5.6	0.3	6.0	5.0

unsuccessful application of the hydrophobicity scale of [5] and did not produce compact globular structures for all proteins.

The most striking result seen in Table 11.5 is that GLOB, which simply crumples the protein by minimizing the greatest interresidue distance, is the most successful function, having $\overline{DME} = 5.6$Å. Statistical data analysis (see Table 11.6) shows that the difference between GLOB and both EMP and MILLER is significant at the 99% level or higher for all five proteins. In addition, GLOB was better at the 98% significance level than HP, HPNX, and WOESE for three out of five proteins. In addition, the average DME_{max} and DME_{min} are lower for GLOB than for any other function except STRUCT. In these results, therefore, an evaluation function only rewarding compact conformations gives better DME values than several functions with presumed biological relevance.

Table 11.6. Hypothesis Confidence Levels

Hypothesis	Protein				
	1CRN	2ETI	1CTI	3ZNF	1PPT
GLOB < EMP	100	100	100	99	100
GLOB < HP	100	100	100	0	0
GLOB < HPNX	100	99	100	0	0
GLOB < WOESE	100	98	100	0	0
WOESE < HP	100	40	100	100	0
WOESE < HPNX	100	0	100	79	0
EMP < HP	0	57	100	0	0
EMP < HPNX	0	0	100	0	0
EMP < WOESE	0	0	40	0	0
HPNX < HP	63	47	0	79	0

It is also notable that the average DME for every tested function (except STRUCT) is too high for useful structure prediction, since a DME above approximately 5Å can only correspond to weak structural similarities. This indiates that none of the functions tested is informative enough to guide the search to correct structure predictions. These functions can therefore at best be used to find approximate solutions to be further refined by more exact methods.

In order to evaluate the accuracy of the evaluation functions, we compared for each evaluation function the fitness of the best evolved solution with the fitness assigned by the same fitness function to the native fold. As can be seen in Table 11.7, evolved structures always have higher or much higher fitness than the native fold, despite having large DME when compared with the native fold, and thus being incorrect solutions. This result indicates that the evaluation functions are misleading, either in the sense that they lead the EA to incorrect minima in search space regions far away from the native fold, or that they lead the EA to "overshoot" the target by overoptimizing the structure past the correct solution. To further investigate the behavior of these functions, we measured the correlation between the fitness values found during the simulations and the DME deviation from the native fold. Table 11.8 shows this correlation for the HP function. As can be seen, the correlation is rather strong (≥ 0.91) for every protein. This indicates that the function does lead the EA towards the correct region of the search space, but either misses or overshoots the target. The correlation levels were similar for all other evaluation functions tested (data not shown).

Table 11.7. Fitness results. For each protein, the first row shows average fitness of the best individual in the final EA1 population, and the second row shows fitness of the native fold. The additional row for $2ETI$ shows average fitness of the best individual in the final EA2 population.

	HP	HPNX	WOESE	MILLER	EMP	GLOB
$1CRN$	107.9	453.6	184.0	168.9	2071.5	0.23
	58.4	251.7	145.7	84.0	1446.3	0.13
$2ETI$	24.8	95.2	69.4	56.2	815.2	0.29
	9.9	51.5	62.0	29.2	643.1	0.20
	23.4	92.2	68.3	44.1	792.3	0.28
$1CTI$	25.3	77.7	71.0	4.1	896.1	0.30
	9.6	38.9	62.3	-28.3	656.6	0.20
$3ZNF$	10.1	20.0	70.8	-68.8	715.4	0.29
	1.7	2.0	59.0	-163.4	536.8	0.16
$1PPT$	52.0	183.0	100.3	-30.1	1219.2	0.27
	27.5	96.4	76.9	-83.6	805.6	0.12

Table 11.8. Correlation Between Fitness (F) and DME (D) for EA1 Using the HP Evaluation Function.

Protein	$corr(F,D)$	$\sigma_{corr(F,D)}$	$corr(F,D)_{max}$	$corr(F,D)_{min}$
$1CRN$	0.94	0.01	0.96	0.92
$2ETI$	0.94	0.01	0.96	0.92
$1CTI$	0.95	0.01	0.96	0.94
$3ZNF$	0.94	0.02	0.95	0.91
$1PPT$	0.91	0.01	0.93	0.90

Table 11.9 shows the results of using fitness sharing in EA2. There is no clear case of improvement in DME values, and on the contrary fitness sharing gave worse DME results on the 2ETI protein for the two evaluation

functions STRUCT and MILLER. One reason for the worse results on these two functions is the choice of sharing parameter value $\sigma_{share} = 16$, which was nonoptimal for these two functions. This σ_{share} value was suitable for other functions, but further experimentation to find values suitable for STRUCT and MILLER was not conducted.

Table 11.9. EA2 versus EA1 on the protein 2ETI. Values within parantheses are from EA1 simulations and are repeated from Table 11.5 and 11.7 to make comparison easier.

Function	$\overline{DME}$	σ_{DME}	DME_{max}	DME_{min}
STRUCT	0.4 (< 0.05)	0.1 (0.2)	0.6 (< 0.05)	0.3 (< 0.05)
HP	4.6 (4.6)	0.3 (0.2)	5.2 (4.9)	4.2 (4.3)
HPNX	4.6 (4.5)	0.4 (0.3)	5.4 (5.2)	4.1 (4.1)
WOESE	4.9 (4.5)	0.8 (0.4)	7.0 (5.4)	4.3 (4.0)
MILLER	9.4 (5.0)	5.4 (0.3)	17.7 (5.6)	4.8 (4.7)
EMP	4.4 (4.5)	0.2 (0.2)	4.8 (4.6)	4.2 (4.1)
GLOB	3.9 (4.0)	0.2 (0.3)	4.1 (4.5)	3.5 (3.5)

Given the lack of improvement when using fitness sharing, it is of interest to study the structural diversity of the populations. We therefore defined the following measure of structural diversity:

$$\delta = \frac{1}{T} \cdot \frac{1}{n} \cdot \sum_{i=1}^{T} \sum_{j=1}^{n} \sum_{k=1}^{n} d_i(s_j, s_k), \tag{11.13}$$

where $d_i(s_j, s_k)$ is the distance between solutions s_j and s_k at iteration step i according to Eq. (11.6). Table 11.10 shows the structural diversity when different evaluation functions with (EA2) and without (EA1) fitness sharing are used. The mean diversity $\overline{\delta}$ is considerably higher for the fitness sharing simulations for all evaluation functions. This shows that the fitness sharing strategy works, in the sense that it gives a higher structural diversity in the population. The fact that this does not result in better DME results (see Table 11.9) can only be attributed to the fitness functions being misleading.

11.4 Conclusions

Our results show that evolutionary algorithms can find correct protein structures given the right fitness function, i.e., the STRUCT function. The problem, of course, is that this function requires that we already know the native structure, and is therefore not of any use for structure prediction. It does indicate,

Table 11.10. Structural diversity (protein 2ETI). For each evaluation function, the first row shows average diversity for EA1 simulations, and the second row shows average diversity for EA2 simulations.

Evaluation function	$\bar{\delta}$	σ_δ	δ_{max}	δ_{min}
HP1	505	11	528	490
	4509	382	5051	3798
HPNX1	477	6	486	469
	5103	672	6167	3961
WOESE1	442	12	462	416
	5109	898	7049	3957
MILLER1	446	5	453	439
	4204	322	4605	3738
EMP1	952	1084	3183	420
	4437	552	5625	3727
DME1	1443	1464	4019	488
	10705	5281	17893	5191
GLOB1	612	142	915	524
	4034	741	6046	3548

however, that EAs are sufficiently powerful search algorithms for eventually solving the protein structure prediction problem.

Our results also show that the simplified models used in much research on protein structure prediction do not give fitness functions informative enough to guide the EA to accurate structure predictions. It is clear from our results that these models are not fruitful abstractions of the folding process. It was suggested in [12] that simplified models (e.g., lattice-based HP) "exhibit many of the features of real folding". However, according to our results, they are far from informative enough for useful structure prediction, since no function gave an average DME below 5Å.

Acknowledgment

This work was supported in part by a grant to the second author from The Foundation for Knowledge and Competence Development (grant 1507/97).

References

1. Anfinsen, C.B. (1973) Principles that govern the folding of proteins chains. Science. **181**, 223-230.
2. Dandekar, T., Argos, P. (1996) Folding the main-chain of small proteins with the genetic algorithm. Journal of Molecular Biology. **236**, 844-861.

3. Doucet, J.P., Weber, J. (1996) Computer-Aided Molecular Design. Academic Press.
4. Lau, K., Dill, K. (1990) Theory for protein mutability and biogenesis. Proceedings of the National Academy of Sciences of the USA. **87**, 638–642
5. Miller, S., Janin, J., Lesk, A.M., Chothia, C. (1987) Interior and surface of monomeric proteins. Journal of Molecular Biology. **196**, 641-656.
6. Michalewicz, Z.,Fogel, D.B. (2000) How to Solve It: Modern Heuristics. Springer-Verlag.
7. Miyazawa, S., Jernigan, R.L. (1996) Journal of Molecular Biology. **256**, 623-644.
8. Patton, A.L., Punch, W.F., Goodman, E.D. (1995) A Standard GA Approach to Native Protein Conformation Prediction. Proc. of the 6th Annual Intern. Conf. on Genetic Algorithms. 574-581.
9. Piccolboni, A., Mauri, G. (1997) Application of evolutionary algorithms to protein folding prediction. Proceedings of ICONIP. Springer.
10. Renner, A., Bornberg-Bauer, E. (1997) Exploring the fitness landscapes of lattice proteins. Pacific Symposium on Biocomputing. **2**, 361-372.
11. Schulze-Kremer, S. (1995) Molecular Bioinformatics: Algorithms and Applications. Walter de Gruyter.
12. Unger, R., Moult, J. (1993) Genetic algorithms for protein folding simulations. Journal of Mol. Biology. **231**, 75-81.
13. Unger, R., Moult, J. A (1993) Genetic Algorithm for 3D Protein Folding Simulations. Proc. of the 5th Annual Intern. Conf. on Genetic Algorithms, 581-588.
14. Unger, R., Moult, J. (1993) Finding the lowest free energy conformation of a protein is a NP-hard problem. Bulletin of Mathematical Biology. **55**(6), 1183–1198
15. Vail, D. (2001) Genetic algorithms as a search strategy and a novel means of potential punction discovery in the protein folding problem. Bowdoin College, Department of Computer Science, report available at www.bowdoin.edu/~dvail2/protein.html
16. Woese, C.R., Dugre, D.H., Dugre, S.A., Kondo, M., Saxinger, W.C. (1966) On the fundamental nature and evolution of the genetic code. Cold Spring Harbor Symp. Quant. Biol. **31**, 723–736

Learning Decision Rules by Means of Hybrid-Encoded Evolutionary Algorithms

J.C. Riquelme and J.S. Aguilar-Ruiz

Summary. This paper describes an approach based on evolutionary algorithms, HIDER (**HI**erarchical **DE**cision **R**ules), for learning rules in continuous and discrete domains. The algorithm produces a hierarchical set of rules, that is, the rules are sequentially obtained and must be therefore tried in order until one is found whose conditions are satisfied. In addition, the algorithm tries to obtain more understandable rules by minimizing the number of attributes involved. The evolutionary algorithm uses binary coding for discrete attributes and integer coding for continuous attributes. The integer coding consists in defining indexes to the values that have greater probability of being used as boundaries in the conditions of the rules. Thus, the individuals handles these indexes instead of the real values. We have tested our system on real data from the UCI Repository, and the results of a 10-fold cross-validation are compared to C4.5s and C4.5Rules. The experiments show that HIDER works well in practice.

12.1 Introduction

Evolutionary Algorithms (EA) are a family of computational models inspired by the concept of evolution. These algorithms employ a randomized search method to find solutions to a particular problem [25]. This search is quite different from the other learning methods mentioned above. An EA is any population-based model that uses selection and recombination operators to generate new sample examples in a search space [22]. EAs have been used in a wide variety of optimization tasks [13] including numerical optimization and combinatorial optimization problems, although the range of problems to which EAs have been applied is quite broad. The main task in applying EAs to any problem consists of selecting an appropriate representation (coding) and an adequate evaluation function (fitness).

Genetic-based searching algorithms for supervised learning, as GABIL [7] or GIL [11], do not handle easily numeric attributes because the method of encoding all possible values would lead to very long rules in the case or real-valued attributes. Concretely, GABIL and GIL are so-called "concept learners" because they are designed for discrete domains. Other approaches, as SIA [19], have been motivated by a real-world data analysis task in a complex domain (continuous and discrete attributes).

The aim of our research was to obtain a set of rules by means of an evolutionary algorithm to classify new examples in the context of supervised learning. With our approach, HIDER, we try to handle efficiently continuous and discrete attributes.

The justification of this method will be discussed in Section 12.2. The characteristics of our approach are presented in section 12.3, where the coding, the algorithm, the selected fitness function, and a particular aspect named *generalization*, are detailed. Section 12.4 shows the experiments, the results and the analysis of them. In Section 12.5 the conclusions are summarized, some of which motivates the future works presented in Section 15.7.

12.2 Motivation

Two artificial two–dimensional databases will be used to clarify the motivation of our approach. The way in which C4.5 splits the space is depicted in Figure 12.1. The figures within the circles describe the level on the tree where the tests (nodes) over these attributes are placed. See the region labeled as B on the bottom left corner of Figure 12.1. C4.5 divides the region into two parts, however, we thought that the region should be completely covered by only one rule. This fact motivates us to design an algorithm able to discover such rule.

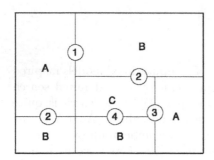
Figure 12.1. C4.5.

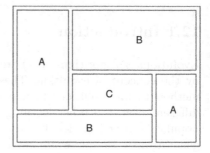
Figure 12.2. HIDER.

HIDER is quite different because it does not divide the space by an attribute, but it extracts sequentially regions from the space. This permits us to obtain *pure* regions, i.e., all examples belong to the same category. As illustrated in Figure 12.2, the region labeled as B on the bottom left corner is discovered by HIDER.

For another artificial two–dimensional database, Figure 12.3 shows the classification that C4.5 gives. Nevertheless, the quality of the rule set would be improved if the algorithm finds rules within others. The most evident feature, graphically observed in Figure 12.4, is the reduction of the number of rules because of the rules overlapping. This characteristic motivates us to use hierarchical decision rules instead of independent (unordered) decision rules.

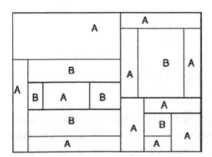

Figure 12.3. C4.5

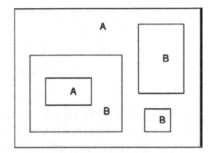

Figure 12.4. HIDER

In short, the obtaining of larger regions (without damaging the prediction accuracy) and the discovery of regions within others are the two main goals that have motivated the development of HIDER.

12.3 HIDER

HIDER (HIerarchical DEcision Rules) uses an EA to search for the best solutions and produces a hierarchical set of rules. According to the hierarchy, an example will be classified by the ith rule if it does not match the conditions of the $(i-1)$th preceding rules. The rules are obtained sequentially until the space is totally covered. The behavior is similar to a *decision list* [17]. As mentioned in [6], the meaning of any single rule is dependent on all the other rules that precede it in the rule list, so that it might be a problem for the expert in understanding the rules (if there are many).

When we want to learn rules in the context of continuous attributes, we need to extend the concept of decision list in two ways: first, for adapting the Boolean functions to interval functions; and second, for representing many classes instead of the true and false values (positives and negatives examples). For each continuous (real) attribute a_i we obtain the boundaries values, called l_i and u_i (lower and upper bounds, respectively), which define the space R_i (range of the attribute i). These intervals allow us to include continuous attributes in a decision list. Our decision list does not have the last constant function true. However, we could interpret the last function as an unknown function, that is, we do not know which class the example belongs to. Therefore, it may be advisable to say "unknown class" instead of making an erroneous decision. From the viewpoint of the experiments, when no induced rules are satisfied, "unknown class" will be considered as an error.

The structure of the set of rules will be as shown in Figure 12.5.

if conditions **then** class
    else if conditions **then** class
        else if conditions **then** class
          ....
        else "unknown class"

Figure 12.5. Hierarchical set of rules.

As mentioned in [8] one of the primary motivation for using real-coded EAs is the precision with which attribute values can be represented and another is the ability to exploit the continuous nature of functions of continuous attributes. We implemented our first versions with binary-coded GAs, but we realized that real-coded EAs were more efficient (time and quality of results).

Before an EA can be run, a suitable *coding* for the problem must be devised. We also require a *fitness function*, which assigns a figure of merit to each coded solution. During the run, parents are *selected* for reproduction and *recombined* to generate *offspring*. These aspects are described below.

12.3.1 Coding

In order to apply EAs to a learning problem, we need to select an internal representation of the space to be searched. These components are critical for the successful application of the EAs to the problem of interest.

Information on the environment comes from a data file, where each example has a class and a number of attributes. We have to codify that information to define the search space, which normally will be dimensionally greater. Each attribute will be formed by several components in the search space, depending on the specific representation. To find out an appropriate coding for the problem is very difficult, but it is almost impossible to get the perfect one. There exist two basic principles for choosing the coding: the principle of meaningful building blocks and the principle of minimal alphabets [25].

In our first approaches, we studied other EA-based classifiers [7, 11] with binary coding. These are generally used as concept learners, where coding assigns a bit to each value of the attribute, i.e., every attribute is symbolic (GABIL and GIL are two well-known systems). For example, an attribute with three possible values would be represented by three bits. A value of one in a bit indicates that the value of the attribute is present so that several bits could be active for the same attribute. This coding is appropriate for symbolic domains. However, it is very difficult to use it in continuous domains, because the number of elements in the alphabet is very large, prohibiting a complete search.

Using binary encoding in continuous domains requires transformations from binary to real for every attribute in order to apply the evaluation function. Moreover, when we convert binary into real, the precision is being lost, so that we have to find the exact number of bits to eliminate the difference between any two values of an attribute. This ensures that a mutation of the less significant bit of an attribute should include or exclude at least one example from the training set. Let l_i and u_i be the lower and upper bounds of an attribute. Let δ_i be the least absolute difference between any two values of the attribute i. The allowed *error* for this attribute must be less than δ_i. Thus, the length of an attribute will depend on that *error*.

Nevertheless, the real coding is more appropriate with real domains, simply because it is more natural to the domain. A number of authors have investigated nonbinary evolutionary algorithms theoretically [3, 4, 12, 20, 21].

The representation for continuous and discrete attributes is best explained by referring to Figure 12.6, where l_i and u_i are values representing an interval for the continuous attribute; b_k are binary values indicating that the value of the discrete attribute is active or not. A last value (omitted in the figure) is for the class.

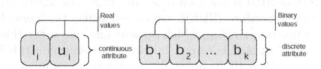

Figure 12.6. Continuous (left) and discrete (right) attributes.

For example, for a database with two attributes, one continuous and one discrete, an individual of the population could be as that depicted in Figure 12.7.

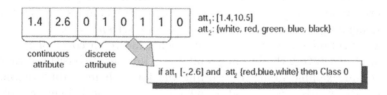

Figure 12.7. Example of coding.

The number of classes determines the set of values to which it belongs, i.e., if there are five classes, the value will belong to the set $\{0, 1, 2, 3, 4\}$. Each rule will be obtained from this representation, but when $l_i = \min(a_i)$ or $u_i = \max(a_i)$, where a_i is an attribute, the rule will not have that value. For example, in the first case the rule would be $[-, v]$ and in the second case $[v, -]$, v being any value within the range of the attribute (see Figure 12.7). If both values are equal to the boundaries, then the rule $[-, -]$ arises for that attribute, which means that it is not relevant because either of the attribute's values will be covered by the whole range of that attribute ($[-, -]$). Under these assumptions, some attributes might not appear in the set of rules. In the same way, when every discrete value is active, that attribute does not appear in the rule.

12.3.2 Algorithm

The algorithm is a typical sequential covering EA [14]. It chooses the best individual of the evolutionary process, transforming it into a rule used to eliminate data from the training file [19]. In this way, the training file is reduced for the following iteration. HIDER searches for only one rule among the possible solutions, that compared to the algorithms based on the Michigan and Pittsburgh approaches, reduces the search space, even if several searches must be performed if several rules are to be learned.

An overview of HIDER is shown in Figure 12.8. The algorithm is divided in two parts: the procedure HIDER, which constructs the hierarchical set of rules, and the function EvoAlg, which obtains one rule every time is called. Initially, the set of rules R is empty, but in each iteration a rule is included (operator $\oplus$) in R; E is the training file, and n is the number of remainder examples that have not been covered yet (exactly $|E|$ at the begining). In each iteration the training file E is reduced (operator $-$), eliminating those examples that have been covered by the description of the rule r (Δ_r), i.e., the left-hand side of the rule, independently of its class. A parameter epf, called *examples pruning factor*, controls the number of examples that will not be covered during the process (ranging from 0% to 5%). This factor ensures that rules covering few examples are not generated. Some authors have pointed out that these rules are undesirable, especially with noise in the domain [6, 10]. The termination criterion is reached when more examples to cover do not exist, depending on epf. For the trials, we have set epf to 0.

The evolutionary algorithm is run each time to discover one rule. The method of generating the initial population (Initialize) consists of randomly selecting an example from the training file for each individual of the population. Afterwards, an interval to which the example belongs is obtained. For example, in one dimension, let l_i and u_i be the lower and upper bounds of the attribute i; then, the range of the attribute is $u_i - l_i$; next, we randomly choose an example $(a_1, \ldots, a_i, \ldots, a_m, class)$ from the training file; $\left(\ldots, a_i - \left(\frac{u_i - l_i}{N}\right)\alpha_1, a_i + \left(\frac{u_i - l_i}{N}\right)\alpha_2, \ldots, class\right)$ could be an individual of the

Procedure HIDER(E, R)
　　$R := \emptyset$
　　$n := |E|$
　　while $|E| > n \times epf$
　　　　$r :=$EvoAlg(E)
　　　　$R := R \oplus \{r\}$
　　　　$E := E - \{e \in E \,|\, e \subseteq \Delta_r\}$
　　end while
　end HIDER

Function EvoAlg(E)
　　$i := 0$
　　$P_0 :=$Initialize()
　　Evaluation(P_0, i)
　　while $i < num\_generations$
　　　　$i := i + 1$
　　　　for $j \in \{1, \ldots, |P_{i-1}|\}$
　　　　　　$\bar{x} :=$Selection(P_{i-1}, i, j)
　　　　　　$P_i := P_i +$Recombination($\bar{x}, P_{i-1}, i, j$)
　　　　end for
　　　　Evaluation(P_i, i)
　　end while
　　return best_of(P_i)
　end EvoAlg

Figure 12.8. Pseudocode of HIDER.

population where α_1 and α_2 are random values belonging to $[0, \frac{N}{C}]$ (N is the size of the training data; C is the number of different classes; and *class* is the same of the example). For discrete attributes, we ensure that the individual has the same active value as the example. The remainder binary values are randomly set to 0 or 1.

For example, let the database be the one used in the Figure 12.7. A possible individual for the initial population is obtained from a randomly selected example $e = (7.6, blue, 0)$. The individual could be $ind = (5.8, 8.2, 1, 0, 0, 1, 0, 0)$. The interval $[5.8, 8.2]$ is for the continuous attribute and the values $(1, 0, 0, 1, 0)$ is for the discrete one. Notice that the value *blue* is active and other value (*white*) has been randomly set to 1. The individual keeps the same class that of the example.

Sometimes, the examples very near to the boundaries are hard to cover during the evolutionary process. To solve this problem, the search space is increased (currently, the lower bound is decreased by 5%, and the upper bound is increased by 5%), for continuous attributes.

The evolutionary module incorporates elitism: the best individual of every generation is replicated to the next one ($j = 1$, see in Figure 12.8 the loop

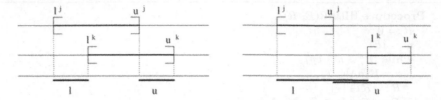

Figure 12.9. Crossover situation 1.   **Figure 12.10.** Crossover situation 2.

controlled by the variable j). A set of children (from $j = 2$ to $j = \frac{|P_{i-1}|}{2}$) is obtained from copies of randomly selected parents, generated by their fitness values and using the roulette wheel selection method. The remainder individuals (from $j = \frac{|P_{i-1}|}{2} + 1$ to $j = |P_{i-1}|$) are formed by means of crossovers (recombination). As half of the new population is created by applying the crossover operator, the probability of selecting an individual for crossing depends on its fitness value. These individuals could be mutated (recombination) later (only the individual from the elite will not be mutated). The evaluation function (evaluation) assigns a value of merit to each individual, which will be further used in the next generation.

Crossover

Wright's linear crossover operator [24] creates three offspring: treating two parents as two points p_1 and p_2, one child is the midpoint of both, and the other two lie on a line determined by $\frac{3}{2}p_1 - \frac{1}{2}p_2$ and $-\frac{1}{2}p_1 + \frac{3}{2}p_2$. Radcliffe's flat crossover [16] chooses values for an offspring by uniformly picking values between (inclusively) the two parents values. Eshelman and Schaffer [8] use a crossover operator that is a generalization of Radcliffe's which is called the blend crossover (BLX-α). It uniformly picks values that lie between two points that contain the two parents, but it may extend equally on either side determined by a user specified EA-parameter α. For example, BLX-0.1 picks values from points that lie on an interval that extends $0.1I$ on either side of the interval I between the parents. Logically, BLX-0.0 is the Radcliffe's flat crossover.

Our crossover operator is an extension of Radcliffes's to parents coded as intervals. Let $[l_i^j, u_i^j]$ and $[l_i^k, u_i^k]$ be the intervals of two parents j and k for the same attribute i. From these parents one children $[l, u]$ is generated by selecting values that satisfy the expression: $l \in [min(l_i^j, l_i^k), max(l_i^j, l_i^k)]$ and $u \in [min(u_i^j, u_i^k), max(u_i^j, u_i^k)]$. This type of crossover could produce two situations, which are illustrated in Figures 12.9 and 12.10. When the intersection of two intervals is not empty, as it is shown in Figure 12.9, the new interval $[l, u]$ is clearly obtained. However, a different situation is produced when the intersection is empty, because l could be greater than u. In this case, the offspring is rejected.

When the attribute is discrete, the crossover operator is like uniform crossover [18].

Mutation

Mutation is applied to continuous attributes as follows: if the randomly selected location (gen) is l_i or u_i, then a quantity is subtracted or added, depending on whether it is the lower or the upper bound, respectively (the quantity is currently the smaller Heterogeneous Overlap-Euclidean Metric (HOEM, [23]) between any two examples). In case of discrete attributes, mutation changes the value from 0 to 1, or viceversa, and it is applied with low probability. We introduce a specific mutation operator to generalize the attribute when nearly all values are 1. In this case, the attribute does not appear in the rule.

Mutation is always applied with probabilities 0.1 (individual) and $\frac{1}{na}$ (attribute), where na is the number of attributes. If the attribute is discrete, the probability of mutating a value is $\frac{1}{ndv}$, where ndv is the number of discrete values of that attribute.

12.3.3 Generalization

Databases used as training files do not have clearly differentiated areas, so that to obtain a totally coherent rule system (without error from the training file) involves a high number of rules. In [1] a system capable of producing a rule set exempt from error (with respect to the training file)is shown; however, sometimes it is interesting to reduce the number of rules in order to get a rule set that may be used like a comprehensible linguistic model. In this way, it could be better to have a system with fewer rules despite some errors than too many rules and no errors. When databases present a distribution of examples very hard to classify, it may be interesting to introduce the relaxing coefficient (RC) for understanding the behavior of databases by decreasing the number of rules [2]. RC indicates what percentage of examples within a rule can have a different class than the rule has. RC behaves like the upper bound of the error with respect to the training file, that is, as an allowed error rate. To deal efficiently with noise and find a good value for RC, the expert should have an estimate of the noise percentage in its data. For example, if a database produces too many rules when RC is 0, we could set RC to 5 to decrease the number of rules and, possibly, the error rate might be very similar.

When an individual tries to expand and it always reaches examples of a different Class, its fitness value cannot be higher, unless a few errors were allowed. In this case, depending on the fitness function, such a value might increase. In Figure 12.11 (right) the individual cannot get bigger, unless one error is allowed, in which case the individual will have four new examples (left), increasing its fitness value.

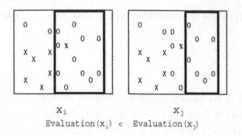

$$x_i \qquad\qquad x_j$$
$$\text{Evaluation}(x_i) \; < \; \text{Evaluation}(x_j)$$

Figure 12.11. Relaxing coefficient.

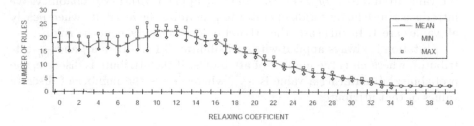

Figure 12.12. Number or rules varying RC for Pima database.

We have tested that the concept of the coefficient relaxation turns out to be useful when the number of rules is greater than expected to understand the information stored in the database.

We used Pima Indians Diabetes database to analyze the influence of the relaxing coefficient on both the error rate and the number of rules. This example showed that the error rate ranges from 18% to 34% depending on the relaxing coefficient (from 0 to 40) and therefore depending on the number of rules (from 26 to 2; see Figure 12.12). When $RC = 36$, HIDER produced only two rules for the Pima database and the error rate mean was about 30%. The lower error rate was achieved when $RC = 16$. All the experiments reported in the next tables were obtained using $RC = 0$.

12.3.4 Fitness Function

The fitness function must be able to discriminate between correct and incorrect classifications of examples. Finding an appropriate function is not a trivial task, due to the noisy nature of most databases.

The evolutionary algorithm maximizes the fitness function f for each individual. It is given by Eq. (12.1):

$$f(i) = 2(N - CE(i)) + G(i) + coverage(i) \tag{12.1}$$

where N is the number of examples being processed; $CE(i)$ is the class error, which is produced when the example i belongs to the region defined by the rule but it does not have the same class; $G(i)$ is the number of examples correctly classified by the rule; and the *coverage* of a rule is the proportion of the search space covered by such rule. Each rule can be quickly expanded to find more examples thanks to the coverage in the fitness function. The reason why $f(i)$ is not $N - CE(i) + G(i) + coverage(i)$ is as follows: for example, when $CE(i) = 7$ and $G(i) = 9$, we will have the same fitness value as when $CE(i) = 15$ and $G(i) = 17$ (the difference is 2; assuming the same coverage for both). Therefore, we decided to penalty the second case ($\frac{9}{7}$ is greater than $\frac{17}{15}$) since fewer errors are preferred.

The coverage of a rule is calculated by dividing the volume of the region defined by the rule by the whole volume of the search space. Let $[l_i, u_i]$ be the interval associated with an attribute i of the rule; k_i the number of active discrete values of an attribute i; $[L_i, U_i]$ the range of a continuous attribute i, and $|A_i|$ the number of different values of a discrete attribute i. Then, the coverage of a rule is given by

$$coverage(x) = \prod_{i=1}^{m} \frac{coverage(x, i)}{range(x, i)},$$

where

$$coverage(x, i) = \begin{cases} u_i - l_i & \text{if the attribute } i \text{ is continuous,} \\ k_i & \text{if it is discrete,} \end{cases}$$

and

$$range(x, i) = \begin{cases} U_i - L_i & \text{if the attribute } i \text{ is continuous,} \\ |A_i| & \text{if it is discrete.} \end{cases}$$

12.4 Results

The experiments described in this section are from the UCI Repository [5]. The results obtained by HIDER have been compared to that of C4.5 Release 8 and C4.5Rules. To measure the performance of each method, a 10-fold cross-validation was achieved with each dataset (18 databases that involve continuous and/or discrete attributes). The algorithms were all run on the same training data and their induced knowledge structures tested using the same test data, so that the 10 resulting performance numbers for C4.5Rules, C4.5, and HIDER are comparable. It is very important to note that the experiments were run with the same default settings for all parameters of the EA: a population size of as little as 100 individuals and 300 generations. In cases of small data sets, like Iris, the results would have been the same using a smaller number of generations (it had been enough around 50). There are very small numbers considering the number of examples and the dimensionality of some databases. HIDER needed about 8 hours to complete the 10-fold cross-validation for the 18 databases in a Pentium 400Mhz with 64 Mb of RAM.

However, C4.5 only needed about 8 minutes in the same machine. C4.5 is an extremely robust algorithm that performs well on many domains. It is very difficult to consistently outperform C4.5 on a variety of data sets.

Table 12.1 gives the values of the parameters involved in the evolutionary process. The results of the trials appear in Tables 12.2, 12.3, 12.4, and 12.5.

Table 12.1. Parameters of HIDER

Parameter	Value
Population size	100
Generations	300
Crossover probability	0.5
Individual mutation probability	0.2
Gen mutation probability	0.1

Table 12.2. Comparing Error Rates

Database	C4.5Rules	C4.5	HIDER
Bupa	34.5 −	34.7 −	35.7
Breast-C (Wisc)	5.2 +	6.28 +	4.3
Cleveland	25.8 +	26.8 +	20.5
German^{5de10}	28.8 −	32.1 +	29.1
Glass^{2de10}	18.5 −	32.7 +	29.4
Heart	20.7 −	21.8 −	22.3
Hepatitis^{8de10}	16.9 −	21.4 +	19.4
Horse Colic	17.5 −	19.0 +	17.6
Iris	4.0 +	4.77 +	3.3
Lenses	16.7 −	29.9 +	25.0
Mushroom	0.0 −	0.0 −	0.8
Pima	26.2 +	32.1 +	25.9
Sonar^{9de10}	29.3 −	30.3 −	43.1
Tic-Tac-Toe	18.8 +	14.2 +	3.8
Vehicle^{8de10}	57.6 +	30.6 +	30.6
Vote	5.3 −	6.2 −	6.4
Wine	6.7 +	6.7 +	3.9
Zoo	29.8 +	7.0 −	8.0
Average	20.1	19.8	18.3

Table 12.2 gives the error rates (numbers of misclassified examples expressed as a percentage) for the C4.5Rules, C4.5, and HIDER algorithms on the selected domains. HIDER outperforms C4.5 and C4.5Rules in 12 out of 18 and 8 out 18 datasets, respectively. If C4.5 produces bad trees, the results from C4.5Rules will not be very good. We can observe that there are four databases whose results generated by C4.5 are about 40% worse than those obtained by

Table 12.3. Comparing Number of Rules

Database	C4.5Rules	C4.5	HIDER
Bupa	14.0 +	28.6 +	11.3
Breast-C (Wisc)	8.1 +	21.9 +	2.6
Cleveland	11.3 +	35.2 +	7.9
German	5.2 −	181.5 +	13.3
Glass	14.0 −	29.0 +	19.0
Heart	10.5 +	29.2 +	9.2
Hepatitis	5.4 +	13.8 +	4.5
Horse Colic	4.1 −	39.3 +	6.0
Iris	4.0 −	5.5 +	4.8
Lenses	3.1 −	4.1 −	6.5
Mushroom	17.2 +	15.7 +	3.1
Pima	9.8 −	93.6 +	16.6
Sonar	5.1 +	16.8 +	2.8
Tic-Tac-Toe	10.7 −	93.9 +	11.9
Vehicle	3.3 −	102.3 +	36.2
Vote	6.6 +	14.7 +	4.0
Wine	4.6 +	5.4 +	3.3
Zoo	5.3 −	9.9 +	7.2
Average	7.9	41.1	9.5

Table 12.4. Comparing Global Results (C4.5/HIDER)

Database	ϵ_{er}	ϵ_{nr}
Bupa	.97	2.53
Breast-C (Wisc)	1.46	8.42
Cleveland	1.31	4.46
German	1.10	13.65
Glass	1.11	1.53
Heart	.98	3.17
Hepatitis	1.10	3.07
Horse Colic	1.08	6.55
Iris	1.40	1.15
Lenses	1.20	.63
Mushroom	.01	5.00
Pima	1.24	5.64
Sonar	.70	6.00
Tic-Tac-Toe	3.69	7.89
Vehicle	1.00	2.83
Vote	.96	3.68
Wine	1.70	1.64
Zoo	.88	1.38
Average	1.22	4.40

Table 12.5. Comparing Global Results (C4.5Rules/HIDER)

Database	ϵ_{er}	ϵ_{nr}
Bupa	.97	1.24
Breast-C (Wisc)	1.21	3.12
Cleveland	1.26	1.43
German	.99	.39
Glass	.63	.74
Heart	.93	1.14
Hepatitis	.87	1.20
Horse Colic	.99	.68
Iris	1.21	.83
Lenses	.67	.48
Mushroom	.01	5.55
Pima	1.01	.59
Sonar	.68	1.82
Tic-Tac-Toe	4.95	.90
Vehicle	1.88	.09
Vote	.83	1.65
Wine	1.72	1.39
Zoo	3.72	.74
Average	1.36	1.33

HIDER (Breast Cancer, Iris, Tic-Tac-Toe and Wine). It is especially worthy the error rate of the Tic-Tac-Toe database. C4.5Rules improves the results of C4.5 for nearly all databases, except three of them (Tic-Tac-Toe, Vehicle and Zoo). C4.5Rules did not achieve to improve those results generated by C4.5, quite the opposite, made results worse, particularly for Tic–Tac–Toe and Zoo databases. As catalogued in the last row of Table 12.2, HIDER is on average better than the others. In Table 12.4 these results will be analyzed by means of the measure (*ratio*) used in the Quinlan's works [15].

Table 12.3 compares the number of rules generated by the three approaches. In order to count the number of rules generated by C4.5, we could sum the leaves on the tree or apply the expression $\frac{s+1}{2}$, where s is the size of the tree. C4.5Rules improves C4.5 in all databases, except Mushrooms. These results are very similar to those generated by HIDER. Nevertheless, although the result for German database is very interesting (5.2 rules), for others databases C4.5Rules reduces the number of rules too much (3.3 rules for Vehicle and 5.3 rules for Zoo), leading to a high error rate (57.6% for Vehicle and 29.8% for Zoo). Due to that reason, although C4.5Rules on average generated fewer rules (7.9) than HIDER (9.5), the error rate increased: C4.5Rules (20.1%) and HIDER (18.3%).

Table 12.4 shows a measure of improvement (ϵ) for the error rate [second and fourth columns: (ϵ_{er})] and the number of rules [third and fifth columns: (ϵ_{nr})]. To calculate those coefficients (ϵ_{er} and ϵ_{nr}, respectively) the error rate (number of rules) for C4.5 (or C4.5Rules) has been divided by the corresponding error rate (number of rules) for HIDER. On average, HIDER found solutions that had less than one fourth of the rules output by C4.5. Surprisingly, C4.5 generated a number of rules five times greater than HIDER for one third of the databases. It is worth noting that applying HIDER, more than two thirds of the databases produce less than half the rules. C4.5 only was better with the Lenses database. C4.5 made the error rate better for six databases, although only three of them improved significantly (Mushrooms, Sonar and Zoo). In summary, the averaged error rate generated by C4.5 is 22% greater and the averaged number of rules 340%. This reason leads to us to make a comparison with C4.5Rules, mainly in regard to the number of rules. The average ratio of the error rate of C4.5 to that of HIDER is 1.22, while the ratio of the number of rules is 4.40. Although the results in Table 12.3 indicated that C4.5Rules improved on average (7.9 rules) to HIDER (9.5 rules), analyzing the relative increase of the number of rules, we can observe that those numbers can be deceptive. C4.5Rules generates an averaged number of rules 33% greater (fourth column), as well as an averaged error rate 36% higher (fifth column), as it is shown in the last row of Table 12.5.

As the overall averages at the bottom of the tables indicate, HIDER is more accurate than C4.5, and C4.5 is more accurate than C4.5Rules. HIDER produces fewer rules than C4.5Rules, which also generates fewer than C4.5.

12.5 Conclusions

An EA-based supervised learning tool to classify databases is presented in this paper. HIDER produces a hierarchical set of rules, where each rule is tried in order until one is found whose conditions are satisfied by the example being classified. The use of hierarchical decision rules led to an overall improvement of the performance on the 18 databases investigated here. In addition, HIDER improves the flexibility to construct a classifier varying the relaxing coefficient. In other words, one can trade off accuracy against understanding. HIDER was compared to C4.5 and C4.5Rules and the number of rules as well as the error rate were decreased. To summarize shortly, the experiments show that HIDER works well in practice.

12.6 Future Works

Evolutionary algorithms are very time-consuming. This aspect is being analyzed from the viewpoint of the coding. We are designing a new type of coding that uses natural numbers for both continuous and discrete attributes, so as the specific genetic operators. This encoding method allows us to reduce the dimensionality of the search space so that the algorithm might converge more quickly.

Another aspect being studied is the way in which the evaluation function analyzes each example from the database. Normally, the information is loaded in a vector, and for each individual of the population the whole vector is processed. Research on improvements to the data structure as input of EAs in order to reduce the time complexity is currently being conducted.

12.7 Acknowledgment

The research was supported by the Spanish Research Agency CICYT under grant TIC2001-1143-C03-02.

References

1. J. S. Aguilar, J. C. Riquelme, and M. Toro (1998) Decision queue classifier for supervised learning using rotated hyperboxes. In *Progress in Artificial Intelligence IBERAMIA '98. Lecture Notes in Artificial Intelligence 1484. Springer-Verlag*, pages 326–336.
2. J. S. Aguilar, J. C. Riquelme, and M. Toro (1998) A tool to obtain a hierarchical qualitative set of rules from quantitative data. In *Lecture Notes in Artificial Intelligence 1415. Springer-Verlag*, pages 336–346.
3. J. Antonisse (1989) A new interpretation of schema notation that overturns the binary encoding constraint. In *Third International Conference on Genetic Algorithms*, pages 86–97. Morgan Kaufmann.
4. S. Bhattacharyya and G.J. Koehler (1994) An analysis of non-binary genetic algorithms with cardinality 2^v. *Complex Systems*, 8:227–256.
5. C. Blake and E. K. Merz (1998) UCI repository of machine learning databases, 1998.
6. P. Clark and R. Boswell (1991) Rule induction with cn2: Some recents improvements. In *Machine Learning: Proceedings of the Fifth European Conference (EWSL-91)*, pages 151–163.
7. K. A. DeJong, W. M. Spears, and D. F. Gordon (1993) Using genetic algorithms for concept learning. *Machine Learning*, 1(13):161–188.
8. L. J. Eshelman and J. D. Schaffer (1993) Real-coded genetic algorithms and interval-schemata. *Foundations of Genetic Algorithms-2*, pages 187–202.
9. D. E. Goldberg (1989) *Genetic Algorithms in Search, Optimization and Machine Learning*. Addison-Wesley.
10. R. C. Holte (1993) Very simple classification rules perform well on most commonly used datasets. *Machine learning*, 11:63–91.
11. C. Z. Janikow (1993) A knowledge-intensive genetic algorithm for supervised learning. *Machine Learning*, 1(13):169–228.
12. G.J. Koehler, S. Bhattacharyya, and M.D. Vose (1998) General cardinality genetic algorithms. *Evolutionary Computation*, 5(4):439–459.
13. Z. Michalewicz (1996) *Genetic Algorithms + Data Structures = Evolution Programs*. Springer-Verlag, 3 ed..
14. T. Mitchell (1997) *Machine Learning*. McGraw Hill.

15. J. R. Quinlan (1996) Improved use of continuous attributes in c4.5. *Journal of Artificial Intelligence Research*, 4:77–90.
16. N. J. Radcliffe (1990) *Genetic Neural Networks on MIMD Computers*. Ph. d., University of Edinburgh.
17. R. L. Rivest (1987) Learning decision lists. *Machine Learning*, 1(2):229–246.
18. G. Syswerda (1989) Uniform crossover in genetic algorithms. In *Proceedings of the Third International Conference on Genetic Algorithms*, pages 2–9.
19. G. Venturini (1993) Sia: a supervised inductive algorithm with genetic search for learning attributes based concepts. In *Proceedings of European Conference on Machine Learning*, pages 281–296.
20. M.D. Vose and A.H. Wright (1998) The simple genetic algorithm and the walsh transform: Part i, theory. *Evolutionary Computation*, 6(3):253–273.
21. M.D. Vose and A.H. Wright (1998) The simple genetic algorithm and the walsh transform: Part ii, the inverse. *Evolutionary Computation*, 6(3):275–289.
22. D. Whitley (1993) A genetic algorithm tutorial. Technical Report CS-93-103, Colorado State University, Fort Collins, CO 80523.
23. D. R. Wilson and T. R. Martinez (1997) Improved heterogeneous distance functions. *Journal of Artificial Intelligence Research*, 6(1):1–34.
24. A. H. Wright (1991) Genetic algorithms for real parameter optimization. *Foundations of Genetic Algorithms-1*, pages 205–218.

13

Evolvable Hardware Techniques for Gate-Level Synthesis of Combinational Circuits

A. Hernández-Aguirre

Summary. This chapter is about the synthesis of combinational logic circuits using evolvable hardware. The chapter introduces several approaches recently followed by a number of researchers to tackle this problem. Research trends, immediate and for years to come, are presented.

13.1 Introduction

A combinational circuit is the implementation of some Boolean function. In real- world applications, the usual goal is to derive that circuit that implements the function using the smallest number of components. There are several interpretations to this problem because in Boolean algebra there are different sets of primitives with the "universal generator" property. Sets of primitive operators with this property are, for instance: {and, or, not },{and, xor, not}, and {nand}. Although any of these sets is sound and complete in Boolean logic, the circuits they generate differ in size. What they share, though, is the top-down strategy used to create the circuit. Human designers derive such minimum circuits by working in a top-down fashion. By a proof process and lots of human ingenuity, all knowledge about principles and valid operations in the Boolean domain have been forged into a few axioms and laws. Human designers repeatedly apply the set of axioms of Boolean logic to a Boolean formula in order to transform it into an equivalent but shorter expression. Therefore, the resulting expression is derived or inferred through this deductive process.

Evolutionary computation techniques are popular design and optimization tools that challenge human designers. Inspired in the Darwinian theory of the evolution of the species, evolutionary techniques mimic the dynamics of a population where the fittest individuals survive and reproduce, and their genes prevail in their children that populate the next generation. Any individual encodes a solution, a Boolean formula in our discussion, which is only a partial solution of the problem. No knowledge other than how well each individual solves the problem is used during the evolution. Evolutionary techniques build upon partial solutions to synthesize the solution. As noted, no knowledge about Boolean domain is precomputed, or axioms used to find equivalent formulas; with no recipes at hand other than surviving, evolutionary computation techniques construct or synthesize circuits. The solutions are quite uncommon since bottom-up mechanisms explore different areas of the search space [29].

Evolvable Hardware (EHW for short) exploits this unique capacity for the synthesis of circuits (which is not easily found on the human side). EHW is, in essence, a combination of evolutionary computation and reconfigurable hardware. In this nascent field there are several approaches that, combined with new technologies and platforms, have spawn a number of modalities.

This chapter presents the most important current and future research trends in evolvable hardware for the synthesis of combinational circuits. The chapter is organized as follows. Section 13.2 deals with different approaches to evolvable hardware and makes a brief introduction to Boolean circuit synthesis. Section 13.3 introduces seven approaches to extrinsic evolvable hardware. Finally, Section 13.4 discusses some of the research trends.

13.2 Basic Concepts in Evolvable Hardware

The utter goals of any full evolvable hardware system are self-reconfiguration and self-adaptation. Self-reconfiguration refers to the ability of a system to modify its structure in order to tackle different tasks (in some closed domain) using the best resources available. Self-adaptation means the use of evolutionary techniques to generate the solution using such resources. Most EHW systems are off-line learning system; therefore, they work in two steps. In step one a new task is presented to the system; thus, a solution is generated by reconfiguration and adaptation. In step two the system responds to new input data in the way it has learned to do so. The adaptation algorithm can be ran in hardware or software. When it runs on hardware the technique is called *intrinsic evolvable hardware*, whereas the other case is called *extrinsic evolvable hardware*. We could say the difference depends on the place where the evolutionary algorithm is run. Figure 13.1 shows the modules of any intrinsic evolvable hardware platform for combinational circuit design [15, 14, 13]. The adaptation module is a GA embedded in hardware, the fitness evaluator module also runs in hardware, and the reconfigurable module is a PLA (an FPGA is frequently used instead of the PLA).

Another issue is the "granularity" level used during the evolutionary process. Granularity refers to how basic the primitive elements used for the synthesis of solutions are. For example, fine granularity evolution could only use {*and*, *or*, *not*} gates, but coarse granularity could combine these primitives

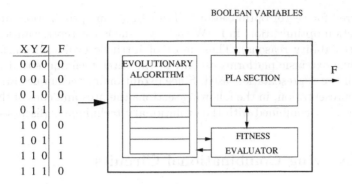

Figure 13.1. Intrinsic evolvable hardware system.

with other components built upon the primitives, say multiplexers and decoders. The fine granularity approach is called "gate-level", whereas the other case is called "functional-level". Granularity must be considered at the time the representation of the individuals is being defined because it has a direct impact on scalability (or capacity to design bigger circuits without changing the algorithm). A clear advantage of extrinsic EHW is the better control of granularity since adjustments are possible at any time. Figure 13.2 shows the modules of an extrinsic evolvable hardware platform. The evolutionary algorithm is implemented in software, the fitness evaluator is also a program tightly coupled with a simulator (HDL, Verilog, or Spice). The simulator "executes" every circuit in the population and the result is used to compute a fitness value. Notice that in this case everything is modeled in software, but combinations of intrinsic and extrinsic are also possible and called *mixtrinsic evolution* [28].

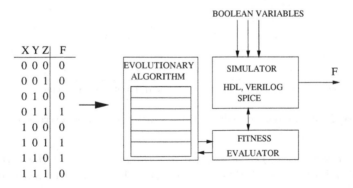

Figure 13.2. Extrinsic evolvable hardware system.

The evolutionary techniques used in EHW are: Genetic Algorithms (GA), Genetic Programming (GP), and Evolutionary Strategies (ES). Although GA is preferred for vector optimization, GP for function optimization, and ES for real function optimization, in EHW the key issue is the representation (again, due to scalability reasons). Thus, most of intrinsic evolution platforms use GAs, while extrinsic platforms use any of the three techniques that best couples with the representation used. Since evolutionary techniques are sensible to the representation, in the following sections the pros and cons of the chosen representation combined with the evolutionary technique is discussed.

13.3 Evolving Combinational Circuits

Louis's dissertation [?] is one of the earliest sources that reports the use of GAs to design combinational logic circuits. The key idea, followed by several researchers, was to represent a circuit inside a matrix of size $n \times m$. Each matrix element is a gate that receives its two inputs from any gate at the previous column. Therefore, each matrix element is a triplet indicating (source of) input 1, input 2, and gate type. The possible gates are chosen from {and, or, not, xor, wire}, but a good selection would include the "wire" that can bypass one column (see row 2, column 1, in Figure 13.3). Any circuit can be represented as a bidimensional array of gates, the same that can be represented as a string of triplets in the chromosome (the string must be created in column order, otherwise the problem becomes disruptive, making it very hard for the GA [?]). Figure 13.3 shows the string encoding a circuit in bidimensional space.

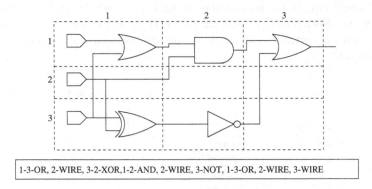

1-3-OR, 2-WIRE, 3-2-XOR,1-2-AND, 2-WIRE, 3-NOT, 1-3-OR, 2-WIRE, 3-WIRE

Figure 13.3. A circuit in bidimensional space encoded by a string of triplets.

In his dissertation, Louis focussed *functional design*, not the optimization of a 2-Bit adder and 4-5-6-Bits parity checker. He introduced a new crossover operator called masked crossover (MX) and the use of a case-based reasoning system (CBR) to assist a GA in the generation of building blocks by reusing past information. The use of a matrix representation spawns a number of approaches discussed next. The statement of the problem is the synthesis of combinational circuits using the smallest number of components.

13.3.1 Gate-Level Synthesis Using Binary GA

Louis proposed the use of a matrix to represent a circuit, but several issues still had to be solved in order to use an evolutionary technique as a design tool. Coello et al. proposed the Binary Genetic Algorithm (BGA), a standard GA with binary representation, and a set of strategies to tackle the problem [1]. Problem statement. Use a GA with binary representation to synthesize a combinational circuit with the smallest number of components. The set of primitive gates is: {and, or, not, xor, wire}. The circuit is evolved inside a matrix, as explained in Section 13.3. The pending issues (not discussed so far) are

- design of a fitness function suitable for both circuit design and optimization
- matrix size

Fitness function. The synthesis of circuits optimized in size is a task controlled by the fitness function. The fitness of a circuit is measured by comparing the expected values defined in the truth table against the real output values. Therefore, the function counts the number of correct matches and returns the proportion of matches as the fitness value. The fitness function works in two stages, therefore called *dynamic*, which are applied at different times of the evolution.

1. Stage one. The fitness function guides the search until the first 100% functional circuit (that fully complies with the truth table) appears in the population.

$$f1 = \frac{correct\ outputs}{total\ number\ of\ outputs}.$$

2. Stage two. Once the first 100% functional circuit is generated, the fitness function is switched to one that counts the number of "wire gates" in the circuit, plus $f1$ (above). This indirect strategy proved very efficient since more wires means fewer "real gates".

$$f2 = f1 + \sum WireGates.$$

Either fitness function is used to measure all the population, that is, it never happens that some circuits are measured with function $f1$ and others with $f2$ at some generation. Some circuits are harder to design when the truth table is unbalanced, that is, the number of outputs in 1 (or 0) is much more than those in 0 (or 1). That kind of circuits presents the "genetic cliff" problem, which is the case of two individuals that are quite close in phenotypic space have an uncomparable distance in genotypic space; for example, a truth table with 15 ones and only 1 zero. The solution is a weighted fitness function that gives to that zero a reasonable or similar importance of any 1. A good strategy is the following:

1. Count the number of 1s and 0s in the truth table.

2. All 1s found represent 50% of the total.
3. All 0s found represent 50% of the total.
4. Compute the weight of each zero, wz, and of each one, wo.
5. $f1 = wz \times No.ofzeros + wo \times No.ofones$.

Matrix size. The matrix serves as a reference for circuit connectivity and works as an environment for the evolution. Therefore, it is important to use the proper size for a circuit, but this is not a simple task. The size of the matrix is determined using the following procedure:

- Start with a square matrix of size 5.
- If no feasible solution is found using this matrix, then increase the number of columns by 1.
- If no feasible solution is found using this matrix, then increase the number of rows by 1.
- Repeat steps 2 and 3 until a suitable matrix is found.

Results and discussion. The BGA design tool has been successfully tested with several circuit design problems, some of them reported in [1, 5, 6]. BGA finds in most cases smaller circuits than those generated by human design-ers using Karnaugh maps. It also finds smaller circuits than those generated by special methods like the one proposed by Sasao that only uses ANDs & XORs gates [25]. BGA seems to favor the use of XOR gates, generating correct circuits but hard for the humans to understand. Also, the "evolutionary trans-formations" that make a functional circuit smaller are hard to understand and follow no apparent logic. The weakness of the method is the poor scalability. Bigger problems are almost impossible to solve since evolution is contained by the matrix, and search space limited to the bidimensional space. Another issue is the *representation bias* due to the binary representation. There are two sources of bias, one comes from the triplet representation, and the other from the matrix size. For instance, when BGA uses 5 primitive gates it needs 3 bits to represent all combinations, thus 3 out of 8 are not used. Similarly, if the matrix size is 5×5, 3 bits are needed to indicate where the input comes from, but again, 3 combinations are not used.

13.3.2 Mending the Representation Bias: Gate-Level Synthesis with NGA

NGA is a GA with N-cardinality encoding. The purpose of using more than one alphabet (of any cardinality) in the genotypic string is to encode the triplets (see Fig. 13.3) in such a way that there are no combinations left with no use. Coello et al. [2] propose such a strategy in an approach called NGA. In Figure 13.4 a triplet using two alphabets is shown. Inputs 1 and 2 are any row out of $\{1,2,3\}$. Therefore, by choosing the cardinality of alphabet $\alpha = 3$ there is a one-to-one mapping between the alphabet symbol and the row number. Same for the specification of the gate type. There are 5 gates, so the alphabet β has cardinality 5.

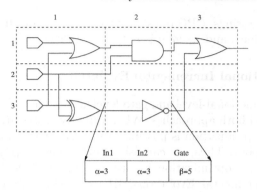

Figure 13.4. A triplet representing a gate and its inputs with two alphabets.

Results and discussion. Genetic operators selection, crossover, and mutation are not affected. NGA proved superior than BGA in most circuits, both in terms of speed of convergence and in terms of total evaluations performed. The reason seems to be less disruption of the building blocks and better reuse of the circuit components. Also, because strings are shorter, the evolutionary algorithm exhibits better behavior.

13.3.3 Functional-Level Synthesis

Miller introduced an extrinsic EHW technique for functional-level design [22, 23, 24]. As noted before, functional techniques are the combination of primitive gates with other components built over the primitive gates. Miller combines ANDs, ORs, XORs, and NOTs, with multiplexers and some more Boolean functions like NANDs, NORs, and the like. His set of 12 Boolean functions pretends to characterize the activity of any subset of a circuit. The adaptation mechanism is implemented by a GA. But the most important aspect is the representation. Using alphabets of cardinality greater than 2, a single gene encodes one of the 12 Boolean functions. This approach, although similar to the NGA, has a drawback: the cardinality of the alphabet grows exponentially with the number of input variables. Miller also models circuit connectivity by a matrix; thus, evolution is contained by some matrix geometry.

Results and discussion. Functional-level synthesis shows good scalability because the granularity is not restricted to only primitive gates. At the same time, for the same reason, the circuit size is harder to optimize (some solutions contrasted with NGA are clearly bigger).

Miller also proposed a special form of Genetic Programming called Cartesian Genetic Programming (CPG), to tackle learning Boolean function problems. Strictly speaking, it must be called GP because it evolves functions, although individuals are not trees as it is common in GP. CPG uses linear integer chromosomes; the advantage of this representation is the easiness of the evaluation of the strings. CPG does not evolve circuits but functional Boolean function expressions, and its goal is not the optimization of functions.

13.3.4 Bidirectional Incremental Evolution

A reflection on functional-level and gate-level makes one to think that what we need is the best of both approaches. When primitive gates are used, scalability is poor but size optimization is possible. When gates are more complex, then optimization is poor. Thus, we can ask: could it not be possible to combine scalability and size optimization in just one method? Kalganova proposes Bidirectional Incremental Evolution (BIE) to tackle this problem [17, 16]. According to her, extrinsic EHW design of *practical* digital circuits (she means real-world applications) involves the following three major problems:

1. limitation in the chromosome length
2. "stalling" effect in the evolution process
3. restriction of the computation time

BIE solves the three of them by combining two main approaches: Divide-and-Conquer and Incremental Evolution. The key notion is to break down a complex task into simpler subtasks, evolve each of the subtasks, and then merge incrementally the evolved subsystems. In essence, BIE is the sound combination of top-down and bottom-up methods. The former stage is conducted by a process called "evolution toward a modularized system", the latter stage by a second process called "evolution toward an optimized system". An alternative way to understand the work of Kalganova is through the work of Gero [9]. Gero's Genetic Engineering system also combines top-down and bottom-up strategies. In the top-down stage, elementary building blocks are targeted and those more likely to produce designs with the required characteristics are evolved. In the second stage, the proper design goals are focussed and the solution is generated by using the evolved primitive building blocks. Several researchers work in this problem, notably Seok, who also proposes a decomposition strategy for EHW [26].

Kalgnova results are encouraging and promising. Further work needs to be done to fully develop a BIE platform for circuit evolution.

13.3.5 Multiobjective EHW Optimization: MGA

The fitness function used by BGA and NGA has been called dynamic since it does change during evolution. The goal is to capture two possible *states* of the circuit (functional or not functional). Looking at the problem in this way, a circuit can have many more states. For instance, if the truth table has three inputs and one output, then there are $2^3 = 8$ output values. A circuit is called in "state 3" if only 3 out of the 8 expected outputs are correct. Thus, the circuit design can be reformulated as the problem of "filling all the states with the correct value". Since there are many states, then the problem is to design the fitness function able to fill all the states. A dynamic fitness function that checks all circuit states is only possible for small circuits. Therefore, the solution is to use a technique that considers each state as an objective, or independent goal.

Coello et al. [7] introduced the Multiobjective Genetic Algorithm (MGA) whose evolutionary algorithm is based on the Vector Evaluated Genetic Algorithm (VEGA) to tackle this problem. The main idea behind the approach is to use a population-based multiobjective optimization technique, such as VEGA, *to handle each of the outputs of a circuit as an objective.* Thus, a circuit with $m = 8$ outputs becomes a problem with 8 restrictions plus a single objective function, that is, $m+1$ goals. VEGA splits the population into $m+1$ subpopulations, assigning each subpopulation to a circuit output and giving to it the mission of matching the correct value specified in the truth table. The issue is how to handle the different situations (or states) that could arise. The fitness of a circuit $\mathbf{X}$ is evaluated as follows:

$$if\ o_j(\mathbf{X}) \neq t_j\ \ then\ \ fitness(\mathbf{X}) = 0,$$
$$else\ if\ v \neq 0\ \ then\ \ fitness = -v,$$
$$else\ fitness = f(\mathbf{X}),$$

where $o_j(\mathbf{X})$ refers to the value of output j for the encoded circuit $\mathbf{X}$; t_j is target value for output j; and v is the number of outputs that are not matched by the circuit $\mathbf{X}$. The fitness function $f(\mathbf{X})$ is calculated as follows:

$$if\ \mathbf{X}\ unfeasible \Rightarrow f(\mathbf{X}) = h(\mathbf{X})\ else\ f(\mathbf{X}) = h(\mathbf{X}) + w(\mathbf{X}).$$

In this equation, $h(\mathbf{X})$ refers to the number of matches between circuit $\mathbf{X}$ and the truth table, and $w(\mathbf{X})$ is the number of wires in circuit $\mathbf{X}$. Kalganova also proposed the use of multiobjective optimization techniques based on the concept of Pareto fronts for the optimization of logic circuits [17].

Results and discussion. MGA was tested with similar complexity circuits used to test BGA and NGA. MGA improves the behavior of NGA, that is, it requires less number of fitness function evaluations. In several cases the circuits are even smaller than NGA (recall the NGA also improved BGA circuits). Another interesting issue is the cooperative effort observed between subpopulations. The fitness function improves as more restrictions are met, and at the same time, the fitness function helps the subpopulations to evolve toward the correct value.

13.3.6 EHW Using the Ant System (AS)

The MGA system considers each circuit output as a restriction and splits the population into subpopulations, assigning one output to one subpopulation. As noted, a cooperative effort is observed between subpopulations. MGA distributes the overall effort among subpopulations, but the cooperation is not under control of the algorithm, neither is knowledge of one subpopulation communicated to either one subpopulation.

Coello et al. used the Ant System (AS) for the first time ever for the design of combinational circuits [3, 4]. The Ant System is a meta-heuristic inspired by colonies of real ants. Ants deposit a chemical substance on the ground (*pheromone*) that influences the behavior of the entire colony: ants will tend to walk over those paths where there is a larger amount of pheromone. Pheromone trails can be seen as a communication mechanism among ants. From the computer science perspective, the AS is a multiagent system where interactions among low-level agents (ants) results in the complex behavior of the colony. The AS can be seen as a distributed knowledge system. Local knowledge collected by the agents (ants) is centralized, analyzed, and redistributed (passed back) to the local agents as an information of the collective behavior. If the colony gets closer to the goal, then the agents will know they are "doing well" and their trails will be reinforced. Otherwise, the trails are abandoned (the pheromone evaporates) and new routes will be inspected. This is called reinforcement learning, a weaker form of supervised learning.

There are three main ideas from real ant colonies that have been adopted by the AS:

1. Indirect communication through pheromone trails.
2. Shortest paths tend to have a higher growth rate of pheromone values.
3. Ants have a higher preference (with certain probability) for paths that have higher amount of pheromones.

The AS was proposed for the traveling salesman problem (TSP), and according to Dorigo [8], to apply efficiently the AS, it is necessary to reformulate the problem as one in which we want to find the optimal path of a graph and to identify a way to measure the distance between nodes. Therefore, in the TSP, the ants traverse a path and try to find the shortest way to the goal. In the circuit design problem, the goal is to produce a fully functional circuit by minimizing a certain payoff function, and "shortest" means "fewer number of gates". Thus, the colony finds a trail from the input to the output of the circuit by assembling local information of low cost paths.

Results and discussion. An important aspect of this application is that it shows the factibility of AS to work in other domains. As noted, the problem is how to translate or reformulate the problem at hand into a graph searching procedure. The advantage of the AS is its robustness; it consistently finds the smallest known circuit for some truth table, having in this respect better behavior than the evolutionary techniques NGA and BGA. Its disadvantage is the performance, which tends to degrade rapidly as the size of the circuit increases.

13.3.7 EWH Using GP and Muxes

All discussed approaches use a matrix to represent circuit connectivity. Although all approaches have tried to improve all sorts of convergence and robustness problems, the matrix itself is the source of the problem. This is so because the search space is restricted to the subset imposed by the matrix representation. In other words, the matrix representation restraints the scalability of the algorithm (it has been told everywhere that the evolutionary technique used is not as important as the representation).

Hernández-Aguirre [12, 11, 10] proposed gate-level EHW using GP and multiplexers to improve the scalability problem by giving more freedom for exploration and exploitation through a representation that could grow and shrink as needed. Thus, the search space is not restricted by the geometry of the representation. The approach is a common GP application since individuals are represented by trees and what is evolved is a function (Boolean). It is not clear though whether this approach is gate-level or functional-level because the multiplexer works as a primitive (but it is built by the primitives {and,or,not}). The problem statement has not changed here: synthesize a circuit using the smallest number of binary multiplexers using GP. An example of a synthesized circuit and its representation is shown in Figure 13.5. Note that entering a multiplexer there are only 1s, 0s, and data from immediate previous multiplexers.

(A2, (B1, (A0, 0, 1), 0), (B0, (B1, 0, 1), (B1, 1, 0)))

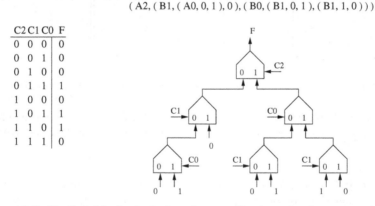

C2	C1	C0	F
0	0	0	0
0	0	1	0
0	1	0	0
0	1	1	1
1	0	0	0
1	0	1	1
1	1	0	1
1	1	1	0

Figure 13.5. Truth table for logic function specification, circuit generated, and its coding.

Many GP applications have been illustrated by Koza [18], but he generates Boolean functions and multiplexers in symbolic form, not gate-level (Koza has many proposals similar to gate-level but for electronic circuits [19]) Multiplexers are sound components for the synthesis of circuits because they are universal logic function generators, thus, an equivalent power shared with the set of primitives {and,or,not} for the synthesis of circuits. A procedure to implement Boolean functions based on multiplexers uses Boolean residues and Shannon's expansion [27], defined next.

The residue of a Boolean function $f(x_1, x_2, \ldots, x_n)$ with respect to a variable x_j is the value of the function for a specific value of x_j. It is denoted by f_{x_j}, for $x_j = 1$ and by $f_{\bar{x}_j}$ for $x_j = 0$.

A Boolean function can then be expressed in terms of these residues in the form of Shannon's expansion:

$$f = \bar{x}_j f|_{\bar{x}_j} + x_j f|_{x_j}$$

Multiplexers can be "active low" or "active high" devices, a quality simply called here *class A* and *class B*. The control line is located on the side of the input to be propagated when the control is *active*. The active state will be "1" for all the examples presented in this paper. Circuits can be synthesized using only one or both mux classes. Figure 13.6 depicts both classes of multiplexers and the construction of larger multiplexers on simpler elements.

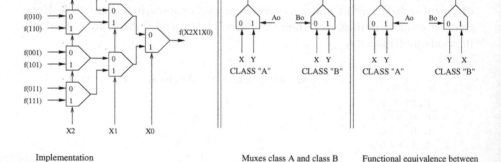

| Implementation | Muxes class A and class B | Functional equivalence between Muxes class A and class B |

Figure 13.6. Implementation of a multiplexer of 3-control lines by means of seven 1-control line. Muxes class "A" and class "B". Functional equivalence between both classes.

A circuit is represented by binary trees, which are encoded as lists. Essentially, each element of the list is the triplet $(mux, left\_child, right\_child)$ that encodes subtrees as nested lists. The tree captures the essence of the circuit topology, allowing only children to feed their parent node (or 1s and 0s as specified in the problem statement). Crossover operator is implemented between node-node, node-leaf (node other than root node), and leaf-leaf. Mutation assigns a random value (in the range) to either node or leaf. The fitness function is also dynamic and works in the same two stages as described in Section 13.3.1.

The following Boolean functions, specified by true terms, are samples of some experiments.

Examples

- $F1(a, b, c) = \sum(1, 2, 4)$.
- $F2(a, b, c, d) = \sum(0, 4, 5, 6, 7, 8, 9, 10, 13, 15)$.
- $F3(a, b, c, d, e) = \sum(0, 1, 3, 6, 7, 8, 10, 13, 15, 18, 20, 21, 25, 26, 28, 30, 31)$.
- $F4(a, b, c, d, e, f) = \sum(0, 1, 3, 6, 7, 8, 10, 13, 15, 18, 20, 21, 25, 27, 28, 30, 31, 32, 33, 35, 38, 39, 42, 42, 45, 47, 50, 52, 53, 57, 59, 60, 62, 63)$.

Table 13.1 condenses the characteristics of the circuits synthesized. Column "Standard implementation" (see Fig. 13.6) is the number of binary muxes needed to implement the Boolean function, "GP" is the number of components in the GP solution, and "Saved" is the difference.

Function	Vars	Standard implementation	GP	Saved
F1	3	7	5	2
F2	4	15	7	8
F3	5	31	15	16
F4	6	63	21	42

Table 13.1. Comparison of the Results Produced by the GP System and the Standard Implementation

The circuit found by the GP system for the function F2 is depicted in Figure 13.7. Another set of interesting experiments is the comparison of GP

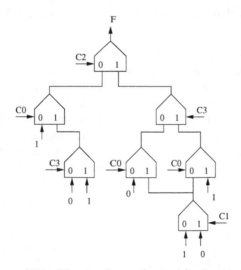

Figure 13.7. The circuit synthesized for function F2.

and Binary Decision Diagramas (BDD). A BDD is a directed acyclic graph where Shannon's decomposition is carried out at each node. There are several classes of BDDs, for instance, Ordered BBDs (OBDD) and Reduced BDDs (RBDD). In OBDD a variable appears at most once on each path from the root to a terminal node. An RBDD does not contain isomorphic subgraphs nor vertices with both edges pointing to the same node.

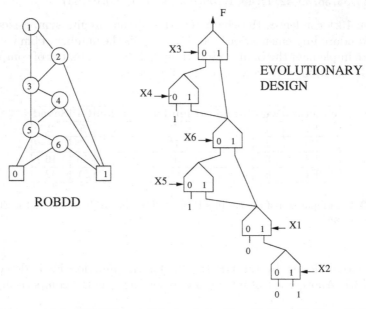

Figure 13.8. ROBDD and GP circuit for $F = X_1X_2 + X_3X_4 + X_5X_6$.

Results and discussion. Extrinsic EHW using GP and multiplexers scales up nicely for Boolean functions of up to 12 variables. The problem that predates GP is "bloat", thus, circuits grow up to contain several hundred nodes before the functional circuit is found. From there, the circuits begin to shrink because the fitness function is changed to its second stage which favors smaller circuits. It is surprising that GP is rather more efficient in shrinking circuits than in growing them. Nonetheless, "introns" appear in the circuit, making it hard for GP to eliminate the redundancy. Introns are part of the ADN chain, and why they are present is not clear, but apparently this redundancy is necessary for life. Contrasting GP and BDDs circuits is interesting. Circuits in Figure 13.8 are similar in size, but what is important to note is their resemblance in topology and difference in node ordering. The circuit generated by GP in Figure 13.9 is smaller because the restriction imposed to the order is not required. Nevertheless, it is not easy for BDD to generate of the GP circuit. Finally, the "odd-parity" circuit shown in Figure 13.10 has minimum size when it is implemented with XOR gates. The GP circuit captures the same topology and matches the smallest possible size.

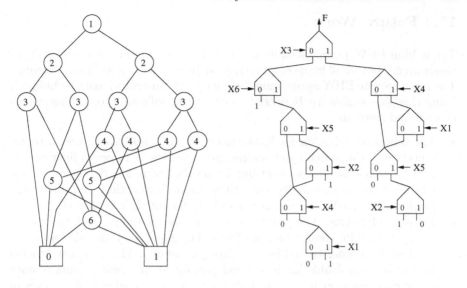

ROBDD   EVOLUTIONARY DESIGN

Figure 13.9. ROBDD and GP circuit for $F = X_1X_4 + X_2X_5 + X_3X_6$.

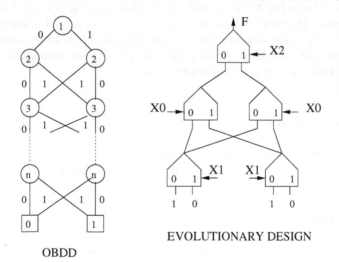

OBDD

EVOLUTIONARY DESIGN

Figure 13.10. "Odd-parity" function with XOR gates and GP circuit.

13.4 Future Work

The field of EHW promises many possibilities, not only in the gate-level synthesis arena, but in all kinds of adaptive hardware, either digital or electronic. The main issue in EHW applications is inherited from evolutionary techniques, being this *poor scalability*. In order to solve it, the following topics deserve attention and research:

- The genotype string length. Evolutionary techniques have to keep a representation of the search space within the organism. A larger or finer granularity search space has a direct impact on the string length, causing "stallation" of the evolution. Shorter strings are desirable; thus, suitable target platforms for EHW are required, specially for intrinsic evolution.
- Suitable platforms. The genotype encodes information about the circuit being evolved for some target platform. The genotype is decoded and "interpreted" in order to find its meaning (or circuit). This is a slow process for extrinsic evolvable hardware and painful for intrinsic evolution since every configuration has to be uploaded on the reconfigurable device in order to have its fitness measured.
- Decomposition and assembling. A combination of top-down and bottom-up procedures has to be assembled and triggered at specific times of the evolution. This is a "natural way" for humans to proceed in the analysis of complex systems; perhaps nature has evolved this trait in human beings for that purpose. If we could evolve this trait, our simulated organisms would be more capable at complex tasks.

Acknowledgment

The author acknowledges partial support for this work from CONCyTEG project No. 01-02-202-111 and CONACyT No. I-39324-A.

References

1. C. Coello, A. Christiansen, and A. Hernández (2000) Use of evolutionary techniques to automate the design of combinational logic circuits. *Intl. Journal of Smart Engineering System Design*, 2:299–314.
2. C. Coello, A. Christiansen, and A. Hernández (2001) Towards automated evolutionary design of combinational circuits. *Computers and Electrical Engineering*, 27:1–28.
3. C. Coello, R. Zavala, B. Mendoza, and A. Hernández-Aguirre (2000) Ant Colony System for the Design of Combinational Logic Circuits. In Miller J., Thompson A., Thomson P., and Forgarty T.C., (eds.), *Evolvable Systems: From Biology to Hardware. Third Intl. Conf., ICES 2000*, pages 21–30, Edinburgh, UK, October, Springer-Verlag.

4. C. Coello, R. Zavala, B. Mendoza, and A. Hernández-Aguirre (2002) Automated design of combinational logic circuits using the ant system. *Engineering Optimization*, 34(2):109–127.

5. C. A. Coello, A. D. Christiansen, and A. Hernández Aguirre (1996) Using genetic algorithms to design combinational logic circuits. In Cihan H. Dagli, Metin Akay, C. L. Philip Chen, B. R. Farnández, and Joydeep Ghosh, (eds.), *Intelligent Engineering Systems Through Artificial Neural Networks. Volume 6. Fuzzy Logic and Evolutionary Programming*, pages 391–396. ASME Press, St. Louis, Missouri, USA.

6. C. A. Coello, A. D. Christiansen, and A. Hernández Aguirre (1997) Automated Design of Combinational Logic Circuits using Genetic Algorithms. In D. G. Smith, N. C. Steele, and R. F. Albrecht, (eds.), *Proceedings of the Intl. Conf. on Artificial Neural Nets and Genetic Algorithms*, pages 335–338. Springer-Verlag, University of East Anglia, England.

7. C. Coello Coello, A. Hernández Aguirre, and B. P. Buckles (2000) Evolutionary Multiobjective Design of Combinational Logic Circuits. In Jason Lohn, Adrian Stoica, Didier Keymeulen, and Silvano Colombano, (eds.), *The Second NASA/DoD Workshop on Evolvable Hardware*, pages 161–170. IEEE Computer Society.

8. M. Dorigo and G. Di Caro (1999) The Ant Colony Optimization Meta-heuristic. In D. Corne, M. Dorigo, and F. Glover, (eds.) *New Ideas in Optimization.* McGraw-Hill, USA.

9. J. S. Gero and V. A. Kazakov (1995) Evolving Building Blocks for Design using Genetic Engineering: A Formal Approach. In J. S. Gero and F. Sudweeks, (eds.), *Advances in Formal Design Methods for CAD*, pages 29–48. University of Sidney, Sidney, Australia.

10. A. Hernández Aguirre, B. P. Buckles, and C. A. Coello Coello (2000) Evolutionary Synthesis of Loolean Functions using Multiplexers. In *Artificial Neural Networks in Engineering Applications, ANNIE2000*, pages 311–316. ASME Press, .

11. A. Hernández Aguirre, B. P. Buckles, and C. A. Coello Coello (2000) Gate-level Synthesis of Boolean Functions using Binary Multiplexers and Genetic Programming. In *Conf. on Evolutionary Computation 2000*, pages 675–682. IEEE Computer Society, .

12. A. Hernández Aguirre, C. A. Coello Coello, and B. P. Buckles (1999) A Genetic Programming Approach to Logic Function Synthesis by means of Multiplexers. In D. Keymeulen A. Stoica and J. Lohn, (eds.), *The First NASA/DoD Workshop on Evolvable Hardware*, pages 46–53. IEEE Computer Society.

13. H. Iba, M. Iwata, and T. Higuchi (1996) Machine Learning Approach to Gate-Level Evolvable Hardware. In T. Higuchi, M. Iwata, and Weixin Liu, (eds.), *Evolvable Systems: From Biology to Hardware. First Intl. Conf. (ICES'96)*, pages 327–343, Tsukuba, Japan, October 1996. Springer-Verlag.

14. H. Iba, M. Iwata, and T. Higuchi (1997) Gate-Level Evolvable Hardware: Empirical Study and Applications. In Dipankar Dasgupta and Zbigniew Michalewicz, (eds.), *Evolutionary Algorithms in Engineering Applications*, pages 259–276. Springer-Verlag, Berlin.

15. M. Iwata, I. Kajitani, Y. Liu, N. Kajihara, and T. Higuchi (2001) Implementation of a Gate Level Evolvable Hardware Chip. In Yong Liu, Kiyoshi Tanaka, and M. Iwata, (eds.), *Evolvable Systems: From Biology to Hardware. Fourth Intl. Conf., ICES 2001*, pages 38–49, Tokio, Japan, Springer-Verlag.

16. T. Kalganova (2000) Bidirectional incremental evolution in extrinsic evolvable hardware. In Jason Lohn, Adrian Stoica, Didier Keymeulen, and Silvano Colombano, (eds.), *The Second NASA/DoD Workshop on Evolvable Hardware*, pages 65–74. IEEE Computer Society.

17. T. G. Kalganova (2000) *Evolvable Hardware Design of Combinational Logic Circuits*. PhD thesis, Napier University, Edinburgh, Scotland.

18. J. R. Koza (1992) *Genetic Programming. On the Programming of Computers by means of Natural Selection*. MIT Press, Massachusetts, USA.

19. J. R. Koza, III F. H. Bennett, D. Andre, and M. A. Keane (1996) Automated WYWIWYG design of both the topology and component values of electrical circuits using genetic programming. In J. R. Koza, D. E. Goldberg, D. B. Fogel, and Rick L. Riolo, (eds.), *Proceedings of the First Annual Conf. on Genetic Programming*, pages 123–131, Cambridge, Masachussetts, Stanford University, The MIT Press.

20. Sushil J. L. (1993) *Genetic Algorithms as a Computational Tool for Design*. PhD thesis, Indiana University, Indiana, USA,.

21. Sushil J. L. and Rawlins G. (1989) Designer Genetic Algorithms: Genetic Algorithms in Structure Design. In Belew R.K. and Booker L.B., (eds.), *Proceedings of the Fourth Intl. Conf. on Genetic Algorithms*, pages 53–60, San Mateo, California. Morgan Kaufmann Publishers.

22. J. F. Miller, P. Thomson, and T. Fogarty (1998) Designing Electronic Circuits Using Evolutionary Algorithms. Arithmetic Circuits: A Case Study. In D. Quagliarella, J. Périaux, C. Poloni, and G. Winter, (eds.), *Genetic Algorithms and Evolution Strategy in Engineering and Computer Science*, pages 105–131. Morgan Kaufmann, Chichester, England.

23. J. F. Miller, D. Job, and V. K. Vassilev (2000) Principles in the Evolutionary Design of Digital Circuits—Part I. *Genetic Programming and Evolvable Machines*, 1(1/2):7–35.

24. J. F. Miller, D. Job, and V. K. Vassilev (2000) Principles in the Evolutionary Design of Digital Circuits—Part II. *Genetic Programming and Evolvable Machines*, 1(3):259–288.

25. T. Sasao. (1993) *Logic Synthesis and Optimization*. Kluwer Academic Press, Dordrecht, The Netherlands.

26. H.-S. Seok, K.-J. Lee, and B.-T. Zhang (2000) Genetic Programming of Process Decomposition Strategies for Evolvable Hardware. In Jason Lohn, A. Stoica, D. Keymeulen, and Silvano Colombano, (eds.), *The Seconf NASA/DoD Workshop on Evolvable Hardware*, pages 25–34. IEEE Computer Society, .

27. C. E. Shannon (1949) The synthesis of two-terminal switching circuits. *Bell System Technical Journal*, 28(1).

28. A. Stoica, R. Zebulum, and D. Keymeulen (2000) Mixtrinsic Evolution. In Miller J., Thompson A., Thomson P., and Forgarty T.C., (eds.), *Evolvable Systems: From Biology to Hardware. Third Intl. Conf., ICES 2000*, pages 208–217, Edinburgh, UK. Springer-Verlag.

29. A. Thompson, P. Layzell, and R. Salem Zebulum (1999) Explorations in Design Space: Unconventional Design Through Artificial Evolution. *IEEE Trans. on Evolutionary Computation*, 3(3):167–196.

14

The Evolutionary Learning Rule in System Identification

Oscar Montiel, Oscar Castillo, Patricia Melin, Roberto Sepulveda

Summary. In this chapter, we are proposing an approach for integrating evolutionary computation applied to the problem of system identification in the well-known statistical signal processing theory. Here, some mathematical expressions are developed in order to justify the learning rule in the adaptive process when a Breeder Genetic Algorithm is used as the optimization technique. In this work, we are including an analysis of errors, energy measures, and stability.

14.1 Introduction

The problem of determining a mathematical model for an unknown system by observing its input-output data pairs is known as system identification, and it is an important step when we wish to design a control law for a specific system. Real systems are non-linear and have time variations; hence the best control laws that we can obtain are those based using real-time data from continuous-time stochastic processes [1].

Traditionally, system identification has been performed in two ways:

1. Using analytic models, i.e., obtaining mathematically the transfer function.
2. Using experimental input-output data. In this way, the identification can be achieved in two forms: nonparametric and parametric.

In this chapter we are interested in parametric models. As we mentioned, there are several well-known techniques to perform the system identification process. Most of the parametric techniques are gradient-guided and are limited in highly multidimensional search spaces. The system identification process generally involves two top-down steps, and these are structure identification and parameter identification. In the first step, we need to apply a priori knowledge about the target system for determining a class of model within the search for the most suitable model is going to be conducted [2] [3].

Here, we are using an evolutionary algorithm known as Breeder Genetic Algorithm (BGA) that lays somehow in between Genetic Algorithms (GAs) and Evolutionary Strategies (ESs). Both methods usually start with a randomly generated population of individuals, which evolves over the time in a quest to get better solutions for a specific problem. GAs are coded in binary forming strings called chromosomes; they produce offsprings by sexual reproduction. Sexual reproduction is achieved when two strings (i.e., parents) are recombined (i.e., crossover). Generally, the parents are selected stochastically, the search process is mainly driven by the recombination operation, and the mutation is used as secondary search operator with low probability, to explore new regions of the search space. An ES is a random search, which models natural evolution by asexual reproduction [4]. It uses direct representation, that is, a gene is a decision variable and its allele is the value of the variable [5] in ES the mutation is used as the search operator, and it uses the (μ, λ)-strategy as a selection method. Thus, the BGA can be seen as a combination of ESs and GAs, because it handles direct real variables, and *truncation selection,* which is very similar to (μ, λ)-strategy, and the search process is mainly driven by recombination making BGAs similar to GAs [6] [7] [8] [9] [10].

14.2 The Generic Identification Problem

Figure 14.1 shows the generic problem of system identification. Here, we have a digital signal input $x(n)$ that is fed to the unknown system and to the adaptive filter at the same time. In this figure there is a "black box" enclosed by dashed lines; its output is called the desired response signal and it is represented by $d(n)$. The adaptive system will compute a corresponding output signal sample $y(n)$ at time n. Both signals, $d(n)$ and $y(n)$, are compared subtracting the two samples at time n, to obtain a desired response signal. This concept is expressed in equation form as

$$e(n) = d(n) - y(n) \tag{14.1}$$

This block might have a pole-zero transfer function, an all-pole or auto-regressive transfer function fixed or time-varying, a nonlinear mapping, or some other complex system. In the dashed "black-box", we have an additive noisy signal known as the observation noise signal because it corrupts the observation of the signal at the output of the unknown system [17]. Thus, the real desired signal $\hat{d}(n)$ is contaminated with noise; hence the signal $d(n)$ is given by Eq. (14.2):

$$d(n) = \hat{d}(n) + \eta(n). \tag{14.2}$$

In the adaptive system block we could have any system with a finite number of parameters that affect how $y(n)$ is computed from $x(n)$. In this work, we are using an adaptive filter with a Finite Impulse Response (FIR filter), and it is represented by the equation

$$y(n) = \sum_{i=0}^{L-1} w_i(n)x(n-i) \tag{14.3}$$

or in vectorial form as

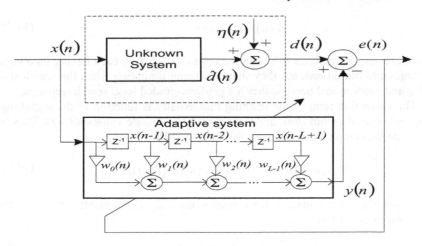

Figure 14.1. System identification with noise presence. The adaptive system uses an adaptive FIR, also known as transversal filter. In this figure z^{-1} represents the unit delay element and each $w_i(n)$ is a multiplicative gain within the system.

$$y(n) = W^T(n)X(n) = X^T(n)W(n), \qquad (14.4)$$

where the coefficient vector $W(n)$ is

$$W(n) = \left[w_0(n), w_1(n), ..., w_{L-1}(n) \right], \qquad (14.5)$$

where $\{ w_i(n); 0 \le i \le L-1 \}$ are the L parameters of the system at time n. The input signal vector is given in vector form by,

$$X(n) = \left[x(n), x(n-1), ..., x(n-L+1) \right]. \qquad (14.6)$$

In the system identification problem, the adaptive filter has the task of representing accurately the signal $\partial(n)$ at its output. This is the case when $y(n) = \hat{d}(n)$. In this stage, the filter has made its work identifying the portion of the unknown system driven by $x(n)$, but frequently this is an ideal goal, because if we are using a linear FIR filter, then the unknown system should be a filter of the same structure. In real-world problems, the identification is successful if we meet with some criterion in the error value. Moreover, in real-world problems, the output of the unknown system $\partial(n)$ is contaminated with noise $\eta(n)$. Generally, we do not have direct access to the uncorrupted output $\hat{d}(n)$ of the plant; instead we have a noisy measurement of it; in this case the output is given by Eq. (14.7). Then, we can say that the adaptive filter has reached the optimum if we find a value $y(n) = d(n)$. This is achieved when we find an optimum weight vector's parameter $W(n)$,

$$W(n) = W_{OPT}(n). \tag{14.7}$$

There are several methods to obtain the optimums values, each having its own advantages and limitations, but they share the same limitation when the search space is big and multi-modal because they are gradient-guided local search techniques.

The correction term of the learning rule usually is function of the signal input $x(n)$, the desired output $d(n)$, and the old weight estimate values $w_i(n-1)$. Thus, we can write the compact expression as follows [11, 12]:

$$W(n) = W(n-1) + f[X(n), d(n), W(n-1)]. \tag{14.8}$$

Following these concepts, the least-mean-square algorithm (LMS) can be written as shown in Eq. (14.9).

$$W(n) = W(n-1) + \mu \cdot X(n) \cdot [e(n)], \tag{14.9}$$

or, expanding the expression for the error, as

$$W(n) = W(n-1) + \mu \cdot X(n) \cdot [d(i) - X_i^T W(n-1)], \tag{14.10}$$

where μ is the step-size parameter.

In order to analyze the learning rule for the BGA in a formal way, we are going to introduce the next notation. We will use $\tilde{W}_r(n)$ to indicate the actual population of r individuals of coefficient vectors $W_r(n)$. By example, one individual is represented as

$$W_0(n) = [w_{0,0}(n), w_{0,1}(n), .., w_{0,L-1}(n)], \tag{14.11}$$

where $w_{0,I}(n)$ belongs to the coefficient 1 of the individual number 0. $W'_r(n)$ belongs to the next generation of coefficient after the evolutionary process. Then we have

$$\tilde{W}_r(n) = \begin{bmatrix} W_0(n) \\ W_1(n) \\ \vdots \\ W_r(n) \end{bmatrix} = \begin{bmatrix} w_{0,0}(n) & w_{0,1}(n) & \cdots & w_{0,L-1}(n) \\ w_{1,0}(n) & w_{1,1}(n) & \cdots & w_{1,L-1}(n) \\ \vdots & \vdots & \ddots & \vdots \\ w_{r,0}(n) & w_{r,1}(n) & \cdots & w_{r,L-1}(n) \end{bmatrix} \tag{14.12}$$

In the evolutionary process, the learning rule is a several step process. The evolutionary learning process begins with the evaluation of every coefficient vector of the population represented in Eq. (14.12) by $\tilde{W}_r(n)$. This process is done using a specific evaluation function "f_i" known as the fitness function. After the whole population has been evaluated, we need to perform a selection of the best of this population. Generally, truncation selection is a good choice; with this process we obtain a pool $\tilde{W}_T(n)$. The whole process, from expression (14.13) to (14.16), is repeated until we reached the optimum value.

$$W_T = T\%\big(feval\big(\tilde{W}_r(n)\big)\big),\tag{14.13}$$

$$W'_r(n) = W_a(n) + f\big[W_a(n), W_b(n)\big],\tag{14.14}$$

$$W'_r(n) = \Delta(W'_r),\tag{14.15}$$

$$\tilde{W}_r(n) = \tilde{W}'_r(n).\tag{14.16}$$

The fitness function (f_i) will guide the search to find the optimum.

14.3 The Breeder Genetic Algorithm

In order to adjust the parameter vector, we used a BGA, which was designed according to the methods and theories used in the science of livestock breeding [11] and is based on advanced statistical methods [12, 13, 14, 15, 16, 17].

The BGA is defined as an eight-tuple

$$BGA = \big(P_g^0, N, T, \Gamma, \Delta, HC, F, term\big),\tag{14.17}$$

where P_g^0 is the initial population of size N, T is the truncation threshold commonly referred as $T\%$, Γ represents the recombination operator, Δ is the mutation operator, HC is a hill-climbing method (by example: the gradient-guided LMS algorithm), F is the fitness function, and $term$ is the termination criterion. In the BGA, $T\%\frac{P}{100}$ best individuals at each generation are selected and mated randomly, until the number of offsprings is equal the size of the population. A basic scheme of a BGA as shown is described in [5, 14].

Referring the BGA procedure to our problem, we need to generate randomly a population with P individuals, where each individual consists of n variables, each of them related with a parameter, i.e., filter's coefficient. By example, an individual might consist of 50 floating-point variables; in this case, the adaptive FIR that we need to use will have 50 coefficients. The whole population is evaluated using a fitness function, specifically designed to measure the aptitude of each individual. This evaluation is done applying a specific signal $x(n)$ (Figure 14.1) to both systems (unknown and adaptive systems) in order to calculate an error signal obtained from the output of the unknown and adaptive systems. This error signal is the core of the fitness function. After each individual of the parent population was evaluated, the best individual should be inserted in the population of the next generation, $P'(t)$. In order to obtain this new population, which will replace the parent population, the BGA uses truncation selection. In truncation selection a percentage of the best individuals are selected to mate, obtaining offsprings; self-mating is prohibited [15].

The mutation operator is applied to each offspring, and the resulting individuals are inserted in the new population $P'(t)$. The process is repeated until a termination criterion is met. There are several recombination operators, but in this work, we used Extended Intermediate Recombination (EIR). In order to use this operator, we have if $x = (x_i,...x_n)$ and $y=(y_1,...,y_n)$ are the parents, then the successor $z=(z_1,...,z_n)$ is calculated by

$$z_i = x_i + \alpha_i(y_i - x_i), \qquad i = 1,...,n, \tag{14.18}$$

where $\alpha_i \in [-d, 1+d]$ is chosen with uniform probability for each i and $d \geq 0$, a good choice is $d = 0.25$, which is the one that we used. The goal of the mutation operator is to modify one or more parameters of z_i, the modified objects (i.e., the offsprings) appear in the landscape within a certain distance of the unmodified objects (i.e., the parents). In this way, an offspring z', where $z'=(z_1,...,z_n)$, is given by

$$z'_i = z_i \pm range_i \cdot \delta \tag{14.19}$$

where $range_i$ defines the mutation range and is calculated as $(\lambda \cdot searchinterval_i)$. In the Discrete Mutation operator (DM) λ is normally set to 0.1 or 0.2 and is very efficient in some functions [4], but also we can set λ to 1. This is the case of the Broad Mutation Operator (BMO) proposed in [16] to solve problems where the distance between the optimums and the actual position is larger than the DM operator could reach. This is the case of Scwefel's function [16]. We will have in one step, that the mutation operator can reach points from z_i only within the distance given by $\pm range_i \cdot \delta$ The sign $+$ or $-$ is chosen with probability of 0.5. The variable δ is computed by

$$\delta = \sum_{i=0}^{K-1} \varphi_i 2^{-i}, \quad \varphi_i \in [0,1]. \tag{14.20}$$

Before mutation we set each φ_i equals to 0, then each φ_i is mutated to 1 with probability $p\_=1/k$, and only $\varphi_i = 1$ contributes to the sum. On the average there will be just one φ_i with value 1, say φ_i. Then δ is given by

$$\delta = 2^{-i}. \tag{14.21}$$

In Eq. (14.20), K is a parameter originally related to the machine precision, i.e., the number of bits used to represent a real variable in the machine we are working with; traditionally K used values of 8 and 16. In practice, however, the value of K is related to the expected value of mutation steps; in other words, the higher K is, the more fine-grained the resultant mutation operator is [5].

14.4 Energy and Error Analysis

The objective of an adaptive scheme is to provide a better model for the unknown system. This is done using the output error sequence given in Eq. (14.1). This error sequence measures how far $d(i)$ is from $y(i)$, in order to update the coefficient vector $W(n)$, providing a better model at each iteration. When the adaptive system is trying to match the unknown system, there exist different sources of errors. The first source is due to the mathematical model that we are using to identify the unknown system. By example, if the unknown plant has the model of the Infinite Impulse Response Filter (IIR) of Eq. (14.22), it is evident that we would need an infinitely long tapped-delay line, whose realization is practically impossible. Therefore, when we are using a finite tapped delay line, the modeling errors are inevitable.

$$y(n) = \sum_{i=0}^{\infty} v_i(n)x(n-i).$$
(14.22)

In this work, we used as an unknown system an IIR filter specified by the second-order difference equation given by (14.23). This problem was taken from [20].

$$d(n)-d(n-1)+0.9d(n-2)=x(n) \qquad \forall n.$$
(14.23)

The adaptive system is an FIR filter with 50 coefficients. As the filter has a higher degree of freedom, the input-output response characteristic of the adaptive model will converge to match closely those of the unknown system.

If we have solved the system identification problem, and the model that we are using is a good one, then we should have a way to measure the parameter errors in the identification process [21]. If we considered that $V(n)$ represents the coefficient vector of the unknown system represented by Eq. (14.22), then we have to measure how far $W(n)$ is from $V(n)$. This quantity, $W_e(n)$, will be referred to as the weight error at time n. The weight vector $W(n)_{OPT}$ is the optimal vector that better will represent $V(n)$.

$$W_e(n) = W_{OPT}(n) - W(n).$$
(14.24)

Using Eq. (14.25), we can obtain the value known as *a priori estimation error* (e_a), which measure how far $X_i^T W(n-1)$ is from the uncorrupted output term $X_i^T W_{OPT}$; hence we have

$$e_a(i) = X^T W_e(n-1).$$
(14.25)

If we use the most recent weight vector, we can define the *a posteriori estimation error* (e_p),

$$e_a(i) = X^T W_e(n-1).$$
(14.26)

A good way to quantify the effect of these errors is the energy and power measures. Then the energy E of a signal $x(n)$ is [17].

$$E_N = \sum_{n=-\infty}^{\infty} |x(n)|^2. \tag{14.27}$$

The energy of a signal can be finite or infinite. The signal $x(n)$ is called an energy signal if E is finite, thus is $0 < E < \infty$.

We can define the signal energy of the sequence $x(n)$ over the finite interval - $0 \leq n \leq N$ as [16]

$$E_N = \sum_{n=0}^{N-1} |x(n)|^2. \tag{14.28}$$

Then we can express the signal energy as [16]

$$E = \lim_{N \to \infty} E_N \tag{14.29}$$

The average power of the signal $x(n)$ is defined as [16]

$$P = \lim_{N \to \infty} \frac{1}{N} E_N \tag{14.30}$$

We will use the definition of power provided in (16) to calculate a short-term average ASE (Average of Squared Error), which will serve us in two ways; one is to estimate the convergence rate of the evolutionary algorithm, and the second way is for using the inverse of this function (1/ASE) as the aptitude function, which will guide the evolutionary algorithm to get the optimums coefficients. The ASE function is defined as

$$ASE(m) = \frac{1}{K} \sum_{k=n+1}^{n+K} e^2(k). \tag{14.31}$$

Here, $m = n/K = 1, 2, \ldots$ The recommended averaging interval K may be selected to be (approximately) $K = 10L$ [16].

14.5 Stability Analysis

In any practical application, an analysis of system's stability is important, since an unstable system usually exhibits erratic and extreme behavior and causes overflow [21]. To prove stability in this work, we used the next theorem, as well as concepts about causal systems:

Theorem. *An arbitrary relaxed system is said to be bounded input-bounded output (BIBO) stable if and only if every bounded input produces a bounded output.*

Considering the previous theorem, if $x(n)$ is the bounded input, there must be a constant M_x such that

$$|x(n)| \leq M_x < \infty, \tag{14.32}$$

and, if the output is bounded, there must be a constant M_y such that

$$|y(n)| \leq M_y < \infty. \tag{14.33}$$

Although we are working with a time-varying system, for analysis purposes we are considering a window time where the system can be treated as a Linear Time invariant system (LTI), and via mathematical induction generalize this result. Then, if we take the absolute value of both sides of Eq. (14.3), we obtain

$$|y(n)| = \left| \sum_{i=0}^{L-1} w_i(n) x(n-i) \right|. \tag{14.34}$$

Then, we have

$$|y(n)| \leq \sum_{i=0}^{L-1} |w_i(n)| |x(n-i)|. \tag{14.35}$$

If the input is bounded, there exists a finite number M_x that satisfies Eq. (14.32), i.e., $|x(n)| \leq M_x$, then we can rewrite Eq. (14.35) as

$$|y(n)| \leq M_x \sum_{i=0}^{L-1} |w_i(n)|. \tag{14.36}$$

From Eq. (14.36), we observe that the output is bounded if the impulse response of the system is absolutely summable, i.e.,

$$\sum_{i=0}^{L-1} |w_i(n)| < \infty. \tag{14.37}$$

In this work, Eq. (14.36) is easily satisfied since we have a finite number of coefficients $w_i(k)$, and their values also are finite. This result implies that any excitation of a finite duration, applied to the input of the system, must produce an output of nature "transient", this is when the system is stable. The input amplitude will decay eventually with time. This condition implies that $W(z)$ must contain the unit circle within its Region of Convergence (ROC). Then,

$$W(z) = \sum_{i=0}^{L-1} w_i(k) z^{-n}.$$

(14.38)

In consequence,

$$|H(z)| \le \left| \sum_{i=0}^{L-1} w_i(k) z^{-n} \right| = \sum_{n=-\infty}^{\infty} |w_i(k)| |z^{-n}|,$$

(14.39)

evaluating on the unit circle (i.e., $|z| = 1$),

$$|H(z)| \le \sum_{n=-\infty}^{\infty} |h(n)|.$$

(14.40)

Then, if the system is BIBO stable, the unit circle is contained in the ROC of $H(z)$. From Eq. (14.2), we can see that the adaptive system is causal because its output at time n depends only on present and past inputs but not on future inputs. An LTI system is causal if and only if the ROC of the system function is the exterior of a circle of radius $r < \infty$, including the point $z = \infty$.

14.6 Experimental Results

This algorithm was realized using the procedure BGA explained in Section 14.3. We selected as the adaptive system an FIR filter (ARMA model), We used as unknown system an IIR filter specified by the second-order difference equation given in (14.23); this problem was taken from [20]. A signal sequence called $x(n)$ is used as the input to the unknown system and the adaptive FIR filter. Then this sequence is the training signal. Using the appropriate training signal, it is very important to be successful in the identification of a system. A good signal should contain at least 10 frequency components. For this reason random signals like white noise and Gaussian white noise are generally used. In this work, we used both signals to train the system, and both are good enough to find optimized parameters. With these signals, we trained the adaptive FIR. In both cases, the tests were made with a population of 300 individuals. In the EIR operator, $d = 0.25$. We used the DM operator with $\lambda = 0.1$, and $\delta = 16$. In order to speed up the processing time we used only 80 samples to calculate ASE; we chose this number experimentally. We ran the BGA for 100 generations.

An important point about the development of this algorithm is that if the fitness function f represents the value of the i-th individual, then

$$f_i = \frac{1}{ASE_i(m)},$$

(14.41)

The training white noise signal $x(n)$ was generated using the Matlab command $x=rand(1,100)*2-1$; in Figure 14.2 we show a histogram of this signal.

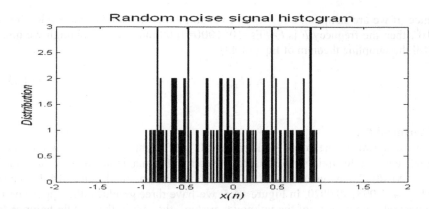

Figure 14.2. For training the ARMA model we generated a sequence of 100 samples of white noise at each generation.

The training Gaussian white noise signal $x(n)$ was generated using the Matlab command $x=wgn(100,1,-6)$; in Figure 14.3 we show a histogram of this signal.

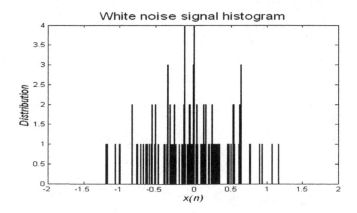

Figure 14.3. Gaussian distribution of 100 samples.

For all the experiments, we analyzed the system response using Bode plots. In the Bode plots we used normalized frequency expressed in radians per sample (rad/samp). The normalized frequency f is calculated using Eq. (14.42), where F is the frequency that we want to normalize and F_s is the sampling frequency.

$$f = \frac{F}{F_s}.$$ (14.42)

Hence, if we are sampling at F_s=1000 rad/samp, and the value in the Bode plot is f=10⁰, then the frequecy F is F=fFs=10⁰·1000=1000 rad/samp. Although we must fulfill the sampling theorem of Eq. (14.43)

$$F_s \geq 2F_{max}.$$ (14.43)

Experiment #1.

In this experiment, the adaptive filter has 50 coefficients. We used a white noise signal sequence for training the adaptive system. The maximal fitness value found was 481.0087, at generation 96. This is shown in Figure 14.4. Then ASE=1/481.0087≈0.0020. In Figure 14.5, we have three graphics; the upper one is the desired output, $d(n)$, of the unknown system, the one in the middle belongs to the output of the adaptive system; and the graphic at the bottom corresponds to the signal error. This graphic represents the value difference at each sample. Figure 14.6 belongs to the unit step response, and the interpretation is similar to Figure 14.5. Figures 14.7 and 14.8 are the Bode plots; here we can analyze the system response in magnitude and phase. In both figures we are using normalized frequency expressed in rad/seg.

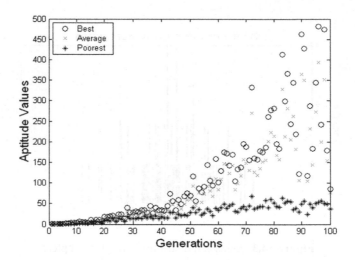

Figure 14.4. Fitness graphic, the "o" belongs to the best fitness found at each generation, as well as the "x" belongs to an average fitness value of the generation, and the symbol "*" is for the poorest fitness.

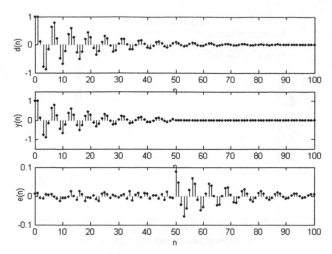

Figure 14.5. Unit impulse response. Experiment 1.

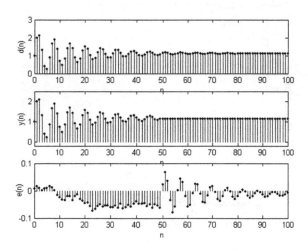

Figure 14.6. Unit step response. Experiment 1.

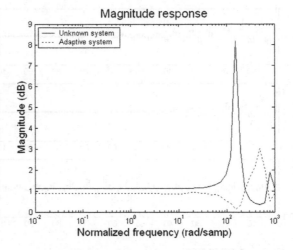

Figure 14.7. Behavior of the adaptive system.

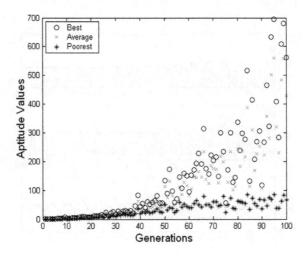

Figure 14.8. Fitness function's values. Experiment 2.

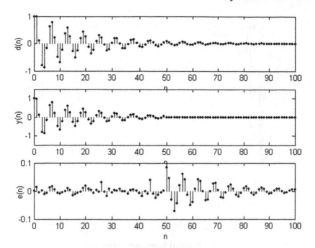

Figure 14.9. Unit impulse response. Experiment 2.

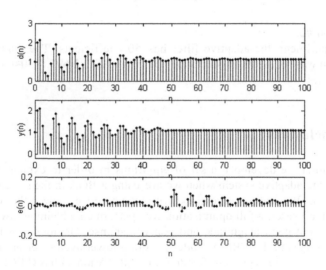

Figure 14.10. Unit step response. Experiment 2.

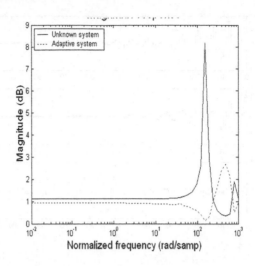

Figure 14.11. Magnitude response. Experiment 2.

Experiment #2.
In this experiment, the adaptive filter has 50 coefficients. The maximal fitness value found was 695.8930, at generation 95. Then ASE=1/695.8930≈0.00144.

14.7 Conclusions

In this chapter we developed a set of equations in order to explain the learning process of the adaptive system when we are using a BGA in the system identification problem. We realized several experiments; here we showed the result of four of them. In all cases, a full optimization was performed, obtaining low rates of average error and good magnitude and phase response. Obviously, when we used more coefficients in the ARMA model we got a lower average error. This is natural, because the more degrees of freedom the ARMA model has (FIR filter), the input-output response characteristic of the adaptive model will converge to match closely the unknown system.

References

1.   C. W. Helstrom (1991) Probability and stochastic processes for engineers. Helstrom U.S.A.
2.   J.-S. R. Jang, C.-T. Sun, E. Mizutani (1997) Neuro-Fuzzy and Soft Computing, A Computational Approach to Learning and Machine Intelligence. Matlab Curriculum Series. Prentice Hall.

3.   S.P. Harris, E.C. Ifeachor, (1996) Nonlinear FIR Filter Design by Genetic Algorithm, in "1st Online Conference on Soft Computing". http://www.lania.mx/~ccoello/EM00/harrisabs.txt
4.   H. Mühlenbein. "6 Genetic Algorithms". Borneo http://citeseer.nj.nec.com/181734.html
5.   L.A. Belanche. (1999) A Study in Function Optimization with the Breeder Genetic Algorithm. Research Report LSI-99-36-R. Universitat Politécnica de Catalunya. http://citeseer.nj.nec.com/belanche99study.html
6.   De Falco, A. Della Cioppa, P. Natale and E. Tarantino. (1997) Artificial Neural Networks Optimization by means of Evolutionary Algorithms, 1997. http://citeseer.nj.nec.com/3503.html.
7.   M.S. White, J.S. Flockton "Adaptive recursive filtering using evolutionary algorithms", http://citeseer.nj.nec.com/392797.html
8.   D. M. Etter, M. J. Hicks, and K. H. Cho. (1982) "Recursive filter design using an adaptive genetic algorithm". In Proceedings of the IEEE International Conference on Acoustics, Speech and Signal Processing (ICASSP 82), volume 2, pp. 635-638, IEEE.
9.   O. Montiel, R. Sepúlveda, O. Castillo, P. Melin. (2001) "Application of a Breeder Genetic Algorithm for Filter Optimization", In Proceedings of the International Conference on Artificial Intelligence IC-AI'2001, volume III, pp. 1199-1205, Las Vegas, Nevada, USA.
10.   O. Montiel, R. Sepúlveda, O. Castillo, P. Melin (2001) A Breeder Genetic Algorithm for Filter Optimization. In World Multiconference on Systemics, Cybernetics an Infomatics (ISAS/SCI 2001), volume IX Industrial Systems: Part I, pp. 556-562, Orlando, Florida, USA.
11.   V. K. Madisetti, D. B. Williams (1997) "The Digital Signal Processing Handbook", A CRC Handbook Published in Cooperation with IEEE Press, pp. 18-1, 18-7, 20-1, 20-4.
12.   O. Montiel, O. Castillo, P. Melin, R. Sepúlveda (2002) "The Evolutionary Learning Rule in System Identification". The 6th. World Multiconference on Systemics, Cybergenics and Informatics (SCI 2002), volume XVII Industrial Systems and Engineering III. pp. 205-210.
13.   H. Mühlenbein. The equation for the response to selection and its use for prediction. http://citeseer.nj.nec.com/181734.html.
14.   H. Mühlenbein, D. Schlierkamp-Voosen (1994) "The science of breeding and its application to the breeder genetic algorithm BGA". Evolutionary Computation, 1(4):335-360.
15.   H. Mühlenbein, J. Bendisch, H.-M. Voigt. (1996) From recombination of genes to the estimation of distribution II. Continuous parameters. Parallel Problem Solving from Nature, Springer: Berlin, pp: 188-197.
16.   I. De Falco. (1997) Sample Contributed Book, John Wiley & Sons. Editor Jenny Smith. http://citeseer.nj.nec.com/cs.
17.   H. Mühlenbein, S.-Voosen (1993) Predictive Model for Breeder Genetic Algorithm. Evolutionary Computation. 1(1): 25-49.
18.   Ralf Salomon. Genetic Algorithms and the O(n ln n) Complexity on Selected Test Functions. http://citesser.nj.nec.com/109962.html.
19.   V. K. Madisetti, D. B. Williams. (1997) The Digital Signal Processing Handbook, A CRC Handbook Published in Cooperation with IEEE Press, pp. 18-1, 18-7, 20-1, 20-4.
20.   V. K. Ingle, J. G. Proakis. (2000) Digital Signal Processing using Matlab. Ed. Brooks/Cole, , pp. 371-377.

21.   O. Montiel, O. Castillo, R. Sepúlveda. (2002) "Error and Energy Measures in System Identification Using an Evolutionary Algorithm", Proceedings of the International Conference on Artificial Intelligence IC-AI'2002. Las Vegas, Nevada, USA.

15

Current and Future Research Trends in Evolutionary Multiobjective Optimization

C.A. Coello Coello, G. Toscano Pulido, E. Mezura Montes

Summary. In this chapter we present a brief analysis of the current research performed on evolutionary multiobjective optimization. After analyzing first- and second-generation multiobjective evolutionary algorithms, we address two important issues: the role of elitism in evolutionary multiobjective optimization and the way in which concepts from multiobjective optimization can be applied to constraint-handling techniques. We conclude with a discussion of some of the most promising research trends in the years to come.

15.1 Introduction

Evolutionary algorithms have become an increasingly popular design and optimization tool in the last few years, with a constantly growing development of new algorithms and applications [1]. Despite this considerably large volume of research, new areas remain to be explored with sufficient depth. One of them is the use of evolutionary algorithms to solve multiobjective optimization problems.

The first reported implementation of a multiobjective evolutionary algorithm (MOEA) dates back to the mid-1980s [45, 46]. Since then, a considerable amount of research has been done in this area, now known as evolutionary multiobjective optimization (EMO for short). The growing importance of this field is reflected by a significant increment (mainly during the last eight years) of technical papers in Intl. Conf.s and peer-reviewed journals, books, special sessions in Intl. Conf.s and interest groups on the Internet [13].[1]

Evolutionary algorithms seem also particularly desirable for solving multiobjective optimization problems because they deal simultaneously with a set

---

[1] The first author maintains an EMO repository with over 900 bibliographical entries at: http://delta.cs.cinvestav.mx/~ccoello/EMOO, with mirrors at http://www.lania.mx/~ccoello/EMOO/ and http://www.jeo.org/emo/.

of possible solutions (the so-called population), which allows us to find several members of the Pareto optimal set in a single run of the algorithm, instead of having to perform a series of separate runs as in the case of the traditional mathematical programming techniques. Additionally, evolutionary algorithms are less susceptible to the shape or continuity of the Pareto front (e.g., they can easily deal with discontinuous and concave Pareto fronts), whereas these two issues are a real concern for mathematical programming techniques [8].

This chapter deals with some of the current and future research trends in evolutionary multiobjective optimization. The perspective adopted is derived from our own research experience in the area and therefore the bias toward certain particular topics of interest. The chapter is organized as follows. Section 15.2 presents some basic concepts used in multiobjective optimization. Section 15.3 briefly describes the origins of evolutionary multiobjective optimization. Section 15.4 introduces the so-called first-generation multiobjective evolutionary algorithms. Second-generation multiobjective evolutionary algorithms are discussed in Section 15.5, emphasizing the role of elitism in evolutionary multiobjective optimization. Section 15.6 discusses ways in which multiobjective optimization concepts have been and could be incorporated into constraint-handling techniques (both for single and for multiobjective optimization). Finally, Section 15.7 discusses some of the research trends that are likely to be predominant in the next few years.

15.2 Basic Concepts

The emphasis of this chapter is the solution of multiobjective optimization problems (MOPs) of the form

$$\text{minimize } [f_1(\mathbf{x}), f_2(\mathbf{x}), \ldots, f_k(\mathbf{x})], \qquad (15.1)$$

subject to the m inequality constraints:

$$g_i(\mathbf{x}) \geq 0 \quad i = 1, 2, \ldots, m, \qquad (15.2)$$

and the p equality constraints:

$$h_i(\mathbf{x}) = 0 \quad i = 1, 2, \ldots, p, \qquad (15.3)$$

where k is the number of objective functions $f_i : \mathbb{R}^n \rightarrow \mathbb{R}$. We call $\mathbf{x} = [x_1, x_2, \ldots, x_n]^T$ the vector of decision variables. We wish to determine from among the set $\mathcal{F}$ of all vectors that satisfy (15.2) and (15.3) the particular set of values $x_1^*, x_2^*, \ldots, x_n^*$ that yield the optimum values of all the objective functions.

15.2.1 Pareto Optimality

It is rarely the case that there is a single point that simultaneously optimizes all the objective functions. Therefore, we normally look for "tradeoffs", rather than single solutions when dealing with multiobjective optimization problems. The notion of "optimality" is, therefore, different in this case. The most commonly adopted notion of optimality is that originally proposed by Francis Ysidro Edgeworth [21] and later generalized by V. Pareto [39]. Although some authors call this notion *Edgeworth–Pareto optimality* (see, for example, [49]), we will use the most commonly accepted term: *Pareto optimality*.

We say that a vector of decision variables $\mathbf{x}^* \in \mathcal{F}$ is *Pareto optimal* if there does not exist another $\mathbf{x} \in \mathcal{F}$ such that $f_i(\mathbf{x}) \leq f_i(\mathbf{x}^*)$ for all $i = 1, \ldots, k$ and $f_j(\mathbf{x}) < f_j(\mathbf{x}^*)$ for at least one j.

In words, this definition says that $\mathbf{x}^*$ is Pareto optimal if there exists no feasible vector of decision variables $\mathbf{x} \in \mathcal{F}$ which would decrease some criterion without causing a simultaneous increase in at least one other criterion. Unfortunately, this concept almost always gives not a single solution, but rather a set of solutions called the *Pareto optimal set*. The vectors $\mathbf{x}^*$ corresponding to the solutions included in the Pareto optimal set are called *nondominated*. The image of the Pareto optimal set under the objective functions is called *Pareto front*.

15.3 How It All Started

The potential of evolutionary algorithms for solving multiobjective optimization problems was hinted as early as the late 1960s by Rosenberg in his Ph.D. thesis [42]. Rosenberg's study contained a suggestion that would have led to multiobjective optimization if he had carried it out as presented. His suggestion was to use multiple *properties* (nearness to some specified chemical composition) in his simulation of the genetics and chemistry of a population of single-celled organisms. Since his actual implementation contained only one single property, the multiobjective approach could not be shown in his work.

The first actual implementation of what it is now called a multiobjective evolutionary algorithm (or MOEA, for short) was Schaffer's *Vector Evaluation Genetic Algorithm* (VEGA), which was introduced in the mid-1980s, mainly aimed for solving problems in machine learning [45, 46, 47].

VEGA basically consisted of a simple genetic algorithm (GA) with a modified selection mechanism. At each generation, a number of subpopulations were generated by performing proportional selection according to each objective function in turn. Thus, for a problem with k objectives, k subpopulations of size N/k each would be generated (assuming a total population size of N). These subpopulations would then be shuffled together to obtain a new population of size N, on which the GA would apply the crossover and mutation operators in the usual way. Schaffer realized that the solutions generated by his system were nondominated in a local sense, because their nondominance was limited to the current population, which was obviously not appropriate. Also, he noted a problem that in genetics is known as "speciation" (i.e., we could have the evolution of "species" within the population which excel on different aspects of performance). This problem arises because this technique selects individuals who excel in one dimension of performance, without looking at the other dimensions. The potential danger doing that is that we could have individuals with what Schaffer called "middling" performance[2] in all dimensions, which could be very useful for compromise solutions, but which will not survive under this selection scheme, since they are not in the extreme for any dimension of performance (i.e., they do not produce the best value for any objective function, but only moderately good values for all of them). Speciation is undesirable because it is opposed to our goal of finding Pareto optimal solutions. Although VEGA's speciation can be dealt with using heuristics or other additional mechanisms, it remained as the main drawback of VEGA.

From the second half of the 1980s up to the first half of the 1990s, few other researchers developed MOEAs. Most of the work reported back then involves rather simple evolutionary algorithms that use an aggregating function (linear in most cases) [33, 54], lexicographic ordering [24], and target-vector approaches [28]. All of these approaches were strongly influenced by the work done in the operations research community and in most cases did not require any major modifications to the evolutionary algorithm adopted.

The algorithms proposed in this initial period are rarely referenced in the current literature except for VEGA (which is still used by some researchers). However, the period is of great importance because it provided the first insights into the possibility of using evolutionary algorithms for multiobjective optimization. The fact that only relatively naive approaches were developed during this stage is natural considering that these were the initial attempts to develop multiobjective extensions of an evolutionary algorithm. Such approaches kept most of the original evolutionary algorithm structure intact (only the fitness function was modified in most cases) to avoid any complex additional coding. The emphasis in incorporating the concept of Pareto dominance into the search mechanism of an evolutionary algorithm would come later.

15.4 MOEAs: First Generation

The major step toward the first generation of MOEAs was given by D. Goldberg on pages 199 to 201 of his famous book on genetic algorithms published in 1989 [25]. In his book, Goldberg analyzes VEGA and proposes a selection scheme based on the concept of Pareto optimality. Goldberg not only suggested what would become the standard first generation MOEA, but also indicated that stochastic noise would make such algorithm useless unless some special mechanism was adopted to block convergence. First-generation MOEAs typically adopt niching or fitness sharing for that sake. The most representative algorithms from the first generation are the following:

---

[2] By "middling", Schaffer meant an individual with acceptable performance, perhaps above average, but not outstanding for any of the objective functions.

1. **Nondominated Sorting Genetic Algorithm** (NSGA): This algorithm was proposed by Srinivas and Deb [48]. The approach is based on several layers of classifications of the individuals as suggested by Goldberg [25]. Before selection is performed, the population is ranked on the basis of nondomination: all nondominated individuals are classified into one category (with a dummy fitness value, which is proportional to the population size, to provide an equal reproductive potential for these individuals). To maintain the diversity of the population, these classified individuals are shared with their dummy fitness values. Then this group of classified individuals is ignored and another layer of nondominated individuals is considered. The process continues until all individuals in the population are classified. Stochastic remainder proportionate selection is adopted for this technique. Since individuals in the first front have the M.imum fitness value, they always get more copies than the rest of the population. This allows us to search for nondominated regions and results in convergence of the population toward such regions. Sharing, by its part, helps to distribute the population over this region (i.e., the Pareto front of the problem).

2. **Niched-Pareto Genetic Algorithm** (NPGA): Proposed by Horn et al. [32]. The NPGA uses the tournament selection scheme based on Pareto dominance. The basic idea of the algorithm is the following: two individuals are randomly chosen and compared against a subset from the entire population (typically, around 10% of the population). If one of them is dominated (by the individuals randomly chosen from the population) and the other is not, then the nondominated individual wins. When both competitors are either dominated or nondominated (i.e., there is a tie), the result of the tournament is decided through fitness sharing [27].

3. **Multiobjective Genetic Algorithm** (MOGA): Proposed by Fonseca and Fleming [23]. In MOGA, the rank of a certain individual corresponds to the number of chromosomes in the current population by which it is dominated. Consider, for example, an individual x_i at generation t, which is dominated by $p_i^{(t)}$ individuals in the current generation.
The rank of an individual is given by [23]

$$\text{rank}(x_i, t) = 1 + p_i^{(t)}. \tag{15.4}$$

All nondominated individuals are assigned rank 1, while dominated ones are penalized according to the population density of the corresponding region of the tradeoff surface.
Fitness assignment is performed in the following way [23]:
   a) Sort population according to rank.
   b) Assign fitness to individuals by interpolating from the best (rank 1) to the worst (rank $n \leq M$) in the way proposed by Goldberg (1989), according to some function, usually linear, but not necessarily.

c) Average the fitnesses of individuals with the same rank, so that all of them are sampled at the same rate. This procedure keeps the global population fitness constant while maintaining appropriate selective pressure, as defined by the function used.

The main questions raised during the first generation were

- Are aggregating functions (so common before and even during the golden years of Pareto ranking) really doomed to fail when the Pareto front is nonconvex [16]? Are there ways to deal with this problem? Is it worth trying? Some recent work seems to indicate that aggregating functions are not death yet [35].
- Can we find ways to maintain diversity in the population without using niches (or fitness sharing), which requires a process $O(M^2)$, where M refers to the population size?
- If we assume that there is no way of reducing the $O(kM^2)$ process required to perform Pareto ranking (k is the number of objectives and M is the population size), how can we design a more efficient MOEA?
- Do we have appropriate test functions and metrics to evaluate quantitatively an MOEA? Not many people worried about this issue until near the end of the first generation. During this first generation, practically all comparisons were done visually (plotting the Pareto fronts produced by different algorithms) or were not provided at all (only the results of the proposed method were reported).
- When will somebody develop theoretical foundations for MOEAs?

Summarizing, the first generation was characterized by the use of selection mechanisms based on Pareto ranking and fitness sharing was the most common approach adopted to maintain diversity. Much work remained to be done, but the first important steps toward a solid research area had been already taken.

15.5 MOEAs: Second Generation

The second generation of MOEAs was born with the introduction of the notion of elitism. In the context of multiobjective optimization, elitism usually (although not necessarily) refers to the use of an external population (also called secondary population) to retain the nondominated individuals. The use of this external file raises several questions:

- How does the external file interact with the main population?
- What do we do when the external file is full?
- Do we impose additional criteria to enter the file instead of just using Pareto dominance?

Elitism can also be introduced through the use of a $(\mu + \lambda)$-selection in which parents compete with their children and those which are nondominated (and possibly comply with some additional criterion such as providing a better distribution of solutions) are selected for the following generation.

The previous points bring us to analyze in more detail the true role of elitism in evolutionary multiobjective optimization. For that sake, we will review next the way in which some of the second-generation MOEAs implement elitism:

1. **Strength Pareto Evolutionary Algorithm** (SPEA): This algorithm was introduced by Zitzler and Thiele [57]. This approach was conceived as a way of integrating different MOEAs. SPEA uses an archive containing nondominated solutions previously found (the so-called external nondominated set). At each generation, nondominated individuals are copied to the external nondominated set. For each individual in this external set, a *strength* value is computed. This strength is similar to the ranking value of MOGA, since it is proportional to the number of solutions to which a certain individual dominates. It should be obvious that the external nondominated set is in this case the elitist mechanism adopted. In SPEA, the fitness of each member of the current population is computed according to the strengths of all external nondominated solutions that dominate it. Additionally, a clustering technique called "average linkage method" [37] is used to keep diversity.

2. **Strength Pareto Evolutionary Algorithm 2** (SPEA2): SPEA2 has three main differences with respect to its predecessor [56]: (1) it incorporates a fine-grained fitness assignment strategy that takes into account for each individual the number of individuals that dominate it and the number of individuals by which it is dominated; (2) it uses a nearest-neighbor density estimation technique that guides the search more efficiently; and (3) it has an enhanced archive truncation method that guarantees the preservation of boundary solutions.
Thefore, in this case the elitist mechanism is just an improved version of the previous.

3. **Pareto Archived Evolution Strategy** (PAES): This algorithm was introduced by Knowles and Corne [36]. PAES consists of a (1+1) evolution strategy (i.e., a single parent that generates a single offspring) in combination with a historical archive that records some of the nondominated solutions previously found. This archive is used as a reference set against which each mutated individual is being compared. Such a historical archive is the elitist mechanism adopted in PAES. However, an interesting aspect of this algorithm is the procedure used to maintain diversity, which consists of a crowding procedure that divides objective space in a recursive manner. Each solution is placed in a certain grid location based on the

values of its objectives (which are used as its "coordinates" or "geographical location"). A map of such grid is maintained, indicating the number of solutions that reside in each grid location. Since the procedure is adaptive, no extra parameters are required (except for the number of divisions of the objective space).

4. **Nondominated Sorting Genetic Algorithm II** (NSGA-II): Deb et al. [18, 19, 20] proposed a revised version of the NSGA [48], called NSGA-II, which is more efficient (computationally speaking), that uses elitism and a crowded comparison operator that keeps diversity without specifying any additional parameters. The NSGA-II does not use an external memory as the previous algorithms. Instead, the elitist mechanism consists of combining the best parents with the best offspring obtained (i.e., a $(\mu + \lambda)$-selection).

5. **Niched Pareto Genetic Algorithm 2** (NPGA 2): E.son et al. [22] proposed a revised version of the NPGA [32] called the NPGA 2. This algorithm uses Pareto ranking but keeps tournament selection (solving ties through fitness sharing as in the original NPGA). In this case, no external memory is used and the elitist mechanism is similar to the one adopted by the NSGA-II. Niche counts in the NPGA 2 are calculated using individuals in the partially filled next generation, rather than using the current generation. This is called continuously updated fitness sharing and was proposed by Oei et al. [38].

6. **Pareto Envelope-based Selection Algorithm** (PESA): This algorithm was proposed by Corne et al. [15]. This approach uses a small internal population and a larger external (or secondary) population. PESA uses the same hypergrid division of phenotype (i.e., objective funcion) space adopted by PAES to maintain diversity. However, its selection mechanism is based on the crowding measure used by the hypergrid previously mentioned. This same crowding measure is used to decide what solutions to introduce into the external population (i.e., the archive of nondominated vectors found along the evolutionary process). Therefore, in PESA, the external memory plays a crucial role in the algorithm since it determines not only the diversity scheme, but also the selection performed by the method. There is also a revised version of this algorithm, called PESA-II [14]. This algorithm is identical to PESA, except for the fact that region-based selection is used in this case. In region-based selection, the unit of selection is a hyperbox rather than an individual. The procedure consists of selecting (using any of the traditional selection techniques [26]) a hyperbox and then randomly select an individual within such a hyperbox. The main motivation of this approach is to reduce the computational costs associated with traditional MOEAs (i.e., those based on Pareto ranking). Again, the role of the external memory in this case is crucial to the per-

formance of the algorithm.

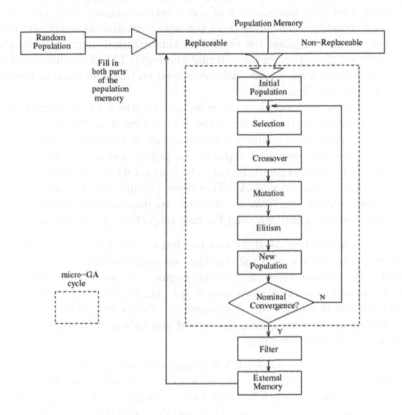

Figure 15.1. Diagram that illustrates the way in which the micro-GA for multiobjective optimization works.

7. **Micro-Genetic Algorithm**: This approach was introduced by Coello Coello and Toscano Pulido [11, 12]. A micro-genetic algorithm is a GA with a small population and a reinitialization process. The way in which the micro-GA works is illustrated in Figure 15.1. First, a random population is generated. This random population feeds the population memory, which is divided in two parts: a replaceable and a nonreplaceable portion. The non-replaceable portion of the population memory never changes during the entire run and is meant to provide the required diversity for the algorithm. In contrast, the replaceable portion experiences changes after each cycle of the micro-GA. The population of the micro-GA at the beginning of each of its cycles is taken (with a certain probability) from both portions of the population memory so that there is a mixture of randomly generated individuals (nonreplaceable portion) and evolved individuals

(replaceable portion). During each cycle, the micro-GA undergoes conventional genetic operators. After the micro-GA finishes one cycle, two nondominated vectors are chosen[3] from the final population and they are compared with the contents of the external memory (this memory is initially empty). If either of them (or both) remains as nondominated after comparing it against the vectors in this external memory, then they are included there (i.e., in the external memory). This is the historical archive of nondominated vectors. All dominated vectors contained in the external memory are eliminated.

The micro-GA uses then three forms of elitism: (1) it retains nondominated solutions found within the internal cycle of the micro-GA; (2) it uses a replaceable memory whose contents is partially "refreshed" at certain intervals; and (3) it replaces the population of the micro-GA by the nominal solutions produced (i.e., the best solutions found after a full internal cycle of the micro-GA). Therefore, the micro-GA is another example of how elitism can play a vital role to improve the performance of an evolutionary algorithm used for multiobjective optimization.

Second-generation MOEAs can be characterized by an emphasis on efficiency and by the use of elitism (in the two main forms previously described). During the second generation, some important theoretical work also took place, mainly related to convergence [43, 44, 29, 30, 53]. Also, metrics and standard test functions were developed to validate new MOEAs [55, 52].

The main concerns during the second generation (which we are still living nowadays) are the following:

- Are our metrics reliable? What about our test functions? We have found out that developing good metrics is in itself a multiobjective optimization problem, too. In fact, it is ironic that nowadays we are going back to trusting more visual comparisons than metrics as during the first generation.
- Are we ready to tackle problems with more than two objective functions efficiently? Is Pareto ranking doomed to fail when dealing with too many objectives? If so, then what is the limit up to which Pareto ranking can be used to select individuals reliably?
- What are the most relevant theoretical aspects of evolutionary multiobjective optimization that are worth exploring in the shortterm?

15.6 Relating Constraint Handling and Multiobjective Optimization

Another research area within evolutionary multiobjective optimization that has not been explored in enough detail in the current literature is constraint

---

[3] This is assuming that there are two or more nondominated vectors. If there is only one, then this vector is the only one selected.

handling (particularly for single-objective optimization). We believe that it is important to study the relationship between constraint handling and multi-objective optimization because of two main reasons: (1) constrained single-objective optimization problems can be restated as multiobjective optimization problems in a natural way; and (2) this sort of constrained single-objective optimization problems can be used to measure performance of MOEAs on a more quantitative basis than when using conventional multiobjective test functions.

The most straightforward approach to use multiobjective optimization techniques to solve a single-objective optimization problems is to redefine the single-objective optimization of $f(\mathbf{x})$ as a multiobjective optimization problem in which we will have $m + 1$ objectives, where m is the number of constraints[4]. Then, we can apply any MOEA to the new vector $\bar{v} = (f(\mathbf{x}), f_1(\mathbf{x}), \ldots, f_m(\mathbf{x}))$, where $f_1(\mathbf{x}), \ldots, f_m(\mathbf{x})$ are the original constraints of the problem. An ideal solution $\mathbf{x}$ would thus have $f_i(\mathbf{x})=0$ for $1 \leq i \leq m$ and $f(\mathbf{x}) \leq f(\mathbf{y})$ for all feasible $\mathbf{y}$ (assuming minimization).

However, it should be clear that in single-objective optimization problems we do not want just good tradeoffs; we want to find the best possible solutions that do not violate any constraints. Therefore, a mechanism such as Pareto ranking may be useful to approach the feasible region, but once we arrive to it, we will need to guide the search with a different mechanism so that we can reach the global optimum. In order to achieve this goal, we should also be able to maintain diversity in the population. Some of the most representative attempts to use multiobjective optimization techniques (or concepts) to handle constraints in single-objective optimization problems are the following:

1. **COMOGA**: Surry et al. [50] proposed the use of Pareto ranking and VEGA to handle constraints. In their approach, called COMOGA, the population is ranked based on constraint violations (counting the number of individuals dominated by each solution). Then, one portion of the population is selected based on constraint ranking, and the rest based on real cost (fitness) of the individuals. COMOGA compared fairly with a penalty-based approach in a pipe-sizing problem, and was less sensitive to changes in the parameters, but the results achieved were not better than those found with a penalty function [50]. It should be added that CO-MOGA requires several extra parameters, although its authors argue that the technique is not particularly sensitive to the values of such parameters.

2. **VEGA**: Parmee and Purchase [40] implemented a version of VEGA that handled the constraints of a gas turbine problem as objectives to allow a GA to locate a feasible region within the highly constrained search space of this application. However, VEGA was not used to further explore the feasible region, and instead the authors used specialized operators that would create a variable-sized hypercube around each feasible point to help the

---

[4] The assumption that we have m constraints will hold throughout this section.

GA to remain within the feasible region at all times. It is important to notice that no real attempt to reach the global optimum was made in this case. Coello [6] also proposed the use of a population-based multiobjective optimization technique such as VEGA to handle each of the constraints of a single-objective optimization problem as an objective. In this case, however, the goal was to approximate the global optimum. At each generation, the population is split into $m + 1$ subpopulations (m is the number of constraints), so that a fraction of the population is selected using the (unconstrained) objective function as its fitness and another fraction uses the first constraint as its fitness and so on. This approach provided good results in several optimization problems [6]. Its main disadvantage was related to scalability issues. However, in a recent application in combinational circuit design we were able to successfully deal with up to 49 objective functions [7]. Furthermore, the approach showed an important improvement (in terms of efficiency) with respect to a previous GA-based approach developed by us for the same task [4].

3. **Line Search and Pareto Dominance**: Camponogara and Talukdar [2] proposed to restate a single-objective optimization problem in such a way that two objectives would be considered: the first would be to optimize the original objective function and the second would be to minimize:

$$\Phi(\mathbf{x}) = \sum_{i=1}^{m} M.[0, g_i(\mathbf{x})]^\beta, \tag{15.5}$$

where β is normally 1 or 2. Once the problem is redefined, nondominated solutions with respect to the two new objectives are generated. The solutions found define a search direction $d = (x_i - x_j)/|x_i - xj|$, where $x_i \in S_i$, $x_j \in S_j$, and S_i and S_j are Pareto sets. The direction search d is intended to simultaneously minimize all the objectives. Line search is performed in this direction so that a solution x can be found such that x dominates x_i and x_j (i.e., x is a better compromise than the two previous solutions found). Line search takes the place of crossover in this approach, and mutation is essentially the same, where the direction d is projected onto the axis of one variable j in the solution space. Additionally, a process of eliminating half of the population is applied at regular intervals (only the less fitted solutions are replaced by randomly generated points). This approach has obvious problems to keep diversity, as it is reflected by the need to discard the worst individuals at each generation. Also, the use of line search increases the computational cost of the approach and what is the impact of the segment chosen to search in the overall performance of the algorithm is not clear.

4. **Min-Max**: Jiménez et al. [34] proposed the use of a Min-Max approach [3] to handle constraints. The main idea of this technique is to apply a set of simple rules to decide the (binary tournament) selection process:
   a) If the two individuals being compared are both feasible, then select based on the minimum value of the objective function.
   b) If one of the two individuals being compared is feasible and the other one is infeasible, then select the feasible individual.
   c) If both individuals are infeasible, then select based on the M.imum constraint violation (M. $g_j(\mathbf{x})$, for $j = 1, \ldots, m$). The individual with the lowest M.imum violation wins.

   A subtle problem with this approach is that the evolutionary process first concentrates only on the constraint satisfaction problem and therefore it samples points in the feasible region essentially at random [51]. This means that in some cases (e.g., when the feasible region is disjoint) we might land in an inappropriate part of the feasible region from which we will not be able to escape. However, this approach may be a good alternative to find a feasible point in a heavily constrained search space. Deb [17] proposed a similar approach but using tournament selection based on feasibility. However, niching was required to maintain diversity in the population.

5. **MOGA**: Coello [5] explored the use of selection based on dominance (defined in terms of feasibility) to handle constraints. In this case, ranking is performed at three different levels: from two feasible individuals the one with the highest fitness is preferred; if one is feasible and the other infeasible, then the first is chosen; if both are infeasible, then the individual with the lowest amount of constraint violation is chosen. This approach uses stochastic universal sampling so that the selection pressure is not too high and no extra procedures are required to maintain diversity. Also, adaptive crossover and mutation rates were adopted as part of the approach.

6. **NPGA**: Coello and Mezura [10] proposed the use of tournaments based on nondominance (as in the NPGA [32]) to handle constraints. An additional parameter, called selection rank (R_s), is added to control the selection pressure of the approach. This parameter makes it unnecessary to use equivalent class sharing (as in the NPGA) to maintain diversity and also decreases the (normally high) selection pressure originated from using tournament selection.

7. **Domain Knowledge and Ranking**: Ray et al. [41] proposed a technique to handle constraints in which the population is ranked both in objective function space and in constraint space. The selection strategy adopted eliminates weaknesses from both spaces and ensures a better constraint satisfaction in the offspring produced. The approach uses niches to maintain diversity with Euclidean distances being the similar measure adopted. It also incorporates mating restrictions based on the information

that each individual has of its own feasibility (this idea was inspired on an earlier approach by Hinterding and Michalewicz [31]), so that the global optimum can be reached through cooperative learning.

Some of the possible trends in this area are the following:

- Use of other MOEAs to handle constraints. Some of these techniques may be rather simple and still remain highly competitive. See, for example, [9].
- Use of online and self-adaptation in constraint-handling techniques both for single- and for multiobjective optimization.
- Extraction and reuse of knowledge obtained from the evolutionary process in order to guide more efficiently the search.
- Design (single-objective optimization) test functions that are particularly difficult for MOEAs to tackle and devise appropriate metrics to measure their performance in this context.

15.7 Where Are We Heading?

Once we have been able to distinguish between the first and second generations in evolutionary multiobjective optimization, a reasonable question is: where are we heading now?

In the last few years, there has been a considerable growth in the number of publications related to evolutionary multiobjective optimization. However, the variety of topics covered is not as rich as the number of publications released each year. The current trend is to either develop new algorithms (validating them with some of the metrics and test functions available) or to develop interesting applications of existing algorithms.

We will finish this section with a list of some of the research topics that we believe that will keep researchers busy during the next few years:

- New metrics with some insightful analysis of their behavior and limitations. Also, metrics that measure not only offline performance, but also online performance are expected to arise.
- More test functions with more than two objectives and with high dimensionality. Concerns about epistasis, deception, dynamic functions, uncertainty, and noise should also be reflected in the upcoming work in this topic.
- Development of a theoretical framework that allows us to analyze the behavior of MOEAs. Topics such as the run-time analysis and bounded convergence times of an MOEA are expected to be tackled in the next few years. We should also expect more work on convergence and on modeling MOEAs using statistical tools.

15.8 Conclusions

This chapter has provided a rather brief and general picture of the past, current, and future research in evolutionary multiobjective optimization. A brief analysis of some of the most popular algorithms reported in the literature has also been provided together with a summary of the main contributions made in this area in the last few years. Finally, some promising areas of future research were also provided.

Our main goal was to provide a motivation for researchers and students to get into this exciting research discipline to tackle the problems that are our main concern right now. Being a young research area, evolutionary multiobjective optimization still has a lot of opportunities to offer to newcomers, and we expect many of them to join us in the next few years.

Acknowledgments

This chapter is representative of the research performed by the Evolutionary Computation Group at CINVESTAV-IPN (EVOCINV). The first author acknowledges support from the mexican Consejo Nacional de Ciencia y Tecnología (CONACyT) through project number 34201-A. The second and third authors acknowledge support from CONACyT through a scholarship to pursue graduate studies at CINVESTAV-IPN's Electrical Engineering Department.

References

1. T. Bäck, D.B. Fogel, and Z. Michalewicz, (1997) (eds.) *Handbook of Evolutionary Computation.* Inst. of Physics Publishing and Oxford University Press, .
2. E. Camponogara and Sarosh N. Talukdar (1997) A genetic algorithm for constrained and multiobjective optimization. In Jarmo T. Alander, (ed.), *3rd Nordic Workshop on Genetic Algorithms and Their Applications (3NWGA)*, pages 49–62, Vaasa, Finland, August 1997. University of Vaasa.
3. V. Chankong and Y.Y. Haimes (1983) *Multiobjective Decision Making: Theory and Methodology.* Systems Science and Engineering. North-Holland.
4. C.A. Coello, A.D. Christiansen, and A. Hernández Aguirre (2000) Use of evolutionary techniques to automate the design of combinational circuits. *Intl. Journal of Smart Engineering System Design*, 2(4):299–314.
5. C.A. Coello Coello (2000) Constraint-handling using an evolutionary multiobjective optimization technique. *Civil Engineering Systems*, 17:319–346.
6. C.A. Coello Coello (2000) Treating Constraints as Objectives for Single-Objective Evolutionary Optimization. *Engineering Optimization*, 32(3):275–308.
7. C.A. Coello Coello, A. Hernández Aguirre, and Bill P. Buckles (2000) Evolutionary multiobjective design of combinational logic circuits. In Jason Lohn, Adrian Stoica, Didier Keymeulen, and Silvano Colombano, (eds.), *Proc. of the Second NASA/DoD Workshop on Evolvable Hardware*, pages 161–170, Los Alamitos, CA, July 2000. IEEE Computer Society.

8. C.A. Coello Coello (1999) A Comprehensive Survey of Evolutionary-Based Multiobjective Optimization Techniques. *Knowledge and Information Systems. An Intl. Journal*, 1(3):269–308.

9. C.A. Coello Coello (2002) Theoretical and Numerical Constraint Handling Techniques used with Evolutionary Algorithms: A Survey of the State of the Art. *Computer Methods in Applied Mechanics and Engineering*, 191(11-12):1245–1287.

10. C.A. Coello Coello and E. Mezura Montes (2002) Handling Constraints in Genetic Algorithms Using Dominance-Based Tournaments. In I.C. Parmee, (ed.), *Proc. of the Fifth Intl. Conf. on Adaptive Computing Design and Manufacture (ACDM 2002)*, volume 5, pages 273–284, University of Exeter, Devon, UK, April 2002. Springer-Verlag.

11. C.A. Coello Coello and G. Toscano Pulido (2001) A Micro-Genetic Algorithm for Multiobjective Optimization. In E. Zitzler, K. Deb, L. Thiele, C.A. Coello Coello, and D. Corne, (eds.), *First Intl. Conf. on Evolutionary Multi-Criterion Optimization*, pages 126–140. Springer-Verlag. Lecture Notes in Computer Science No. 1993, 2001.

12. C.A. Coello Coello and G. Toscano Pulido (2001) Multiobjective Optimization using a Micro-Genetic Algorithm. In L. Spector, E. D. Goodman, A. Wu, W.B. Langdon, H.M. Voigt, M. Gen, S. Sen, M. Dorigo, S. Pezeshk, M. H. Garzon, and E. Burke, (eds.), *Proc. of the Genetic and Evolutionary Computation Conf. (GECCO'2001)*, pages 274–282, San Francisco, California, 2001. Morgan Kaufmann Pub.

13. C.A. Coello Coello, D.A. Van Veldhuizen, and G. B. Lamont (2002) *Evolutionary Algorithms for Solving Multi-Objective Problems*. Kluwer Academic Pub., New York. ISBN 0-3064-6762-3.

14. D.W. Corne, N. R. Jerram, J. D. Knowles, and M. J. Oates (2001) PESA-II: Region-based Selection in Evolutionary Multiobjective Optimization. In Lee Spector, E. D. Goodman, A. Wu, W.B. Langdon, H.M. Voigt, M. Gen, S. Sen, M. Dorigo, S. Pezeshk, M. H. Garzon, and E. Burke, (eds.), *Proc. of the Genetic and Evolutionary Computation Conf. (GECCO'2001)*, pages 283–290, San Francisco, California, 2001. Morgan Kaufmann Pub.

15. D.W. Corne, J. D. Knowles, and M. J. Oates (2000) The Pareto Envelope-based Selection Algorithm for Multiobjective Optimization. In Marc Schoenauer, K. Deb, Günter Rudolph, Xin Yao, Evelyne Lutton, J. J. Merelo, and H.-P. Schwefel, (eds.), *Proc. of the Parallel Problem Solving from Nature VI Conf.*, pages 839–848, Paris, France, 2000. Springer. Lecture Notes in Computer Science No. 1917.

16. I. Das and J. Dennis (1997) A closer look at drawbacks of minimizing weighted sums of objectives for pareto set generation in multicriteria optimization problems. *Structural Optimization*, 14(1):63–69, 1997.

17. K. Deb (2000) An Efficient Constraint Handling Method for Genetic Algorithms. *Computer Methods in Applied Mechanics and Engineering*, 186(2/4):311–338, 2000.

18. K. Deb, S. Agrawal, A. Pratab, and T. Meyarivan (2000) A fast elitist non-dominated sorting genetic algorithm for multi-objective optimization: NSGA-II. KanGAL report 200001, Indian Inst. of Technology, Kanpur, India, 2000.

19. K. Deb, S. Agrawal, A. Pratab, and T. Meyarivan (2000) A fast elitist non-dominated sorting genetic algorithm for multi-objective optimization: NSGA-II. In Marc Schoenauer, K. Deb, Günter Rudolph, Xin Yao, Evelyne Lutton, J. J. Merelo, and H.-P. Schwefel, (eds.), *Proc. of the Parallel Problem Solving from*

Nature VI Conf., pages 849–858, Paris, France, 2000. Springer. Lecture Notes in Computer Science No. 1917.

20. K. Deb, A. Pratap, Sameer Agarwal, and T. Meyarivan (2002) A Fast and Elitist Multiobjective Genetic Algorithm: NSGA–II. *IEEE Trans. on Evolutionary Computation*, 6(2):182–197.

21. F. Y. Edgeworth (1981) *Mathematical Physics*. P. Keagan, London, England, 1881.

22. M. E.son, A. Mayer, and J. Horn (2001) The Niched Pareto Genetic Algorithm 2 Applied to the Design of Groundwater Remediation Systems. In E. Zitzler, K. Deb, L. Thiele, C.A. Coello Coello, and D. Corne, (eds.), *First Intl. Conf. on Evolutionary Multi-Criterion Optimization*, pages 681–695. Springer-Verlag. Lecture Notes in Computer Science No. 1993, 2001.

23. C.M. Fonseca and P. J. Fleming (1993) Genetic algorithms for multiobjective optimization: Formulation, discussion and generalization. In S. Forrest, (ed.), *Proc. of the Fifth Intl. Conf. on Genetic Algorithms*, pages 416–423, San Mateo, CA, 1993. Morgan Kaufmann Pub.

24. M.P. Fourman (1985) Compaction of symbolic layout using genetic algorithms. In *Genetic Algorithms and their Applications: Proc. of the First Intl. Conf. on Genetic Algorithms*, pages 141–153, Hillsdale, NJ, 1985. Lawrence Erlbaum.

25. D.E. Goldberg (1989) *Genetic Algorithms in Search, Optimization and Machine Learning*. Addison-Wesley Publishing Company, Reading, MA.

26. D.E. Goldberg and K. Deb (1991) A comparison of selection schemes used in genetic algorithms. In G.J. E. Rawlins, (ed.), *Foundations of Genetic Algorithms*, pages 69–93. Morgan Kaufmann, San Mateo, CA, 1991.

27. D.E. Goldberg and J. Richardson (1987) Genetic algorithm with sharing for multimodal function optimization. In J. J. Grefenstette, (ed.), *Genetic Algorithms and Their Applications: Proc. of the Second Intl. Conf. on Genetic Algorithms*, pages 41–49, Hillsdale, NJ, 1987. Lawrence Erlbaum.

28. P. Hajela and C. Y. Lin (1992) Genetic search strategies in multicriterion optimal design. *Structural Optimization*, 4:99–107.

29. T. Hanne (2000) On the convergence of multiobjective evolutionary algorithms. *European Journal of Operational Research*, 117(3):553–564.

30. T.Hanne (2000) Global multiobjective optimization using evolutionary algorithms. *Journal of Heuristics*, 6(3):347–360.

31. R. Hinterding and Z. Michalewicz (1998) Your brains and my beauty: Parent matching for constrained optimisation. In *Proc. of the 5th Intl. Conf. on Evolutionary Computation*, pages 810–815, Anchorage, Alaska, May 1998.

32. J. Horn, N. Nafpliotis, and D.E. Goldberg (1994) A niched pareto genetic algorithm for multiobjective optimization. In *Proc. of the First IEEE Conf. on Evolutionary Computation, IEEE World Cong. on Computational Intelligence*, volume 1, pages 82–87, Piscataway, NJ, June 1994. IEEE Service Center.

33. W. Jakob, M. Gorges-Schleuter, and C. Blume (1992) Application of genetic algorithms to task planning and learning. In R. Männer and B. MandE., (eds.), *Parallel Problem Solving from Nature, 2nd Workshop*, Lecture Notes in Computer Science, pages 291–300, Amsterdam, 1992. North-Holland Publishing Company.

34. F. Jiménez, J.L. Verdegay, and A.F. Gómez-Skarmeta (1999) Evolutionary techniques for constrained multiobjective optimization problems. In A. S. Wu, (ed.), *Proc. of the 1999 Genetic and Evolutionary Computation Conf. Workshop Program*, pages 115–116, Orlando, Florida, July 1999.

35. Y. Jin, T. Okabe, and B. Sendhoff (2001) Dynamic Weighted Aggregation for Evolutionary Multi-Objective Optimization: Why Does It Work and How? In Lee Spector, E. D. Goodman, A. Wu, W.B. Langdon, H.M. Voigt, M. Gen, S. Sen, M. Dorigo, S. Pezeshk, M. H. Garzon, and E. Burke, (eds.), *Proc. of the Genetic and Evolutionary Computation Conf. (GECCO'2001)*, pages 1042–1049, San Francisco, California, 2001. Morgan Kaufmann Pub.
36. J. D. Knowles and D.W. Corne (2000) Approximating the nondominated front using the pareto archived evolution strategy. *Evolutionary Computation*, 8(2):149–172.
37. J.N. Morse (1980) Reducing the size of the nondominated set: Pruning by clustering. *Computers and Operations Research*, 7(1–2):55–66.
38. C.K. Oei, D.E. Goldberg, and S.J. Chang (1991) Tournament Selection, Niching, and the Preservation of Diversity. Technical Report 91011, Illinois Genetic Algorithms Laboratory, University of Illinois at Urbana-Champaign, Urbana, Illinois, December 1991.
39. V. Pareto (1896) *Cours D'Economie Politique*, volume I and II. F. Rouge, Lausanne.
40. I. C. Parmee and G. Purchase (1994) The development of a directed genetic search technique for heavily constrained design spaces. In I. C. Parmee, (ed.), *Adaptive Computing in Engineering Design and Control-'94*, pages 97–102, Plymouth, UK, 1994. University of Plymouth, University of Plymouth.
41. T. Ray, T. Kang, and S.K. Chye (2000) An evolutionary algorithm for constrained optimization. In D. Whitley, D. Goldberg, E. Cantú-Paz, L. Spector, I. Parmee, and H.-G. Beyer, (eds.), *Proc. of the Genetic and Evolutionary Computation Conf. (GECCO'2000)*, pages 771–777, San Francisco, California, 2000. Morgan Kaufmann.
42. R. S. Rosenberg (1967) *Simulation of genetic populations with biochemical properties*. PhD thesis, University of Michigan, Ann Arbor, MI.
43. G. Rudolph (1998) On a Multi-Objective Evolutionary Algorithm and Its Convergence to the Pareto Set. In *Proc. of the 5th IEEE Conf. on Evolutionary Computation*, pages 511–516, Piscataway, NJ, 1998. IEEE Press.
44. G. Rudolph and A. Agapie (2000) Convergence Properties of Some Multi-Objective Evolutionary Algorithms. In *Proc. of the 2000 Conf. on Evolutionary Computation*, volume 2, pages 1010–1016, Piscataway, NJ, July 2000. IEEE Press.
45. J.D. Schaffer (1984) *Multiple Objective Optimization with Vector Evaluated Genetic Algorithms*. PhD thesis, Vanderbilt University, Nashville, TN.
46. J.D. Schaffer (1985) Multiple objective optimization with vector evaluated genetic algorithms. In *Genetic Algorithms and their Applications: Proc. of the First Intl. Conf. on Genetic Algorithms*, pages 93–100, Hillsdale, NJ, 1985. Lawrence Erlbaum.
47. J.D. Schaffer and J.J. Grefenstette (1985) Multiobjective learning via genetic algorithms. In *Proc. of the 9th Intl. Joint Conf. on Artificial Intelligence (IJCAI-85)*, pages 593–595, Los Angeles, CA, 1985. AAAI.
48. N. Srinivas and K. Deb (1994) Multiobjective optimization using nondominated sorting in genetic algorithms. *Evolutionary Computation*, 2(3):221–248.
49. W. Stadler (1988) Fundamentals of multicriteria optimization. In W. Stadler, (ed.), *Multicriteria Optimization in Engineering and the Sciences*, pages 1–25. Plenum Press, New York, NY.

50. P.D. Surry and N.J. Radcliffe (1997) The COMOGA method: Constrained optimisation by multiobjective genetic algorithms. *Control and Cybernetics*, 26(3):391–412.
51. P.D. Surry, N.J. Radcliffe, and I.D. Boyd (1995) A multi-objective approach to constrained optimisation of gas supply networks : The COMOGA method. In Terence C. Fogarty, (ed.), *Evolutionary Computing. AISB Workshop. Selected Papers*, pages 166–180, Sheffield, U.K., 1995. Springer-Verlag. Lecture Notes in Computer Science No. 993.
52. D.A. Van Veldhuizen (1999) *Multiobjective Evolutionary Algorithms: Classifications, Analyses, and New Innovations*. PhD thesis, Department of Electrical and Computer Engineering. Graduate School of Engineering. Air Force Inst. of Technology, Wright-Patterson AFB, OH, May 1999.
53. D.A. Van Veldhuizen and G.B. Lamont (1998) Evolutionary computation and convergence to a pareto front. In J.R. Koza, (ed.), *Late Breaking Papers at the Genetic Programming 1998 Conf.*, pages 221–228, Stanford, CA, July 1998. Stanford University Bookstore.
54. P.B. Wilson and M.D. Macleod (1993) Low implementation cost IIR digital filter design using genetic algorithms. In *IEE/IEEE Workshop on Natural Algorithms in Signal Processing*, pages 4/1–4/8, Chelmsford, U.K., 1993.
55. E. Zitzler, K. Deb, and L. Thiele (2000) Comparison of Multiobjective Evolutionary Algorithms: Empirical Results. *Evolutionary Computation*, 8(2):173–195.
56. E. Zitzler, M. Laumanns, and L. Thiele (2001) SPEA2: Improving the Strength Pareto Evolutionary Algorithm. Technical Report 103, Computer Engineering and Networks Laboratory (TIK), Swiss Fed. Inst. of Technology (ETH) Zurich, Gloriastrasse 35, CH-8092 Zurich, Switzerland, May 2001.
57. E. Zitzler and L. Thiele (1999) Multiobjective evolutionary algorithms: A comparative case study and the strength pareto approach. *IEEE Trans. on Evolutionary Computation*, 3(4):257-271.

16

Genetic Algorithms with Limited Convergence

J. Kubalík and L. Rothkrantz, J. Lažanský

16.1 Introduction

Genetic algorithms (GAs) are probabilistic search and optimization techniques, which operate on a population of chromosomes, representing potential solutions of the given problem [10]. In a standard GA, binary strings of ones and zeros represent the chromosomes. Each chromosome is assigned a fitness value that expresses its quality considering the given objective function. Such a population is evolved by means of reproduction and recombination operators in order to breed the optimal solution's chromosome. The evolution is running until some termination condition is fulfilled. The best chromosome encountered so far is then considered as the found solution.

The basic analysis of GA's behavior is based on a notion of a *schema* [15] as a template, which matches a certain class of chromosomes. As the population evolves, some good schemata are represented by increasing number of chromosomes while bad schemata disappear. The fixed positions of those good schemata constitute so-called building blocks (BBs), which represent important components of the final solution. The optimum solution emerges when these building blocks are mixed together in an optimal way in some chromosome.

GAs simultaneously carry out exploitation of the promising regions found so far and exploration of other areas for potentially better solution. The weak point of a GA is that it often suffers from so-called premature convergence, which is caused by an early homogenization of genetic material in the population. This means that no more exploration can be performed. There are many factors affecting the convergence of a GA: the used population size, type and rate of application of crossover and mutation operators, encoding used and many others. Inadequate population size cannot provide the GA with sufficient amount of genetic material to evolve the optimal chromosome. Improperly designed and set genetic operators cannot maintain an optimal balance between exploitation and exploration of the GA.

This paper introduces a novel approach to protect GAs from getting stuck in local optima and so extending the search power of GAs. To achieve this we have proposed a GA where only limited convergence of the population genotype can take place.

The paper starts with an overview of some recent approaches to the problems related somehow to prevent premature convergence, preserving the population diversity (or better the multimodal diversity), and improving the performance of GAs in general. The next section introduces the proposed genetic algorithm with limited convergence and discusses its aspects. Section 16.4 briefly describes the test problems used for experimental evaluation of the proposed algorithm. Empirical results presented in Section 16.5 show that the algorithm performs very well across the representative set of search problems. Especially its explorative power and the ability to keep useful diversity of the population are demonstrated there. Section 16.6 summarizes and concludes the paper and mentions interesting topics to be studied in future in this area.

16.2 Related Work

There are many factors that affect the convergence of a GA. The most influencing and the most frequently studied are the used reproduction strategy, the size of the evolved population, the representation, i.e., the mapping of the problem parameters on a binary string in conventional GAs, and last but not least the used recombination operators and the frequency with which they are applied and other problem-dependent parameters. Let us briefly list some of the approaches that have been recently proposed to tackle the aspects mentioned above.

Dual GAs [3], [4] represent one possible way to introduce some kind of redundancy into the evolved genetic material. The dual GAs use a standard binary representation extended with just one bit, called the head bit or meta bit, which is added to every individual in the population. This bit does not code any information of the represented solution. Instead this extra bit is used to determine the way the informative part of the chromosome will be interpreted. If the value of the head bit is 0, then the rest of the chromosome is taken as it is. Otherwise if the head bit is 1 the string is interpreted as its binary complement. This means that two binary complementary strings represent the same solution. In other words, the population may contain individuals with completely different genotype but with the same phenotype and so the same fitness values.

It has been obvious from the very beginning of the GA's use that the population size plays a crucial role in determining the convergence quality of GAs. The population should be large enough to provide an adequate initial supply of BBs. Another aspect of population sizing involves the decision making between competing BBs. De Jong [5] recognized that the decision making for a particular BB is strongly affected by contributions of other BBs. There are several studies that try to estimate an adequate population size [8], [12], [14]. However, a user should know much information about the problem at hand like the size of the considered BBs, the number of BBs in the problem, the average fitness variance of the considered BB, and some other conservative assumptions in order to be able to use the theoretical estimates.

Another factor that affects the convergence of GA is the selection scheme. Generally, the selection should work so that the chromosomes representing better solutions are given a bigger chance to take part in the process of generating a new and hopefully better population. The extent to which the better chromosomes are favored is measured by so-called selection pressure. However, if the selection pressure is too low, then the convergence to the optimal solution is too slow. In the opposite case, i.e., if the selection pressure is too high, the population is prone to converge very fast toward some suboptimal solution. So commensurate efforts have been spent to analyze various selection schemes and to develop the convergence models of GAs under those selection schemes [1], [11], [13], [23]. In order to keep the desired distribution of fitness values in the population during the whole run, a proper scaling technique [22] might be engaged in GA as well.

GAs are very often engaged in solving multimodal optimization problems. This implies that the ability of the GA to keep just the "raw" diversity is not good enough. Instead the multimodal diversity covering many niches of the search space is required. One early approach to maintain many niches in the GA was based on utilization of so-called shared fitness values that were calculated using a sharing function [9]. The general concept of fitness sharing is based on the idea that each individual's fitness is divided by the number of neighbors within the niche to which the given individual belongs. Thus the goal desired state is such that the population is distributed over a number of different peaks in the search space, with each peak receiving a fraction of the population in proportion to the height of that peak. It results in a situation that the convergence occurs within a niche, but convergence of the full population is avoided.

Other works dealing with maintenance of the population diversity date back to the 1970s. Cavicchio [2] and De Jong [5] came up with techniques called preselection and crowding, respectively. Both are inspired by an ecological phenomenon that similar individuals in the natural population compete against each other for limited resources. Dissimilar individuals tend to occupy different niches, so they typically do not compete. As a result, the number of members of a particular niche does not change during the evolution of the whole population of fixed size. In preselection and crowding this is achieved so that the newly created individuals, which are to be inserted into the population replace the most similar individuals in the current population. The two methods differ in that how the individuals to be replaced are found. In crowding the replacement is found among randomly chosen CF individuals. Preselection assumes that a parent is one of the closest individuals to the generated offspring so the parent is replaced if the competing child is better. Mahfoud studied several strategies of crowding and preselection in [20] and proposed a variation of preselection called deterministic crowding that processes two parents and two offspring at a time and uses phenotypic similarity measure to determine which offspring competes against which parent. He shows that his method is better in clustering solutions about all peaks of the tested problems.

Mengshoel and Goldberg [21] proposed a niching algorithm called probabilistic crowding, which is a successor of the deterministic crowding. The two core ideas in probabilistic crowding are (1) to hold tournaments between similar individuals and (2) to let tournaments be probabilistic. Theoretical analysis and empirical results showed that probabilistic crowding is a simple, stable, predictable, and fast niching algorithm.

A search performance of the GA can be also measured in terms of the size of the search space explored during the run. To efficiently sample the whole search space is the task for recombination operators, i.e., crossover and mutation operators. In standard genetic algorithms the crossover is considered to be of the primary role in an exploration process while the mutation is used to preserve the diversity in the population and to preserve a loss of information [10], [22]. However, the utility of crossover and mutation changes with a population size. A mutation can be more useful than crossover when the population size is small while a crossover is more useful when the population is large.

A proper use of recombination operators is even harder since there are many different variants of crossover. The implementations differ between each other in many aspects. The disruption effect of crossover, first analyzed for 1-point crossover in [15], is the probability that the crossover will disrupt long schemata. This is important to predict how the promising schemata will be propagated to subsequent populations. De Jong and Spears [6] characterized recombination in terms of productivity and exploration power. Those characteristics describe the ability of crossover to generate new sample points in the search space. De Jong and Spears also derived a heuristics that the more disruptive crossovers (which are also more productive and explorative) are better when the population is small and less disruptive operators are better when the population is large relative to the problem size. For more recent work on the role of recombination operators, see [26].

Another approach is to dynamically adapt the rates of the utilization of multiple operators during the run. Spears [25] used an extra tag-bit attached to every individual to store the information about which crossover (1 is 2-point and 0 is uniform crossover) should be preferred when crossing two parental chromosomes. So if the parents both have 1 at the tag-bit position, then the 2-point crossover is used. Similarly, if both have 0, then uniform is used. Otherwise one of the two operators is chosen with a probability 0.5. Spears found that this adaptive approach always had a performance intermediate between the best and worst of the two single recombination operators.

Srinivas and Patnaik [27] used adaptive probabilities of crossover and mutation to achieve the twin goals of maintaining diversity in the population and sustaining convergence capacity of the GA. They increased the probability of crossover and mutation when the population was stuck at local optima and decreased the probabilities when the population was scattered in the solution space. They also considered the need to preserve "good" solutions. This was attempted by having low probabilities for highly fit individuals while poor solutions will encounter high probability of crossover and mutation rate.

Kubalík and Lažanský proposed so-called partially randomized crossover operators (PRX) as an enhancement of the traditional crossover operators used for binary representation [16], [17], [18]. The enhancement of the crossover functionality is in a modified treatment of a common schema of the parents, which are the bits common to both parental chromosomes. Standard operators work so that both offspring inherit unchanged all the bits of the common schema. As the population converges, the common schema occupies a growing portion of the parent chromosomes and so the crossover can produce only little new. The PRX operators do not strictly preserve the common schema of the parents, since in one of the two generated offspring, a portion of the common schema is changed with the probability that evolves during the run. Thus, the population is not saturated with superior building blocks but also with their randomly chosen binary complements. The diversity of the population is permanently maintained, which helps to preserve the SGA from getting stuck in a local optimum and enhance the exploration of the search space beyond the limits imposed by the pure evolution.

The PRX operators were engaged in genetic algorithms with permanent re-initialization of parental common schemata proposed in [19]. The algorithm forks the search into two directions when creating a new population from the old one. To do so the main generation cycle consists of two steps. First, the primary population is evolved for M generations with the use of the PRX crossover in order to produce both the direct and randomized offspring. The randomized offspring are stored in the secondary population. Since it is derived from the primary population, it still has much in common with the "main stream" evolution so it does not represent quite random samples of the search space. As such the secondary population represents a source of hopefully useful diverse genetic material. Then the secondary population is refined through a short evolution running for N generations. Finally, these two populations are merged together into one new primary population and the new main iteration can be launched. The empirical results show that in such a way a diversity of the population can easily be maintained while converging faster and to better solutions than with the standard GA.

16.3 Genetic Algorithms with Limited Convergence

This section describes a novel approach to improve the performance of GAs. The main goal of the proposed algorithm, called the *genetic algorithm with limited convergence* (GALCO), is to maintain the fruitful diversity of the evolved population during the whole run and so to preserve a GA from getting stuck in local optima. To achieve this a concept of imposing limits on the convergence of the population is adopted.

The algorithm inherits most of the features from the standard GA working on a binary representation. In fact it is a type of the incremental GA where only one crossover operation is performed in each generation cycle (the step from the old to the new population). As such it uses a standard selection strategy to choose the parents, a classical crossover operator (2-point crossover is used here, as commented further) for generating new chromosomes, and special rule for inserting of the offspring chromosomes into the population. What makes the GALCO unique is just the way the convergence of the population is maintained within specified boundaries.

There is a limit imposed on the maximum convergence of every position of the representation. Let us denote the vector of genes at the ith position of the chromosome over the whole population as the ith column of the population. Then the limit is expressed as a symmetric integer interval $[PopSize/2 - C, PopSize/2 + C]$, where $PopSize$ is the population size. The parameter C denotes the *convergence rate*. Its value is the input parameter to the algorithm and can be chosen from the range 0 to $PopSize/2$. Strictly speaking, $2 \times C$ defines the maximal allowed difference of the frequency of ones and zeros in every column of the population. So the ratio of ones and zeros must be $1 : 1$ during the whole run in the case of $C = 0$ or the ratio can change up to $0 : PopSize$ in favor of either ones or zeros for $C = PopSize/2$. This is a principal condition of the algorithm. To keep the condition valid during the whole run a special insertion rule for incorporating offspring into the population has been used.

The functional scheme of the GALCO is shown in Figure 16.3. First an initial population of chromosomes is generated. It is made sure that the distribution of ones and zeros does not violates the convergence constraint at any position of the chromosome. In our case the evolution starts from maximally diverse population, i.e., every column of the population consists of an equal number $PopSize/2$ of ones and zeros regardless of the chosen convergence range. The body of the algorithm is through steps 2–5, which realizes the generation cycle of the incremental GA. In step 2 a pair of parental chromosomes is chosen according to the used selection strategy (a tournament selection is used here). Then the parents are crossed over using the 2-point crossover to yield two new chromosomes. Note that there is no parameter specifying the rate of application of the crossover needed since the parents always undergo this operation. The 2-point crossover was chosen intentionally since it is the least disruptive recombination operator among the standard

```
Step 1   Generate initial population of size PopSize
Step 2   Choose parents
Step 3   Create offspring using the 2-point crossover
Step 4   Insert the offspring into the population according
         to the following rule
         if (max(child1,child2) > max(parent1,parent2))
         then replace both parents with the children
         else{
           find(current_worst)
           replace_with_mask(child1, current_worst)
           find(current_worst)
           replace_with_mask(child2, current_worst)
         }
Step 5   if (not finished) then go to Step 2
```

Figure 16.1. A functional schema of the GALCO algorithm.

operators. So it is best suited for preserving the promising building blocks when mixing genes of two parental chromosomes. It is supposed to be a good counterpart to the artificially maintained rather high diversity in the population (as will be shown in Section 16.5, the best performance of the algorithm is achieved with the convergence rate $C << PopSize/2$). There is no explicit mutation operator used in the algorithm.

The most important action of the algorithm comes in step 4. Here the offspring is inserted to the population according to the insertion rule, which follows two main objectives: (1) to use as much of the genetic material of the newly generated individuals as possible and (2) not to violate the maximal allowed convergence rate. In practice this is implemented so that both children replace their parents iff at least one of the children has better fitness than both parents. Otherwise the children replace the worst individuals of the current population using the *replace_ with_ mask* operator described below.

The effect of replacing the parents with both offspring in the "then part of the rule" is such that the distributions of ones and zeros do not change in any column of the population. This is obvious since the genetic material of parents and their children is invariant through the application of the crossover operation. Thus it is ensured that if the old population does comply with the desired convergence range the new population must comply with the convergence range as well.

A slightly more complicated situation arises when the children are both of rather poor quality. Replacing the parents with their offspring irrespectively of the offspring quality would cause problems with a slow convergence to the optimal solution. Note that the case the parents produce fitter offspring is much less frequent than the opposite case, i.e., that both offspring are worse than the better parent. So the breeding phase (crossover plus replacement of parents) would be in most cases counterproductive. Moreover the elitism,

```
for(i=0;i<chrom_length;i++){
    change = child.genes[i]-current_worst.genes[i]
    if(PopSize/2 - C < conv[i] + change < PopSize/2 + C) then{
        convergence[i] = convergence[i] + change
        current_worst.genes[i] = child.genes[i]
    }
}
```

Figure 16.2. A functional schema of the *replace_ with_ mask* operator.

i.e., preserving of the best individual in the population could not be ensured. Apparently if the best individual in the population was selected as a parent and did not succeed to generate at least the same fit offspring, the best so far solution would disappear from the population when replaced by the offspring. On the other hand, the evolution should not be restricted only to those rather singular moments when the parents breed something better than they are. Some reasonable way to use the newly generated chromosomes whatever good they are might be very useful since it would considerably increase the rate of sampling of the search space.

The tradeoff between exploration power and exploitation ability of the algorithm is accomplished by placing the generated offspring into the population using the *replace_ with_ mask* operator. Generally any chromosome of the population can be replaced. Here, the chromosomes representing the least-fit solutions are chosen in order to reduce the loss of quality due to the operation performed on the replaced individual. Note that it is necessary to start seeking for the worst individual from a randomly chosen position in the population in order to ensure that any out of the multiple worst individuals can be chosen with an equal probability. If one did not take care of it, the first or the last (depending on the implementation of the search routine) worst individual in the population would be chosen all the time that would restrict the sampling effect of the operator.

The operator works so that it traverses the chromosome of the worst individual and replaces its ith gene with a corresponding gene of the child's chromosome if and only if such a change is legal. So the bit is replaced if this does not make the frequency of ones and zeros of the corresponding column of the population to exceed the allowed convergence range. Otherwise the original gene of the worst chromosome retains in the population. It is apparent that the role of the *replace_ with_ mask* operator is twofold: it enables the pair of offspring, which do not improve the parents' best as well as the worst individual in the population to contribute to the population genotype. Note that usually neither the inserted nor the replaced chromosome remains unchanged when the operator is applied. Instead the genetic material of the two chromosomes is mixed in the resultant chromosome. So the operation should be seen as a merging of two chromosomes rather than an inserting of a new one in the population. One should expect that at the beginning of the run the genes of the new offspring would dominate in the so-composed chromosome while in the later stages of the run more and more genes of the old chromosome would be retained. Particular characteristics depend on many factors such as the used value of the parameter C, the character of the solved problem, etc. Apparently the greater the C is the more of the offspring's genes are used in the early phase of the run, and vice versa. An example of how the bias can change during the run will be shown in Section 16.5 with experiments. Also the impact of the use of the operator on the performance of the whole algorithm will be empirically tested there.

From this point of view such an operation of merging of two chromosomes can be considered as a kind of biased uniform crossover as well, where the bias is in favor of either the old or the new chromosome. In this sense the whole algorithm belongs to the class of approaches, which try to profit from simultaneous utilization of the most and the least explorative crossover operators uniform and 2-point [25]. Here the 2-point crossover is used as lets say primary or explicit recombination operator while the form of uniform crossover appears as a side effect of preventing the population from becoming too homogenous. Last but not least an implicit elitism embodied in the algorithm should be mentioned. Any worse individual can replace the best individual of the current population neither by replacing the parents with their offspring (since it happens only if the offspring is better) nor by application of the *replace_with_mask* operator. So the best-so-far fitness value can only improve during the evolution.

To implement those decision makings performed within the operator *replace_with_mask* an integer vector convergence is used to store the gene distribution statistics of all columns of the population. The ith vector element is updated whenever a corresponding gene changes its value. Note that all vector elements must be from $[PopSize/2 - C,\ PopSize/2 + C]$ during the whole run. The vector of convergence statistics can be considered as a mask (this is where the name of the operator is derived from), specifying for each position of the replaced chromosome whether it can be changed or not.

16.4 Test Problems

This section briefly describes the test problems that were used in the experiments described in the next section. The presented selection of the problems was made with intention to cover nonlinear function optimizations, deceptive, royal road, hierarchically decomposable, and multiple-optima problems.

The first test problem is based on function F101(x,y) taken from [31]. The function is defined as follows:

$$F101(x, y) = -x \cdot \sin(\sqrt{|x - y - 47|}) - (y + 47) \cdot \sin(\sqrt{|y + 47 + x/2|}),$$

where the parameters x and y are coded on 10 bits and converted to integer values from the interval $(-512, 511)$.

The function is used as basic building block of the problem. It is nonlinear nonseparable, and highly multimodal function of two variables. This means that the optimal value of one variable cannot be determined independently of the other parameter. Here the whole problem is constructed in such a way that it consists of 7 triples $x_1 - y - x_2$, where each one contributes to the overall fitness with the value $F101(x_1, y) + F101(x_2, y)$. So the parameter y is nonlinearly bound with two other parameters x_1 and x_2, which makes the problem even more difficult. The total length of the chromosome is 210 bits. The fitness of the whole chromosome is calculated as the average value of those 7 function contributions. The global minimum value of the problem composed of $F101(x, y)$ is –955.96.

The next test problem is a representative of the deceptive problems, i.e., problems that are intentionally designed to make GAs converge toward some local deceptive optimum. Here, the problem is composed of the deceptive function DF3 taken from [30], which is 4-bit fully deceptive function with one global optimum in the string 1110 of the fitness 30. The function has a deceptive attractor 0000 of fitness 10, which is surrounded, in the search space, by four strings containing just one 1 with quite high fitness values 28, 27, 26, and 25. The problem is formed as concatenation of 50 DF3 functions resulting in a 200-bit-long chromosome. Thus the global optimum of the problem is 1500. The definition of the search space of the DF3 function is shown in Figure 16.4.

The used Royal Road problem (RR) is a 16-bit version of the RR1 single-level royal road problem described in [7]. The problem is defined by enumerating the schemata, where each schema s_i has assigned its contribution coefficient c_i. The evaluation of an arbitrary chromosome is given as a sum of all contributions of those schemata that are covered by the chromosome. The used RR problem is defined as a concatenation of 10 16-bit schemata of all ones. All building blocks have the equal contribution 16. Only the combination of all ones on the bits pertinent to a given schema contributes to

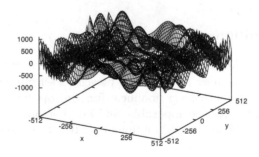

Figure 16.3. Nonlinear and highly multimodal function $F101(x, y)$.

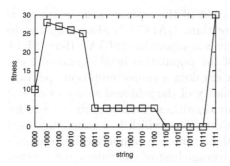

Figure 16.4. Deceptive function DF3.

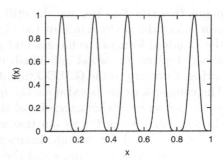

Figure 16.5. Deb's periodic function $F1(x)$.

the fitness with the nonzero value, any other combination has value 0. So the optimal solution is the string of all ones with its fitness 160.

Another test problem used in our experiments is a representative of hierarchically decomposable problems, namely the hierarchical-if-and-only-if function (H-IFF) proposed in [29]. The hierarchical block structure of the function is a balanced binary tree. Each block, consisting of two subblocks (a pair of its children), contributes to the overall fitness by the value, which depends on its interpretation (*meaning*) and its level in the tree. Each leaf node, corresponding to a single gene, contributes to the fitness by 1. Each inner node x is interpreted as 1 if and only if its children are both 1s, as 0 iff they are both 0s. In such a case the node contributes to the fitness by value $2^{height(x)}$, where $height(x)$ is the distance from the node x to its antecedent leaves. Otherwise the node is interpreted as *null* and its contribution is 0. It follows from its definition that the function has two global optima, one consists of all 1s and one of all 0s. For our purposes the 256-bit H-IFF function with the global optima of value 2304 was used.

The last test function is the function F1 taken from [20] that was used to analyze the ability of the GALCO algorithm to maintain multiple optimal solutions in the population. The function is defined in the interval (0.0, 1.0) as follows:

$$F1(x) = \sin^6(5\pi x),$$

where the parameter x is coded on 30 bits so that the string of all zeros represents 0.0 and the string of all ones represent 1.0. The function is periodic with 5 equally spaced maxima of equal height; see Figure 16.5.

16.5 Experiments

This section presents an empirical analysis of the GALCO algorithm and shows some interesting aspects of this approach. The series of experiments were carried out to reveal how the factors such as the convergence rate C, the population size *PopSize*, and the utilization of the *replace_with_mask* operator affect the performance of the algorithm. GALCO is also compared to the standard form of the incremental genetic algorithm (SIGA). Here, SIGA always replaces the worst individuals of the population by the generated offspring. Contrary to the GALCO, SIGA employs a simple mutation operator. The comparisons are based upon the quality of the achieved solutions as well as the convergence characteristics of the algorithms. Both algorithms run for the same number of fitness function evaluations, which is a commonly used condition when different evolutionary algorithms are compared. Each experiment were replicated 20 times and the average best-of-run values and average convergence courses are presented in tables and graphs.

Let us first focus on how the performance of the algorithm depends on the chosen convergence rate C. Results achieved with various values of C are in Table 16.1. We can observe that small values of C (means that rather low convergence is allowed) give better results than the bigger ones in general. This confirms our assumption that the less the population can get homogenous the higher the chance that better results will be generated is. However, this assertion holds just when rather extreme values of C are considered. The trend across the whole interval of C is such that starting from big C the performance improves as the C decreases until some optimum value of C is reached (results written in bold). Further when the C decreases, the quality of the obtained solutions does not improve any more while the time needed to find the optimal solution increases.

Apparently this is caused by the fact that the more diverse the population is kept (an extreme case $C = 0$ is discussed further) the more the convergence toward the optimal solution slows down. Thus we can see that the average best-of-run value achieved with $C = 1$ is worse than that achieved with the optimal $C = 20$ in the case of F101. In the case of DF3 and H-IFF problems the optimal average best-of-run values were achieved even with $C = 1$ but it

Table 16.1. An Effect of Varying Convergence Range on a Performance of the GALCO

C	F101	DF3	H-IFF	RR
225	-918	1480	1344	26
200	-920	1490	1675	37
100	-930	1496	2304	56
50	-941	1500	2304	140
20	**-943**	**1500**	**2304**	150
10	-942	1500	2304	152
5	-942	1500	2304	154
1	-941	1500	2304	**160**
0	-927	1498.5	1453	86

* The population size 500 was used.

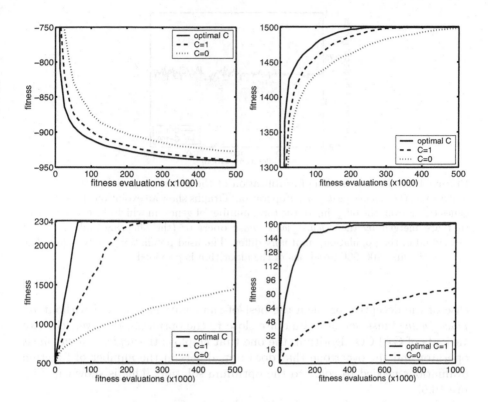

Figure 16.6a–d. Mean convergence curves obtained with the optimal convergence rate C, convergence rate $C=1$ and $C=0$ on the problem F101 (**a**), DF3 (**b**), H-IFF (**c**), and RR (**d**). The population size 500 was used.

took considerably longer time to find them. See Figure 16.6, where the average convergence curves with the optimal C and $C = 1$ are shown.

Let us have a look at the results on the RR problem now. This is the problem that requires the least convergence rate to get the best results. This results from the nature of the benchmark. There are no smaller building blocks available besides those predefined 16-bits ones, which would guide the algorithm toward the complete optimal solution. So the algorithm can only rely on maximal diversity of individuals that would maximize a chance that all building blocks will be generated and combined in one optimal chromosome.

It is also interesting to see the effect of the *replace_with_mask* operator. The results of experiments carried out with disabled replacement operator are in the last row of Table 16.1, where $C = 0$. It is evident that the operator greatly improves the performance of GALCO if used with a reasonable frequency. There are considerable differences in average best-of-run values obtained on problems F101, H-IFF, and especially on RR. In the

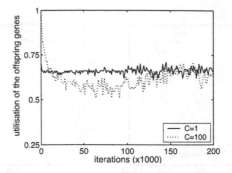

Figure 16.7. Demonstration of a utilization of the genetic material of the offspring undergoing the *replace_ with_ mask* operation. Graphs show an evolution of the ratio of genes taken from the offspring to the total number of genes, in which the chromosomes that are merged by the *replace_ with_ mask* operator (the offspring and the worst individual in the population), mutually differ. The used population size was 250. The view of the first 200, 000 iterations of the algorithm is provided.

case of the deceptive problem the best-of-run solutions achieved without *re-place_ with_ mask* operator are quite close to the optimum. However, the two variants of GALCO algorithm, the one that employs the *replace_ with_ mask* operator and the other one that does not, differs in the number of function evaluations needed to come to the optimum solution. This is shown in Figure 16.6.

These results confirm our intuition that not only a crossover operator applied explicitly to promising parents enables the good building blocks to combine. Also a mixing of the genetic information of two rather poor chromosomes by the replacement operator is very fruitful. One should see that in this way the worst individual in the population is given a high chance that its genes or complete building blocks will be combined with other genetic material. Note that without the replacement operator such a chance would be very small since the worst individual is almost unlikely to be chosen as a parent.

Figure 16.7 shows an evolution of a utilization of genes taken from the offspring chromosome. We can see that the characteristics differ from each other in a way one would expect. When a small convergence rate is used (i.e., $C = 1$) the proportion of genes taken from the offspring is stable (around the value 2/3) during the whole run. The bigger C is used (situation for $C = 100$ is shown here) the more of the offspring genes can be used in the early stages of the run. At the beginning of the run the offspring chromosome completely replaces the worst chromosome of the population. As the population converges i.e., the distribution of ones and zeros in the population columns reaches the boundary values (either $PopSize - C$ or $PopSize + C$) the utilization of the offspring genes drops down and then stabilizes around the value 2/3 as in the former case. Note that the proportion of the worst individual genes is the

Table 16.2. An Effect of Varying Population Size on a Performance of the GALCO

PopSize	F101	DF3	H-IFF	RR
20	-928	1500	2304	68
50	-937	1500	2304	147
100	-943	1500	**2304**	154
150	**-949**	**1500**	2304	159
200	-946	1500	2304	160
250	-945	1500	2304	160
500	-941	1500	2304	160
1000	-928	1500	2304	**160**

* The convergence range $C = 1$ was used in these experiments.

complement to 1.0. So a considerable number of genes of the worst individual are used as well.

Another factor, which strongly affects a performance of GAs, is the size of the population. General trend in standard GAs is that the bigger the used population is, the better results can be achieved. This is because the big population provides better supply of necessary fundamental building blocks when it is initialized and is less subject to premature convergence. On the other hand, the evolution of large population toward high-quality solutions may be too slow and at the expense of more computations performed (measured for instance by a number of performed fitness function evaluations or crossover operations).

The results of experiments carried out in order to investigate a sensitivity of the GALCO to population size are presented in Table 16.2.

There are two important observations. First, the performance of the algorithm depends on the population size in a similar way as other GAs. As the population size increases, the quality of the obtained results improves until an optimal population size is reached (the results written in bold). Further increasing of the size slows down the convergence to the optimal solution. In the case of F101 much worse solutions were found with population size 1000 than with the population size 150. Similarly, much slower convergence

Table 16.3. Results of the SIGA Algorithm with Varying Population Sizes

PopSize	F101	DF3	H-IFF	RR
500	-877	1449	1234	149
1000	-907	1464	1348	150
1500	-909	1473	1382	144
2000	**-912**	**1476**	**1501**	147

* Other parameters of the SIGA were $P_{cross} = 1.0$, $P_{mut} = 0.01$, and the number of fitness function evaluations was 500,000.

to optimal solutions were observed when large populations ($PopSize > 200$) were used on DF3 and H-IFF problems. Again when solving the RR problem the best results were achieved with the biggest tested population size. A strange phenomenon can be observed on the DF3 problem. There, the optimal solution was found even with a small population of 20 individuals. Such an unusual success of the algorithm on this benchmark could be easily explained. Recall that the DF3 function is a fully deceptive function with the deceptive attractor in the string, which is a binary complement of the global desired optimum. This means that the deceptive building blocks (those with all 0s or at most one 1) tend to gradually proliferate in the population. However the saturation of the population with those building blocks is limited due to the $C = 1$. So in reaction to the increased number of deceptive building blocks the number of building blocks composed of all 1s grows as well in order to keep the balance of 1s and 0s in the population. Obviously such a mechanism should work whenever a string representing a local optimum is close to the binary complement of the global optimum string.

The second observation is that the algorithm does not require very large populations to be able to solve the problems. In fact, rather small populations (100–200 for our test problems, except the RR problem) can be used with GALCO to effectively search a complex solution space. This becomes evident when compared to the results obtained with the standard incremental GA (SIGA), see Table 16.3. While the SIGA needs a large population to come up with good solutions, the GALCO profits from its inherent explorative power described above. A comparison of the GALCO and SIGA in terms of the average convergence characteristics is shown in Figure 16.8. We can see that the GALCO outperforms the SIGA on all test problems. An especially remarkable difference between the two algorithms can be observed on F101, DF3, and H-IFF problems, where SIGA did not give any comparably good result even with population size 2000.

As we mentioned in the previous section some experiments were performed to test the GALCO algorithm on its ability to discover many different global optima. The plots in Figure 16.9 show how the population samples the solution space of the F1 function after 50,000 and 500,000 performed fitness function evaluations. It turned out that the algorithm is able to maintain a number of samples for each peak of the function. As the evolution goes on the individuals in the population become better and better. An important observation is that the proportions of the population are almost stable during this process.

16.6 Summary and Conclusions

We have introduced a novel approach for preserving population diversity. It is based on an idea that the population is explicitly prevented from becoming too homogenous by simply imposing limits on its convergence. This is done by specifying the maximum difference between frequency of ones and zeros

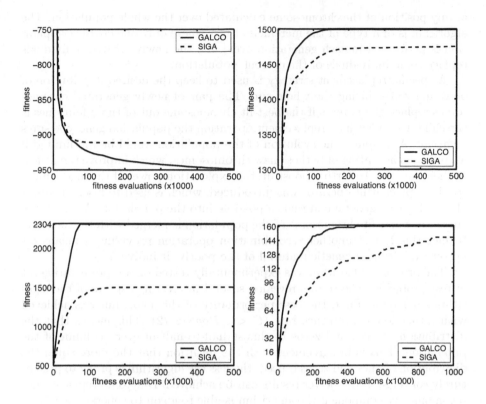

Figure 16.8a–d. Comparison of the convergence characteristics of GALCO and SIGA on the problem F101 (**a**), DF3 (**b**), H-IFF (**c**), and RR (**d**). It shows the convergence characteristics corresponding to the experiments marked bold in Table 16.2 and Table 16.3, respectively.

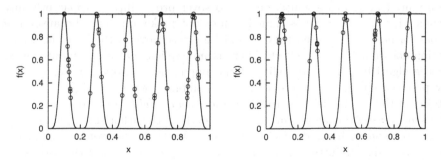

Figure 16.9a–b. The final distribution of 100 solutions after 50,000 (**a**) and 500,000 (**b**) fitness function evaluations. Proportions of the population after 50,000 and 500,000 evaluations are 24-18-19-19-20 and 26-16-22-17-19, respectively.

at any position of the chromosome calculated over the whole population. The algorithm is of a type of the incremental GA where only one crossover operation is performed in each generation cycle and the newly created individuals replace some individuals of the current population.

A specific replacement strategy is used to keep the desired distribution of ones and zeros during the whole run. The pair of newly generated chromosomes replace the parents if the best-fit chromosome out of those four ones is the child. Under such an replacement operation the population genotype stays invariant. Apparently the evolution of the population would be too limited if we relied on accepting only those new chromosomes, which improve the fitness of their parents. To further boost up the exploration power of the algorithm a special replacement operator was introduced, which is used to insert as much of the offspring genetic material as possible into the population. Actually the currently worst-fit chromosome of the population is merged with the new one. In fact this is just another recombination operation providing a means for better exploiting of genetic material of the poorly fit individuals.

The proposed algorithm was experimentally tested on a representative set of test problems. The results revealed several interesting aspects of the algorithm's behavior. First, the best performance of the algorithm was achieved with rather low convergence rate ($C << PopSize/2$). This means that the distribution of ones and zeros is almost half-to-half in every column of the population. This is in agreement with the intuition that the more equal the distribution of ones and zeros is used, the less the algorithm is prone to prematurely converge so the better results can be achieved. Due to its replacement–recombinative component the algorithm is able to go on to generate new sample points of the search space even after the global optimum has been found. It was also shown that the algorithm is capable of maintaining multimodal diversity of the population. So representatives of various optima can co-exist in the population during the whole evolution.

An interesting aspect of the proposed algorithm is that it does not require any tuning of the mutation or crossover probabilities. Apparently any probability of crossover less than 1.0 does not make any sense because once a pair of parents is chosen they should be crossed over, otherwise the whole action does not have any effect. There is no explicit mutation operator used in the algorithm. The variability of the population genotype is maintained by preservation of the gene distribution combined with the high generative ability of the recombination crossover and *replace_ with_ mask* operators. For the same reason the algorithm works efficiently with rather small populations in comparison with standard GA. It was shown that from some value of the population size its further increasing is counterproductive and the process of finding the optimum solution slows down.

Concluding this chapter we can say that the GALCO algorithm exhibits many nice features. However, they were presented and confirmed only in an empirical way. Future research in this area should focus on theoretical analysis of the algorithm. That would help us to better understand its behavior and to estimate its convergence characteristics. Note that for our evaluation purposes we have used test problems composed of tightly linked building blocks. The applicability of the algorithm to the problems with low linkage, i.e., the problems with building blocks spread across the chromosome, should be studied as well.

Acknowledgments

The authors would like to thank Petr Posik for many valuable comments and Stepan Janda for his help with carrying out the experiments.

The first author acknowledges the support provided by the TU Delft within a frame of the Research Fellowship Program. The research was funded by the project No. 102/02/0132 of the Grant Agency of the Czech Republic.

References

1. Baker, J.E. (1987) Reducing Bias and Inefficiency in the Selection Algorithm. In *Proceedings of the Fourth International Conference on Genetic Algorithms*, Lawrence Erlbaum Associates, Hillsdale, pp. 14–21
2. Cavicchio, D.J. (1970) *Adaptive search using simulated evolution*, Ph.D. Thesis, Univ. of Michigan, Ann Arbor.
3. Collard, P., Gaspar, A. (1996) Royal-road landscapes for a dual genetic algorithm, in W. Wahlster, editor, *ECAI 96: 12th European Conference on Artificial Intelligence*, Wiley & Son, pp 214–217
4. Collard, P., Escazut, C. (1996) Fitness Distance Correlation in a Dual Genetic Algorithm, in W. Wahlster, ed., *ECAI 96: 12th European Conference on Artificial Intelligence*, Wiley & Son, pp. 218–222
5. De Jong, K.A. (1975) *An Analysis of the Behavior of a Class of Genetic Adaptive Systems*, Doctoral Thesis, Dept. of Computer and Communication Sciences, Univ. of Michigan, Ann Arbor,
6. De Jong, K.A., Spears, W. (1992) A formal analysis of the role of multi-point crossover in genetic algorithms, *Annals of Mathematics and Artificial Intelligence* (Switzerland: J C Baltzer A G Scientific Publishing Company), pp. 1-26.
7. Forrest, S., and M. Mitchell. (1993) Relative building-block fitness and the Building Block Hypothesis, in Whitley, L.D. (Ed.), *Foundations of Genetic Algorithms 2*, pp. 109-126. San Mateo, CA: Morgan Kaufmann.
8. Goldberg, D.E. (1985) Optimal Initial Population Size for Binary-Coded Genetic Algorithms,. TCGA Report No. 85001, University of Alabama, Department of Engineering Mechanics.
9. Goldberg, D.E., Richardson, J.J. (1987) Genetic algorithms with sharing for multimodal function optimization, *Genetic Algorithms and Their Applications: Proceedings of the Second ICGA*, Lawrence Erlbaum Associates, Hillsdale, NJ, pp 41-49
10. Goldberg D.E. (1989) *Genetic Algorithms in Search, Optimization and Machine Learning*, Addison-Wesley, Reading, MA.

11. Goldberg, D.E., Deb, K. (1991) A comparative analysis of selection schemes used in genetic algorithms, in Rawlins, G. J. E. (Ed.), *Foundations of Genetic Algorithms*, San Mateo, CA: Morgan Kaufmann, pp. 69-93

12. Goldberg, D.E., Deb, K., Clark, J.H. (1992) Genetic algorithms, noise, and the sizing of populations. *Complex Systems*, 6:333-362,

13. Goldberg, D.E., Sastry, K. (2001) A Practical Schema Theorem for Genetic Algorithms Design and Tuning, IlliGAL Report No. 2001017, Illinois Genetic Algorithms Laboratory, University of Illinois at Urbana-Champaign,

14. Harik, G., Cantu-Paz, E., Goldberg, D.E., and Miller, B. L: (1999) The gambler's ruin problem, genetic algorithms, and the sizing of populations, *Evolutionary Computation*, 7(3):231-253

15. Holland J.H. (1975) *Adaptation in Natural and Artificial Systems*. University of Michigan Press, Ann Arbor.

16. Kubalík, J., Lažanský, J. (2000) Partially randomised Crossover Operators, In: *Advances in Soft Computing*, R. John & R. Birkenhead (Eds.), Heidelberg: Physica-Verlag, pp 93-98.

17. Kubalík, J., Lažanský, J. (2001) A New Genetic Operator Maintaining Population Diversity, in *AIP Conference Proceedings of CASYS '2000*, Dubois, D. (Ed.), American Institute of Physics, pp. 338-348.

18. Kubalík, J., Lažanský, J. (2000) A New Genetic Operator with Enhanced Capabilities. In: *Quo Vadis Computational Intelligence?* Sincák, P. (ed.), Physica-Verlag, Heidelberg, Germany, pp. 305-310.

19. Kubalík, J., Lažanský, J., Rothkrantz, L.J.M. (2001) On Extending of Search Power of Genetic Algorithms by Means of Permanent Re-initialisation of Parental Common Schema, in *Proceeding of Mendel 2001*, Brno University of Technology, pp. 1-6.

20. Mahfoud, S.W. (1992) Crowding and Preselection Revisited, *Parallel Problem Solving From Nature*, 2, R. Manner and B. Manderick (Eds), Elsevier Science Publishers (North Holland), Amsterdam, pp. 27-36.

21. Mengshoel, O.J., Goldberg, D.E. (1999) Probabilistic Crowding: Deterministic Crowding with Probabilistic Replacement, in *Proceedings of the Genetic and Evolutionary Computation Conference*, W. Banzhaf, J. Daida, A. E. Eiben, M. H. Garzon, V. Honavar, M. Jakiela, R. E. Smith (Eds), Morgan Kaufmann Publishers, California,

22. Michalewicz Z. (1994) *Genetic Algorithms + Data Structures = Evolution Programs*, Springer-Verlag, Berlin Heidelberg, Second edition.

23. Miller, B., Goldberg, D.E. (1995) Genetic Algorithms, Tournament Selection, and the Effects of Noise. IlliGAL Report No. 95006, Urbana: University of Illinois, Illinois Genetic Algorithms Laboratory.

24. Oei, C.K., Goldberg, D.E., Chang, S. J. (1991) Tournament selection, niching, and the preservation of diversity, IlliGAL Report No. 91011, Illinois Genetic Algorithms Laboratory, University of Illinois at Urbana-Champaign.

25. Spears, W.M. (1995) Adapting Crossover in Evolutionary Algorithms, in *Proceedings of the Fourth Annual Conference on Evolutionary Programming*, J.R. McDonnel, R. G. Reynolds and D.B. Fogel, eds., MIT press, Cambridge, 1995, pp 367-384

26. Spears, W.M. (1997)Recombination Parameters, in *Handbook of Evolutionary Computation*, T. Back, D.B. Fogel, and Z. Michalewicz, eds., New York: Oxford Univ. Press and Institute of Physics, pp E1:3:1-11

27. Srinivas,M., and Patnaik, L. M. (1994) Adaptive Probabilities of Crossover and Mutation in Genetic Algorithms, in *IEEE Transaction of Systems, Man and Cybernetics*, 24:656-667

28. Thierens, D., Goldberg, D.E.: (1994) Elitist Recombination: an integrated selection recombination GA. In *Proceedings of The First IEEE Conference on Evolutionary Computation*, Vol 1, pp 508-512.

29. Watson, R.A., Hornby, G.S. and Pollack, J.B. (1998) Modeling Building-Block Interdependency. *Parallel Problem Solving from Nature*, proceedings of Fifth International Conference PPSN V, Springer, pp.97-106.

30. Whitley D. (1991) Fundamental Principles of Deception in Genetic Search. In: *Foundations of Genetic Algorithms*, G. Rawlins ed., Morgan Kaufmann, pp. 221-241.

31. Whitley D., Mathias, K., Rana, S., Dzubera, J. (1996) Evaluating Evolutionary Algorithms, *Artificial Intelligence*, 85:245-276.

17

Evolution with Sampled Fitness Functions

F. Bellas, J. A. Becerra and R. J. Duro

Summary: In this chapter we study the effect of different parameters and algorithmic strategies on the problem of working with sampled fitness functions in evolutionary processes. Some results are presented on the effect of the size of the short-term memory and the number of generations of evolution in between updates. From these results it can be observed that there are some critical points that may be considered in order to define the limits to which one can simplify the computations when working with sampled fitness functions while maintaining the same representative power.

We provide a study of different proposals for the construction of short-term memories and their replacement strategies in order to obtain the maximum information with the minimum use of resources when operating evolutionary algorithms in problems where the fitness functions cannot be fully known and thus need to be sampled. We provide results for different functions and study the effect of the level of randomness of the replacement of a maximum-minimum replacement strategy.

17.1 Introduction

In the realm of evolutionary computation many applications involve obtaining fitness data from partial samplings of the fitness function [2-8]. This fitness determination may be carried out through an explicit mathematical function that is partially sampled or some type of environment that provides performance information for different actions carried out by the entity resulting from the phenotypic representation of the genotype. In any case, for every individual and determination of fitness, the data employed is different, although part of the same function. Consequently, if the required optimal individual must achieve optimality for the whole fitness function, obtaining it implies the integration of series of partial snapshots of the fitness function. These snapshots depend on how the evolutionary process is presented with the information on fitness.

If we translate this into a more formal computational environment, we have a problem of obtaining a general representation of some type of function through the presentation of sequences of partial data samples or frames. The traditional approach to the problem has been to wait until enough frames had been compiled and use the whole of the information to obtain the representation [3]. This is what we would call a full (or very close to full) information fitness function. In the case of the agent-environment interaction, each agent would be made to interact with the environment for a very long period of time. This is all so well when we have a simple and static process that does not change, independently of how long it takes us to gather the information, and where the relevant data that must be considered to adequately model the process can be gathered and stored in reasonable time and space. It does not perform so well when we are working with complex dynamic processes. In this case, performing evolution with anything close to full information fitness functions becomes computationally very expensive, in fact, it becomes unapproachable.

In this paper we will try to provide some insight into the problem and present some results that will help to decide how to apply sampled fitness functions in order to obtain results that are often as good as with the complete fitness function.

17.2 Our Problem

The problem we have considered is to obtain world and internal models for autonomous robots through their online interaction with the world, whether real or simulated. The information the agent receives from the environment in any given instant of time and which it must use to evaluate its models is partial and, in many cases, noisy or irrelevant. Any model it extracts from this instantaneous information will, in most cases, be useless for other instants of time. To generalize appropriate models the agent will have to consider and relate information obtained in many different instants of time in an efficient manner.

In more mathematical terms and considering a set of data that define a function, the fitness of the model is given by how well it fits the whole function and not by how well it fits the individual point or the subset of points it is considering in a given instant of time. This is what we have called a Sparse Fitness Function (SFF), the fitness of the individual is given by its response to several different instantaneous local fitness functions, which together conform the desired global one.

In order to illustrate the problems encountered, we have performed tests on three benchmark functions of increasing difficulty in order to obtain generalizable indications.

- Sin function: $y = \sin(x)$
- Logistic series: $x(t) = 4x(t-1)/1-x(t-1)$
- 3D function: $z = x\sin(x) + y\sin(y)$

The idea was to obtain a neural network that would model these functions through evolution. Each network consisted of one input neuron, two hidden layers with four nodes, and one output neuron both for the sin and the logistic functions. In the case of the 3D function we have used a neural network with two input neurons, two hidden layers of six neurons each, and one output neuron. The evolution was carried out using 350 individuals (700 for the 3D function). The fitness of each individual was obtained by determining the mean squared error (MSE) between the output of the network and each one of the points of the signals contained in a ShortTerm Memory (STM). This STM contains a window of data of the signal that is fed to the STM replacement mechanism one item per instant of time.

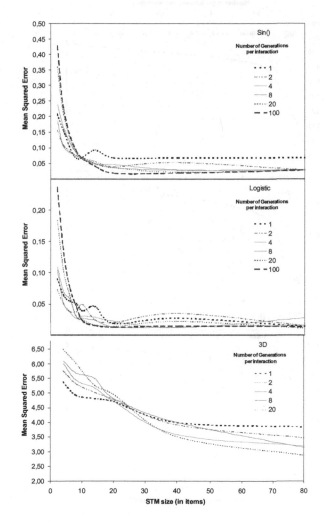

Figure 17.1. MSE of the output of the network after evolution with respect to the real function for different number of generations of evolution per interaction and STM sizes.

How big the STM is and how many generations of the evolutionary algorithm we perform per data input are the main two parameters in terms of computing resource usage. Each item in the STM must be run through the current model once per individual per generation so as to obtain an error term. Obviously, the smaller the number of individuals in a population, the smaller the STM and the less generations per data input cycle we run the evolutionary algorithm the better in terms of resources. The problem regarding population size is that, as commented in [1], there is a lower limit to the size of the populations we can use before running into premature convergence problems. Consequently, we will have to concentrate on the other two terms.

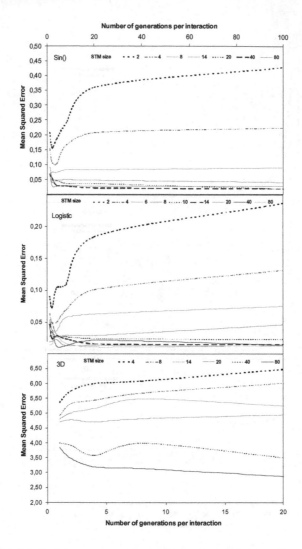

Figure 17.2. MSE of the output of the network after evolution with respect to the real function for different STM sizes and number of generations of evolution per interaction.

17.3 Short-Term Memory Size and Number of Generations per Interaction with the World

Figure 17.1 displays the evolution of the MSE of the output of the network with respect to the real function for different STM sizes and number of generations of evolution per interaction. The three graphs that make up the picture correspond to the three functions. The MSE is calculated by running the resulting networks over the whole signal and comparing the result to the original one. It is clear that for STMs larger than 8 the MSE becomes almost a constant, independently of the number of generations per update. This implies that for a randomly filled STM on average, eight points of the signal provide enough information to model the whole signal. Obviously, if we take, for example, a STM of 10, we will be on the safe side, no matter how many generations of the evolutionary process we run. This is not necessarily the optimal solution, just the safest one. If we look at this graph more closely, we see that for a STM of 4 and running 2 generations per iteration we obtain almost the same error, but now, the computing required is much less. Let us take a look at this graph in another way (Figure 17.2). Now we can see that there are two types of behaviors with the number of generations per interaction with the world. In the first case, for STMs, smaller than the critical size, if we carry out few generations per interaction, that is, if we evolve very little with a given frame of the STM, the results improve with the number of generations up to a point, in this case about 4 or 6 generations per interaction. More evolution without changing data items in the STM leads to a problem of overfitting the current STM frame and not generalizing to the whole fitness function. In short, for these values of the STM, we have a concave function with a minimum for a given number of generations per iteration. After the critical STM value is surpassed, there is no minimum, the function is monotonously decreasing with the number of generations, implying that it is very difficult to overfit to the current STM as it provides a good enough representation of the signal to model it correctly without having to use many frames.

Figure 17.3 displays the variation of the MSE during evolution for six cases. We have first considered an STM of 2 and have evolved the networks for 2 generations per interaction. There is a certain improvement, but, as two points is a very poor representation of the signal, evolution on two points just leads to oscillations in MSE, with very poor values. The networks never really learn the fitness function; they tend to evolve toward the contents of the STM in a given instant of time. This is more marked if we take 100 generations per interaction for a short-term memory of 2, now the MSE is basically pure noise. The network evolves to predict the STM contents very well (two points) but not the signal. Consequently, the MSE with respect to the signal becomes really deficient. As STM increases in size, as in the case of the second set of graphs for STM 8 (middle graphs), we see that now the information in the STM starts to be relevant. There is an evolution toward a reasonable representation of the signal (low MSE). With new interactions with the world the STM changes, and some oscillations in the behavior of the MSE can be observed, but, especially in the case where not many generations of the evolutionary algorithm are run between interactions, the networks are not overfitted to the instantaneous contents of the STM but tend to obtain a more general solution. Obviously, the more generations per interaction we run the evolution, the more marked the overfitting of the instantaneous STM becomes. Finally, in the third case, we present an STM of 20 (top graphs), well above the critical point for this function. Now the networks evolve to a good prediction of the whole signal (low MSE) with very little difference between running many or few generations of the evolutionary process between interactions with the world. The only appreciable difference is that with more generations, the process is evidently faster.

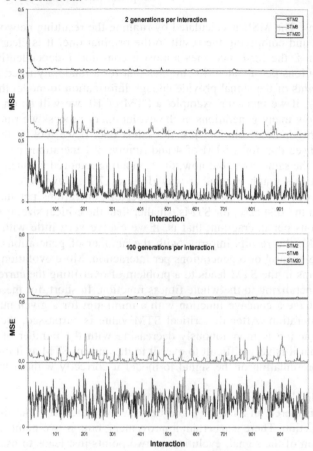

Fig ure17.3. Evolution of the MSE for STMs of sizes 2, 8, and 20 using the logistic function. The top figure shows 2 generation per update of the STM, and the bottom figure shows 100 generations per update.

This is all very well for the logistic function, but what happens with other types of functions? We have considered a simpler and a more difficult function (sin and 3D). If we produce the same representations for these functions as we did for the logistic one (Figures 17.1 and 17.2, top and bottom), it can be clearly seen that the behavior is basically the same. On one hand, the sin() function provides representations that are almost indistinguishable from those of the logistic function except, maybe, for the fact that they are smoother. This is a surprising result, indicating that for the network we are using, a sin() function is about as hard, or easy to model, as a logistic function. Well, if one looks at the state space this is probably true. Thus, it is good to see that for similar modeling difficulty, we obtain basically the same results.

On the other hand, if we go to a much harder function to model, such as the 3D one we indicated above, we see that, although the general behavior is similar, now the critical point has changed; it has gone up to an STM of about 20. What is really interesting about this is that by looking at the slope of the MSE function as a function of the number of generations per interaction, one knows what side of the critical STM point one is for a given function. As commented above for the logistic function, if one is below the critical point, a small number of generations per interaction will provide better results in the global error. If one is above the critical point, two considerations may be made. On one hand, a smaller STM could probably be used, thus reducing computational load, on the other, the number of generations per interaction will not really affect the outcome. Consequently, by delimiting where the critical point is located, one could think of tweaking with parameters such as the size of the STM, the evolutionary pressure of the process as well as the number of generations per interaction with the world in order to optimize the computational load and the probability of obtaining a successful evolution. Take into account that if these parameters are not properly set, two consequences may arise. If the STM is too small or the evolutionary pressure per interaction too high (through many generations per interaction or an evolutionary algorithm with a high pressure), the network will never learn the global function and will overfit the current STM frame, thus producing a global oscillating MSE. On the other hand, large STMs will lead to very long processing times.

17.4 Critical Points

In the previous sections we have seen that when one studies the evolution of the mean squared error of the model of a signal provided by an evolved ANN when the fitness function during evolution was sampled, a critical point arises for STM size whereby the behavior over this critical point is quite different from that below it. Below, the MSE is very dependent on STM size and evolutionary pressure. Above it, this dependence disappears. In fact, above it, it seems that no matter how many generations we evolve on a given frame of the STM, the results remain the same; there is no overfitting. Consequently, if the STM is above the critical point, why not just evolve for a very large number of generations on a static STM without introducing any new data?. Well, there are two answers to this. First, this strategy would provide no capability of dealing with changing environments. Second, the critical point we are considering is what we would call a dynamic sampling critical point, this is, the contents of the STM are enough to model the signal if they change at a reasonable rate.

In fact, one could define three different types of critical STM sizes. On one hand, we could define what we would call static consecutive sampling critical point (SCS-CP). This critical size indicates what the minimum size of the STM must be in order to provide a good enough representation of the signal if the STM does not input any new data and the data it contains are consecutive samples of the signal. This point obviously depends on how good a representation of the signal one desires and on the sampling frequency. For a 63 sample per cycle representation of the sin() function, in our case it results that an STM of 63 is required as SCS-CP.

The second type of critical point is given by the average STM required to reliably represent the signal when this STM is static (no updating) and the points in it are random samples of the signal. This is what we call the static random sampling critical point (SRS-CP), For the sin() function, the SRS-CP would be around 20.

Finally, we have the critical point we have derived in Part I, that is, the Dynamic Sampling Critical Point (DS-CP). In this case, the STM will be updated with some criterion. As in the case of static critical points, it will also depend on how we sample the signals or environments. Obviously a DCS-CP (dynamic consecutive sampling critical point) will in general present a higher value than a DRS-CP (dynamic random sampling critical point) given the better probability of a random sampling of providing a good representation of the signal. In fact, for the sin() function, the DRS-CP turns out to be about 10 for the same sampling frequency as above.

From a practical point of view, all of the above comments lead to the consideration that the minimum size necessary for the STM to be able to provide a good enough representation of the signal to permit obtaining a model within a given error margin depends on two factors: sampling frequency and dynamicity. Sampling frequency, if above the frequency established by Shannon's theorem, is only relevant if the data are taken in a consecutive manner. Any other STM updating strategy will reduce the influence of this factor.

Regarding dynamicity, any evolutionary strategy acting on a dynamic STM, that is a STM that is updated with new information as new interactions with the function or environment occur, will see a virtual STM that is larger than the real one just as long as the evolutionary pressure on a single frame of the STM is not too large. Thus, for practical use one would think that the optimal usage of an STM would occur when the maximum information on the signal is introduced in it through an appropriate update or replacement strategy and when this information changes with time at a rate compatible with the number of generations and evolutionary pressure of the algorithm in between interactions with the function or environment. When evolving between interactions or updates of a dynamically changing STM, one does not want the population to converge to the current frame of the STM; otherwise, when the next frame comes in, unless the STM is well above the static critical point, the performance of the solution evolved will be very poor. The result of something like this would be to have an algorithm that is constantly converging to the contents of the STMs but never really modeling the underlying function or environment.

17.5 Replacement Mechanism

One of the most relevant aspects in managing dynamic STMs, as mentioned above, is the replacement mechanism. The better the replacement strategy, the better the representative power of each frame. Thus, a good replacement strategy maximizes the information content of the memory.

To achieve this objective we have studied the effect of introducing a strategy that maximizes the minimum distance from every item in the STM to every other item. This approach implies defining a distance between items. In our case we have just used a standard Euclidean distance taking each item in the STM as an n-

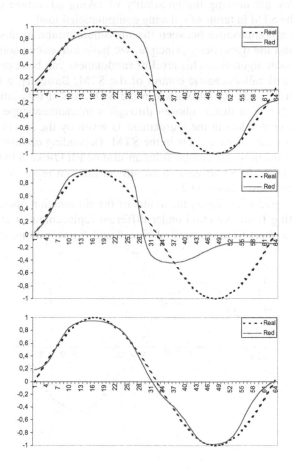

Figure 17.4. Model of the sin() function provided by the best network evolved using different replacement strategies for the STM. It is a size 4 STM with 8 generations of evolution per update. The strategies considered are static (top), FIFO (middle), and maximum-minimum replacement (bottom). The functions were sampled randomly.

dimensional vector.

This approach usually results in a very good distribution of the items in the *n*-dimensional space conformed by the representations of the items in the short-term memory. Evidently, this strategy does not imply any relation to the importance of the items towards the task in hand; it is just a maximization of the coverage of the *n*-dimensional space by a limited number of vectors. It is just a geometric property. Notwithstanding this fact, this type of approach has provided a good selection of the points to be used for the evolution of representations as shown in Figure 17.7.

The problem with this approach is that after a maximum/minimum distance configuration of the STM has been achieved, no changes occur in the STM, thus obviating the dynamicity principle. We are basically obtaining the best static STM possible, but we are missing the possibility of taking advantage of the dynamic properties of the STM in terms of reducing computational load.

To achieve a compromise between the maximum/minimum distance criterion for the STM and the dynamicity principle, we have introduced some stochasticity in the replacement algorithm. This level of randomness can be regulated through a parameter we will call stochastic control of the STM. Basically, a new item has a certain probability of being introduced in the STM, and if it is introduced, it will substitute another item that is chosen through a tournament-type selection. The strength of the contenders in the tournament is given by the inverse of their minimum distance to the other elements in the STM. Depending on how large we make the tournament window, we can go from an almost FIFO-like STM by setting the tournament window to STMsize-1 to an almost random replacement strategy by setting the tournament window to 2.

Figures 17.4 and 17.5 display the model of the sin function obtained by the best network resulting from evolution under different replacement strategies. In every case we used a short-term memory of size 4 and 8 generations of evolution be-

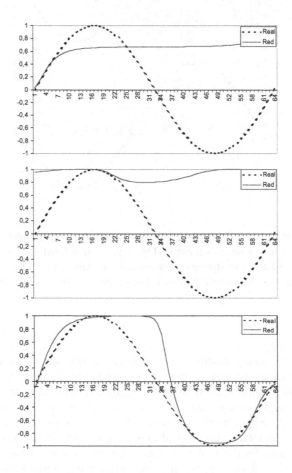

Figure 17.5. Model of the sin() function provided by the best network evolved using different replacement strategies for the STM. It is a size 4 STM with 8 generations of evolution per update. The strategies considered are static (top), FIFO (middle), and maximum/minimum replacement (bottom). The functions were sampled sequentially.

tween updates . For the three models on Figure 17.4, the samples of the function were taken randomly. For the three of Figure 17.5, the samples were taken consecutively. If one is working with real problems, both cases may arise. When an agent is exploring an environment, what it will perceive will be relatively random depending on its actions. On the other hand, when a signal is being analyzed, it is usually received in a consecutive fashion.

The top two graphs in both figures correspond to a static STM, that is, once it is filled there is no replacement. As we see, in the case of the sequential sampling strategy, the network learns to model the first points of the sin() function perfectly, as they are the only ones in the STM. Obviously, the model with respect to the whole signal is very poor. When a randomly filled static STM is used, the model improves, but, as it only considers four points of the signal, it is quite sensitive to the randomness of the points and usually overfits them without really modeling the signal. This is shown in the top graph of Figure 17.4. In the middle graphs of both figures, the STM works as a FIFO. The oldest element is substituted by the new input, without considering if the information provided by the new element is useful. It could be thought that this would be an appropriate strategy in autonomous robotics, where older information is usually considered less relevant. The results are not much better than in the previous case. The network tends to overfit the local contents of the STMs and, as these change continuously, it does not obtain a general representation of the signal.

Finally, in the bottom two graphs we display the case of the replacement strategy we introduced above. Now the models obtained are much better, even in the case of the sequential sampling of the signal. This is mainly due to the fact that now a new data item has a low probability of being input to the STM if it provides little information (if it is not different from those present in the STM), but this probability is not zero, so the STM does not become static after a while.

The same results can be obtained for other functions. In figure 17.6 we display the evolution of fitness of the best network for a $xsin(x)+ysin(y)$ function. We have used an STM size of 40. The top figure displays the case of using a FIFO-like replacement strategy. For this case the overfit of the current contents of the STM leads to very large oscillations in the fitness with respect to the global function.

If we consider a maximum-minimum replacement strategy, as shown in the bottom part of the figure, the fitness of the model in terms of the MSE improves until it reaches a relatively constant value. If the network is tested, the model it provides is quite good. As an illustration of the effects of this strategy, in Figure 17.7 we present the final contents of the short-term memory for this last function. The homogeneity of the distribution of the data points within the [-10,10] interval, both on the x- and on the y-axes (inputs) is clear. We have also represented the z-value (output) as bars and it can be seen that when points are close in the x-y-plane, their z values are quite different. The replacement strategy obviously maximizes the descriptive power of the STM, and, as it never stops being updated, the process contemplates a larger virtual STM than the actual real one.

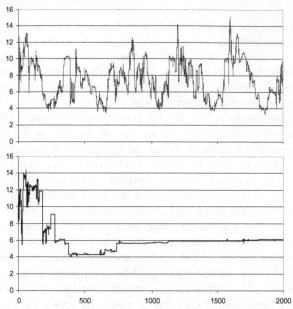

Figure 17.6 Evolution of the fitness of the best individual for the sin*(x)*+ysin*(y)* function using a FIFO (top) and a maximum minimum replacement (bottom) over an STM size of 40.

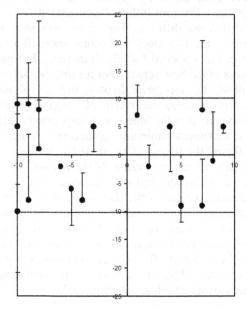

Figure 17.7. Contents of the STM for the case of Figure 17.6. The points on the *x-y*-plane correspond to the two inputs to the network in the interval [-10,10]. The bars provide the *z*-values (outputs).

17.6 Conclusions

In this chapter we have provided a general view of some aspects to take into account when designing evolutionary processes that require the use of sampled fitness functions. The study has concentrated on the size and replacement strategy of the contents of the short-term memory. From these results it can be inferred that by appropriately choosing STM size, evolutionary pressure of the algorithm and STM replacement strategies in dynamic STMs, the quality of the results improve drastically, leading to processes that require much less computational resources for the same result quality.

Acknowledgments

This work was supported by the FEDER through project PROTECAS N. 1FD1997-1262 MAR. and by the MCYT of Spain through project TIC2000-0739C0404.

References

1. Santos, J., Duro, R.J., Becerra, J.A., Crespo, J.L., and Bellas F. (2001) Considerations in the Application of Evolution to the Generation of Robot Controllers, *Information Sciences* 133:127-148.
2. Beer, R.D. and Gallagher, J.C. (1992) Evolving Dynamical Neural Networks for Adaptive Behavior, *Adaptive Behavior,* 1(1):91-122.
3. Cheng, M.Y. and Lin, C.S. (1997) Genetic Algorithm for Control Design of Biped Locomotion, *Journal of Robotic Systems*, 14(5):365-373.
4. Dain, R. A. (1998) Developing Mobile Robot Wall-Following Algorithms Using Genetic Programming, *Applied Intelligence*, 8:33-41.
5. Floreano, D. and Mondada, F. (1998) Evolutionary Neurocontrollers for Autonomous Mobile Robots, *Neural Networks*, 11:1461-1478.
6. Gomez, F. and Miikkulainen, R. (1997), Incremental Evolution of Complex General Behavior, *Adaptive Behavior,* 5(3/4):317-342.
7. Jakobi, N. (1997) Evolutionary Robotics and the Radical Envelope of Noise Hypothesis, *Adaptive Behavior,* 6(2):325-368.
8. Nolfi, S. and Parisi, D. (1997) Learning to Adapt to Changing Environments in Evolving Neural Networks, *Adaptive Behavior,* 5(1):75-98.

18

Molecular Computing by Signaling Pathways

J.-Q. Liu and K. Shimohara

Summary. To reduce the computing cost (i.e., the molecular number and time) of molecular computers by using DNA, RNA, and other biomolecules is an important task for enhancing their computing performance with parallelism obtained by biological implementation. For this purpose, we propose a new molecular computing method, namely, computing with Rho family GTPases, which differs from the Adleman-Lipton paradigm of DNA computing [1,9] and surfaced-based techniques [2]. This method employs the signaling pathways (the pathways of Rho family GTPases) of *in situ* cells that are formalized as a special kind of hypergraph rewriting, thus forming "conceptualized pathway objects" that systematically guarantee the rigorousness of massive parallel computing processes.

The 3-SAT problem is used as a benchmark for testing the algorithm of our method. The initial values, the given clauses of the 3-SAT problem, are encoded as signaling molecules and treated as cell input by means of inter-cell communication. Then, after being transmitted by the sender molecules of the cells' skeleton, these molecules are accepted by the receptor molecules within the cells. Consequently, the pathways of the cells are activated to generate candidate solutions in the reactant molecules' form in parallel. The process of making these molecules interact in a stepwise manner is carried out recursively based on the implicit constraints within the problem solving itself. Depending on the complexity of the biological mechanism of the molecules for biochemical reactions in the cells, a high degree of autonomy, both in computation theory and in biological faithfulness, is obtained by the entire computing process. By applying our method to solve 3-SAT problems, we have obtained a space complexity of $O(m \times n)$ and a time complexity of $O(m)$, where m is the number of clauses and n is the number of variables.

The experimental results obtained from a corresponding software simulator (impleme n-tation) of our method show that the algorithm that we have obtained is efficient from the viewpoint of computing costs and that it also has reasonable biological faithfulness with a strong potential for further biological implementation by cells *in situ*.

18.1 Introduction

Biomolecular computing by DNA, RNA, or other biomolecules offers a new and unconventional computational paradigm and promises strong advantages in applications for NP problem solving [1-9]. One of the most important challenges in molecular computing is how to obtain an efficient degree of spatial complexity, e.g., how to obtain a linear order in space (the number of molecules), while keeping the merits of the DNA computing in the linear time. For a 3-SAT problem [10], which is one of the most important benchmarks for testing DNA computing algorithms, two recent advances directly relate to this subject:

(1) The concurrent version of Schöning's algorithm [7] implemented by a DNA computation algorithm: Sergio Díaz, Juan Luis Esteban, and Mitsunori Ogihara [8] have realized a space complexity of $O((2-2/k)^n)$ and a time complexity of $O(kmn+n^3)$, where k is the literal number.

(2) Qinghua Liu et al. [2] have devised surfaced-based DNA computing for a 3-SAT (4,4) problem. Its time complexity would be $O(m)$ and its space complexity would be $O(2^n)$ if their method were scaled. It is well known that linear time complexity is feasible in most forms of DNA computing [6]. But with respect to space complexity, M. Ogihara and A. Ray pointed out that in surface-based DNA computing, the DNA number used for solving a 3-SAT problem is at least 10^{15} [3]. In the important work of "DNA computing on surface" in [2], DNA computing was successful in handling an intractable problem (3-SAT). However, open problems still remain, such as, from a theoretical aspect, those described in the comments on surface-based DNA computing in [3]: "From a computer-science perspective these results are remarkable, but . . . The most serious remaining issue is the exponentially increasing number of DNA molecules needed to compute even small 3-SAT problems...". The motivation for our work is to achieve molecular computing with biological signaling pathways in cells where the complexity increases by the mechanism itself, so that we can obtain results at a linear cost both in space and time. Here, parallelism and auto-growing of the molecular computing mechanisms are the kernels that support this efficiency. Our concrete target is to explore the internal pathway mechanism in cells and to construct an efficient algorithm using them. In this paper, we propose a new model for molecular computing, in which computing is carried out by pathway objects and related signaling molecules in cells.

The original contributions of our work are

(1) The use of the pathways in cells (functional proteins and kinases) as computing units, focusing our efforts on the Rho family GTPases for potential implementation.

(2) We obtain an efficient algorithm with linear cost both in space and in time.

(3) Systematic parallelism guaranteed by hypergraph rewriting and a high degree of autonomy within the computing mechanism, which is used for the formal reasoning about the ability to guarantee the validity of the theory.

This chapter is organized as follows: Section 18.2 gives an explanation of biological faithfulness and potential implementation, Section 18.3 describes a computing process that includes the representation and formal definition, Section 18.4 presents experimental results of software simulator implementation, and Section 18.5 outlines the main points of our work.

18.2 Biological Faithfulness

For use as further benchmarks, we have verified the following materials by means of software simulation for potential implementation by Rho family GTPases of *in situ* cells (here, a 23-variable, 8-clause 3-SAT is taken as an example):

(1) The clause of the 3-SAT problem with three variables in the 3-SAT is constructed by MLC (Myosin Light Chain) regulated by Rho, Rho-kinase, and myosin phosphatase. The three literals for variables (e.g., X,Y,Z) are expressed by MLC-p, MBS-cat-Rho-GTP, and Rho-kinase+Rho+GTP, and the negative forms of the three variables, e.g., $(\neg X, \neg Y, \neg Z)$, are expressed by MLC, MBS-cat, and Rho-kinase. The molecular complexes that satisfy those clauses will be "output" by signaling senders and receptors through different channels in cells and will transit between different cells by inter-cell communication.

(2) The pathways of Rho family GTPases are regulated by the targets of the Rho family GTPases = {Rho, Rac, Cdc42} corresponding to the three literals. The signaling molecules that encode the combined form of the candidate solutions for the 3-SAT are {PIP 5-kinase, Rhophilin, Rhotekin, PKN, PRK2, citron, citron-kinase, Rho-kinase, MBS, MLC, p140mDia, p140 Sra-1, Por1, PI 3-kinase, S 6-kinase, IQGAP, PAKs, MLK3, MEKK4, MRCKs, WASP, N-WASP, and Ack}.

(3) Biologically faithful verification of our software simulator that comes from the experimental samples for cells *in situ* is based on the objects of rats. Because the detection of the signaling molecules is feasible by the fluorescent strength of hippocampal neurons regulated at the CRMP-2/TOAD-64/Ulip2/DRP-2 level by the Rho effector, Rho-kinase/ROK/ROCK [22]. This is the most appropriate I/O approach for molecular computing by kinase-regulated pathways.

The I/O interface is different for input and output. The input clauses are regulated by the target of the Rho family GTPases. The candidates are activated within the cells in uniform concentrations. We expect that the outputs will be verified by two-dimensional gel electrophoresis for the proteom (protein sequences/kinases) expressions.

The main points of the computing processes are

(1) Input: signaling molecules.
(2) Output: signaling molecules.
(3) Information encoded: the alphabetic symbols from (the name of the) molecule complex (e.g., the combined forms of the encoded molecules for the candidates shown in Figure 18.4). The combined forms of these molecules for special representations in a specific problem, in a more general sense, are the program codes for computing where they are carried out as computing programs whose abstract forms are coupled hypergraphs with the biological faithfulness of signaling pathways.
(4) The computing units: in physical form, they are multicells in a living state, i.e., *in situ* cells. The computing principles:
     "input -> pathway 0 -> ... -> pathway *m* -> output".

In the underlying computing processes, a "computing unit" is a "pathway," which is defined as a special kind of hypergraph with a topological constraint in space; the computing is the rewriting on the hypergraphs with coupled relations among the objects and interactions. The core mechanisms of computing on structures are biochemical reactions for structural rewriting. From this, consequently, we can see that the complexity within the underlying system itself is increased due to the interactions of pathways in the computing processes. Therefore, the computing cost has been cut into the linear order. In the 3-SAT, the pathway objects are selected as candidates of combined forms of variables with assigned truth values (i.e., the forms in Section 18.3 by formal representation).

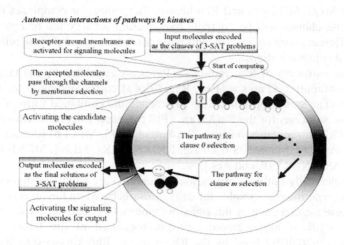

Figure 18.1. Autonomous interactions of pathways by kinases.

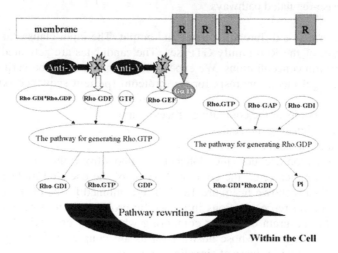

Figure 18.2. Rho family GTPases pathway in cells.

The information flow in Rho family GTPases can be expressed in terms of computer science as illustrated in Figure 18.2. The green parts show the reactions, and the brown parts show the equivalent rewriting relationship in theoretical computer science. The material that we selected to make our kinase-based pathway mechanism for computing is the Rho-family GTPases of *in situ* cells, which consist of a series of biochemical reactions whose output is determined by the input based on chains of coupled reactions with interactions. Here, the pathways are controlled/regulated by kinases, i.e., Rho family GTPases in our case. The related computing is carried out by the pathways and signaling molecules in cells, which here refers to molecular computing by kinases and their related molecules in living cells (Figure 18.2). Kinase here refers to a phosphorylation enzyme that can activate the pathway in cells: substrate + ATP --> substrate-O-P + ADP. The kinase speeds up biochemical reaction by more than 100 times. Also, under the regulation of kinases, a huge number of pathways can efficiently operate in parallel. More importantly, the kinases' phosphorylation is closely related to ATP, which is the core of energy cycling in living cells. This key factor enables the "pathway" architecture to be autonomous "computing" that consists of kinase-regulated reactions.

18.3 The Computing Process

The basic terms of graph rewriting [18] include:
- A- an alphabet set;
- $\tau(a)$ - the rank associated to a symbol, $a \in A$;
- H - a hypergraph, which consists of vetex set V_H and hyperedge set E_H, i.e., $H = < V_H, E_H >$ where $V_H \cap E_H = \varnothing$;
- $lab_H(e)$ - the label assigned to a hyperedge e in A;
- $\tau(lab_H(e))$ - the length of the sequence of vertices with $lab_H(e)$.

Now we define the formal system of hypergraph rewriting with topological constraints [19] based on the relation of a structure and algebraic operators developed especially for the "pathway" objects. For the object set of pathways, we define a relation $R_p(A) = \{pah_a \mid a \in A\}$, where pah_a is $(\tau(a)+2)$-ary.

The hypergraph H definition is given by the structure

$$|H|_3 := \left\langle V_H \cup E_H \cup K_H, (pah_{aH})_{a \in A} \right\rangle \in STR(R_p(A))$$ (18.1)

where we select the index 3 for $|H|_3$ in order to distinguish it from the $|H|_1$ and $|H|_2$ in [18] defined by Bruno Courcelle. The related predicate becomes

$$pah\ (x, y_1, ..., y_m, z_1, ..., z_n),$$ (18.2)

where $x \in E_H$, $y_1, ..., y_m \in V_H$, $lab_H(x) = a$, $n = \tau(a)$, $z_1, ..., z_n$ are the controls in K_H. Controls $z_1, ..., z_n$ are contained in the category Cag_H, and the related functor is given as $F_h : z_i \to z_j; i, j \in N$. Notice that all of the operations are carried out on a set of pathways that are a special kind of hypergraph under certain topological conditions that will be defined later in this section. The formal system we propose here is a kind of molecular computing operation reflecting the idea of modeling from pathway to pathway, where pathway rewriting is conceptualized by operators defined by rules.

Let L be a category, and we define a construct $< Ob(L), Mor(X,Y), M >$, where $Ob(L)$ denotes the set of pathway objects, $Mor(X,Y)$ is the morphism of X into Y (X, $Y \in Ob(L)$), and M is the law of composition designed by rule Q here. This is the core of the formal system. The model can be formalized by the following construct:

$$W_{cells} = < V, T, D, U, E, Y, Z, PTs, Q >$$ (18.3)

where V is the alphabet set; T is the terminal set ($T \subset V$); D is the set of $\{0, 1\}$; U is the set of vertexes ($U \subset V$); E is the set of edges; Y is the set of hypergraphs $<HE, U>$ in which HE is the set of hyperedges in Y, and the corresponding HR (hyperedge replacement) and VR (vertex replacement) are defined based on HE; Z is the set of local concentrations (discrete values); ($Z \subset V$); PTs is the set of pathways, i.e., the directed graphs that have inputs and outputs in U and contain hyperedges in HE with interactions that fall into HE. The pathway is designated as a class of special directed hypergraphs. Each one is defined as

[pathway] ::= [pathway] $\cup$ [single-hyperedge-with-two-vertexes]   (18.4)

under the operation of Q; Q is the set of operators for operations on hypergraphs in HE from V and E, i.e., we have the set of $Q = \{ Q1, Q2, Q3, Q4 \}$ for the objects in PTs. For the interactions in the set of all pathways, the operational processes carried out by the operator set of Q are formalized as the following four rules in terms of rewriting on hypergraphs that include (1) Rule $Q1$ (the rule of interaction) for the interactions of pathways as defined in PTs; (2) Rule $Q2$ (the rule of feedback-making) for the addition of feedback in the pathways; (3) Rule $Q3$ for the addition of new pathways; and (4) Rule $Q4$ for pathway deletion. From the above model, we can derive the following forms of rewriting on "pathways": (i) $PTs(Gh) \rightarrow PTs(Gh')$ s.t. the objects of rewriting are limited to pathways obtained by Q, and (ii) $Gh'' \rightarrow Gh'''$ s.t. the objects of rewriting are limited to hypergraphs by Q, where Gh, Gh', Gh'' and Gh''' refer to hypergraphs in Y and rewriting is carried out through executing the Q operators (more details on the operations of Q rules can be found in [17]).

Our method can conduct the following three forms of computing:

(1) The unified form of abstract computation: In the definition of theoretical computers [11], the formal model obtained from our method equals the hypergraph rewriting: H $\Rightarrow$ H' s.t. Q rules, where H and H' refer to the hypergraph before and after rewriting, respectively. We have proven it to be equivalent to a Turing machine in [12].

(2)   Molecular computing as ALU (Algorithmic and Logic Unit): let the input and output of the model be encoded by alphabetical symbols as binary numbers. We have proposed and proven that the model can perform arith-

metic operations such as addition, subtraction, multiplication, and division, and logic operations such as AND, OR, NOT, and XOR in [13].

(3) Molecular computation for NP problem solving: the application of our method to the 3-SAT problem is the main topic in this paper as a new paradigm for NP problem solving.

According to the convention of model description for DNA computing [8], the model is presented in the following form (a formal definition has been given in this section):

Let $\Psi_i = C_{i1} \vee C_{i2} \vee C_{i3}$ be a clause in a 3-SAT problem ($i=1, ..., m$). The union of all clauses $\{\Psi_i\}$ takes the form $\Psi_1 \wedge \Psi_2 \wedge ... \wedge \Psi_m$. C_{ij} ($j=1,2,3$) the variables taking different truth assignments. Here, we define the positive form of the variable as the signaling molecule X_{ij} with the phosphorylation attached components $O\text{-}X_{ij}$, and the negative form is with de-phosphorylation $N\text{-}X_{ij}$:

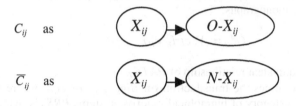

Figure 18.3. Representation of truth assignments to variables.

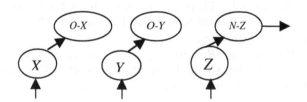

From the related channel Ch $(X,Y,\_Z)$

Figure 18.4. Representation of candidates.

By the structure of $|H|_3$, the rewriting on hypergraphs can be transferred into the rewriting on the combined RPO (relative pushout)s, i.e., RPOs$_H$ w.r.t. Cag$_H$. Equivalently, the rewriting on hypergraphs is denoted as GRiT, i.e., $G \rightarrow G'$, where G, G' refer to the hypergraphs, and transferred into the transductions among the bigraphs in terms of the following operator Q^H set on relation structure $|H|_i$ (here, i=3): $\{Q^H_{Scope}, Q^H_{Binding}, Q^H_{Elision}\}$ w.r.t. ζ, where ζ refers to topological constraints such as homotopy and homology.

Let Tog_H, Mog_H, and Big_H be the categories of topographs, monographs, and bigraphs, wherein the bigraph [20] for hypergraphs is given as

$$G_H = G (U_H, ctrl_H, G^T_H, G^M_H): I \rightarrow J, \tag{18.5}$$

where $U_H \in V_H \cup E_H$, $ctrl_H \in K_H$, G^T_H in Tog_H, G^M_H in Mog_H, G_H in Big_H.
Within the equivalent class PAT_H of pathways, the transductions are exerted on the topographs:

$$G^T_H = (V, ctrl_H, prt): m \rightarrow n, \tag{18.6}$$

where prt is the parent of the vertexes in rewriting, $m, n \in N$.

Among the different equivalent classes $PATs_H$ of pathways, the transductions are exerted on the monographs:

$$G^M_H = (V, ctrl_H, \equiv_H), \tag{18.7}$$

where $\equiv_H$ is the equivalent relationship of $PATs_H$.

Then GRiT becomes the transduction on $Big_H(K_H, react_H)$, where the interaction $react_H$ in the category of bigraphical reactive systems BRS_H is made by the interactions of bigraphs based on the Q^H_{Scope}.

We have the following propositions and theorem according to [21]:

Proposition 18.1: $GRiT(|H|_3, Big_H(K_H, react_H))$ is congruent iff the transductions on $Big_H(K_H, react_H)$ are definable by the homotopy group for $\equiv_H$.

Proposition 18.2: $GRiT(|H|_3, Big_H(K_H, react_H))$ is congruent iff the transductions on $Big_H(K_H, react_H)$ are definable by the homologous group for $\equiv_H$.

Proposition 18.3: $GRiT(|H|_3, Big_H(K_H, react_H))$ with redex of completeness on $(pah_{aH})_{a \in A}$ is capable of being represented by extended RPL. Here, RPL refers to Rescher Probabilistic Logic.

Theorem 18.1: Homological $GRiT(|H|_3, Big_H(K_H, react_H))$ is capable of generating a recursive enumerable set iff the input and output of the pathways $PATs_H$ satisfies the constraint caused by $\equiv_H$.

Here, "homological $GRiT(|H|_3, Big_H (K_H, react_H))$" is also denoted as $hGRiT(|H|_3, Big_H (K_H, react_H))$. Therefore, we obtain that signaling molecules with variant concentrations under the robustness constraints are mapped into the set characterized by the homotopy group and transductions on the pathways $G_H = G (U_H, ctrl_H, G^T_H, G^M_H): I \rightarrow J$ for $hGRiT(|H|_3, Big_H(K_H, react_H))$ given in Theorem 18.1.

The input of the model is $\{\Psi_i\}$. Let $Ch_1, Ch_2, \dots, Ch_m$ be the signaling molecule channel in the membranes of cells, and $C_{ij} = 1$ and $C_{ij} = 0$ are represented as the phosphorylation and de-phosphorylation forms, respectively. The computation is carried out by a set of corresponding pathways consisting of biochemical reactants in the cells. The pathways are interacted and sustained in cells. The output of the model is the solution of the 3-SAT problem.

Here, the channel refers to the RECEPTOR molecules in the cells' membrane that recognize the molecules encoded as clauses in 3-SAT and activate the corresponding pathways in the cells. Pathways refer to the mechanism for cell communication [14-16] that consists of a series of biochemical reactions and whose output is determined by the input reactants and kinases used in the related computing processes. The relationship of molecular names between input and output is determined by the corresponding concentrations that guarantee the sustaining of the pathway.

The four basic operations in the computing model are arranged as the following

steps:

Step 0: Initial pathway for clause input:

The clauses $\{\Psi_i\}$ in 3-SAT are encoded as the input of the pathways. Then, based on the basic set of pathways we made in advance, the channels Ch_1, Ch_2, ..., Ch_m work as RECEPTORs $RP_j(Ch_i)$ for SENDERs defined as variables $\{X_j(Ch_i)\}$, where $i = 1, 2, ..., m$, $j = 1, 2, ..., m$, and where $X_j(Ch_i)$ denotes the channel Ch_i for X_j. Therefore, it is necessary to initialize the population of the candidates $\{\Psi_i\}$, $\{Ch_{ij}\}$ and $\{W_{cell}\}_v$ $(i, j, v = 0,1...)$.

Step 1: Interaction of pathways:

Pathways are generated (to grow in the biological sense) and encoded for candidate solutions by interactions of the existing pathways under the hypergraph rewriting rules. Here, the neighboring pathways are selected as the objects for interactions (the measurement for neighborhood Θ is defined as the minimum Hamming distance of the variables of candidates).

Let φ_k $(k = 0, 1...)$ and φ_l $(l = 0,1, ...)$ be two different RECEPTOR molecules in cells represented for clauses $\{\Psi_i\}$. They activate the input reactants in pathways δ_k and δ_l.

Let W_{kl} be the neighborhood of pathways δ_k and δ_l. The interaction of δ_k and δ_l in W_{kl} is made by connecting their pathways to couple the common reactants for biochemical reactions. This means that φ_k and φ_l activate δ_k and δ_l, respectively, in W_{kl} for $k = 0,1...$, and $l = 0,1, ...$.

Then we apply Q rules (i.e., the four rules that are discussed in this section for the formalization) on the pathway $\{\delta_k\}$ $(k = 0,1,...)$ in the neighborhood Θ and activate the related signaling mechanism of the pathways.

For the quantitative representation, the three main predicates that we define for *GRiT* are:

(1) *VALPATH()* --- To test for valid pathway, i.e.,

$$VALPATH(pah \ (x, y_1, ..., y_m, z_1, ..., z_n))$$
$$= True \quad \text{if} \quad pah \text{ in } hGRiT(|H|_3, Big_H(K_H, react_H)),$$
$$= False \quad \text{if} \quad pah \text{ NOT in } hGRiT(|H|_3, Big_H(K_H, react_H)).$$

(2) *ELELSN(pah* $(x, y_1, ..., y_m, z_1, ..., z_n))$ --- This shows the situation of eliminating elision in pathways in $hGRiT(|H|_3, Big_H(K_H, react_H))$, i.e.,

$$ELELSN(pah \ (x, y_1, ..., y_m, z_1, ..., z_n))$$

$= True$ if sequence $\{z_1, ..., z_n\}$ is free of elision sequences
            in $pah(x, y_1, ..., y_m, z_1, ..., z_n)$
$= False$ if sequence $\{z_1, ..., z_n\}$ covers certain elisions
            in $pah(x, y_1, ..., y_m, z_1, ..., z_n)$

(3) $TRANDN()$ --- This is for transduction, i.e.,

    $TRANDN(pah(x, y_1, ..., y_m, z_1, ..., z_n))$

    $= True$ if the sequence $\{z_1, ..., z_n\}$ can deduce the redexed RPO,

    $= False$ else.

For the $m \rightarrow n$ in $GRiT(|H|_3, Big_H(K_H, react_H), \Im_H)$, the formula

    $TRANDN(pah(x, y_1, ..., y_m, z_1, ..., z_n))$

    $\wedge ELELSN(pah(x, y_1, ..., y_m, z_1, ..., z_n))$

    $\wedge VALPATH(pah(x, y_1, ..., y_m, z_1, ..., z_n))$

guarantees that the arities in $Big_H(K_H, react_H), \Im_H)$ corresponding to sequence $\{z_1, .., z_n\}$ are complete in the meaning of the m-recursive function. For the mapping: $\iota_m \rightarrow \iota_n$ in the G_H, the input and output of pathways pah(.) in $R_p(A)$ are defined in terms of category cag_ζ. The category cag_ζ for the $Big_H(K_H, react_H), \Im_H)$ holds the homology group for the transductions among different hypergraphs and the homotopy groups for the same hypergraphs with the variant parameters (i.e., concentration) under the sustaining constraints with robustness. Let $Dom(pah)$ and $Cod(pah)$ be the domain of $pah(.)$ and codomain of $pah(.)$, respectively. The three basic operations can be derived from Q^H:

$$\{Q^H_{Scope}, Q^H_{Binding}, Q^H_{Elision}\} \quad \text{w.r.t. } \zeta,$$

From $Q^H_{Elision}$, the composition infers that

    $ELELSN(pah(x, y_1, ..., y_m, z_1, ..., z_{n-1-k}))$

    $\wedge ELELSN(pah(x, y_1, ..., y_m, z_1, ..., z_{n-k}))$

    $\wedge ELELSN(pah(x, y_1, ..., y_m, z_1, ..., z_n))$

    $\rightarrow$

    $(pah(x, y_1, ..., y_m, z_1, ..., z_{n-1-k})$
    $-> pah(x, y_1, ..., y_m, z_1, ..., z_{n-k}))$

    AND

    $(pah(x, y_1, ..., y_m, z_1, ..., z_{n-k})$
    $-> pah(x, y_1, ..., y_m, z_1, ..., z_n))$

-------------------- --

    $(pah(x, y_1, ..., y_m, z_1, ..., z_{n-1-k})$
    $-> pah(x, y_1, ..., y_m, z_1, ..., z_n))$.

From $Q^H_{Binding}$, the tensor in cag_ζ becomes that

    $VALPATH(pah_a(x, y_1, ..., y_m, z_1, ..., z_n)$

    $\wedge VALPATH(pah_b(x, y_1, ..., y_m, z_1, ..., z_n)$

    $\wedge VALPATH(pah_c(x, y_1, ..., y_m, z_1, ..., z_n)$

    $\rightarrow$

    $TRANDN(pah_{a\_b\_c}(x, y_1, ..., y_m, z_1, ..., z_n)$.

From $Q^H{}_{Scope,}$ we can get that

TRANDN (pah (x, y_1, ..., y_m, z_1, ..., z_p ...z_q, ..., z_m))
∧ *ELELSN (pah (x, y_1, ..., y_m, z_1, ..., z_p ...z_q ... ,z_n))*
→
VALPATH (pah (x, y_1, ..., y_m, z_1, ..., z_p ...z_q, ..., z_k)).
    where $p,q,m,n,k \in N$.

For *GRiT($|H|_3$, $Big_H(K_H$, $react_H)$, $\Im_H)$, GRiT($|H|_3$, $Big_H(K_H$, $react_H)$, $\Im_H)$* where $\Im_H$ is the equivalence given by the homological group, and the interactions of pathways are carried out for exploring the potential solutions of the 3-SAT problem.

Step 2: Pathway generation:

Let input node(δ_k) be the input reactant of pathway δ_k, let output node(δ_k) be the output reactant of pathway δ_k, and let internal node(δ_k) be the internal reactants of pathway δ_k, where δ_k is in the set of all pathways, e.g., $X \vee Y \vee \neg Z$ implies that pathway δ_k covers the reactant molecules that correspond to the candidates as the sets of subpathways. The same parts are kept only once, and these are sustained by pathway δ_k. Therefore, after the signaling feedback is executed on the pathways, the remaining parts are the candidates represented by the signaling molecules, where the reactants are designed to produce the additional chemicals $\{\varphi'_s\}$ $(s=0,1,...)$ to feed the energy (e.g., ATP). The same is also true for another pathway δ_k'. When δ_k and $\delta'_{k'}$ interact by the operations of Q rules, different components are deleted due to the fact that they cannot be sustained. Then we get the final result. The advantage of this scheme is that the number of candidates has no relation to the molecules we set in advance. The recursive generation of pathways is executed to sift out the less suitable candidates. In the meantime, according to the rules defined in this section for formalization, the common reactants in pathway δ_k $(k = 0,1, ...)$ with feedback ensure that the related pathways are sustained. This continues to loop until rewriting stops at the final stage, i.e., biochemical reactions do not produce any more new reactants.

At this point, we need to check whether the solution has been obtained according to the terminal criterion:

If yes, the computing process goes to the next step.

If no, we must update the population and let the computing process go to Step 1.

Step 3: Judging by terminal criterion:

The criterion to judge the halting of the entire process is that the final variable form of the candidate is confirmed as the solution to the 3-SAT problem when no more new pathways emerge. At this point, the existing pathways are identical in all of the cells. Finally, after the result is confirmed, the final solution will be decided as the output.

We have proven that the algorithm can solve the 3-SAT problem with a linear complexity cost both in time and in space. The full proof can be found in [17].

Theorem 18.2 [17]: Its space complexity is $O(m \times n)$ and time complexity is $O(m)$ when it is applied to solve a 3-SAT problem.

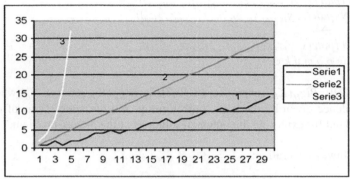

Number of variables

Figure 18.5. Relationship among the number of molecules to the number of variables in 3-SAT.

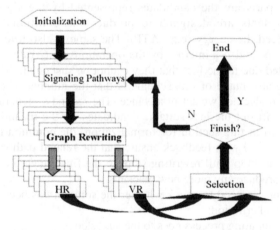

Figure 18.6. A brief flow chart of the main part of our simulator.

18.4 Experimental Result

In the sense of biological plausibility supported by real objects, our simulator is based on feasible biological signaling pathways in cells that are constructed by Rho family GTPases [15,16,22]. We have verified that our method based on pathways with interactions is biologically faithful by simulation using biological supporting software in [16]. Confirmed by the benchworks in biolabs, the kinase-based bio-chemical systems in living cells are an excellent biomachine for molecular com-

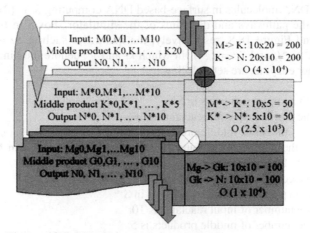

Figure 18.7. The diagrams of computation.

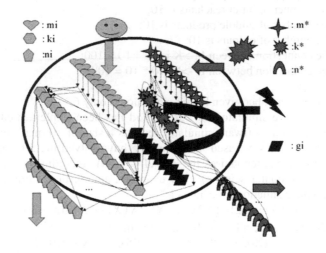

Figure 18.8. The outline of pathways in cells.

puting. The engine of this process is the assembly of kinases that keep the information flowing and energy cycling (e.g., ATP and metabolism) in order to achieve self-maintenance with robustness in an unknown dynamic environment. Parallelism for complexity, fine-grained architecture for speed, and robustness for fault/defect tolerance can be expected by exploring the above-mentioned mechanism.

Figure 18.5 shows the relationship between the molecular number (in vertical coordinates) and variable number (in horizontal coordinates). Series 1 is our result.

Series 2 is the number of variables in the 3-SAT. Series 3 is the exponential number of DNA molecules in surface-based DNA computing (e.g. [2]).

In the pathways and diagrams of the simulator shown in Figure 18.6 , Figure 18.7 and Figure 18.8, respectively, the quantities such as $Si = \{mi, ki, ni\}$, $S^* = \{m^*, k^*, n^*\}$, and $Sg = \{g^*\}$, in which ki and g^* denote the kinases and k^* denotes the other enzyme, are set as follows:

(i) for the normal pathways in Si:
   the number of input reactants is 10;
   the number of middle products is 20;
      the number of outputs is 10. the connection between M->K is 10 * 20 = 200;
   the connection between K ->N: 20 * 10 = 200;
(ii) for the pathways with disturbance in S^*:
   the number of input reactants is 10;
   the number of middle products is 5;
   the number of outputs is 10;
   the connection between M*->K* is 10 * 5 = 50;
   the connection between K* ->N*: 5 * 10 = 50;
(iii) for the graph rewriting in Sg:
   the number of input reactants is 10;
   the number of middle products is 10;
   the number of outputs is 10;
   the connection between M->K is 10 * 10 = 100;
   the connection between K ->N: 10 * 10 = 100;

But the kinase number given by our simulator is only 6.

The software simulator for our method has been implemented in C++. In the current stage, our software simulator reaches a size of 10 quadrillion (10^{16}) molecules. Using pathway-based modeling, we have solved the 50-variable, 30-clause 3-SAT problem, (denoted as the 3-SAT (50,30), according to the convention of theoretical computer science). For example, among the examples in our experiment, a typical situation for clauses is

$$(X0 \vee X1 \vee X2) \wedge (X3 \vee ... \vee X11) \wedge (X12 \vee X13) \wedge (\neg X12 \vee \neg X13),$$

where 28 clauses use all 7 combined forms in

(X0, X1, X2), (X3, X4, X5), ..., (X9, X10, X11)

except $(\neg X0 \vee \neg X1 \vee \neg X2),....,(\neg X9 \vee \neg X10 \vee \neg X11)$ and the other two clauses $=(X12 \vee X13)$ and $(\neg X12 \vee \neg X13)$. The solution is X0 = X1 = ... = X11 = 1 and $\{(X12 = 0$ and X13 = 1) or (X12 = 1 and X13 = 0)$\}$, and X14, ..., X49 takes values in the set of $\{1,0\}$. The number of signaling enzyme molecules is 14. This small cost is affordable for molecular computing and the corresponding algorithm is thus efficient. Furthermore, the robustness of the scalable schemes is achieved in order to maintain the identity of the pathways when the concentrations vary in the domain of thresholds. The cost will fluctuate slightly around the theoretical curve. Figure 18.9 shows the relationship between the molecular number (vertical coordinates) and the variable number (horizontal coordinates). It illustrates a performance comparison, with the best, average, and worst cases given in series 1, series 2 and series 3, respectively.

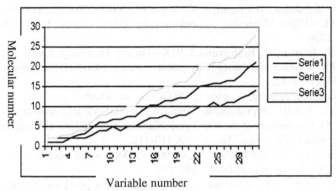

Figure 18.9. The relationship between the molecular number and the variable number.

18.5 Conclusion

In this chapter, we have proposed a new method of molecular computing constructed by "Rho family GTPases"-based pathways and formalized as hypergraph rewriting. With regard to biological faithfulness, performance as a formal system, and the application of its algorithm to the 3-SAT problem, we have discussed our method by explaining its functional factors. Furthermore, we have confirmed that the method is actually feasible for reducing the computing costs needed to solve the 3-SAT problem and for potential biochemical implementation. Future work will mainly focus on biologically realizing the method by using *in situ* cells with "Rho family GTPases"-regulated signaling pathways.

Acknowledgments

The authors sincerely thank Prof. Kozo Kaibuchi and his lab for their invaluable academic help; Prof. Masami Ito, Prof. Manuel Graña Romay, Prof. Naoyuki Inagaki, Dr. Shinya Kuroda, and Dr. Mutsuki Amano for their advice and suggestions. This research was conducted as part of "Research on Human Communication" with funding from the Telecommunications Advancement Organization of Japan. The work is also partly supported by the Foh Ying Tung Education Foundation (Project No. 71063).

References

1. Adleman, L.M. (1994) Molecular computation of solutions to combinatorial problems. Science, 266:1021-1024.
2. Liu, Q., Wang, L., Frutos, A.Q., Condon, A.E., Corn, R.M., and Smith, L.M. (2000) DNA computing on surfaces. Nature, 403:175-179.

3. Ogihara, M. and Ray, A. (2000) DNA computing on a chip. Nature, 403:143-144.
4. Sakamoto, K., Gouzu, H., Komiya, K., Kiga, D., Yokoyama, S., Yokomori, T., and Hagiya, M. (2000) Molecular computation by DNA hairpin formation. Science, 288:1223-1226.
5. Braich, R.S., Johnson, C., Rothemund, P.W.K., Hwang, D., Chelyapov, N. and Adleman, L.M. (2000) Solution of a satisfiability problem on a gel-based DNA computer. In Pre-proc. of DNA 6:31-42.
6. Condon, A., and Rozenberg, G., editors, (2000) Proc. of DNA6.
7. Schöning, U. (1999) A probabilistic algorithm for k-SAT and constraint satisfaction problems. In Proceedings of the 40th Symposium on Foundations of Computer Science, IEEE Computer Society, Los Alamitos, CA 410-414.
8. Díaz, S., Esteban, J.L., and Ogihara, M. (2000) A DNA-based random walk method for solving k-SAT. In Pre-proc. of DNA 6:181-191.
9. Lipton, R. (1995) DNA solutions of hard computational problems. Science, 268:542-545.
10. Garey, M.R., Johnson, D.S. (1979) Computers and intractability - a guide to the theory of NP-completeness. Freeman.
11. Rozenberg, G., Salomaa, A., eds. (1997) Handbook of formal languages. Springer-Verlag, Heidelberg.
12. Liu, J.-Q., and Shimohara, K. (2001) Pathway graph models for molecular computing in situ. RIMS Kokyuroku 1222, RIMS, Kyoto University 128-137.
13. Liu, J.-Q., and Shimohara, K. (2001) On arithmetic units and logic operators of kinase-based molecular computers. IPSJ SIG Notes, Vol. 2001, No. 93 25-32.
14. Scott, J.D., and Pawson, T. (2000) Cell communication: the inside story. Scientific American 54-61.
15. Kaibuchi, K., Kuroda, S., and Amano, M. (1999) Regulation of the cytoskeleton and cell adhesion by the Rho family GTPases in mammalian cells. Annu. Rev. Biochem. 68:459-486.
16. Liu, J.-Q., and Shimohara, K. (2001) Kinase computing in GTPases: analysis and simulation. IPSJ SIG Notes, Vol. 2001, No. 91:29-32.
17. Liu, J.-Q., and Shimohara, K. (2003) On the computational complexity of molecular computing by pathways. ATR-HIS Technical Report.
18. Courcelle, B. (1997) The expression of graph properties and graph transformations in monadic second-order logic. Chapter 5 of the "Handbook of graph grammars and computing by graph transformations, Vol. 1: Foundations", Rozenberg, R., (ed.), World Scientific (New-Jersey, London), 313-400.
19. Liu, J.-Q., and Shimohara, K. (2001) Graph rewriting in topology I: operators and the grammar. SIG-FAI-A101-4 (9/21):21-26.
20. Milner, R. (2001) Bigraphical reactive systems: basic theory. (http://www.cl.cam.ac.uk/users/rm135/bigraphs.ps.gz).
21. Liu, J.-Q., and Shimohara, K. (2001) Graph rewriting in topology II: computability. Proc. of the 5th Symposium on Algebra, Language and Computation, Edited by Imaoka, T., and Shoji, K., (Shimane, Japan), 63-68.
22. Inagaki, N., Chihara, K., Arimura, N., et al., (2001) CRMP-2 induces axons in cultured hippocampal neurons. Nature Neuroscience, 4(8):781-782.

Strategy-Oriented Evolutionary Games:
Toward a Grammatical Model of Games

B. Cases and S.O. Anchorena

Summary. We generalize evolutionary games to have strategy oriented payoff: for each strategy h, $\Pi_h(i,j) \in \mathbb{R}$ is the number of survival offspring of the specie h produced by a contest (i,j). This minor change allows the natural extension of strategy-oriented games G to a strategy-oriented replicator $\mathcal{S}_G$ that extends the classical replicator $\mathcal{R}_G$ of evolutionary games. We prove that the extension is strict by modeling the logistic equation as an $\mathcal{S}_G$ replicator. After that, we sketch the definition of a grammatical model of games implementing the logistic replicator.

19.1 Theory of Games: a Background

In 1944 Von Neumman and Morgenstern [7] elaborated the principles of a Theory of Games that was conceived as a mathematical theory of human economic behavior. They developed a contrast between the "Robinson Crusoe" model of economy, of an isolated single person, and a social exchange economy, with a moderate number of participants. Their aim was to establish the foundation of economy in the rational behavior of agents that play strategy games performing the optimization of some self-interest criterion.

Since that time [11], the Theory of Games has suffered wide development. A first step was the introduction in 1950 of the concept of Nash equilibrium: the mathematical characterization of the sets of strategies that drive to the maximization of profits and the minimization of losses in games. A second qualitative step was the application of the Theory of Games to study and simulate the biological evolution of species in 1973 by John M. Smith and Price [5, 6, 4]. In economy, the players are rational agents in a market competition. The payoff of games is measured in terms of goods or money. In biology, the games model pairwise contests between animals in a large population, and the payoff is measured in terms of Darwinian fitness (the expected number of surviving offspring).

In this section, we set the background of Theory of Games following the precise notation of Weibull [11]. In Subsection 19.1.1 games in normal form and their pure strategies are introduced. In Subsection 19.1.2 we introduce mixed strategies and the concepts of best reply and Nash equilibrium. Section 19.2 explains the principles of evolutionary games and the approaches to their study. In subsection 19.2.1 the approach based on mutations brings to the definition of "evolutionarily stable strategy". In Subsection 19.2.2 the dynamical approach based on replication and selection is described.

The classical replicator $\mathcal{R}_G$ of an evolutionary game G determines the dynamic of concentrations $x(t)$, $t = 0, 1, 2, \ldots$, of a population of individuals that contest pairwise, following k common strategies. The replicator is defined by the equations:

$$x_h(t+1) = \frac{u(e^h, x(t))}{u(x(t), x(t))} x_h(t) = \frac{e^h A x(t)}{x(t) A x(t)} x_h(t),$$

where u is the payoff for mixed strategies, e^h represents the pure strategy h vector, and A is the matrix of the game.

Our contributions begin in Section 19.3. We generalize the evolutionary games G of M. Smith and Price to have strategy, oriented replicators $\mathcal{S}_G$. The modification is minor: for each strategy h, $\Pi_h(i, j) \in \mathbb{R}$ is the number of surviving offspring of the specie h produced by a contest (i, j), represented by a matrix A_h. For example: modeling the encounter of rabbits r and carrots c, the contest (r, c) produces 1.2 rabbits and indirectly 2 carrots if the rabbit transports the seeds to a good substrate. Hence, $\Pi_r(r, c) = 1.2$ and $\Pi_c(r, c) = 2$.

This is a refinement of evolutionary games because the global payoff of a game G, $\pi = \sum_{h=1}^{k} \Pi_h$, is identical to the payoff of classical evolutionary games. Instead of playing a two-person symmetric game defined by the matrix A, there is a different payoff, in fact a different game G_h, for each strategy h, represented by the matrix A_h. The matrix A is the global payoff $\sum_{i=1}^{k} A_h = A$. The equations of a strategy-oriented replicator become to:

$$x_h(t+1) = \frac{v_h(x(t), x(t))}{u(x(t), x(t))} = \frac{x(t) A_h x(t)}{x(t) A x(t)},$$

where v_h is the payoff extended to mixed strategies of subgame G_h.

In Sections 19.4 and 19.5 we make a double contribution. First, we prove that the class of evolutionary games with classical replicators is strictly contained in the class of evolutionary games with strategy-oriented replicators. Second, we base our proof on the representation of the logistic equation as a strategy-oriented replicator:

$$x_1(t+1) = \mu x_1(t)(1 - x_1(t)), \tag{19.1}$$

$$x_2(t+1) = 1 - \mu x_1(t)(1 - x_1(t)). \tag{19.2}$$

We represent the logistic equation by an $\mathcal{S}_G$ replicator in Section 19.4, and we prove in Section 19.5 the impossibility of representing it as a classical replicator $\mathcal{R}_G$.

Finally, in Section 19.6 we describe a grammatical model that fits exactly to the notion of strategy-oriented replicator. We implement the logistic replicator of Section of section 19.5 using strategy-oriented grammars.

19.1.1 Games in Normal Form: Pure Strategies

Following [11] the elements of the Theory of Games are

- A set of players, $I = \{i_1, \ldots, i_n\}$, $n \geq 1$.
- For each player i, a set of pure strategies $S_i = \{1, 2, \ldots, m_i\}$ for some integer $m_i \geq 1$.
- A vector $s = (s_1, \ldots, s_n)$, where $s_i \in S_i$ is the pure strategy selected by player $i \in I$, called the pure strategy profile.
- The pure strategy space $S = S_1 \times \ldots \times S_n$ is the Cartesian product of pure strategies sets.
- For any pure strategy profile $s \in S$ and player $i \in I$ the payoff function of ith player is $\pi_i : S \to \mathbb{R}$. The associated payoff to player i is $\pi_i(s) \in \mathbb{R}$.
- The combined pure strategy payoff function is $\pi : S \to \mathbb{R}^n$ such that $\pi(s) = (\pi_1(s), \ldots, \pi_n(s))$ gives a payoff $\pi_1(s)$ to each player i.
- A game in normal form is, in terms of pure strategies, a triplet $G = (I, S, \pi)$.

Example 1. The "hawk–dove" game designed by M. Smith and Price [5, 6, 4] is a model of animals contesting a resource, for example, a territory, of value v, or victory, with a cost c. The value is measured in terms of Darwinian fitness: it means that winning the contest will increase the number of survival offspring of the winner by v. The cost of the fight (the player gets hurt or tired) has a value of $-c$. Both players have probability $1/2$ of winning the contest.

Let the set of individuals be $I = \{1, 2\}$. Individuals are birds of the same specie. The behaviors of the animals in the contest, the pure strategies, are fight like a hawk, escalating and continuing until injured or until opponent retreats; or fight like a dove, who displays without injuring the opponent unless the other escalates and in this case retreats. The sets of strategies are $S_1 = S_2 = \{H, D\}$. The space of pure strategies is $S = \{(H, H), (H, D), (D, H), (D, D)\}$.

When the number of players is two, the game is called a two-person game. In this cases, the payoff of the game for player 1 is given in a matrix A representing $\pi_1(s)$ with $s \in S$. Matrix B represents the payoff $\pi_2(s)$. The game is symmetric since $B = A^T$. Note that symmetry is referred to players 1 and 2.

Matrix C represents the combined payoff since the value in row i and column j, $C_{ij} = \pi(s) = \pi(i, j)$ when $s = (i, j)$. Rows correspond to strategies

H and D of player 1, while columns represent the strategies H and D of player 2 in all the matrices.

$$A = \begin{pmatrix} \frac{v-c}{2} & v \\ 0 & \frac{v}{2} \end{pmatrix}, B = \begin{pmatrix} \frac{v-c}{2} & 0 \\ v & \frac{v}{2} \end{pmatrix}, C = \begin{pmatrix} (\frac{v-c}{2}, \frac{v-c}{2}) & (v,0) \\ (0,v) & (\frac{v}{2}, \frac{v}{2}) \end{pmatrix}.$$

If both players fight like hawks, the payoff $\pi(H,H) = (\frac{v-c}{2}, \frac{v-c}{2})$ is low (and even negative if $v < c$) for both players. If they both select the strategy of the dove, the result is positive for the two players, $\pi(D,D) = (\frac{v}{2}, \frac{v}{2})$. If they select different strategies, the result is very good for the hawk and bad for the player that selects the role of dove.

19.1.2 Mixed Strategies Extensions of Games

An alternative to pure strategies are mixed strategies [11]:

- Mixed strategies are based on a probability distribution over the set S_i of pure strategies of player i: a vector $x_i = (x_{i1}, \ldots, x_{ij}, \ldots, x_{im_i})$ with $x_{ij} \in [0,1] \subseteq \mathbb{R}$ and $\sum_{j=1}^{m_i} x_{ij} = 1$.
- The set of all the mixed strategies of the ith player is $\Delta_i \subseteq [0,1]^{m_i}$.
- A mixed-strategy profile is a vector: $x = (x_1, \ldots, x_n) \in \Delta_1 \times \ldots \times \Delta_n = \Theta$. The set Θ is the mixed-strategy space.
- $u_i(x) = \sum_{s \in S} x(s)\pi_i(s)$ is the expected value of the payoff to the ith player associated to x. We call u_i the utility function of player i.
- The combined mixed-strategy payoff function, or utility function of the game, is $u(x) = (u_1(x), \ldots, u_n(x))$.
- The mixed strategy extension of game $G = (I, S, \pi)$ is the triplet $\mathcal{G} = (I, \Theta, u)$.

The word "utility" is avoided by Weibull in [11] but is the object of a deep discussion by Von Neumann and Morgenstern in [7]. We use "utility" here to abbreviate *combined mixed-strategy payoff function*.

Example 2. Consider the hawk–dove game in Example 1. The utility function in a two-player game, where matrix A represents the payoff of player 1 and matrix B is the payoff of player 2, is

$$u_1(x) = u_1(x_1, x_2) = x_1 A x_2 = (x_{11}, x_{12}) \begin{pmatrix} \frac{v-c}{2} & v \\ 0 & \frac{v}{2} \end{pmatrix} \begin{pmatrix} x_{21} \\ x_{22} \end{pmatrix},$$

$$u_2(x) = u_2(x_1, x_2) = x_1 B x_2 = (x_{11}, x_{12}) \begin{pmatrix} \frac{v-c}{2} & 0 \\ v & \frac{v}{2} \end{pmatrix} \begin{pmatrix} x_{21} \\ x_{22} \end{pmatrix}.$$

Note that $x = (x_1, x_2)$ is a mixed-strategy profile, that is a vector of strategies. Each x_i is a mixed strategy $x_i = (x_{i1}, x_{i2}) = (x_{i1}, 1 - x_{i1})$, a vector of probabilities.

Noncooperative Games Theory haas two main concepts:

- *Best reply:* The best reply of player i to a strategy profile

$$y = (y_1, \ldots, y_i, \ldots y_n) \in \Theta$$

is the set of mixed strategies

$$\tilde{\beta}_i(y) = \{x_i : (y_1, \ldots, y_{i-1}, x_i, y_{i+1}, \ldots, y_n) = z \in \Theta$$

and $u_i(y) \leq u_i(z)\}$. The combined best reply correspondence is $\tilde{\beta}(y) = \tilde{\beta}_1(y) \times \ldots \times \tilde{\beta}_n(y)$.

- *Nash equilibrium:* The set of Nash equilibrium $\Theta^{NE} \subseteq \Theta$ is the set of mixed-strategy profiles x such that $x \in \tilde{\beta}(x)$, that is the set of mixed-strategy profiles giving optimal results when played against themselves. Nash proved in 1950 that for any finite game $\Theta^{NE} \neq \emptyset$.

19.2 The Approaches to Study Evolutionary Games

Evolutionary games are symmetric two-person games based on the concept of *evolutionarily stable strategies*. Symmetric two-player games, widely studied in [7], are an important subset of games. We say, following again the notation of Weibull [11], that $G = (I, S, \pi)$ is a symmetric game if the set of players is $I = \{1, 2\}$, $S_1 = S_2 = K = \{1, \ldots, k\}$ is a common set of pure strategies and $\pi_2(s_1, s_2) = \pi_1(s_2, s_1)$ for all $s_1, s_2 \in S$, meaning that the matrix B representing π_2 is the transpose of the matrix A representing the payoff π_1, that is $A^T = B$.

The space of mixed strategies is $\Theta = \Delta^2$. In nonsymmetric, two-person games the utility of strategy x against strategy y is denoted

$$u(x, y) = (u_1(x, y), u_2(x, y)) = (xAy^T, xBy^T),$$

where $s = (x, y) \in \Delta^2$ is a mixed-strategy profile.

Notice that xAy is a bilinear form. For any two matrices A, B:

- $xAy + xBy = x(A + B)y$.
- $(x + x\prime)A(y + y\prime) = xAy + xAy\prime + x\prime Ay + x\prime Ay\prime$.
- For all scalar r, $r \times xAy^T = x\,(r \times A)\,y^T$.
- $xAy^T = yA^T x^T$.

In symmetric games, $A^T = B$, the utility functions of the players are symmetric $u_1(x, y) = xAy^T = yA^T x^T = u_2(y, x)$. Because of this, we identify $u(x, y) = u_1(x, y)$. The utility of the second player is denoted $u_2(x, y) = u(y, x)$ when necessary. Hence, the utility of strategy x when played against itself is $u_1(x, x) = u_2(x, x) = u(x, x)$.

Consider any 2×2 matrix A (if the common set of strategies has k elements the dimension of A is $k \times k$) the utility $u(x, x) = xAx^T$ is calculated in Eqs. (19.3) to (19.5).

$$xAx^T = (x_1, (1 - x_1)) \begin{pmatrix} a & b \\ c & d \end{pmatrix} \begin{pmatrix} x_1 \\ (1 - x_1) \end{pmatrix} \tag{19.3}$$

$$= ax_1^2 + (b + c)x_1(1 - x_1) + d(1 - x_1)^2 \tag{19.4}$$

$$= (a + d - (b + c)) x_1^2 + ((b + c) + 2d) x_1 + d. \tag{19.5}$$

The payoff to pure strategy $i \in K$ is $u(e^i, x) = e^i Ax^T$, where e^i is the vector that assigns 1 to component i and 0 to the resting $k - 1$ components.

The set of best replies to any opponent strategy $y \in \Delta$ is $\beta^*(y) = \{x \in \Delta : \forall x\prime \in \Delta,\ u(x\prime, y) \le u(x, y)\}$.

Finally, a Nash equilibrium $(x, y) \in \Theta^{NE}$ is symmetric if $x = y$. The set of strategies in Nash equilibrium is $\Delta^{NE} = \{x \in \Delta : x \in \beta^*(x)\} = \{x \in \Delta : \forall y \in \Delta,\ u(y, x) \le u(x, x)\}$.

Example 3. Consider the hawk–dove game in Examples 1 and 2.

$$u(y, x) = (y_1, 1 - y_1) \begin{pmatrix} \frac{v-c}{2} & 0 \\ v & \frac{v}{2} \end{pmatrix} \begin{pmatrix} x_1 \\ 1 - x_1 \end{pmatrix} = y_1 x_1 \frac{v - c}{2} + \frac{v}{2}(1 + y_1)(1 - x_1).$$

By definition, $x \in \beta^*(x)$ is in Nash equilibrium iff $\forall y\ \ u(y, x) \le u(x, x)$ iff for all y_1, $0 \le y_1 \le 1$:

$$(x_1 - y_1) \left(x_1 \frac{v - c}{2} + \frac{v}{2}(1 - x_1) \right) \ge 0 \leftrightarrow$$

$$(x_1 - y_1) \frac{v}{2} \left(1 - \frac{c}{v} x_1 \right) \ge 0 \leftrightarrow$$

$$\begin{cases} x_1 = 1 \ \wedge\ v \ge c, \\ \quad\quad \vee \\ x_1 = \frac{v}{c} \ \wedge\ c \ge v. \end{cases}$$

The set of strategies in Nash equilibrium for the hawk–dove game is

$$\Delta^{NE} = \left\{ x = (x_1, 1 - x_1) \in \Delta : \left(x_1 = \frac{v}{c} \le 1 \right) \vee \left(x_1 = 1 \le \frac{v}{c} \right) \right\}.$$

The "hawk-dove" game is the original reference to explain evolutionary games. The evolution of populations is simulated from the pairwise (first and second players) interaction and reproduction of the individuals in the interior of populations. In evolutionary games the mixed strategy of both players depends on the concentration of individuals in the population accumulated over time, because the pair of strategists contesting are drawn at random in the whole population and payoff is made in terms of Darwinian fitness. The rationality of individuals is limited, without any observation or learning and without any genetic algorithm.

There are two approaches to the evolution of populations: the approach based on mutations and the approach based on replication and selection.

19.2.1 The Approach Based on Mutations

There exists a population of individuals "programmed" to play some pure or mixed strategy. A small population share $\epsilon \in (0,1)$ of "mutant" individuals that play a different strategy is injected. The incumbent strategy is evolutionarily stable if it gets a higher payoff whenever the mutant strategy falls below a certain limit.

The strategy $x \in \Delta$ is an evolutionarily stable strategy (ESS) if for every strategy $y \neq x$, there exists some $\bar{\epsilon}_y \in (0,1)$ such that for all $\epsilon \in (0, \bar{\epsilon}_y)$:

$$u[x, \epsilon y + (1 - \epsilon)x] > u[y, \epsilon y + (1 - \epsilon)x].$$

.

The condition above is equivalent to the following two conditions:

- $\forall y \in \Delta, \ u(y,x) \leq u(x,x),$
- $\forall y \in \Delta, \ y \neq x \ (u(y,x) = u(x,x) \Rightarrow u(y,y) < u(x,y)).$

19.2.2 The Approach Based on Selection: The Replicator

Let $p_h(t)$ be the population of individuals programmed to pure strategy $h \in K$ at time step t. The total population is $p(t) = \sum_{h \in K} p_h(t) > 0$. The associated population state is the vector $x(t) = (x_1(t), \dots, x_k(t))$ where $x_h(t) = p_h(t)/p(t)$ is the population share programmed to strategy $h \in K$ at time t. A population state $x(t) \in \Delta$ is formally equal to a mixed strategy: a vector that assigns a probability to each strategy, but in this case the probability is identified to the frequency of the strategists in the population.

The expected payoff to any pure strategy h if the state of the population is x is denoted $u(e^h, x) = e^h A x^T$. The associated population average payoff, that is the average of any individual drawn at random, is $u(x,x) = \sum_{h=1}^{k} x_h u(e^h, x)$.

The dynamic of a population is determined by the iterations $t = 0, 1, 2, \dots$:

$$p_h(t+1) = \left(\alpha + u\left[e^h, x(t)\right]\right) p_h(t), \quad (19.6)$$

$$p(t+1) = \sum_{h=1}^{k} \left(\alpha + u\left[e^h, x(t)\right]\right) p_h(t) = (\alpha + u\left[x(t), x(t)\right]) p(t). \quad (19.7)$$

G defines the replicator $\mathcal{R}_G(t, x(0))$, which determines, starting at any initial condition $x(0) = (x_1(0), \dots, x_n(0))$. the state of the population $\mathcal{R}_G(t, x(0)) = x(t)$ at time step t by the equations

$$x_h(t+1) = \frac{\alpha + u\left[e^h, x(t)\right]}{\alpha + u\left[x(t), x(t)\right]} x_h(t). \quad (19.8)$$

Example 4. This example extends Example 3. Consider a population of $p(0) = 20$ strategists. The initial number of hawks is $p_1(0) = 20\lambda$ and the initial doves are $p_2(0) = 20(1 - \lambda)$, where $\lambda = v/c \leq 1$. We will iterate the replicator from $x(0) = (\lambda, 1 - \lambda)$ with parameter $\alpha = 0$. As shown in Example 3, $x(0)$ is a Nash equilibrium and for every strategy y, $u(y, x(0)) = \frac{v}{2}(1 - \lambda) = u(x(0), x(0))$. Hence, the population at step $t = 1$ is

- $p_1(1) = u\left[e^1, x(0)\right] p_1(0) = \frac{v}{2}(1 - \lambda)20\lambda = 10v\lambda(1 - \lambda)$,
- $p_2(1) = u\left[e^2, x(0)\right] p_0(t) = \frac{v}{2}(1 - \lambda)20(1 - \lambda) = 10v(1 - \lambda)^2$,
- $p(1) = 10v\lambda(1 - \lambda) + 10v(1 - \lambda)^2 = 10v(1 - \lambda)$.

The replicator $\mathcal{R}_G$ gives the state of the population at step $t = 1$:

- $x_1(1) = \frac{u[e^1, x(0)]}{u[x(0), x(0)]} x_1(0) = \frac{10v\lambda(1-\lambda)}{10v(1-\lambda)} = \lambda = x_1(0)$,
- $x_2(1) = \frac{u[e^2, x(0)]}{u[x(0), x(0)]} x_1(0) = \frac{10v(1-\lambda)^2}{10v(1-\lambda)} = 1 - \lambda = x_2(0)$.

Then, every Nash equilibrium $x(0) = \lambda = v/c \leq 1$ is a fixed point of the replicator replicator since $x(1) = x(0)$.

If $v/c \geq 1$, the only Nash equilibrium is $x(0) = (1, 0)$, a fixed point to the replicator:

$$x_1(1) = 1 = x_1(0), \qquad x_2(1) = 0 = 1 - x_1(0) = x_2(0).$$

It can be easily proved that every game G can be reduced to an equivalent game $G\prime$ with nonnegative payoffs. In the following, we assume nonnegative values for the matrix of the game.

19.3 Strategy-Oriented Replicators

In this section we deal with a generalization of the replicator model of evolutionary games that we call the replicator oriented to strategy. This generalization comes from a refinement of the payoff function inspired in grammars: consider a population $rrcccr$ of rabbits, determined by symbol r, and carrots, symbol c. A grammar is basically a set of rewriting rules, for example, $P = \{r \rightarrow rrccc, c \rightarrow ccc\}$. In a step of derivation one rule is applied to any symbol in the string matching the left-hand side of the rule, replacing the symbol by the right-hand side. For example: $r\ \overgroup{r}\ cccr \Rightarrow r\ \overgroup{rrccc}\ cccr$. Consider a different grammar defined by the rules $P\prime = \{r \rightarrow rrr, c \rightarrow cc\}$.

Interpreting a rewriting step as a game, assume that player 1 selects a grammar, P or $P\prime$ while player 2 selects a symbol in the string. If the contest is (P, r), the payoff is determined by the rule $r \rightarrow rrccc \in P$. Note that each symbol is like a coin: the payoff is composed of two rabbits and three carrots. Hence, we need a function $\Pi_r(P, r) = 2$ that defines the payoff of the contest (P, r) in "rabbit coins" and $\Pi_c(P, r) = 3$ means "carrot coins". In [1] we present a formalization of the hawk–dove game using Eco-grammar systems [2].

Definition 1. $G = (I, S, \pi, \Pi_1, \dots, \Pi_k)$ *is an evolutionary game oriented to strategy if*

- *The triplet (I, S, π) is a symmetric two-person game where $K = S_1 = S_2 = \{1, 2, \dots, k\}$ is a common set of strategies, $S = K \times K$ is the pure strategy space, and the payoff is $\pi = \sum_{i=1}^{k} \Pi_i$. We call π the global payoff of G.*
- *For each contest (i, j) and each strategy $h \in K$, $\Pi_h(i, j) \in \mathbb{R}$ is the payoff of (i, j) to strategy h.*
- *Each triplet $G_h = (I, S, \Pi_h)$ is a symmetric two-person game with utility function v_h called the subgame for strategy h.*

An evolutionary game oriented to strategy $G = (I, S, \pi, \Pi_1, \dots, \Pi_k)$ is a refinement of the global game $G = (I, S, \pi)$ that we denote with the same name without loss of generality. With $\mathcal{R}_G$ we denote the classical replicator defined by the global game G.

The payoff of the global game is determined by the matrix A, which gives for contest (i, j) the payoff $\pi(i, j) = A_{ij}$, the component of row i and column j of the matrix of the game A.

Matrix A_h represents the payoff to strategy $h \in K$ of contest (i, j) being $\Pi_h(i, j) = A_{h_{ij}} \in \mathbb{R}$ the component of row i and column j of A_h. The matrix of the game is $A = \sum_{h=1}^{k} A_h$.

Let $v_h(x, y) = x A_h y^T$ be the utility function of subgame G_h, where $x, y \in \Delta$ are mixed strategies. The utility function of game G is $u(x, y) = \sum_{h=1}^{k} v_h(x, y) = \sum_{h=1}^{k} x A_h y^T = x A y^T$.

Definition 2. *Let $G = (I, S, \pi, \Pi_1, \dots, \Pi_k)$ be an evolutionary game oriented to strategy. The dynamic of populations of G is defined as the iteration with $h \in K$:*

$$p_h(t+1) = (\alpha + v_h(x(t), x(t))) p_h(t), \qquad (19.9)$$

$$p(t+1) = \sum_{h=1}^{k} p_h(t+1) = (\alpha + u(x(t), x(t))) p_h(t). \qquad (19.10)$$

We say that G defines the strategy-oriented replicator denoted $\mathcal{S}_{G_1 + \dots + G_k}$ or simply $\mathcal{S}_G$. The expression $\mathcal{S}_G(t, x(0))$ determines, starting at any initial condition $x(0) = (x_1(0), \dots, x_n(0))$, the state of the population $\mathcal{S}_G(t, x(0)) = x(t)$ at time step t by the equations:

$$x_h(t+1) = \frac{p_h(t+1)}{p(t+1)} = \frac{\alpha + v_h(x(t), x(t))}{\alpha + u(x(t), x(t))} = \frac{\alpha + x(t) A_h x(t)^T}{\alpha + x(t) A x(t)^T}. \qquad (19.11)$$

Compare Eq. (19.11) to the classical replicator in Section 19.2 Eq. (19.8). Now, there is a different matrix A_h for each strategy h and hence, the polynomial $x(t) A_h x(t)^T$ is quadratic. In the classical replicator, $u[e^h, x(t)]$ is linear and becomes quadratic when multiplied by $x_h(t)$.

Example 5. Consider the hawk–dove game oriented to strategy: $G = (I, S, \pi,$ $\Pi_1, \Pi_2)$ where $A_1 = \begin{pmatrix} \frac{v-c}{2} & v \\ 0 & 0 \end{pmatrix}$ represents the payoff Π_1 to hawks, while $A_2 = \begin{pmatrix} 0 & 0 \\ 0 & \frac{v}{2} \end{pmatrix}$ represents the payoff Π_2 to doves. $A = A_1 + A_2$ is the matrix of the game.

Let $x(t) = (x_1(t), x_2(t))$ where $x_2(t) = 1 - x_1(t)$ is a mixed strategy representing the state of population at time step t.

By Eq. (19.5):

$$u[x(t), x(t)] = \frac{-c}{2}x_1^2(t) + 2vx_1(t) + \frac{v}{2}$$

and

$$u[e^1, x(t)]\, x_1(t) = (1,0)Ax(t)^T x_1(t) = x(t)A_1 x(t)^T$$
$$= \left(-\frac{v+c}{2}x_1(t) + v\right)x_1(t)$$
$$u[e^2, x(t)]\, x_2(t) = (0,1)Ax(t)^T x_2(t)$$
$$= x(t)A_2 x(t)^T = \frac{v}{2}(1 - x_1(t))^2$$

The strategy-oriented replicator $S_G = S_{G_1+G_2}$ is just the "hawk-dove" game replicator $\mathcal{R}_G$ of the global game, considering $G = (I, S, \pi)$:

$$x_1(t+1) = \frac{\left(-\frac{v+c}{2}x_1(t) + v\right)x_1(t)}{\frac{-c}{2}x_1^2(t) + 2vx_1(t) + \frac{v}{2}},$$
$$x_2(t+1) = \frac{\frac{v}{2}(1 - x_1(t))^2}{\frac{-c}{2}x_1^2(t) + 2vx_1(t) + \frac{v}{2}}.$$

The following proposition proves that the class of strategy-oriented replicators is a generalization of the class of classical replicators. We say that two replicators of any type ($\mathcal{X}$ means classical or strategy oriented) $\mathcal{X}_G$ and $\mathcal{X}\prime_{G\prime}$ are equivalent if for all initial state of the population $x(0)$ and for all time step t, $\mathcal{X}_G(t, x(0)) = \mathcal{X}\prime_{G\prime}(t, x(0)) = x(t)$.

Proposition 1. *Let $G = (I, S, \pi)$ be an evolutionary game and $\mathcal{R}_G$ its classical replicator. There exists a strategy-oriented game $G = (I, S, \pi, \Pi_k, \ldots, \Pi_k)$ such that $S_{G_1+\ldots+G_k} = \mathcal{R}_G$.*

Proof. If $\mathcal{R}_G$ is a replicator determining the state dynamic $x(t)$, to build an equivalent strategy-oriented replicator S_G determining $x\prime(t)$, we identify $v_h(x, x) = xA_h x^T = u(e^h, x)x_h$, where

$$A_h = \begin{pmatrix} 0 & \cdots & 0 \\ A_{h1} & \cdots & A_{hm} \\ 0 & \cdots & 0 \end{pmatrix}$$

is a matrix of components 0, except the hth row is copied from matrix A. By only this identification the population state dynamics become identical:

$$x_h(t+1) = \frac{(\alpha + u\,[e^h, x])\,x_h}{u(x(t), x(t))} = \frac{(\alpha + v_h(x(t), x(t)))}{u(x(t), x(t))} = x\prime_h(t+1).$$

Proposition 2. *Let $\mathcal{S}_G$ be a strategy oriented replicator where*

$$x_h(t) = \frac{\alpha + v_h(x(t), x(t))}{\alpha + u(x(t), x(t))}$$

is the state of the population of h strategists at time t. There exists an equivalent strategy-oriented replicator $\mathcal{S}_{G\prime}$ that for all time step t,

$$x_h(t) = x\prime_h(t) = \frac{v\prime_h(x(t), x(t))}{u\prime(x(t), x(t))},$$

i.e., produces the same dynamics with $\alpha = 0$.

Proof. The state population dynamics of G are determined by

$$x_h(t) = \frac{\alpha + x(t)A_h x^T(t)}{\alpha + x(t)Ax^T(t)}$$

, where A is the matrix of the game and A_h is the payoff to strategy h.

Consider the matrix $Z_\alpha = \begin{pmatrix} \alpha \dots \alpha \\ \vdots \ddots \vdots \\ \alpha \dots \alpha \end{pmatrix}$.

Then $x(t)Z_\alpha x^T(t) = \alpha$ for all time step t. .

Let $A\prime = A + Z_\alpha$ be the matrix of the game $G\prime$, and let $A\prime_h = A_h + Z_\alpha$ be the payoff to strategy h. Then, $v\prime_h(x(t), x(t)) = x(t)(A_h + Z_\alpha)x^T(t) = x(t)Z_\alpha x^T(t) + x(t)A_h x^T(t)$ and

$$u\prime(x(t), x(t)) = x(t)(A + Z)x^T(t) = x(t)Zx^T(t) + x(t)Ax^T(t).$$

Consequently, for all time step t, $x_h(t) = x\prime_h(t)$.

19.4 Modeling the Logistic Equation as a Strategy Oriented Replicator

The logistic equation developed by May in 1976 [10, 3] has the form

$$z(t+1) = \mu z(t)(1 - z(t)) \text{ with } 0 \le \mu \le 4, \tag{19.12}$$

where $z(t) \in [0, 1]$ means the relative frequency of an organism, for example, a population of rabbits, μ is the rate of reproduction of rabbits and $1 - z(t) \in [0, 1]$ is the probability of resources, for example, carrots. This equation has been widely studied because of its ecological interest and because it is paradigm of chaotic behavior. In this section we present a strategy-oriented replicator that models the logistic equation. The logistic equation has values $z(t) \in [0, 1]$ for all t if $0 \leq \mu \leq 4$.

Consider the game in normal form $G = (I, S, \pi)$ where $I = \{1, 2\}$ are the players, $K = \{R, C\}$, where $R = 1$ and $C = 2$, is the set of pure strategies common to both players, and $S = \{(R, R), (R, C), (C, R), (C, C)\}$ is the space of pure strategy profiles. The matrix of the game is A, and the matrices representing the payoff to strategies R and C are A_R and A_C, with

$$A = A_R + A_C = \begin{pmatrix} a & b \\ c & d \end{pmatrix}. \tag{19.13}$$

By Proposition 2 the equations that govern the state of the population in the strategy-oriented replicator have $\alpha = 0$, and they are

$$x_R(t+1) = \frac{v_R(x(t), x(t))}{u(x(t), x(t))} = \frac{x(t)A_R x(t)^T}{x(t)A x(t)^T} \tag{19.14}$$
$$= \mu x_R(t)(1 - x_R(t)),$$

$$x_C(t+1) = \frac{v_C(x(t), x(t))}{u(x(t), x(t))} = \frac{x(t)A_C x(t)^T}{x(t)A x(t)^T} \tag{19.15}$$
$$= 1 - \mu x_R(t)(1 - x_R(t)).$$

Notice that $x_R(t+1) = \mu x_R(t)(1 - x_R(t))$ is the quotient of two quadratic polynomials. The only possibility of obtaining Eqs. (19.14) and (19.15) is when $u(x(t), x(t)) = \gamma$ is constant. From Eq. (19.5):

$$u(x(t), x(t)) = (a + d - b - c)x_R^2 + (b + c - 2d)x_R + d = \gamma \longleftrightarrow \tag{19.16}$$
$$a + d = b + c = 2d \quad \wedge \quad d = \gamma \longleftrightarrow \tag{19.17}$$
$$a = d = \gamma \quad \wedge \quad b + c = 2\gamma. \tag{19.18}$$

From Eq. (19.18) we conclude that $A = A_R + A_C$ is a matrix:

$$A = \begin{pmatrix} \gamma & \gamma - \gamma\prime \\ \gamma + \gamma\prime & \gamma \end{pmatrix} \quad \vee \quad A = \begin{pmatrix} \gamma & \gamma + \gamma\prime \\ \gamma - \gamma\prime & \gamma \end{pmatrix} \tag{19.19}$$

If the matrix of the game looks like matrices in Eq. (19.19) we ensure that the whole population evolves in a constant rate $u(x(t), x(t)) = \gamma$. From the definition of the logistic equation Eq. (19.12), the parameters $k, k\prime$ are bounded by $0 \leq \mu = \frac{\gamma\prime}{\gamma} \leq 4$.

Consider $A_R = \begin{pmatrix} 0 & \gamma' \\ 0 & 0 \end{pmatrix}$ and $A_C = \begin{pmatrix} \gamma & \gamma \\ \gamma - \gamma' & \gamma \end{pmatrix}$.

Notice that $A_R + A_C = A$ and $A_R^T + A_C^T = A^T$ have the form deduced in Eq. (19.19). From the matrices we get the logistic equation represented as the population state of a strategy-oriented replicator, when $\mu = \gamma'/\gamma$:

$$x_R(t+1) = \frac{v_R(x(t), x(t))}{\gamma} = \frac{x(t)A_R x(t)^T}{\gamma} \qquad (19.20)$$

$$= \mu x_R(t)(1 - x_R(t)),$$

$$x_C(t+1) = \frac{v_C(x(t), x(t))}{\gamma} = \frac{x(t)A_C x^T(t)}{\gamma} \qquad (19.21)$$

$$= 1 - \mu x_R(t)(1 - x_R(t)).$$

We call $\mathcal{L}_G$ to the logistic replicator oriented to strategy $\mathcal{S}_{G_R + G_C} = \mathcal{S}_G$ built in this section.

19.5 The Impossibility of Modeling the Logistic Equation as a Classical Replicator

We attempt in this section to model the logistic equation by means of the classical replicator. The equation that defines the concentration of strategy h in a population is

$$x_R(t) = \left(\alpha + \frac{u\left[e^1, x(t)\right]}{\alpha + u(x(t), x(t))} \right) x_R(t) = \mu x_R(t)(1 - x_R(t)), \quad (19.22)$$

$$x_C(t) = \left(\alpha + \frac{u\left[e^2, x(t)\right]}{\alpha + u(x(t), x(t))} = 1 - \mu x_R(t) \right) (1 - x_R(t)). \quad (19.23)$$

Reasoning like in Section 19.4, the only possibility to obtain that result is making $\alpha + u(x(t), x(t)) = r$ constant. The parameter $\alpha = 0$ has null value by proposition 2, since Proposition 1 ensures that classical replicators are a subclass of strategy-oriented replicators.

Hence the matrix A of the game is the same of the logistic replicator oriented to strategy given in section 19.4, Eq. (19.19).

Applying matrix A to the Eqs. (19.22) and (19.23) that model concentrations:

$$x_R(t) = \frac{u\left[e^1, x(t)\right] x_R(t)}{\gamma} \qquad (19.24)$$

$$= \left(x_R(t) + \frac{\gamma'}{\gamma}(1 - x_R(t)) \right) x_R(t)$$

$$= \mu(1 - x_R(t))x_R(t),$$

$$x_C(t) = \frac{u\left[e^2, x(t)\right] x_C(t)}{\gamma} \tag{19.25}$$

$$= \left(\left(1 - \frac{\gamma\prime}{\gamma}\right) x_R(t) + (1 - x_R(t))\right)(1 - x_R(t))$$

$$= 1 - \mu(1 - x_R(t))x_R(t).$$

Equations (19.24) and (19.25) are unsolvable if we look for values $\mu, \gamma, \gamma\prime$ that make the expression true for any population state $x_R(t)$. Thus, the logistic equation cannot be obtained as the dynamic of concentrations of a classical replicator.

19.6 Towards a Grammatical Model of Games

The work above has been though related to grammars. Formal language theory [9] is a branch of theoretical computer sciences that develops abstract models of computation based on rewriting symbols in strings according to a finite set of rules.

In [1] we defined a grammatical model of the hawk–dove game using Eco-grammars systems, but this work attempts to make a more general approach to a grammatical model of games. Eco-Grammar systems [8, 2] are an abstract model of computation with universal computation capability proposed as a formal frame to study systems composed of interdependent agents acting on a common environment. This model was developed by Csuhaj-Varjú, Kelemen, Kelemenova and Paŭn [2] as a formal model of ecosystems. The six basic postulates intended by the authors for the development of EG systems are

1. An ecosystem consists of an environment and a set of agents. The internal states of the agents and the state of the environment are described by strings of symbols, called words, over certain alphabets.
2. In an ecosystems there exists a universal clock that sets units of time, common to the agents and to the environment, and according to them the development of the agents and of the environment is considered.
3. The agent and the environment have developmental rules that correspond to context-free Lindenmayer systems, which are applied in parallel to all the symbols that describe the state of the agents and of the environment. All the agents and the environment perform a parallel step of derivation at each unit of time.
4. The environmental rules are independent or the agents and independent of the state of the environment. Agents' developmental rules depend on the state of the environment, which determines a subset of developmental rules that is applicable to the internal state of the agent.

5. Agents act in the environment (and possible in the internal words of other agents) according to action rules, which are rewriting rules used in chomskyan (sequential) mode. At each instant of time, each agent uses a rule selected from a set that depends on the internal state of the agent.
6. The action of the agents in the environment has greater priority than the development of the environment. Only the symbols of the environmental string that are not affected by the agents will be rewritten by the environmental rules.

A rewriting grammar scheme is basically a pair $\Sigma = (V, P)$ formed of an alphabet V (a nonempty and finite set of symbols) and a set P of rewriting rules with the form $a \to \alpha$, where $a \in V^+$ (the set of nonempty words over V) and $\alpha \in V^*$ (the set of all the words over the alphabet including the empty word denoted by ε). The set of rules is context-free if all the left-hand sides of the rules are symbols $a \in V$.

We work in this paper only with context-free rules. A set of rules P is deterministic if there exists at most one rule $a \to \alpha$ with left-hand side $a \in V$. The set is complete if for each $a \in V$ there is a rule with left-hand side a.

A grammar scheme $\Sigma = (V, P)$ is CF chomskyan if P is a set of context-free sequential rules. A step of derivation in CF sequential mode is denoted by the expression $xay \Rightarrow x\alpha y$, where $xay \in V^+$ and $x\alpha y \in V^*$ iff the rule $a \to \alpha$ is in P.

A grammar scheme $\Sigma = (V, P)$ is 0L if P is a set of context-free parallel rules. The expression $a_{h_1} \ldots a_{h_n} \Rightarrow_{\Sigma_i} \alpha_{h_1} \ldots \alpha_{h_n}$ is a step of derivation in 0L mode iff for each h_i the rule $a_{h_i} \to \alpha_{h_i}$ is in P.

Example 6. Consider the alphabet $V = \{r, c\}$, where r means a rabbit and c a carrot. A word $crcrc \in V^*$ represents a population of two rabbits and three carrots. Let $P = \{c \to crc, r \to \varepsilon, r \to cc\}$ be the set of rules and $\Sigma = (V, P)$ a grammar scheme.

The expression $crcrc \Rightarrow crcrcrc$ is a step of derivation in CF chomskyan mode since $cr\underline{c}rc \Rightarrow cr\underline{crc}rc$ and the rule $c \to crc$ is in P. The rule $r \to \varepsilon$ produces derivation steps $crcrc \Rightarrow ccrc = c\varepsilon crc$ and $crcrc \Rightarrow crcc$.

The expression $\underline{c}\ r\ \underline{c}\ r\ \underline{c} \Rightarrow \underline{crc}\ \varepsilon\ \underline{crc}\ cc\ \underline{crc}$ is a step of derivation in 0L mode. Notice that rules $c \to crc$, $r \to \varepsilon$, $c \to crc$, $r \to cc$, and $c \to crc$ are applied each one to one symbol in the word.

Let $\Sigma = (V, P)$ be a grammar scheme. The number of rules in P with the same left-hand side $a \in V$ is denoted r_a. A grammar scheme $\Sigma = (V, P)$ is deterministic if $r_a \le 1$, and Σ is complete if $r_a \ge 1$ for all symbols a. In the following assume that every grammar Σ is deterministic and complete (denoted DCF or $D0L$).

While a grammar scheme is a pair $G = (V, P)$, a grammar is a triplet $G_w = (V, P, w)$ where $w = w(0)$ is a word called the axiom representing an initial population of symbols. A k-step derivation is a sequence $w(0) \Rightarrow w(1) \Rightarrow \ldots \Rightarrow w(k)$ of derivation steps starting at the axiom.

An interpretation of grammars as games comes immediately. Consider a game $G = (I, S, \pi)$, where $I = \{1, 2\}$, the strategies of the first player are grammars $S_1 = \{\Sigma_1, \ldots, \Sigma_k\}$, and the strategies of the second $S_2 = V$ are the symbols of the alphabet. The rules determine the payoff matrix represented below. Notice that each entry is occupied by exactly one rule because the grammars are deterministic and complete.

global	a_1	$\ldots$	a_m
Σ_1	$a_1 \to \alpha_{11}$	$\ldots$	$a_m \to \alpha_{1m}$
$\vdots$			
Σ_k	$a_1 \to \alpha_{k1}$	$\ldots$	$a_m \to \alpha_{km}$

The mixed strategies are determined by the state of the derived string. Each derivation step represents a move in the game. Let $\bar{w} = \psi(w) = (|w|_{a_1}, \ldots, |w|_{a_m})$ be the vector that counts the occurrences of symbol a_i in the word w, denoted $|w|_{a_i} \in \mathbb{N}^m$. Let $|w|$ be the length of w.

If player 1 selects a grammar Σ_i (a pure strategy i) and player 2 a symbol a_h at random in the population, $w = x a_h x\prime$, the probability of a_h is determined by $x_h = |w|_{a_h}/|w|$. The state of the population is $x = \psi(w)/|w|$, just the mixed strategy of player two due to the mechanism of selection.

If the selected grammar Σ_i is DCF, the population at the following step becomes $x a_h x\prime \Rightarrow_{\Sigma_i} x \alpha_{ih} x\prime$. If grammars are $D0L$, then $w = a_{h_1} \ldots a_{h_n} \Rightarrow_{\Sigma_i} \alpha_{ih_1} \ldots \alpha_{ih_n}$. Thus, the mixed strategy of the second player varies in the next step. Notice that a game with only one strategy for the first player is simply a DCF or a $D0L$ grammar. If the number of grammars is greater than one, the first player could elaborate mixed strategies selecting grammar Σ_i with probability z_i.

The coefficients of the matrix of payoffs are words composed of different symbols and consequently the payoff is a natural number. For example, rule $r \to rrccr$ produces $|rrccr|_r = 3$ rabbits and $|rrccr|_c = 2$ carrots. This is a minor problem since we can obtain any real nonnegative payoff using nondeterministic and probabilistic sets of a-rules (rules with the same left-hand side a), that allow the selection of a rule $a \to \alpha_i$ with probability q_i when there is more than one rule with left-hand side a. The discrete case is enough to illustrate an approach toward game grammars.

19.7 Strategy-Oriented Game Grammars: Implementing the Logistic Replicator

In this section we will specify more our model of a game grammar. For this purpose, we will represent the logistic game developed in Section 19.4 in grammatical terms.

We call a strategy oriented game grammar to a strategy-oriented game $G = (I, S, \pi, \Pi_1, \ldots, \Pi_k)$, where $I = \{1, 2\}$, the strategies of the first player are sequential grammars $S_1 = \{\Sigma_{a_1}, \ldots, \Sigma_{a_k}\}$, and the strategies of the second player $S_2 = V = \{a_1, \ldots, a_k\}$ are the symbols of the alphabet. Notation x^i means the concatenation i times of x and $x^0 = \varepsilon$. The rules determine the payoff matrix for the logistic game:

π	$x_r(t)$ r	$x_c(t)$ c
$x_r(t)\ \Sigma_r$	$r \to c^\gamma$	$c \to c^\gamma r^{\gamma\prime}$
$x_c(t)\ \Sigma_c$	$r \to c^{\gamma-\gamma\prime}$	$r \to c^\gamma$

A	r	c
Σ_r	γ	$\gamma + \gamma\prime$
Σ_c	$\gamma - \gamma\prime$	γ

$$(19.26)$$

The payoff Π_h is separated for each strategy h:

Π_r	$x_r(t)$ r	$x_c(t)$ c
$x_r(t)\ \Sigma_{r,r}$	$r \to \varepsilon$	$c \to r^{\gamma\prime}$
$x_c(t)\ \Sigma_{c,r}$	$r \to \varepsilon$	$c \to \varepsilon$

A_r	$x_r(t)$ r	$x_c(t)$ c
$x_r(t)\ \Sigma_{r,r}$	0	$\gamma\prime$
$x_c(t)\ \Sigma_{c,r}$	0	0

Π_c	r	c
$\Sigma_{r,c}$	$r \to c^\gamma$	$c \to c^\gamma$
$\Sigma_{c,c}$	$r \to c^{\gamma-\gamma\prime}$	$r \to c^\gamma$

A_c	r	c
$\Sigma_{r,c}$	γ	γ
$\Sigma_{c,c}$	$\gamma - \gamma\prime$	γ

In strategy-oriented game grammars, each strategy h is identified to a DCF grammar Σ_h. This makes natural the use of the state of the population as a mixed strategy: to simulate a move, we interpret every symbol r in the string w as an agent Σ_r while a carrot c is the agent Σ_c. Each agent selects at random a symbol to combat in the population and applies the corresponding rule.

	Σ_c	Σ_r	Σ_c	Σ_c	Σ_r
	$\downarrow$	$\downarrow$	$\downarrow$	$\downarrow$	$\downarrow$
$r\,c\,c\,r\,c \mapsto$	r	c	c	r	c
	$\Downarrow$	$\Downarrow$	$\Downarrow$	$\Downarrow$	$\Downarrow$
	$c^{\gamma-\gamma\prime}$	$r^{\gamma\prime}c^\gamma$	c^γ	$c^{\gamma-\gamma\prime}$	$r^{\gamma\prime}c^\gamma$

This is the step of derivation:

$$r c c r c \Rightarrow c^{\gamma-\gamma\prime} r^{\gamma\prime} c^{3\gamma-\gamma\prime} r^{\gamma\prime} c^\gamma.$$

The mechanism of derivation corresponds to the class of reproductive simple Eco-grammar systems, as will be proved in a different paper. If all the grammars are equal, $\Sigma_1 = \ldots = \Sigma_k$, the grammar is formally identical to a $D0L$ grammar.

The derivation step can be subdivided to see the effect of separating the payoff of each strategy in a different grammar: each encounter (i, j) produces $\Pi_r(i, j) + \Pi_c(i, j) = \pi(i, j)$ new individuals.

$\Sigma_{c,r} - \Sigma_{c,c}$	$\Sigma_{r,r} - \Sigma_{r,c}$	$\Sigma_{c,r} - \Sigma_{c,c}$	$\Sigma_{c,r} - \Sigma_{c,c}$	$\Sigma_{r,r} - \Sigma_{r,c}$
$\downarrow$	$\downarrow$	$\downarrow$	$\downarrow$	$\downarrow$

$$r\ c\ c\ r\ c \mapsto$$

r	c	c	r	c
$\Downarrow$	$\Downarrow$	$\Downarrow$	$\Downarrow$	$\Downarrow$
$r^0 c^{\gamma-\gamma'}$	$r^{\gamma'} c^{\gamma}$	$r^0 c^{\gamma}$	$r^0 c^{\gamma-\gamma'}$	$r^{\gamma'} c^{\gamma}$

Interpreting grammars in the free commutative monoid $(V^{\oplus}, \cdot, \varepsilon)$, a word $rrccc = r^2 c^3$ is equivalent to any permutation $crrcc$, we only are interested in the number of occurrences of symbols and not in their positions. A step of derivation starting at w can be defined as the sequence $w \Rightarrow_G xy$ iff $w \Rightarrow_{\Pi_r} x$ and $w \Rightarrow_{\Pi_c} x$.

With respect to the strategies used for each player, they are Indicated by the matrix of the game in Eq. (19.26). At time step t, the probability of a contest (Σ_i, j) equals the probability of independently selecting at random a symbol i from the string $w(t)$ that represents the population at time t. The first player becomes to an agent Σ_i, and the second player (agent Σ_i is the second player) selects the passive individual j from $w(t)$. This probability is $x_i(t) x_j(t) = \frac{|w(t)|_i}{|w(t)|} \frac{|w(t)|_j}{|w(t)|}$. The contest produces $A_{r_{ij}}$ new rabbits and $A_{c_{ij}}$ new carrots.

At time $t + 1$, the expected survival offspring of rabbits and carrots are

$$x_r(t+1) = \frac{x(t) A_r x(t)^T}{x(t) A x(t)^T} = \frac{\sum_{i,j \in K} x_i(t) x_j(t) A_{r_{ij}}}{\sum_{i,j \in K} x_i(t) x_j(t) A_{ij}},$$

$$x_c(t+1) = \frac{x(t) A_c x(t)^T}{x(t) A x(t)^T} = \frac{\sum_{i,j \in K} x_i(t) x_j(t) A_{c_{ij}}}{\sum_{i,j \in K} x_i(t) x_j(t) A_{ij}}.$$

19.8 Conclusions

In this paper we extend evolutionary games to strategy-oriented evolutionary games. We prove that this extension is strict. This approach is different of the multipopulation models described in [11], based on the increment of the number of players and the elimination of symmetry.

We generalize the payoff of games to strategies. For each strategy h, $\Pi_h(i,j) \in \mathbb{R}$ is the number of survival offspring of the specie h produced by a contest (i, j). The global payoff is the sum of the payoffs to strategies $\pi(i, j) = \sum_h \Pi_h(i, j)$. Each Pi_h defines in fact a different evolutionary game G_h, and the global game G is the sum of the partial games. In the extension to mixed strategies x, y, the utility function $u(x, y) = \sum_h v_h(x, y)$ of G is the sum of the utilities of the partial games G_h.

We generalize the classical replicators $\mathcal{R}_G$ of evolutionary games to strategy-oriented replicators $\mathcal{S}_G$, such that $x_h(t+1) = \frac{v_h(x(t), x(t))}{u(x(t), x(t))}$. We proved that this replicator is a strict extension of the classical replicator. We based our proof on the representation as a strategy-oriented replicator of the logistic equation called the logistic replicator $\mathcal{L}_G$.

Finally, we sketch a grammatical model of two-person games that fits exactly to the notion of strategy-oriented replicator. We implement the logistic replicator using strategy-oriented grammars.

This work requires two extensions: the first direction, exploring the properties of the Nash equilibrium, ESS and Lyapunov stable strategies. It seems clear that the strategies in Nash equilibrium for two-person symmetric games and for strategy-oriented games are identical. In fact, they depend on the global payoff and not on the replicators. Respecting to ESS, and Lyapunov stable strategies, they both depend on the dynamical properties of the replicators; this suggests that the results that are valid for classical replicators will extend to strategy-oriented replicators.

The second direction to extend this work is relating formally Strategy-oriented games to the hierarchy of Eco-grammar systems, a work initiated in [1] representing the "hawk-dove" game as an eco-grammar system with a constant number of agents. Strategy-oriented game grammars are qualitatively different, since each symbol in the population has a dual interpretation: it is an agent and it is a passive individual.

Finally, the main contribution of this work is opening a way to study the sequences of moves in two-person games from the point of view of their complexity as formal languages, and relate it to the expected payoff. This is a step toward a hierarchy of dynamical systems in relation to a hierarchy of grammars that we consider necessary to unify concepts in complex systems and artificial life.

Acknowledgments

Acknowledgment: This paper has been sponsored by the Spanish Interdepartmental Commission of Science and Technology (CICYT), project number TEL1999-0181. And the University of the Basque Country project number 9/upv 00003.230-13707/2001.

References

1. S. Anchorena and B. Cases. "Eco-grammars to model biological systems: adding probabilities to agents". Proceedings of the European Conference on Artificial Life, ECAL 2002. Springer. Berlin (2001)
2. E. Csuhaj-Varju, J. Kelemen; A. Kelemenova and G. Paǔn (1997) Eco-Grammar Systems: A Grammatical Framework for Life-Like Interactions". Artificial Life, 3(1):1-38
3. R.L. Devaney (1992) A first course in chaotic dynamical systems. Theory and experiment. Studies in Nonlinearity. Addison-Wesley. U.S.A.

4. M. Smith, J. (1982) Evolution and Theory of Games. Cambridge University Press. Cambridge MA.
5. M. Smith, J. and Price, G.R. (1973) The logic of animal conflict. Nature 246:15-18
6. M. Smith, J. (1978) La evolución del comportamiento in Evolución, Libros de Investigación y Ciencia, Ed. Prensa Científica,Barcelona pp. 116-126
7. J. Von Neumann; O. Morgenstern. (1944) Theory of Games and economic behavior.Princeton University Press. U.S.A
8. Paŭn, G. (Ed.) (1995) Artificial Life: Grammatical Models. Black Sea University. Bucharest, Romania
9. Rozenberg, G. y A. Salomaa (Eds).(1997) Handbook of Formal Languages. Vol.1, 2 3. Springer, Berlin
10. Sole, R., Manrubia, S. (1996)Orden y caos en sistemas complejos. Edicions UPC, Barcelona
11. Weibull, J. W. (1996) Evolutionary Game Theory. The MIT Press. Cambridge, MA.

20

Discrete Multi-Phase Particle Swarm Optimization

B. Al-kazemi, C.K. Mohan

Summary. This chapter proposes the Discrete Multi-Phase Particle Swarm Optimization (DiMuPSO) algorithm, extending the PSO approach to problems coded with discrete binary representations. The main features of DiMuPSO are in utilizing multiple groups of particles with different goals that are allowed to change with time, alternately moving toward or away from the best solutions found recently. DiMuPSO also enforces steady improvement in solution quality, accepting only moves that improve fitness. Experimental simulations show that DiMuPSO outperforms a genetic algorithm and a previous discrete version of PSO on several benchmark problems.

20.1 Introduction

The Particle Swarm Optimization *(PSO)* algorithm is a stochastic population-based algorithm, derived from bird flocking simulations [8, 17, 19]. This chapter proposes the Discrete Multi-Phase Particle Swarm Optimization (DiMuPSO) algorithm, successful in applying the PSO approach to problems coded with discrete binary representations. The main features of DiMuPSO are in utilizing multiple groups of particles with different goals that are allowed to change with time, alternately moving toward or away from the best solutions found recently. DiMuPSO also enforces steady improvement in solution quality, accepting only moves that improve fitness.

The rest of this section describes the PSO algorithm. Section 20.2 presents the DiMuPSO algorithm. Section 20.3 presents experimental results comparing DiMuPSO with a genetic algorithm and with a previous discrete version of PSO [15], on several deceptive optimization problems. Section 20.4 describes similar comparisons for continuous optimization problems whose parameters are encoded using discrete (binary vector) representations. Section 20.5 presents concluding remarks.

20.1.1 Particle Swarm Optimization Algorithm

The PSO algorithm uses a population of individuals called "particles." Each particle has its own position and velocity to move around the search space. When a particle wants to calculate its new position, it takes into account its own previous best value, and the best value found so far by all other particles (the *global PSO* model [17, 27]) or its neighbors (the *local PSO* model [10, 15, 28]). Our experiments presume the global version, believed to offer a faster rate of convergence, though at greater risk of premature convergence than the local version.

We use the following notation, and assume a discrete-time updating model:

1. N: the maximum number of swarms (generations).
2. M: the number of particles in each swarm.
3. n: the dimension of the problem.
4. $X_m(t)$: the position of the mth particle at time t, a vector whose ith component is $x_{m,i}(t)$.
5. $V_m(t)$: the current velocity of the mth particle at time t, a vector whose ith component is $v_{m,i}(t)$.
6. $G(t)$: the best of all positions discovered by all particles at time t or earlier, with components $g_i(t)$.
7. $L_m(t)$: best position of particle m discovered at time t or earlier, with components $l_{m,i}(t.)$

We use the term "fitness" as synonymous with "solution quality," not to imply a proportion of offspring allocated to individuals as in genetic algorithms.

Each particle moves around in space using the following PSO update equations:

1. The following equation updates the velocity for each dimension i of the particle m :

$$v_{m,i}(t+1) = v_{m,i}(t) + C_1 * rand() * \left(l_{m,i}(t) - x_{m,i}(t)\right)$$
$$+ C_2 * rand() * \left(g_{m,i}(t) - x_{m,i}(t)\right), \qquad (20.1)$$

    where C_1 and C_2 are two positive constants called acceleration coefficients, and they affect the maximum size step that each particle can take in a single iteration, and *rand()* is a function that generates random numbers uniformly from the interval [0,1].

2. The ith component of the position of particle m is updated as follows:

$$x_{m,i}(t+1) = x_{m,i}(t) + v_{m,i}(t+1). \qquad (20.2)$$

The magnitude of each position component is restricted by a predetermined problem-specific upper bound (*Xmax*). Similarly, velocity component magnitudes are upper-bounded by a parameter (*Vmax*), which is no greater than *Xmax*. Even for unconstrained problems, this approach can be used, successively increasing (perhaps doubling) these upper bounds and widening the scope of the search.

The PSO algorithm is as follows:

1. Initialize the population, randomly assigning each particle's position and velocity, which also provide initial values for $l_{m,i}$ components; the best initial particle's position provides the initial G.
2. Repeatedly calculate the new velocity and then the new position for all particles, using equations (20.1) and (20.2), and updating G and l_m components until a satisfactory solution G is found or computation limits are exceeded.

20.2 Discrete Multiphase Particle Swarm Optimization

In several problems, PSO finds the optimum value more quickly than when using traditional evolutionary algorithms. This is explained by the fact that PSO uses a combination of local and global searches. The DiMuPSO algorithm is obtained by modifying the PSO algorithm in three ways:

1. Dividing particles into multiple groups, increasing the diversity and exploration of the space.
2. Introducing different phases, between which the direction of particle movement changes.
3. Moving only to positions that will increase fitness.

To begin with, our research attempts to increase population diversity and problem space exploration capabilities of PSO, beginning by addressing the following question: instead of the particles working in one group that flies toward the best position found so far, what if the particles are divided into groups and each group searches differently? That is, one group is directed toward the globally best position found so far, and the other flies in the opposite direction. This was the first step to developing the DiMuPSO algorithm, dividing the particles into working groups with different temporary goals.

In addition, we also observed that a considerable amount of computational effort is wasted by PSO in visiting states of poor fitness values. Although this is often necessary for a stochastic algorithm to avoid being trapped in local minima, enlarging the notion of "neighborhood" in the search space is a possible approach that allows pursuit of global optima using hill-climbing algorithms. We hence investigated a variation of the PSO that restricts each particle to move only to a position with better fitness (than that particle's current position). Hill-climbing has been found to be helpful in other evolutionary algorithms such as memetic algorithms [21].

Another observation was that each particle in PSO often continues to move roughly in the same direction (toward G) especially when there is no change in G [3, 9, 14]. This leads to convergence of all particles toward local optima whose fitness may be low. Changing direction could lead to a better solution, and this is done by allowing particles to vary their current goals or directions of search, depending on the current *phase* of each particle. If a particle finds no improvement in fitness for a prespecified period of time, it changes phase and continues search in a different direction.

Directions for particle movement are provided by the global and local best, as in PSO, except that the hill-climbing strategy implies that the local best is the same as the current position. These two positions act as opposite poles for the velocity vector, with one acting as attractor and the other as repellor, depending on the phase. A related, but different, diversity improvement scheme is adopted by the Shepherd and Sheepdog algorithm [24].

20.2.1 Update Equations

In DiMuPSO, the mth particle updates its jth velocity as follows:

$$v_{m.i}(t+1) = min(Vmax, max(-Vmax, \ v_{m.i}(t) + C_m(t) \ x_{m.i}(t) - C_m(t) \ g_i(t))), \quad (20.3)$$

where $C_m(t)$ equals either 1 or -1 depending on the current phase of the particle.

Comparing with Eq. (20.1), we observe the disappearance of $l_{m,i}$, not needed since the hill-climbing strategy ensures that the current position of each particle is also its best local position found so far. Separate memory for storing the best local position is not needed.

The position update equation is a simple discretized version of Eq. (20.2), except that it is considered only a *tentative* position update, not to be accepted if such an update diminishes a particle's fitness:

$$Tentative\_x_{m,j}(t+1) = \begin{cases} 1 & \text{if } \left(v_{m,j}(t+1) + x_{m,j}(t+1)\right) > 0.5, \\ 0 & \text{otherwise.} \end{cases}$$

20.2.2 Which Components to Update?

For multidimensional problems, the new position update equation poses a new issue:

1. Should we iteratively compare the previous fitness with the result of updating a single component (dimension) of the particle's position at a time?
2. Or should we compare the previous fitness with the result of updating all the components?

These two choices may be considered the extremes in answering the question of what constitutes the neighborhood of a position in the search process—note that a neighborhood in this sense depends on the definition of the moves or operators used, not just on a predetermined problem space topology. The first choice is plagued by the problem that the particle can be trapped in local minima of the problem space topology; this also requires one additional fitness evaluation per problem dimension, increasing the computational expense significantly. The second choice leads to the possibility that very large moves are made that lead very far away from the previous position, since the problem space is discrete, violating the paradigm of particles moving to nearby points at each successive instant.

We address this issue by using a new *sublength (sl)* parameter in the DiMuPSO algorithm. The *sl* parameter will determine how many dimensions are considered for update at a time before evaluating the fitness of the tentatively changed particle position. For example, if *sl* = 3, then the tentative updates to the particle velocity and the position will be calculated for dimensions i to $i+3$. If fitness is improved by updating the tentative new positions for the calculated dimensions, the particle will move to its new position, updating *sl* components at a time. If no improvement is found, there will be no change of the particles' position along those dimensions. Similar calculations are performed for other tuples of *sl* components of the position vector. In our experiments, *sl* was chosen randomly from the interval [1, $min(10, n)$], where n is the dimensionality of the search space..

20.2.3 Phase Changes

In Eq. (20.3), $x_{m,j}(t)$ and $g_j(t)$ have opposite signs, so that the particle moves toward or away from the current global best position, depending on its current phase. Phase change may be enforced after a fixed number of generations (phase change frequency, *pcf*). Alternatively, in the adaptive version of this algorithm, phase is changed when there is no improvement within the current phase for a prespecified number of generations, referred to as the *pcf*.

20.2.4 Velocity Change

Many evolutionary algorithms rely on a restart mechanism to reduce the probability of being stuck in local optima of the objective function. This was done for particle positions in the random particle approach [6]. A similar idea is applied in the DiMuPSO algorithm, periodically reinitializing all particle velocities (rather than positions) after a predetermined number *(VC)* of generations.

Figure 20.1 presents details of the DiMuPSO algorithm. The next two sections describe experimental results obtained using this algorithm.

20.3 Benchmark Problems and Results

This section describes the application of DiMuPSO algorithm to several discrete binary benchmark optimization problems. Section 20.3.1 describes each of the functions, Section 20.3.2 gives details of the experiments, and Section 20.3.3 shows the results. Results are discussed in Section 20.3.4.

Initialize algorithm parameters such as pcf and N;
Create and initialize positions and velocities of M particles;
Initialize coefficients C_m to 1 for half the particles, and –1 for the rest
Initialize g to be the position of the particle with highest fitness;

for each swarm $t \in [1...N]$
    If (t is a multiple of VC)
        Reinitialize particle velocities;

    For each particle $m \in [1...M]$
        Reverse the sign of C_m if $X_m(t)= X_m(t\text{-}pcf)$;
        Copy $X_m(t)$ into Temp, the tentative new position vector;
        Let sl be a randomly drawn integer from [1, min(10,N)];
        for each j in 0...(n/sl –1),
            for each i in [j*sl ... min(n, j*sl+sl-1)],
                Update
                    $v_{m,i}(t+1) = min(Vmax, max(\text{-}Vmax,$
                        $v_{m,i}(t) + C_m(t) x_{m,i}(t) - C_m(t) g_i(t)))$;
                and
                $Temp_i = 1$ if $(v_{m,i}(t+1) + x_{m,i}(t)) > 0.5,$
                        and 0 otherwise;

        If $(fitness(Temp) > fitness(X_m))$
            for each i in [j*sl ... min(n, j*sl+sl-1)]
                $x_{m,i}(t+1) = Temp_i;$
        else for each i in [j*sl ... min(n, j*sl+sl-1)]
                $Temp_{i = } x_{m,i}(t);$

        If $fitness(X_m)>fitness(g)$
            Update $g=X_m;$
        Exit if fitness(g) meets prespecified solution quality criteria;

Figure 20.1. Details of the DiMuPSO algorithm.

20.3.1 Test Functions

Three different deceptive problems, each characterized by a large number of local optima, were used for evaluation of the DiMuPSO algorithm: Goldberg's order-3, Bipolar order-6, and Mühlenbein's order-5 concatenation problems, described in detail below.

20.3.1.1 Order-3 Deceptive Problem

Goldberg's deceptive order-3 problem [12] is presented here. The fitness of each particle is calculated as follows:

$$f(X) = \sum_{i=1}^{n/3} f_3(x_i),$$ where each x_i is a disjoint 3-bit substring of X and

$$f_3(x_i) = \begin{cases} 0.9 & if \quad |x_i| = 0, \\ 0.6 & if \quad |x_i| = 1, \\ 0.3 & if \quad |x_i| = 2, \\ 1.0 & if \quad |x_i| = 3, \end{cases} \tag{20.4}$$

where $|x_i|$ denotes the sum of the bits in the 3-bit substring.

20.3.1.2 Bipolar Deceptive Problem

The Bipolar order-6 function [11] computes the fitness of a particle as the sum of the partial fitness functions obtained by applying a function f_6 to disjoint six-bit substrings of the particle position. Function f_6 has two optima with $f_6(X)=1$ if $X=000000$ or $X=111111$. Local optima occur with $f_6(X)=0.8$ if $|X|=3$. Finally, these local optima are rendered deceptive by setting $f_6(X)=0.4$ if $|X|=2$ or 4, and $f_6(X)=0.0$ if $|X|=1$ or 5.

20.3.1.3 Mühlenbein's Order-5 Problem

The last deceptive problem to be tested is Mühlenbein's order-5 problem [22]. As in the above two problems, the fitness of a particle is computed as the sum of a function f_5 applied to disjoint five-bit substrings of the particle position. But the optimization task is rendered much more difficult by setting $f_5(X)=0$ everywhere except at five positions: $f_5(00000) = 4$, $f_5(00001) = 3$, $f_5(00011) = 2$, $f_5(00111) = 1$, and $f_5(11111) = 3.5$.

20.3.2 Details of Experiments

DiMuPSO was compared to two other algorithms: traditional GA using one-point crossover and a discrete variation of the standard PSO developed by Kennedy and Eberhart [2], referred to as KE-PSO here (elsewhere referred to as Q-DiPSO [1, 20]). Each of the algorithms has special settings for its parameters that are presented in the following subsections.

20.3.2.1 GA Settings

Table 20.1 shows a summary of parameter settings for GA algorithms used in our experiments. The *one-point crossover* operator was used, along with a bitwise mutation operator. The *mutation probability* was set to be the reciprocal of the bitstring length n (problem dimensionality). The crossover probability (*px*) was set to 0.9.

The population size was increased proportionally to the problem dimensionality, and the maximum number of generations was limited to 1000.

Binary tournament selection mechanism [7] was used; two individuals are selected at random and the fittest is selected [25].

20.3.2.2 KE-PSO Settings

Table 20.2 summarizes the parameter settings. The velocity equation was the same as Eq. (20.1), with the only difference being in the position calculations (Eq. 20.2): KE-PSO uses velocity components to compute the probability with which each position component is determined to be 1. The new equation is as follows:

$$\text{if}\left(rand(\;) < \left(1/e^{-v_{m,i}}\right)\right), \text{ then } x_{m,i} = 1; \text{ else } x_{m,i} = 0, \qquad (20.5)$$

where $rand$ () is a random number generator using the interval [0, 1].

$Vmax$ was set to 5 and both coefficients were set to 2, as in [10, 27, 28].

As with the GA algorithm, the swarm size varies according to the length of the problem, and the maximum swarm number that can be reached is limited to 1000.

20.3.2.3 DiMuPSO Settings

Table 20.3 is a summary of the following DiMuPSO parameters used in the experiments.

1. Phase changes were determined adaptively: a particle changes phase if no improvement in fitness is observed in pcf=50 successive swarms (generations).
2. Sl was randomly generated for each individual in each swarm, in the range [1, min (10, n)].
3. $VC = 5$.

The swarm size is set to 30. The maximum number of swarms is set to 1000, as in the other algorithms. $Vmax$ is set to 1, since discrete-binary functions are being tested. Also, $Xmax$ is set to 1.

20.3.3 Results

The results for each of the defined test problems are given in the following subsections.

20.3.3.1 Goldberg's Order-3 Problem

The results obtained were averaged over 20 runs. As shown in Table 20.5, the GA and the DiMuPSO algorithm reached optimum fitness for the problem's size equal to 30, with the DiMuPSO algorithm requiring fewer fitness evaluations. The DiMuPSO algorithm used fewer fitness evaluations than the GA.

Table 20.1 GA Parameters

Parameter	GA
Pm	$1/n$
Px	0.9
N	1000

Table 20.2 KE-PSO Parameters

Parameter	KE-PSO
Vmax	5
M	100
N	1,000
C_1	2
C_2	2

Table 20.3 DiMuPSO Parameters

Parameter	DiMuPSO
M	30
N	1000
C_m	1 or −1
$Vmax$	1
Sl	Randomly generated for each particle in each swarm, From the interval [1, min(10, M)]
pcf	50 (adaptive)
VC	5

Table 20.4 Population Sizes Used by GA and PSO for the Three Testing Problems.

n	Goldberg		Bipolar		Mühlenbein	
	GA	PSO	GA	PSO	GA	PSO
30	50	50	50	50	30	30
60	50	50	100	50	60	60
90	100	100	100	100	90	90
120	120	120	120	120	120	120
150	120	120	150	150	150	150

As the dimensionality of the problem increased, the DiMuPSO algorithm was still able to reach better fitness than the GA. On the other hand, KE-PSO was unable to reach optimum fitness for all different problem sizes.

Figure 20.2 shows the performance of each algorithm for a problem size of 150 bits. The DiMuPSO algorithm reached optimum fitness. The GA and the KE-PSO algorithm were unable to reach optimum fitness.

20.3.3.2 Bipolar Order-6 Problem

The results were averaged over 20 runs. As observed from Table 20.6, the DiMuPSO algorithm reached optimum fitness for all the dimensions. The GA was able to reach the best fitness for 30- and 60-bit problems. For a problem size of 30 bits, the GA used fewer fitness evaluations than the DiMuPSO, but for 60 bits the DiMuPSO algorithm used fewer fitness evaluations than the GA. The KE-PSO was unable to reach the best fitness for all the different instances of the problem.

Figure 20.3 shows the performance of the three algorithms for the 150-bit problem. From the figure, and as mentioned earlier, the DiMuPSO algorithm was the only one that reached optimum fitness. In addition, the population size used by the DiMuPSO algorithm was much smaller than that used by the GA and the KE-PSO algorithm. The DiMuPSO algorithm used 30 particles, whereas GA and KE-PSO used 150 individuals. Even though they used a larger number of individuals, both were unable to reach optimum fitness.

20.3.3.3 Mühlenbein's order-5 Problem

What was observed earlier is true here as well. The DiMuPSO algorithm reached optimum fitness for all the dimensions. None of the other algorithms was able to reach the best fitness. Table 20.7 shows the results for all the algorithms for different dimensions. As before, the DiMuPSO used fewer fitness evaluations to reach optimum fitness.

Figure 20.4 shows the results obtained for 150 bits. As mentioned earlier, the DiMuPSO was the only one that reached optimum fitness.

Table 20.5 Best Fitness Found Using GA, KE-PSO and DiMuPSO for Goldberg's Order-3 Deceptive Problem Instances of Different Dimensionality, Averaged over 20 Trials

	GA		KE-PSO		DiMuPSO	
n	*Best Fitness*	*Fitness Evals*	*Best Fitness*	*Fitness Evals*	*Best Fitness*	*Fitness Evals*
30	10	8,800	9.375	49,200	10	5,624
60	19.845	43,175	16.725	48,300	20	17,046
90	29.515	99,500	23.895	99,100	30	32,988
120	39.025	120,000	30.78	117,840	40	39,509
150	47.995	116,640	37.495	111,840	50	60,616

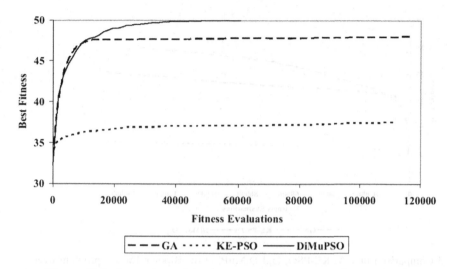

Figure 20.2: Comparison of GA, KE-PSO, and DiMuPSO for Goldberg's 150-bit problem over 20 runs.

Table 20.6 Best Fitness Found Using GA, KE-PSO and DiMuPSO for Bipolar order-6 Deceptive Problem Instances of Different Dimensionality, Averaged over 20 Trials.

n	*GA* Best Fitness	Fitness Evals	*KE-PSO* Best Fitness	Fitness Evals	*DiMuPSO* Best Fitness	Fitness Evals
3 0	5	8,070	4.67	48,450	5	9,310
6 0	10	44,925	8.24	48,800	10	35,118
9 0	14.82	94,745	11.71	99,300	15	68,811
120	18.97	119,520	14.92	117,840	20	98,406
150	23.17	149,700	18	145,950	25	136,547

Table 20.7: Best Fitness Found Using GA, KE-PSO, and DiMuPSO for Mühlenbein's Order-5 Deceptive Problem Instances of Different Dimensionality, Averaged over 20 Trials.

n	*GA* Best Fitness	Fitness Evals	*KE-PSO* Best Fitness	Fitness Evals	*DiMuPSO* Best Fitness	Fitness Evals
3 0	23.75	12,602	20.875	29,880	24	9,323
6 0	46.675	48,705	33.575	58,200	48	13,248
9 0	70.2	81,990	44.425	89,460	96	39,361
120	93.5	120,000	55	119,640	120	52,590
150	116.575	140,000	63.175	144,750	148	55,069

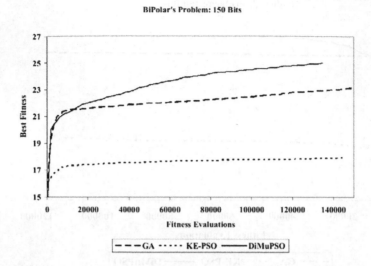

Figure 20.3 Comparison of GA, KE-PSO, and DiMuPSO for Bipolar 150-bit problem over 20 runs.

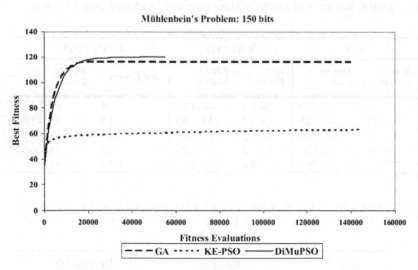

Figure 20.4 Comparison of GA, KE-PSO, and DiMuPSO for Mühlenbein's 150-bit problem using the same maximum generation: 1,000 over 20 runs.

20.3.4   Discussion

Experimental results show that DiMuPSO is a very efficient algorithm. It reached optimum fitness each time it was run, and it used fewer fitness evaluations to reach optimum fitness each time. As problem dimensionality increased, the algorithm still used fewer fitness evaluations and managed to reach optimum fitness each time.

Another observable factor is the time required by DiMuPSO to reach the best fitness over the 20 runs. Table 20.8 shows the time needed for each algorithm to finish the execution for the 20 runs for a 30-bit dimension. To be able to compare results, all these numbers were obtained using a population size equal to 30 and a maximum generation of 1,000. As observed from the table, the DiMuPSO algorithm required less time than the other two algorithms.

Table 20.8 Time Needed for Each Algorithm to Be Executed 20 Times in Seconds for 30-bit Problems; Population Size Was Set to 30 and the Maximum Number of Generations to 1000.

Algorithm	Goldberg	Bipolar	Mühlenbein
GA	26.718	22.692	32.056
KE-PSO	82.839	180.930	90.209
DiMuPSO	2.213	9.633	5.374

Table 20.9 Time Needed for Each Algorithm to Be Executed 20 Times in Seconds for 120-bit Problems; Population Size Was Set to 120 and the Maximum Number of Generations to 1000.

Algorithm	Goldberg	Bipolar	Mühlenbein
GA	425.351	452.660	444.579
KE-PSO	748.438	727.225	711.402
DiMuPSO	27.669	88.887	23.924

In order to observe the difference, the experiments were also conducted for higher-dimensional problems. In Table 20.9, when the problem dimensionality is increased to 120, the time needed by the other two algorithms is much more than the time needed by the DiMuPSO. It is important to note that only DiMuPSO reached the best fitness for this problem. The population size here was set to 120, and the maximum number of generations was limited to 1000. Experiments were performed on a Pentium III machine with 800MHz and 640Mb RAM.

20.4. Discrete Encoding, Continuous Space

The previous section addressed the application of DiMuPSO to discrete binary functions. In this section, we describe how continuous optimization problems may also be solved using DiMuPSO, using a discrete encoding for problem parameters. The overall methodology is similar to that of Kennedy and Eberhart [16], who encoded particle position components using binary numbers. The calculations were carried out using these binary numbers, and results were converted back to real numbers. The same experimental settings were used as in Section 20.3, except that the population sizes for GA and PSO were set to 100, and DiMuPSO's population size was set to 100 for one of the test functions (Rosenbrock) and 20 for the rest of the test functions; VC was set to 10 while pcf was set to 5. Section 20.4.1 describes the test functions, and Section 20.4.2 shows the results for the various functions, discussed further in Section 20.4.3.

20.4.1 Test Functions

Four benchmark problems were used to test the algorithms: DeJong F1 (Sphere function), DeJong F2 (Rosenbrock), DeJong F5 (Foxholes), and Rastrigin. These functions were chosen because they represent the common difficulties in optimization problems. These problems are described in the rest of this subsection.

20.4.1.1 Sphere Function (DeJong F1)

Sphere function [13] is a continuous, unimodal function generally used to measure the efficiency of an algorithm. The graph of this function is shown in Figure 20.5 [29]. The function is defined as follows:

$$f(x) = \sum_{i=1}^{n} x_i^2, \quad \text{where } -100 < x_i < 100,$$

where x is an n-dimensional, real-valued vector and x_i is the ith element of that vector. It has a global minimum of 0 at $(x_i) = 0$.

20.4.1.2 Rosenbrock Function (DeJong F2)

The Rosenbrock function [26] is a smooth function with a sharp ridge that distracts ordinary optimization algorithms. This function can be quite difficult for algorithms that are unable to identify promising search directions with little information. Algorithms that take good direction for the search will perform well in this function. The function is depicted in Figure 20.6, and the description is as follows:

$$f(x) = 100(x_1^2 - x_2)^2 + (1 - x_1)^2, \quad \text{where } -2.048 \le x_i \le 2.048.$$

The function has a minimum value of 0 at $(x_1, x_2) = (1,1)$.

20.4.1.3. Foxhole Function (DeJong F5)

The Foxhole function [23] has many nonuniformly distributed local optima, and many optimization algorithms get stuck at the first peak. Figure 20.7 shows the function graphically. The function is described as follows:

$$f(x) = \frac{1}{1/k + \sum_{j=1}^{25} f_j^1(x)}, \text{ where } f_j(x) = C_j + \sum_{i=1}^{n} (x_i - a_{i,j}),$$

where $-65.536 \le x_i \le 65.536$, $k = 500$, $C_j = j$, and

$$[a_{i,j}] = \begin{bmatrix} -32 & -16 & 0 & 16 & 32 & -32 & \dots & 0 & 16 & 32 \\ -32 & -32 & -32 & -32 & -32 & -16 & \dots & 32 & 32 & 32 \end{bmatrix}.$$

The function has a minimum global value of 0.998 at $(x_1, x_2) = (-32, -32)$.

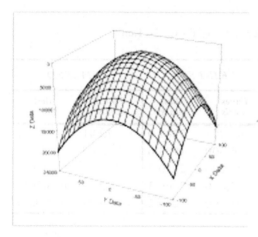

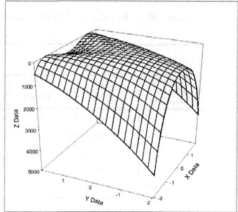

Figure 20.5. Sphere function (DeJong F1).

Figure 20.6. Rosenbrock function (DeJong F2).

20.4.1.4 Rastrigin Function

The Rastrigin function [4] has many local optima that are uniformly distributed through the space. The function is shown in Figure 20.8. Its description is as follows:

$$f(x) = \sum_{i=1}^{n} (x_i^2 - 10\cos(2\pi x_i) + 10), \text{ where } -5.12 \le x_i \le 5.12$$

where x is an n-dimensional real-valued vector and x_i is the ith element of that vector. It has a global minimum of 0 at $(x_i) = 0$.

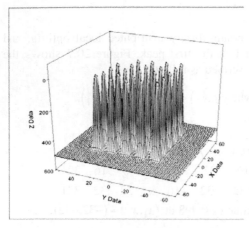

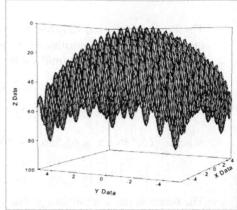

Figure 20.7. Foxhole Function (DeJong F5).

Figure 20.8. Rastrigin Function.

Table 20.10 Results for Sphere Function, Averaged over 20 Runs.

	GA		KE-PSO		DiMuPSO	
Number of bits for encoding	Fitness evals	Best fitness	Fitness evals	Best fitness	Fitness evals	Best fitness
5	99,200	129.0	98,000	2281.0	7,641	104.1
1 0	99,100	47.6	86,600	1983.0	12,947	0.096
1 5	97,600	14.3	93,000	2170.2	19,673	0.000093
2 0	98,460	11.1	97,600	2169.3	22,515	0.000014
2 5	99,530	48.4	91,700	2249.2	30,618	0.000017

Table 20.11 Results for Rosenbrock (DeJong F2) Function, Averaged over 20 Runs.

	GA		KE-PSO		DiMuPSO	
Number of bits for encoding	Fitness evals	Best fitness	Fitness evals	Best fitness	Fitness evals	Best fitness
5	1,100	0.029	5,700	0.0081	83,100	0.0086
10	4,4400	0.027	94,500	0.00050	87,118	0.00019
15	84,260	0.031	70,030	0.00025	69,160	0.00015
20	91,430	0.046	78,975	0.00034	64,769	0.00012
25	95,180	0.043	64,935	0.00031	63,945	0.00029

20.4.2 Results

The results of each of the test problems are given in the following subsections.

20.4.2.1 Sphere Problem

The results obtained here were averaged over 20 runs, and the problem's dimensionality was set to 10. When the number of bits used to encode each unknown was small, not all of the algorithms reached optimum fitness. Comparing those results, the DiMuPSO reached the best fitness any of them found. When the number of bits that encodes each unknown increased, it was clearly found that the DiMuPSO was the best. It managed to reach optimum fitness each time, but not the GA and the KE-PSO. It was surprising that the GA and the KE-PSO did not reach a value near the optima, a possible reason being the high range of the values for the problem parameters.

Table 20.10 shows the results of the different sizes used to encode the problem parameters. Figure 20.9 shows the performance of the three algorithms, using 25 bits for encoding.

20.4.2.2 Rosenbrock Problem (DeJong F2)

The results obtained here were averaged over 20 runs. Table 20.11 shows the results obtained for different encoding lengths. When the encoding length is small (five bits for each unknown), the KE-PSO reached better fitness than the DiMuPSO because the DiMuPSO uses the *sl* parameter to cut hill-climbing's cost, which for a small number of bits uses more fitness evaluations than a large number of bits.

For all other encoding lengths, the DiMuPSO was able to reach near the optimum fitness with fewer fitness evaluations. KE-PSO reached near the optimum with more fitness evaluations. The GA performed worse than both of these algorithms. Figure 20.10 shows the performance of the three algorithms for 25 bits of encoding length.

20.4.2.3. Foxhole Problem (DeJong F5)

For this problem, the DiMuPSO and the KE-PSO were able to reach optimum fitness each time. For 5-bit encoding, the KE-PSO used fewer fitness evaluations than the DiMuPSO because, as mentioned earlier, the DiMuPSO incorporated hill-climbing, which, when using few bits for encoding, tended to require more fitness evaluations. When the number of bits for encoding increased, the DiMuPSO used fewer fitness evaluations than the KE-PSO. The GA was unable to reach the optimum fitness. Table 20.12 shows the results obtained for different encoding lengths. Figure 20.11 shows the performance of three algorithms for 25-bit encoding.

Table 20.12 Results for Foxhole (DeJong F5) Function Averaged over 20 Runs.

	GA		KE-PSO		DiMuPSO	
Number of bits for encoding	Fitness evals	Best fitness	Fitness evals	Best fitness	Fitness evals	Best fitness
5	2,600	0.999	1,800	0.999	9,866	0.999
1 0	4,920	1.197	9,340	0.998	3,532	0.998
1 5	43,830	1.189	12,595	0.998	5,703	0.998
2 0	52,865	1.189	17,200	0.998	6,561	0.998
2 5	60,395	1.324	12,355	0.998	8,814	0.998

20.4.2.4 Rastrigin Problem

The Rastrigin function with dimensionality 10 was used. Table 20.13 shows the results obtained for the different sizes used for encoding. When 5-bit encoding was used, the same observation mentioned earlier applied here. Although DiMuPSO was unable to reach the optimum fitness, it reached the best fitness among the three algorithms. When the number of bits used in the encoding increased, the DiMuPSO was able to reach the optimum fitness. Neither the KE-PSO nor the GA reached the optimum fitness.

Figure 20.12 shows the performance of the three algorithms using 25 bits for the encoding and 100,000 as the maximum number of fitness evaluations. The highest value for the DiMuPSO shown in the graph was equal to 0.178649 for the best fitness and 86,973 for the fitness evaluations.

Table 20.13 Results for Rastrigin Problem, Averaged over 20 Runs.

	GA		KE-PSO		DiMuPSO	
Number of bits for encoding	Fitness evals	Best fitness	Fitness evals	Best fitness	Fitness evals	Best fitness
5	56,300	52.3	94,000	62.5	27,639	49.5
1 0	97,900	10.9	86,400	49.9	67,006	0.0497
1 5	98,800	10.8	92,000	51.7	54,078	0.000056
2 0	99,900	9.7	98,800	52.0	93,016	0.000012
2 5	99,800	11.0	99,000	51.3	100,332	0.000009

20.4.3 Discussion

Experimental results show that the DiMuPSO algorithm is much more efficient than the other two algorithms. The KE-PSO algorithm performed well in two sets of problems; namely, the Rosenbrock and the Foxhole problems. But even for these two problems, the DiMuPSO algorithm required fewer fitness evaluations.

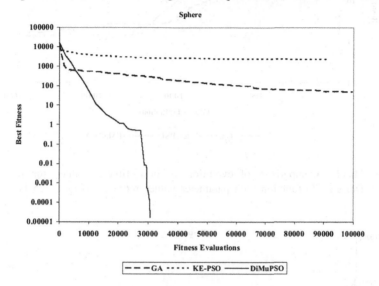

Figure 20.9 Comparison of evolution of best fitness values for minimizing sphere function with parameter values represented using 25 bits over 20 runs.

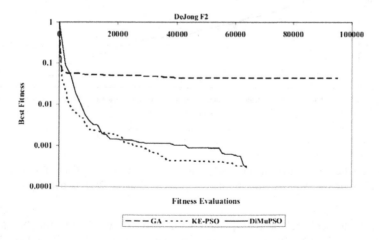

Figure 20.10 Comparison of evolution of best fitness values for minimizing Rosenbrock (DeJong F2) function with parameter values represented using 25 bits over 20 runs.

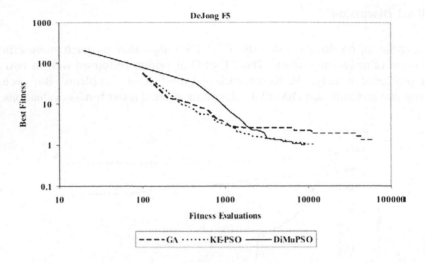

Figure 20.11 Comparison of evolution of best fitness values for minimizing Foxhole (DeJong F5) function with parameter values represented using 25 bits over 20 runs.

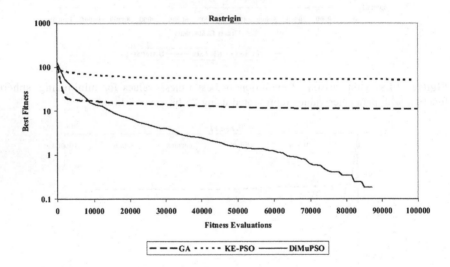

Figure 20.12 Comparison of evolution of best fitness values for minimizing Rastrigin's function with parameter values represented using 25 bits over 20 runs.

For the Rosenbrock problem, when using only a few (5) bits for the encoding mechanism, the DiMuPSO algorithm approached (0.1% difference) but did not reach the level of fitness that the KE-PSO algorithm reached. For the Foxhole function, both algorithms reached the best fitness when using five bits for the encoding, but the DiMuPSO required more fitness evaluations, possibly because DiMuPSO incorporates hill-climbing. When using more bits for encoding, the problem is harder, and use of the sl parameter helps reduce the number of fitness evaluations required instead of degrading the performance.

As described in the previous section, the time used to execute 20 runs was recorded. DiMuPSO used less time than the two other algorithms. Table 20.14 shows the time needed for each of the algorithms to be executed 20 times using a population size of 100 and maximum generation of 1,000.

Table 20.14 The Time Needed for Each Algorithm to Be Executed 20 Times in Seconds for 25-bit Encoding; Population Size Was Set to 100 and Maximum Generation to 1,000

Algorithm	Sphere (DeJong F1)	Rosenbrock (DeJong F2)	Foxhole (DeJong F5)	Rastrigin
GA	858,574	174,851	162,183	771,249
KE-PSO	1149,332	178,606	39,777	1128,212
DiMuPSO	35,691	132,390	6,789	110,548

20.5 Concluding Remarks

We have presented DiMuPSO, a variation of the particle swarm optimization algorithm for discrete optimization tasks. The main features of the new algorithm are the incorporation of hill climbing, the use of multiple groups of particles with different search parameters, and the adaptive modification of particle goals as they cycle through different phases. Extensive experimental results show that the new algorithm outperforms traditional GA and PSO algorithms for difficult benchmark discrete and continuous optimization problems.

The modifications to PSO proposed in this paper are largely orthogonal to other improvements to PSO suggested in the literature [5, 18], and we expect that several of those improvements can also be incorporated into the DiMuPSO approach.

In related recent work [2], we have shown the applicability of this approach directly to continuous optimization tasks without discrete encoding, e.g., successfully training the weights of feedforward neural networks for classification problems using a continuous version of DiMuPSO.

References

1.   B. Al-kazemi and C. K. Mohan, (2002) Multi-Phase Discrete Particle Swarm Optimization, Proc. The Fourth International Workshop on Frontiers in Evolutionary Algorithms (FEA 2002).
2.   B. Al-kazemi and C. K. Mohan, (2002) Multi-Phase Generalization of the Particle Swarm Optimization Algorithm," Proc. Congress on Evolutionary Computation, Honolulu, Hawaii.

3.   P. J. Angeline, (1998) Evolutionary Optimization Versus Particle Swarm Optimization: Philosophical and Performance Differences," Proc. Evolutionary Programming VII (EP98) LNCS 1447.

4.   T. Bäck, G. Rudolph, and H. P. Schwefel, (1993) Evolutionary Programming and Evolution Strategies: Similarities and Differences," Proc. 2nd Annual Conference on Evolutionary Programming, San Diego, CA.

5.   F. van den Bergh and A.P Engelbrecht, (2001) Effects of Swarm Size on Cooperative Particle Swarm Optimizers," Proc. GECCO 2001, San Francisco, USA.

6.   Frans van den Bergh, (2001) An Analysis of Particle Swarm Optimizers," (Ph.D. Dissertation, University of Pretoria, Pretoria).

7.   Tobias Blickle and Lothar Thiele, (1995) A Comparison of Selection Schemes used in Genetic Algorithms, Computer Engineering and Communication Networks Lab (TIK), Zurich.

8.   Roy W. Dobbins, Russell C. Eberhart, and Patrick K. Simpson, (1996) in *Computational Intelligence PC Tools*: Academic Press Professional, pp. 212-226.

9.   R. C. Eberhart and Y Shi, (1998) Comparison between Genetic Algorithms and Particle Swarm Optimization, Proc. 7th international Conference on Evolutionary Programming, San diego, California, USA.

10.   R. C. Eberhart and J. Kennedy, (1995) A New Optimizer using Particle Swarm Theory," Proc. the Sixth International Symposium on Micro Machine and Human Science, Nagoya, Japan.

11.   D. E. Goldberg, K. Deb, and J. Horn, (1992) Massive Multimodality, Deception, and Genetic Algorithms, *Parallel Problem Solving from Nature*, vol. 2, pp. 37-46.

12.   D. E. Goldberg, K. Deb, and B. Korb, (1990) Messy Genetic Algorithms Revisited: Studies in mixed size and scale, *Complex Systems*, vol. 4, pp. 415-444.

13.   K. De Jong, (1975) An Analysis of the Behaviour of a Class of Genetic Adaptive Systems, (Ph.D. Dissertation, University of Michigan).

14.   J. Kennedy, (1998) The Behavior of Particles, Proc. Evolutionary Programming VII: 7th International Conference on Evolutionary Programming, San Diego, California, USA.

15.   J. Kennedy, (1999) Small Worlds and Mega-Minds: Effects of Neighborhood Topology on Particle Swarm Performance, Proc. Congress on Evolutionary Computation, Washington, DC, USA.

16.   J. Kennedy and R. C. Eberhart, (1997) A Discrete Binary Version of the Particle Swarm Algorithm, Proc. Conf. on Systems, Man, and Cybernetics, Piscataway, NJ.

17.   J. Kennedy and R. C. Eberhart, (1995) Particle Swarm Optimization, Proc. IEEE International Conference on Neural Networks.

18.   M. Løvbjerg, T. K. Rasmussen, and T. Krink, (2001) "Hybrid Particle Swarm Optimizer with breeding and subpopulations," Proc. Third Genetic and Evolutionary Computation Conference.

19.   M.M. Millonas, (1994) "Swarms, Phase Transitions, and Collective Intelligence," in *Artificial Life III*, S. S. i. t. S. o. Complexity, Ed.: Addison Wesley Longman, pp. 417-445.

20.   C. K. Mohan and B. Al-kazemi, (2001) Discrete Particle Swarm Optimization, Proc. Workshop on Particle Swarm Optimization, Indianapolis, IN: Purdue School of Engineering and Technology, IUPUI, 2001.

21.   Pablo Moscato, (1989) On Evolution, Search, Optimization, Genetic Algorithms and Martial Arts: Towards Memetic Algorithms, California Institute of Technology, Pasadena, California, USA 826, 1989.

22.   H. Mühlenbein, T. Mahnig, and A. O. Rodrigues, (1999) Schemata, Distributions and Graphical Modes in Evolutionary Optimization, *Journal of Heuristics*, vol. 5.

23.   R. Patil, (1995) Intervals in Evolutionary Algorithms for Global Optimization," Los Alamos National Laboratory Unclassified 1196.

24.   Denis Robilliard and Cyril Fonlupt, (1999) A Shepherd and a Sheepdog to Guide Evolutionary Computation, Proc. Evolutionary Computation, France.

25.   A. Rogers and A. Prügel-Bennett, (1999) Genetic Drift in Genetic Algorithm Selection Schemes, *IEEE Transactions on Evolutionary Computation*, vol. 3, pp. 298-303, 1999.

26.   F. Seredynski, P. Bouvry, and F. Arbab, (1997) Distributed Evolutionary Optimization in Manifold: the Rosenbrock's Function Case Study, Proc. First International Workshop on Frontiers in Evolutionary Algorithms, Duke University , USA.

27.   Y. Shi and R. C. Eberhart, (1999) Empirical study of Particle Swarm Optimization, Proc. Congress on Evolutionary Computation, Piscataway, NJ.

28.   P. N. Suganthan, (1999) Particle Swarm Optimizer with Neighborhood Operator," Proc. Congress on Evolutionary Computation, Piscataway, NJ: IEEE Service Center.

29.   Deniz Yuret, (1994) From Genetic Algorithms to Efficient Optimization, (Master of Science Thesis, Massachusetts Institute Of Technology).

Index